DATE DUE

GAYLORD   PRINTED IN U.S.A.

Laws of Heaven

Books by Michael Gallagher

Bombs and Ginko Leaves
Laws of Heaven

Books Translated by Michael Gallagher

The Pornographers by Akiyuki Nozaka
Sea and Poison by Shusaku Endo
Spring Snow by Yukio Mishima
Runaway Horses by Yukio Mishima
Japan Sinks by Sakyo Komatsu

LAWS
— *of* —
HEAVEN

Catholic Activists Today

MICHAEL GALLAGHER

TICKNOR & FIELDS

New York

1992

For information about permission to reproduce selections
from this book, write to Permissions, Ticknor & Fields,
215 Park Avenue South, New York, New York 10003.

Library of Congress Cataloging-in-Publication Data

Gallagher, Michael.
Laws of heaven : Catholic activists today / Michael
Gallagher.
p.   cm.
Includes index.
ISBN 0–89919–982–8
1. Catholics — United States — Political activity.
2. Radicalism — United States.   I. Title.
BX1407.P63G35   1992
282′.092′273 — dc20
[B]   92–3181
CIP

"Here I Am, Lord", © 1981, Daniel L. Schutte and
New Dawn Music. P.O. 13248, Portland, OR 97213.
All Rights Reserved. Used with permission.

Printed in the United States of America

HAD   10   9   8   7   6   5   4   3   2   1

To Rosemary, Maureen, Julie, and Kevin

You will remember what things I suffer and at
what men's hands because I would not
transgress the laws of heaven.
— *Antigone's final words*

_____

We must obey God rather than men.
— *Acts of the Apostles 5:13*

Contents

Laws of Heaven

Would Jesus Run
for Congress?

Christians like to think that Christianity has civilized politics, whatever that might mean. If it has, the price has been a heavy one. For politics, in its turn, from the days of Constantine to the days of George Bush, has taken its toll of Christianity. Politicians, secular and ecclesiastic, have tried their best to diminish Christianity to a creed that knows its place, to a piety that never, never gets in the way.

Unfortunately for politicians, however, the real thing seems to be still at large, dangerous and unpredictable, ready to strike without warning to the discomfiture of many in high places, Rome included.

Oddly enough, outrageously enough, people still believe. They believe even though faith is a terribly troublesome thing. Faith, real faith, is something quite different from an allegiance to a church or party. The latter is all too often a once-for-all commitment that relieves you forever after of the need to think for yourself and act on your own — no matter how far your church or party strays from its professed ideals, no matter how willing it becomes to go along in order to get along. Faith, on the contrary, spares the believer nothing, and wherever it appears — and it appears in the most unexpected places — it presents a clear and present danger to the status quo. Even a touch of real faith makes difficult, perhaps impossible, what we persist in calling normal life. So it was when Jesus nodded to James and John on the shore of the Sea of Galilee and they got up and left their father and his hired men to finish mending the net. And so is it now. Not least of all here in the United States in the past decade, the focus of my story.

On December 2, 1980, Ita Ford, Maura Clarke, Dorothy Kazel, and Jean Donovan, four American churchwomen who had been working with selfless dedication for the poor and oppressed peasants of war-ravaged El Salvador, were sexually assaulted and murdered by soldiers of the National Guard, and their bodies were thrown into a single unmarked grave beside a lonely road. Salvadoran soil was already soaked with innocent blood, but this time there was a difference. This was innocent North American blood.

In May of 1983, the Catholic bishops of the United States issued a pastoral letter on modern war, "The Challenge of Peace," a document that, despite its waffling in the end, expressed grave misgivings about the morality of nuclear deterrence, the cornerstone of American defense policy.

Two quite diverse events. But together with two others no less diverse of the decade previous — the Vietnam War and the 1973 *Roe vs. Wade* Supreme Court decision striking down anti-abortion laws — they have had a profound effect on the Catholic Church in the United States, giving rise to a transformation, however halting and incomplete, that might yet leave its mark on a secular history that would prefer to ignore the role of faith.

All four of these events were signs of contradiction, something that has but intensified their impact. For those who had eyes to see, everything was changed, utterly changed, and if a terrible beauty wasn't born, it was, I think, conceived.

The relatives of the El Salvador victims were shocked and appalled by the brusque lack of concern shown by most American officials, including fellow Catholics. Secretary of State Alexander Haig, a Catholic who would later be elevated to the dignity of a Papal Knight of Malta, declared in the course of some exceptionally convoluted testimony before a congressional committee that the women may have tried to run a roadblock and died in an "exchange of fire" — this after Haig had in hand FBI evidence that showed that each woman had been shot through the head at close range.

Nor did the words of our ambassador to the United Nations, Jeane Kirkpatrick, sit well with those who mourned. Although she was a member of the faculty of a renowned university that not only was Catholic but, exquisite irony, was run by a Jesuit order that had recently lost three priests to savage repression in Latin America — one in El Salvador itself, two after prolonged torture and mutilation — Madame Ambassador nonetheless insisted in her precise, meant-to-daunt fashion that one should bear in mind that the victims were not really missionaries but "political activists."

Her arrogance miscarried. Bereaved mothers and fathers, sisters and brothers don't take kindly to the insinuation that their beloved dead were outside agitators who deserved what they got, whether it comes from the mouth of a semiliterate Klansman or a lady with impeccable academic credentials.

The peace pastoral, for its part, drove onto the rocks the perfect marriage between Cross and Flag over whose consummation churchmen such as Francis Cardinal Spellman had presided with such pious glee — the kind of patriotism caught in purest form by an unforgettable news photo from Vietnam showing the cardinal seated behind a machine gun, his pudgy hands on the stock, as he declared, "My country right or wrong," a theological opinion derived not from Aquinas or Augustine but from Stephen Decatur, the hero of one of our first small wars.

Many American Catholics, strongly affected by one or more of these signs of contradiction, began to realize that they couldn't be uncritical patriots and true to the demands of their faith. This book tells the stories of some of them. Politics figures prominently in it, but it's not really about politics per se. It's about faith. I happen to find the latter even more fascinating than the former.

Finally — this is fair warning — the book is also about me in a sense. My admiration for the people I'm writing about is not a detached admiration. What they represent, each in his or her own way, challenges me. Telling their stories in this manner represents my attempt to come to grips with a question that has troubled me most of my life, a disturbing question that leads to a host of other questions.

What does it mean to be a Christian in the United States of America in the latter part of the twentieth century? How do you live an essentially simple faith in an essentially complex society that is part of a still more complex world? How, especially, when a variety of evils of unprecedented dimension threatens both society and world? How, especially, when not only outright unbelievers but even many of those who retain some attachment to Christianity reject, however wistfully, its supernatural claims?

Each of those whom I write about — from shy, soft-spoken Joan Andrews, who spent three years in solitary confinement rather than acknowledge the state of Florida's right to imprison her for anti-abortion activism, to born leader of men Charles Liteky, who laid down his Medal of Honor before the Vietnam Veterans Memorial and went on a water-only fast of forty-nine days to protest aid to the Contras — represents an intensely personal answer to these questions.

Each, finally, as I have good reason to know, is quite formidable in his or her own way. As the Duke of Wellington said of his soldiers: "I don't know what they do to the enemy, but they terrify me."

The Rebel Priest

Bob Begin

It was a hot and humid August afternoon, the kind that the climate of Cleveland lavishly affords. I got out of my station wagon with its New Jersey plates and began to walk along Clinton Street, a street of old frame houses. It was narrow and lined on both sides with parked cars, many of them the ancient gas guzzlers that allow the poor to make a major contribution to our economy. There was still a touch of grace to Clinton Street, however. It was lined with trees as well as cars, large, leafy trees, not the scrawny, doomed saplings of most inner-city neighborhoods.

I had an appointment with a priest named Bob Begin at the West Side Ecumenical Ministry, which occupied one of Clinton Street's frame houses.

It was an odd sensation to be walking along Clinton Street, odd but somehow reassuring. I had in my time been a harvest hand in South Dakota, a paratrooper in Korea, a Jesuit high school teacher in Cincinnati, a day laborer in Osaka, an instructor in English at Tokyo University, a translator of Japanese novels, a movie critic, and, most recently, a moral theologian of sorts. Now this afternoon, rather late in life this time, I was again starting something new. But since I was beginning with Begin, I was starting on a street whose name was so familiar to me that I couldn't remember when I first heard it.

Two or three generations earlier, Clinton Street had been a middle-class Irish neighborhood. The children of the impoverished refugees from the Potato Famine who had settled in the Flats and on the slopes overlooking the Cuyahoga River three miles to the east aspired to Clinton Street and, if they prospered, often moved here. The transition was from St. Malachi's

Parish to St. Patrick's on Bridge, from shanty Irish to lace curtain.

My grandfather and namesake was one of those who made it. Despite being but a generation removed from the Great Hunger and the peat bogs of Mayo, he became a coal company executive and a Republican, and, at the turn of the century, he built a good-sized house on Clinton Street for his wife and four children. And though he hadn't gone to high school, he used to close the door of his study at night, according to family lore, and recite Shakespeare.

In 1900, my father at ten was the oldest of my grandfather's children. Aunt Helen, who became an Ursuline nun, was the youngest, and all her life she would remember being remembered as the new baby in the new house in the new century. A fifth child, Stewart, named for the Protestant president of the coal company, was born on Clinton Street in 1901. Prosperity turned out to be fleeting, however. Panics were frequent when laissez-faire was in flower, but, whatever the cause, by the time my father disgraced the family in 1917 by joining the Cleveland Fire Department, my grandfather was dead and the money and the house were gone. Four years later, the brilliant Stewart, who might have restored the family's fortunes, drowned in the Mississippi at Prairie du Chien, Wisconsin. He was visiting his brother Jim, a Jesuit seminarian who, to his lifelong regret, persuaded Stewart, tired from the long train ride from Cleveland, to go for a swim.

Begin's father was also a fireman, and we had some other things in common, though the size of our families wasn't one of them. I had been an only child. Bob Begin, born in 1938, eight years after me, was one of twelve children. He grew up on the far western edge of Cleveland in St. Patrick's Parish, called St. Patrick's West Park to distinguish it from the other St. Patrick's, several miles to the east. West Park was and still is a pleasant residential neighborhood of single houses with almost nothing in the way of commercial buildings or apartments, more like a suburb than a part of the city.

I remembered it fondly. My mother and father rented a house on Elsienna, which was just a few blocks from Larchwood, Begin's street. It had a big front porch, and I sat out on it on sunny days one Depression-era spring while recuperating from diphtheria.

My stay in West Park and Bob Begin's overlapped by only a year. In the fateful month of August 1939, when I was going into fourth grade and he was just a year old, my family moved to East Cleveland.

Begin's path and mine wouldn't cross for more than thirty years, but when, home on a visit to my parents in January of 1969, I picked up *The Plain Dealer* one morning to see a picture of two young priests being arrested for staging an antiwar Mass at St. John's Cathedral, the story was of special interest because one of the priests was named Begin. Begin being so uncommon a name, I concluded at once that the young priest must be Chief Begin's son.

When Begin and I did meet in 1972 at the home of a close friend who taught at John Carroll, the local Jesuit university, we didn't hit it off famously. Begin, very much the rebel priest, was full of hotly expressed idealism, and I, on the brink of middle age, found his certainty and self-righteousness grating. But Bob Begin had mellowed over the years, my brother and sister-in-law had assured me, moderating his indignation enough to become a consultant to the Junior League.

My grandfather's house still stood this sultry August afternoon a few blocks east of the West Side Ecumenical Ministry, but once genteel Clinton Street was now part of the inner city, an ominous designation born of our era, and it was home to Hispanics, blacks, Appalachian whites, Palestinians, Gypsies, and Cambodians. New and more turbulent sorrows had come to displace the old, and Bob Begin lived in the midst of them.

He shook my hand warmly, congratulating me once again, as he had on the phone, on Archbishop Raymond Hunthausen's having quoted extensively from an article of mine on nuclear deterrence in his speech at the Pax Christi convention in Chicago the previous week. Begin's photo had just appeared on the front page of an alternative paper below a headline reading, inevitably, THE REBEL PRIEST. The photo had shown a weathered face quite different from that of the man I had met twenty years before, and the likeness was an accurate one. I had remembered his expression as petulant, but now he looked like a more rugged Van Heflin, and the smile, warm but tinged with what could be irony, hardly recalled the humorless zealot who had rubbed me the wrong way. When I mentioned Philip Berrigan in passing, I saw I had been right in detecting irony in Begin's cover photo smile. "Phil gives me a call once in a while," he said, with a laugh, "and wants to know when I'm going to stop spinning my wheels here."

Despite the mordant irony, despite the self-mockery, his intensity seemed as strong as ever. His frequent laugh was loud, and it had a harsh edge. "Hickey," said Begin, referring to His Eminence Cardinal James Hickey of Washington, who as bishop of Cleveland had reinstated him in the diocese after he had been suspended from the priesthood, "is about as liberal as an ambitious man can be. Saul Alinsky once met with some priests who said that they wanted to organize. He told them that all he wanted at the second meeting were those who didn't want to become bishops." Another loud laugh. "There was no second meeting."

Our experiences at St. Patrick's grade school turned out to have had a significant difference. I had had the Ursuline nuns as teachers, Aunt Helen's order. The brutal rape and murder of Sister Dorothy Kazel in El Salvador, an epochal event, was far in the future. Like Begin, Dorothy Kazel was only a baby in 1939, the delight of her parents, no doubt, in a Lithuanian neighborhood on the near East Side. So despite the martyrdom of their patron, St. Ursula, at the hands of the Goths — according to pious legend no less than ten thousand other virgins perished with her — there was no air of danger and risk about the Ursulines I knew. No one dreamed, it seemed, that what had happened long ages past could happen again. Even on a more modest scale, not with ten thousand companions but just three.

The Ursulines were gone by the time Bob Begin entered St. Patrick's at the end of World War II, and in their place were the Incarnate Word nuns, an Irish order thrown out of Mexico. Being Irish-Irish, with a sense of history shared at best only imperfectly by Irish-Americans, and refugees from government-directed persecution, the Incarnate Word sisters had considerably less trust in Caesar than had the Ursulines. They were willing to render him his due, but they weren't inclined to give him an unlimited line of credit.

"One of them," said Begin, "had actually saved the Host from the tabernacle during an anticlerical outbreak." How astonished, I thought, would Begin's detractors be, conservative Catholics that they were, to hear him relate with such enthusiasm the kind of story that had stirred hearts long ago in parochial school classrooms all over America. Begin's corollary, however, would have confirmed their worst fears: "Living in Mexico, they knew all about civil disobedience, though nobody called it that at the time. I remember distinctly my third grade teacher, Sr. Fidelis. You know what she said? Do what you should do no matter what the law says. I asked her about it years later. She said: 'Yes, I probably did teach you that because that's how I looked on rules.' "

Nuns, even in those days, harbored disturbing thoughts, it seemed, thanks perhaps to their being in intimate contact with a messy and unruly world. Vatican officials, on the other hand, the rule makers, were rarely called upon to save the Host from desecration — or to move fast under any circumstances for that matter.

When Begin was in the seventh grade, two Maryknoll priests came to St. Patrick's to talk about vocations. Maryknoll's image in the early fifties was quite different from what it would be twenty years later. The marriage of Cross and Flag was still a loving, untroubled union. With cold war in Europe and hot war in Korea, Rome and Washington had a common enemy: atheism in arms under the crimson banner of international communism. The Maryknollers, more so than other American religious orders, had suffered much at the hands of Red tyranny. Their many martyrs in China and Korea included two bishops (one of whom, Francis X. Ford, was a cousin of Ita Ford, who would die with Dorothy Kazel on the road to San Pedro Nonualco a generation later), and they had a living martyr in Bishop James Walsh, imprisoned for life in Shanghai for alleged crimes against the people. What could be more inspiring to a red-blooded American Catholic boy?

"The Maryknoll recruiters hooked me good," said Begin. "I was all set to go." There was no need for him to explain his enthusiasm to me. I had felt it too. At twenty-four, however, my feelings had been more complex than Begin's at twelve. Serving Christ as had Paul and Francis Xavier in faraway places, braving dangers by sea and by land, not only represented a far more thrilling challenge than a quiet life in a rectory or school but had struck me as the best way to keep my mind off sex.

Begin's parents weren't enthusiastic about his wanting to join Maryknoll. Having a son a priest was one thing. Having a son a missionary was another. In the first case, you gave up grandchildren. In the second, you gave up your son as well, though, God knows, Begin's parents, unlike my own mother and father, had sons to spare.

His uncle, Floyd Begin, then a monsignor of the diocese of Cleveland and later the bishop of Oakland, felt the same way. More so in fact. He wasn't at all eager to see the diocese lose so promising a candidate, especially one who was his nephew. The joint decision of parents and uncle was that young Robert should enter the diocesan minor seminary and then think again about Maryknoll when he was more mature.

So it was that he entered St. Francis Borromeo Seminary at thirteen, a decision that he characterized as "a real bad mistake." He did not find the seminary curriculum very challenging, either then or later. To escape the prevailing boredom, he turned to literature, making his way through all of O'Neill, Dostoyevsky, and Tolstoy. When he reread many of these works as an adult, he confessed, he came upon ideas that he had thought were of his own creation, a humbling experience. Seven years later, when he was about to begin the four years of theology that led to ordination, he still felt that he had a vocation to the missions, and he wrote a letter to the Maryknoll superior. The response was that Maryknoll would be happy to accept him but first he had to produce a letter of recommendation from his uncle. "I called them and said: 'Do you ask for a letter of recommendation from everybody's uncle?' 'No,' they said, 'but we want one from yours.' "

The Jesuits wouldn't have shown anything like so tender a regard for the feelings of the local hierarchy, but a small order, even one with Maryknoll's laurels, had to be prudent in dealing with bishops.

Floyd Begin was an auxiliary bishop by that time and the pastor of St. Agnes's Parish on the East Side. Its church was an enormous domed structure that stood on Euclid Avenue at the edge of downtown Cleveland. Since no mortal act is free of some trace of pride and self-interest, churches, whatever the pretense, are never built to honor God alone. Thus St. Agnes's, as late as the forties when I used to ride by it on the streetcar on the way to St. Ignatius High School, stood as the proud symbol of a thriving Catholic community. In the decade following World War II, however, it lost most of its congregation and all of its prosperity. Only its slender bell tower would survive a disastrous fire in the seventies, and today, like Shelley's Ozymandias, it stands as a symbol of quite another sort. The vanity of human endeavor.

When Bishop Begin invited his nephew over for a visit in the late fifties, his parish included one of the most dangerous neighborhoods in Cleveland, Hough (as in rough and tough), which would lend its name to one of the major riots of the mid-sixties.

The bishop took the seminarian for a little walk. He let him see the poverty and squalor all around and the boarded-up storefronts. They went into two or three bars. Then when they got back, he said to his nephew: "I'm not going to write your damn letter. What do you want to go to China for? There's plenty of work for a priest right here, right here in Cleveland." Then he said to Begin, reflecting the pride of the era that had formed him: "If we do it right here, everybody will do it right because everybody wants to be like us." It was 1959, some years before the painful realization began to penetrate the American awareness that perhaps we had something to learn, whether from Vietnamese generals, Japanese industrialists, or Latin American theologians.

Begin wrote back to Maryknoll explaining his problem, and they relented to some extent, telling him that they might agree to his joining even without his uncle's letter. He had had enough temporizing by then, however, and he told Maryknoll to forget it. He began his theological studies at the local major seminary, and in 1962 he became a priest of the diocese of Cleveland. Though it hardly seemed so at the time, becoming a diocesan priest rather than a Maryknoller was a fateful decision. Before the end of the decade, radical priests would become so common among the Maryknollers that even the pious faithful would become used to them. Not so with radical diocesan priests. They would retain a greater power to shock, especially since bishops as a class tend to prize tranquillity and good order above all else.

Begin was assigned to St. Gregory's Parish in South Euclid, an eastern suburb, whose parishioners ranged from blue collar to upper middle class. It was to some extent a white-flight suburb since it bordered on Cleveland Heights and East Cleveland, into which blacks were moving at a rapid rate. My old neighborhood, East Cleveland, in particular, a blue-collar suburb almost surrounded by Cleveland and filled with older and inexpensive single-family houses, was well on its way to becoming entirely black and would one day gain the unfortunate distinction of having the highest poverty rate in Ohio. The climate of South Euclid, then, was not congenial to liberal ideas.

For the first two years at St. Gregory's, Begin was a model priest, doing exactly what was expected of him. But then a classmate of his from the seminary, Len Ferrante, joined the staff of St. Gregory's. Begin had great respect for Ferrante and thought he was very talented. After Ferrante had been at St. Gregory's for about six months, he came to Begin's room one night after midnight and said to him: "I just have to tell you that you're going to grow up and be just like this asshole who's the pastor. You're beginning to be just like him. Treating everybody equally. Not being passionate, not allowing yourself to fall in love with anybody, loving people generically. . . ."

The wisdom of Ferrante's speech, as recounted, impressed me somewhat less than it had Begin. I had been as he had wanted Begin to be, and that's why I was no longer a Jesuit. I asked who the pastor was, and when Begin told me his name, I felt a small stab of pain. I had known the man, a simple, good-natured Irish-American of my father's generation. I had once served his Mass, and he had tried to make conversation afterward in a bluff, awkward way. Somehow he saw fit to convey to his thirteen-year-old altar boy that what he thought about most was bills.

Next a parishioner named Bill Corrigan told Begin that what the parish needed was a discussion group dealing with the documents of the Vatican Council. Begin had read them, Corrigan had read them, but hardly anybody else had.

Begin put Corrigan off, telling him that he would think about it. But then Corrigan came up to him one day and said: "Okay, we're going to have our first meeting. Nine o'clock Friday night." Thus was born the St. Gregory's Discussion Group. They began with five or six couples and before long Begin, contrary to parish policy, was going out every night. The group was ecumenical. Begin promised not to try to convert spouses, and everyone enjoyed getting together and exchanging ideas in a relaxed atmosphere. Some of the participants started thinking in terms of how to teach religion to children, and so Sunday school teachers began to come to meetings. A community of about 150 people formed. They went so far as to propose a reorganization of the parish based on Vatican II, but the pastor turned it down.

Then after three or four years, some of the boys Begin had taught in his religion classes began to return from Vietnam. One in particular had come home an emotional and mental wreck. He had been a helicopter gunner; after a napalm attack on a grove of trees or other shelter, the helicopter would swoop down, and it was this boy's job to shoot whoever came out.

Bill Corrigan, who had taken a German bullet in the Battle of the Bulge, asked Begin when he was going to talk about the war in his sermons. "I told him next Sunday. So I did, and he came up to me afterward and said that that was a nice talk about war and how bad it was, but how about the Vietnam War? When was I going to talk about that?" Soon after, Begin did talk about the Vietnam War, but that still wasn't good enough for Corrigan. It wasn't a bad sermon, he told Begin, but when was he going to talk about the Vietnam War and call it the Vietnam War?

Bill Corrigan didn't favor the Pius XII school of circumlocution. In the forties, the *Universe Bulletin,* Cleveland's Catholic paper, had tirelessly hailed Pius XII as the Pope of Peace, but even I, a simple Catholic school-boy, had my doubts. Why, I wondered, couldn't the pope get down to brass tacks? He was always deploring war, but it was never too clear that he had anything against World War II in particular.

Goaded by Corrigan, Begin did get specific the next Sunday, and people started walking out of church. The Rebel Priest was on his way and discovering, it seemed, that he enjoyed this sort of thing. "One Sunday we had a Mass devoted to forgiveness. During the petitions, I sang out" — he sang — " 'For Ho Chi Min who is seriously ill, let us pray to the Lord,' and instead of the response 'Lord hear us,' a big gasp filled the church." He laughed a harsh, raucous laugh.

Begin also began to preach against racism, a theme that was, if possible, even more volatile, given the racial circumstances of South Euclid. Begin's community formed a committee on suburban human relations. They trained people on how to become active by getting five couples together and showing them movies and giving them tapes to take home. They invited guest speakers such as Philip Berrigan and George Mischi of the Catonsville

Nine, who were able to tell them what those with like concerns were doing elsewhere.

It was an exciting time, said Begin. People would stand up at meetings and make statements. Members of the community that they had formed, which never had a name, went to the draft file-burning trials of both the Catonsville Nine and the Milwaukee Fourteen. Bernie Meyer, a curate in a black parish, started what he was rash enough to call the Catholic Peace Movement and so incurred the displeasure of the bishop of Cleveland, Clarence Issenman. "Issenman was pissed about the 'Catholic' in the name and told him to take it out," said Begin. Peace wasn't an official apostolate of the diocese, said Issenman sternly, betraying no sense of incongruity despite his presumed familiarity with the Sermon on the Mount.

It was 1968, and everybody agreed that something had to be done in Cleveland too. Begin and Meyer intended at first to make a statement at the Christmas midnight Mass at St. John's Cathedral, but since there wasn't enough time to plan it properly, they put their action off a month, selecting one of the midnight Masses held at the Cathedral every Saturday, the so-called printers' Mass. And instead of merely making a statement, they decided to have a Mass of their own, preempting the scheduled one by beginning ten minutes earlier.

Begin and Meyer weren't at all secretive about their intentions, and word soon got around that something was up. When Bishop William Cosgrove, an auxiliary bishop of Cleveland, called Begin and asked him about his plans, Begin answered quite frankly that they were going to have a Mass and read a statement condemning the war and calling for action on racial and social justice issues.

Cosgrove asked Begin not to do it. He was about to get Bishop Issenman to approve a new organization dedicated to social concerns, he said — the Commission on Catholic Community Action. "He told me," said Begin, "that he thought we were going to screw everything up." Begin replied that he didn't think so. In fact, he told him, he and Meyer might give Cosgrove some leverage. Harassed by restive clerics and lay people like Begin and Meyer and their friends, Issenman should be able to see the advantage of being able to hold up the commission as an example of how the diocese of Cleveland really was concerned about social issues and was getting seriously involved.

Cosgrove remained unconvinced. Familiar as he was with the hierarchical mind, he probably knew all too well that bold logic like this was beyond men like Issenman. Holding the line was all they knew. But he told Begin to go ahead and do what he thought he had to do and hung up.

Begin paused in his account, reflecting on what had happened twenty years before. Cosgrove, he said, was probably too much of an Irish Catholic to think of using the Mass in the way that Begin and Meyer intended. "You know, it's a real problem, the balance between compassion and anger. Cosgrove was full of compassion, but he wasn't angry enough to go against the system."

Bishop William Cosgrove, in his mid-fifties at the time, was an intellectual with a deep sense of social concern who was firmly committed to racial justice. He was loved and admired by clergy and laity alike. Rome would pass over him again and again, and when he finally received a see of his own, it would be that of Belleville, Illinois, best known as an affluent suburb of tragic East St. Louis. The bishop of Cleveland in 1969, Clarence Issenman, was an affable, kindly man, but, as was the case with so many of his fellow shepherds, myopic when it came to reading the signs of the times.

On Saturday night, January 25, ten minutes before the midnight printers' Mass was to begin, Begin and Bernie Meyer, in full vestments, entered St. John's Cathedral at East 9th and Superior through its massive front door and walked up the center aisle in procession with a dozen or so of their supporters. More were in the congregation. The conspirators were confident they would be able to carry out their plan without any major confrontation. True, they had seen several police cars on their way to the cathedral, but they thought that once they had started the Mass, no one would dare interrupt them.

About five minutes after they had begun, however, a priest from the cathedral parish climbed into the pulpit and announced to the startled faithful — whether printers or romantic youths intent on sleeping in on Sunday after late dates — that the supposed celebrants weren't real priests. He asked the congregation to leave at once, and then, after telling an outright lie in the house of God, he flaunted the legalism so dear to the clerical heart by informing them that he was forthwith dispensing them from their Sunday Mass obligation. Some of the congregation left, but most stayed, perhaps just to see what was going to happen.

What followed, played out on the stage of St. John's sanctuary, combined elements of farce, tragedy, and melodrama — a moral play, in other words. The marriage of Cross and Flag may have been breaking up, but the Church and the theater, lovers centuries estranged, were reaching out to each other once again.

A second priest came up to the altar and told Begin and Meyer that they were suspended and that they should cease and desist. Begin countered by informing him that canon law required a priest to continue a Mass once begun. After the Gospel, Begin read a statement that expressed the sentiments of the St. Gregory's group. No one thought to save a copy of the statement, but, though its focus was the Vietnam War, Begin recalled that it also addressed the responsibility that all Christians share with regard to poverty and racism.

The back of the church had begun to fill up with police, about fifty of them, but Begin and Meyer had heard one of the cathedral priests tell the police to arrest them once they left the altar, and they felt that they had nothing to worry about until the Mass was over. When Begin came down to distribute Communion, however, two policemen grabbed him and a general struggle ensued, with the priests from the cathedral and some of the St. Gregory contingent joining the fray. Never had liturgical renewal gone quite so far, at least in Cleveland.

"One of the women in our group," said Begin, "knelt down and started to pick up some hosts that had fallen to the floor, and one of the priests, Jim Griffin, who's now the bishop of Columbus, yelled at her not to touch them. One cop still had hold of me by the arm. I said I wasn't leaving until I got the hosts back into the tabernacle, and a Dominican nun in our group grabbed my other arm and yelled at the cop to let me do it. Bernie Meyer, who had had nonviolence training, just sat down when it all started. I said to Griffin: 'Jim, these hosts are going to spill, and it will be your responsibility,' and he finally told the cops to let us finish the Mass. So we finished the Mass, and then we all sat down, and the police came up and carried us out."

The other demonstrators were released, but Begin and Meyer were charged with "disturbing a church service," an ironic accusation in the light of events. Whoever had alerted the police had gotten it wrong, and the police had framed the charges accordingly.

The police told them that the diocese was willing to drop the charges if they would meet with the bishop. The diocese, in fact, had little choice but to back down, given the inaccuracy of the charges, but getting Issenman's full attention had been one of Begin and Meyer's objectives, and so they readily agreed. The next day they met with a distraught Bishop Issenman.

"He told us that we'd been disobedient. He forgave us, though, and then he said: 'Kneel down, and I'll give you my blessing.' "

The two wayward clerics, both over thirty, knelt down like naughty schoolboys who had been reprieved, and the bishop of Cleveland gave them his blessing. After they had walked out of his office, the episcopal benefaction flush upon them, they were greeted by representatives of Cleveland's finest, who rearrested them on the new charge of trespassing. It took several motions and $900 in legal fees before the diocese finally relented and dropped the charges.

The memory still rankled for Begin. "What they did was totally out of line," he said. "Once a deal is made, you don't back down on it like that."

Years later Cosgrove came back to Cleveland to receive the annual award of the Commission on Catholic Community Action. Begin belonged to the organization by then and was in the audience. Reminiscing in his acceptance speech about the events surrounding the founding of the commission, Cosgrove acknowledged the contribution made by Begin and Meyer and their supporters — "the activists," as he called them. Their statement, he said, had in fact well expressed the ideals of the commission. Then, confiding to an audience he knew was sympathetic, he went on to say that the last thing Bishop Issenman said to him before he died was that if he had been able to handle things himself, Begin and Meyer wouldn't have been treated as they had.

Issenman, a good and decent man, had yielded to the hard-liners as American bishops invariably did. It was the kind of sad little tragedy that has been enacted again and again in the history of the Church: a splendid opportunity to speak truth to power thrown away because of timidity — a fearful reaction in the name of a political expediency that took no account of the demands of faith. The abiding irony, little noted nor long remembered, was that the course of events usually showed that the faith-inspired action would have been politically sound as well and the politically motivated action, or failure to act, had in fact been ill considered and disastrous in its consequences. So it was with the French Church's ardent embrace of the Bourbons, the enthusiastic support of Cardinal James Gibbons of Baltimore, the de facto primate of the American Church, for the United States' entry into World War I, the failure of the American Church to denounce slavery in the nineteenth century, its tardiness in speaking out for civil rights in the twentieth, and, the issue here, its vacillation on the Vietnam War. In due time, I think, Pius XII's failure to condemn the Holocaust, the American Church's silence on U.S. involvement in Grenada, Panama, and the Persian Gulf, and its mere hand-wringing on nuclear weapons and on American policy in Latin America will also emerge from the heat and smoke of controversy as not only moral lapses but political lapses as well. As Chesterton observed, Christianity hasn't failed; it's never really been tried.

Most of Begin and Meyer's fellow priests sided with the chancery. They were shocked. "How could you do something like this to your mothers?" they asked.

"The funny thing," said Begin, "is that priests in the missions are much more likely to do radical things than priests at home. And parents who'd be happy about things their sons might do on the other side of an ocean are horrified when they do them in their own backyard." John Groppi, he said, had once given a talk in Cleveland on this very theme. Groppi, a Milwaukee priest who eventually left the priesthood, had come out strongly against racial injustice in the early sixties and accused the Church of what amounted to criminal neglect. In his talk, he said that the Church counts on the families of young priests to keep them in line because they'll hesitate to do anything that might disgrace their mothers.

Actually, Begin's mother took her son's situation quite well. It was his father, the fire chief, who took it to heart. "My father was really pissed. He was ready to kill me. He went so far as to take out and shine up an old .22 that he used to shoot rats in the chicken coop, this time with me in mind. 'I'll shoot that son of a bitch if he comes around here,' he said. My sister called me" — Begin raised his pitch — " 'Don't come home. Daddy's going to shoot you.' " He laughed. "He knew all the policemen who arrested me. They hated my guts for making them arrest a priest, and many still do. Given the racism of the police at the time, our singing 'We Shall Overcome' as they carried us out didn't help matters. My father was an officer of the fire department union, and he had to work with them, and he was also the chief's secretary. He had to go to work the next Monday and face everybody."

My father, I said, had never had a good word for the police.

"Oh, my father didn't either," replied Begin. "He said they were a bunch of thieves." He imitated his father's strident tone: " 'Don't leave anything out when the police are around. They'll steal the tablecloth off your table.' But even so, my father was a man who believed that you had to work within organizations, and so when I opted out, it not only upset him emotionally, it was also something that he disagreed with intellectually. It wasn't the way to operate, he thought. But it almost killed him sometimes to do it his way. Whenever he had to go down to Columbus to lobby for a bill for both police and firemen, he'd be sick about it ahead of time."

As spectacular as his father's rage was, it didn't last long. "I hitchhiked out to California while the charges were still pending," said Begin, "and I talked with my uncle, the bishop, and I also visited an aunt who was a Notre Dame nun. I think she called my father. Anyway, when I came back, he was a changed man. He came to see that the diocese had gone too far."

When Begin's father lay dying in the hospital ten years later, a close friend of Begin's later told me, he kept telling his nurse how proud he was of him, but he never told his son.

Begin and Meyer, so sure that right reason was on their side in the face of the manifest wrong of the Vietnam War, had not expected their protest to provoke so intense and hostile a reaction. To make matters worse, said Begin, they found themselves the men of the hour for "every kook who ever had any kind of problem with the Church." Despite the problems their action engendered, however, some good came of it. Paul Hritz, a highly respected priest of the diocese, spoke out in favor of Begin and Meyer, and he and some others finally persuaded the Priests Council, a post–Vatican II innovation, to ask the bishop to drop the charges. The council set up a committee for priests concerned about social justice, which functioned effectively for a short time. But then when everybody began to join it just to find out what was going on in the diocese, its focus became blurred and the group lost sight of the Vietnam War, among other things.

It was at that juncture, in March 1969, that Bernie Meyer called up Phil Berrigan and told him how things stood. The brothers Berrigan, Dan the Jesuit and Phil the Josephite priest, were in the forefront of the antiwar movement, heroes not only to the so-called Catholic left but to secular activists as well, including members of the radical and irreligious Students for a Democratic Society, who endorsed the use of violence, something the Berrigans would have no part of. Phil Berrigan advised a retreat, and so Meyer and Begin went on a retreat with Bill Corrigan and his wife, Judy. The setting was a farmhouse on the outskirts of Milwaukee, and Phil Berrigan came by for a day to talk with them.

Making a retreat, a withdrawal from everyday life for an extended period of prayer and reflection on the course of one's life, was a practice that at the time was almost exclusively a Catholic one, though it has since become popular in other denominations and, *mutatis mutandis,* even among secular organizations. It was a staple of the pre–Vatican II Church that not only survived the council's traumatic aftermath but flourished. In the sixties, the Berrigans' secular admirers might have wondered at the efficacy of something so suggestive of navel gazing in times that demanded radical action, but making retreats was something that came naturally to Catholic peace activists, even though they seemed to be at odds with their Church in so many other respects. The world might not have understood this, but it was a Christian tradition older than the Church itself, one that Jesus began by going out into the desert.

The Catholic peace movement wasn't by any means born with the Vietnam War. Dorothy Day and her Catholic Worker movement and then Gordon Zahn had provided a Catholic presence among those working for peace for more than thirty years, and they too had had predecessors. Despite the prevalence of the just war theory in Catholic theology, there has always been a pacifist current in Catholic thought, something that the 1983 peace pastoral of the American bishops, "The Challenge of Peace," would at last acknowledge despite the grumblings of some of the more bellicose shepherds.

The Berrigan brothers urged retreats as a means for activists to test their resolve and spiritual commitment. It was this spiritual dimension, in fact, that made Catholic peace activists among the most tenacious opponents of the war. They were willing to take the greatest risks and perform the most radical actions, as long as they were nonviolent. Many of them, the Berrigans first and foremost, would carry this same commitment into the struggle against nuclear arms and intervention in Central America once the Vietnam War was over, even though the media would cease to care by then.

After their return to Cleveland, Meyer received a phone call from a fellow retreatant. There was to be a meeting in Washington for those interested in taking part in a protest that could have serious consequences.

He and Begin were ready for something of just that sort, and they went to Washington. Twenty-one people participated, divided into two groups. The target of Begin and Meyer's group, which consisted of nine people, was Dow Chemical. They were to gain entry to its corporate headquarters and throw their blood wherever it seemed most appropriate.

Dow was one of the favorite villains of the antiwar movement; its recruiters were harassed on campuses all over the country. It made napalm, and its corporate image would be forever linked with the famous photo of the naked and scarred Vietnamese girl fleeing a village destroyed by its flagship product. For good measure, Dow also made the body bags that some 58,000 young Americans would wear on their return stateside.

The other group was to seize files from a draft office and burn them in front of the White House. Each group had a prepared statement which, among other things, said that all twenty-one people were acting in conspiracy. Just as the government and industry were in conspiracy to carry on war, they were in a conspiracy on behalf of peace.

One of their number, unfortunately, was an FBI infiltrator. He warned the targeted draft office, and the files were moved. The informer was also the one assigned to case Dow, and he assured the group there was no security alarm at Dow Headquarters when in fact there was, a bit of deception that was to have ironic consequences.

Begin's job was to go up to the twelfth floor of Dow's offices and, after signing in as a visitor, open a window to the fire escape. When he opened the window, the alarm that wasn't supposed to be there went off. Dow security responded promptly, but they did so by rushing down to the basement, allowing Begin's companions ample time to reach the twelfth floor unhindered, each carrying a plastic container of blood. After throwing the blood on the walls and floor, they broke a window and threw out whatever papers they could lay hands on. The *Washington Post*'s offices were just across the street, and photographers shot some pictures.

Then Begin, Meyer, and the others, in accordance with the principles of nonviolence, waited for the police to come to arrest them. When they finally did, the protesters sang "Glory, Glory, Hallelujah" as they were carried out.

Among the group, besides Begin and Meyer, were Arthur Melville, a former Maryknoll priest in Guatemala like his brother Thomas of Catonsville Nine fame; Mike Doherty and Joe O'Rourke, two Jesuits about to be ordained, the latter expelled from the order in later years because of an aggressive pro-abortion stance; Joanne Malone, a Sister of Loretto from St. Louis; and Mike Slasky, a young draft resister, and a priest named Denny Maloney, both from Detroit. Sister Joanne had a connection with the Teamsters, and it was an official of the Teamsters, an organization little noted for leftist sympathies, who bailed out the group after ten days in the notorious Washington city jail.

The first trial ended with a conviction, but the verdict was overturned on the grounds that the accused had not been permitted to defend themselves as they had requested, and a new trial was ordered. By the time the second trial was held, the war was practically over as far as the United States was concerned and the soldiers were coming home. The defendants were offered a deal by the government. If they pleaded guilty to simple trespassing, a misdemeanor, they could get off with a suspended sentence. They accepted. A misdemeanor conviction wouldn't prevent Begin from going to law school, and that's what he had decided to do.

The Church was not as forgiving as the government, however, despite the well-known injunction of its founder and despite Begin and Meyer's having acted against a war that the American hierarchy, however tardily and halfheartedly, had come out against. The two were forbidden to say Mass or otherwise function as priests.

Though reviled by many, especially among their coreligionists, Begin and Meyer found themselves hailed as heroes in some highly respectable circles. After their first trial, they went on a speaking tour that included most of the prep schools of New England, Harvard Divinity School, and hundreds of churches. Everyone wanted to hear why they had done it.

Once back in Cleveland, they settled into a more prosaic existence. Begin had to find a new place to live. He had been staying with a married couple sympathetic to his ideals, but the husband, an engineer, was the head of the bombsight division of a major local company. "When I went to Washington," he said, "they thought that it was simply to burn draft files. But when it turned out that we had hit Dow, implicating all war profiteers, I had to go." He found a room not far from St. Patrick's on Bridge, in a neighborhood so wild at night that sometimes he was afraid to get out of his car when he came home.

Begin and Meyer were still intent on starting a Catholic peace movement, and their efforts over the next few months led to the founding of the Thomas Merton Community, a group based on the ideals of the Catholic Worker movement. Each Catholic Worker community did things a little differently, and the Thomas Merton Community, instead of having its own soup kitchen, ran one in a different church each week.

Begin had been working as a cook, and he and Meyer still got some income from speaking at colleges, but most of their financial support came from the community that Begin and Bill and Judy Corrigan had begun at St. Gregory's Parish in the mid-sixties. Many of its members were appalled by what Begin and Meyer had done, but they nevertheless felt obliged to help them, and they raised enough money to provide a living allowance of about ten dollars a day. Begin, in the meantime, had begun classes at Cleveland State Law School.

James Hickey became the bishop of Cleveland in 1973, and one of the first things he did was to call Begin. They had dinner together at Kiefer's, a German restaurant on the near West Side that, despite its drab decor and undistinguished food, was a favorite gathering place of priests, lawyers, and politicians. Hickey wanted to know what Begin and Meyer were doing, and Begin told him about their work in the neighborhood and his going to law school. "We'd like to start paying you if we can," said Hickey. "Suppose we give you one hundred dollars a month for law school, and then we can talk again. But first, how about your prayer life?"

Begin answered that with his crowded schedule he was more inclined to nap than to pray, getting in at least twenty minutes a day. It was a response that would have severely tested my patience had I been Hickey, but the future cardinal-archbishop of Washington persisted. What, he asked, was Begin's idea of obedience?

Begin was quite prepared. "Well," he told the bishop of Cleveland, "I think we have to be obedient to the needs of the people because that's where Christ is, and when what you tell me is in agreement with the needs of the people, then I'm also obedient to you. Sometimes, though, I might know more about the needs of the people than you do because I'm here, and then I might not be willing to do it your way."

Hickey had evidently come to Kiefer's determined to be patient. That was certainly a novel idea of obedience, he replied. Was that what Begin had had in mind when he put his hands in his bishop's hands at his ordination and promised obedience and reverence?

"No," Begin replied, "it's what I mean now."

Thanks to Hickey's remarkable forbearance, Begin was on his way to becoming once more a priest in good standing in the Diocese of Cleveland. Bernie Meyer, on the other hand, was to leave the priesthood, and I would later meet him in Seattle when I went there to interview Archbishop Raymond Hunthausen, who had given him a job in the archdiocese.

The West Side Ecumenical Ministry, Begin's current base of operations, is made up of four clusters of churches for a total of thirty-five embracing nine denominations. Unlike most grassroots organizations that flourished in the sixties only to wither in the seventies, it has survived. Some three thousand families in the area make use of its emergency food program, which allows a family to obtain a three-day supply of food three times a year. In 1970, the ministry fed only two hundred families, an indication, said Begin, of how the poor had fared under Reagan.

The ministry also tries to help families cope with the causes of their distress. Have they been compelled to take money from their food budget to buy a refrigerator or pay the rent or has it gone for a purchase that wasn't really necessary? Do they know how to manage what money they have? Are they eligible for some kind of benefit or work program? Would going to school help? The idea, Begin said, is to give people the means to help themselves so that they will no longer be dependent on the hunger program.

Another program of the ministry gathers people into groups of nine or ten to set up their own food co-ops. Most of the inner-city poor have never been at any kind of meeting or belonged to any kind of organization. They had no idea how to cooperate. "What we found," said Begin, "was that being in need is something that really isolates people, and the skills for coming out of isolation don't even exist. So we try to help them to develop these skills." The people in the groups began to babysit for one another and to give one another rides. With the help of the ministry, they also try to find piecework that they can do at home and earn money for their treasury.

Another strategy is to partner an inner-city group with a suburban group. A group from Gesu Parish in University Heights, for example, is the partner of the West Side Women's Center. Members of the suburban group and the inner-city group attend each other's meetings. The participation of the suburban group helps give a sense of esteem and importance to the inner-city group. Their presence shows that they have confidence in and respect for what the inner-city group is doing. The suburban group also matches any sum the inner-city group puts into its treasury.

Begin went on recounting the details. He had an easy command of facts and figures. There had been a 40 percent cut in federal grants the year before. In 1970 there had been seven thousand people in prison in Ohio. In 1988 there were twenty-four thousand. By 1990 there would probably be thirty thousand, he said, and, as it turned out, he was right on the mark. The rate of recidivism among young offenders was 80 percent. More impressive yet were his insights. Because there were no extracurricular activities in inner-city schools, young adults knew nothing about cooperation. Just competition.

Despite Begin's mastery of his subject, his account did not make for easy listening. It was at once unsettling and tedious. He was describing a national disaster of frightening proportions, but unlike most disasters it wasn't exciting. There wasn't the frisson that comes of reading about a plane crash, the surge of pity and distress provoked by an account of a cyclone in Bangladesh. There was a drabness and dailiness to the tragedy he recounted. It wasn't over and done with. It just kept going on. Nor did there seem to be much hope.

The Democratic programs of the sixties were not perfect, Begin said, but now they were gone; what used to be emergency measures, like soup kitchens and shelters, had become institutionalized. Five years ago, the people the ministry was helping were just entering into poverty, but now they had become part of a whole subclass. The recovery, if indeed there ever were one, would take a long time. Begin realized that the big problems were beyond him. All he could do was try to help some people help themselves through the programs that the ministry had developed, noting what worked and what didn't work and hoping that the ministry's successes might be emulated elsewhere if the government ever again started to show some concern for the poor.

The Rebel Priest had, it seemed, immersed himself in noncontroversial good works, which included the founding of Templum House, a shelter for battered women, the project that had led to his relationship with the Junior League as a consultant on inner-city matters. But despite Begin's ability to make himself useful and even agreeable when it suited him, his conversation turned easily from the need to cope and make do to assessments calculated to set pious Catholic teeth on edge.

"There are two tendencies in the world," he said. "One is to concentrate wealth and power in the hands of fewer and fewer people. The other is to try and give every man, woman, and child his or her just share. I see the Church lining up with the wrong process. From their statements, the pope and the bishops seem to be on the side of the people, but by what they're doing and not doing they're definitely lining up on the other side."

For Begin St. Patrick's Parish was a microcosm. What was writ small in its neighborhoods was writ large in the world. To understand what was going on in the near West Side was to begin to understand what was going on in the Third World. Though St. Patrick's was the focus of his work, his concerns extended much farther, particularly to Central America.

He had been there once before, and now he was preparing to go again. He would fly to Mexico City, get a bus to Guatemala City, and then, after a stay there, get another bus to San Salvador. In El Salvador, he would link up with the Cleveland mission team in La Libertad, to which the two martyrs Jean Donovan and Dorothy Kazel had belonged.

An organization called Peace Brigades International ran an escort service for the leaders of a Salvadoran group that documented the atrocities of the death squads, publicizing the names of the victims and the circumstances of their deaths or disappearance. The organization's first leader, a young man, was found beaten to death. The second was a young woman. She was very careful and never went out alone, but she too was found beaten to death and raped as well, with her two-year-old son lying dead beside her. Peace Brigades provided Europeans or North Americans to stay with families who had reason to feel threatened.

There was really nothing much to it, Begin said. You just sat there and nobody paid much attention to you, though the people you stayed with were obviously grateful for your presence. It was nerve-wracking at first, he confessed. You tensed up every time a car passed, afraid that it might stop and a death squad would get out.

His trips to Central America were, he thought, his way of trying to deal with living in a superpower. The people in Guatemala and El Salvador were essentially the same as the people on the near West Side, but there were differences as well. "You have to find some way of identifying with the victims," said Begin. "You have to get to know them." The West Side Ecumenical Ministry got to know the prisoners it worked with by obtaining bail bonds for them. Begin had been drawn into the antiwar movement because he knew the boys from St. Gregory's who had come home traumatized. It was the same with the poor, he said. You have to find some means of identifying with them before they would trust you to struggle with them. "I wanted to identify with people who were the victims of our foreign policy. I could say all I wanted about Central America, but unless I've been there, I'm not speaking from my own hurts."

He had not always thought this way, he said. Begin was a man altogether open to experience, a rare characteristic in any case and one quite foreign to the clerical mind, and his thinking had evolved accordingly over the years. He had disagreed with Bill and Judy Corrigan in the sixties when they and others in the group at St. Gregory's decided to move to St. Patrick's Parish and start a Catholic Worker community.

"I thought they were crazy, and I said as much. You have to change society by being in the middle of society, I told them. If you move into the city, your energy will be taken up with surviving and helping others survive."

The Corrigans answered that they had to start practicing what they preached. Instead of doing for the poor, they said, they had to start doing *with* the poor. Their best argument, though, one that eventually persuaded Begin, was that they had tried to move society from the middle of society, and society hadn't budged. Their fellow parishioners at St. Gregory's had written them off as kooks.

The Corrigans and their friends differed from the average Catholic in that they saw the struggle for social justice as a constitutive part of Christianity. By the sixties, many Catholics had advanced to the stage where they felt an obligation to contribute money to help promote justice throughout the world, but the Corrigans' thinking had gone far beyond that. They believed that you had to become personally involved and that you had to challenge those who had conspired to institutionalize injustice, whether they were in government, in business, or in the Church itself. This, Begin said, was the crime that they had crucified Jesus for. They didn't mind his feeding the poor.

Most of the Catholics whom Begin depended on for support, however, didn't live in St. Patrick's on the near West Side but far away, in St.

Gregory's in South Euclid and Gesu in University Heights. They were as success-oriented as their fellow Americans of the same social class, but now they felt an obligation to do something about the critical state of American society. The winner-loser gap had widened to proportions that no reasonably intelligent person could ignore. Nor were they altogether disinterested in their yearning to do something constructive. They were confronting the unpleasant truth that their children stood a good chance of being less well off than they were. They wanted to do something, but they weren't keen on challenging authority, and they hadn't the least inclination to move in next to the Corrigans on Clinton Street.

This made for a certain amount of tension. "It's hard," said Begin, "when you're sitting in somebody's living room in University Heights to make even the most matter-of-fact and commonsense statement without it seeming to be a personal attack — even to say that America should join the ranks of civilized nations and establish a comprehensive system of national health care, because there'll probably be a doctor or two in the group."

Perhaps it was easier to lay down one's life than one's lifestyle for another. And maybe the tension was a good thing. In sensing, however unwillingly, how great a threat the demands of faith posed to a pleasant and well-ordered existence, these Catholics were, after all, far ahead of their coreligionists. Too many of the latter were like the wealthy businessman Begin had an exchange with at a wedding. He told the man that the United States spent so much on armaments because we wanted them to defend our economic interests in the Third World, and the man agreed wholeheartedly. That was exactly why he was willing to pay his taxes, he said.

What about the Church? I asked. It was a question I had asked many times and would continue to ask — David Copperfield's friend Mr. Dick had his King Charles's head and I had my Church — and each time I asked it, the question would grow more plaintive.

Begin felt that it was naive to expect the Church to call Catholics like the businessman to task, just as it would have been naive in the Middle Ages to expect the Church to confront the social inequities of the time. A new Church had to emerge, and that's what came about, however imperfectly, through St. Francis of Assisi and St. Dominic and the founding of the mendicant orders. Unlike monks, Franciscan and Dominican friars traveled about preaching the Gospel, wholly dependent on charity for their living, not bound to a particular monastery whose abbot, like any secular prince, was the master of vast lands worked by serfs.

There was, in fact, a historical parallel for the actions of Begin and other disturbers of the peace within the Catholic Church. The various popular movements embracing evangelical poverty and decrying ecclesiastical and secular corruption that sprung up in twelfth-century Europe were at least as threatening to the status quo as liberation theology in Latin America would be in the twentieth. Bishops and princes alike dreaded such movements. They saw their adherents as a heretical rabble who had blasphemously laid hold of the sharp, two-edged sword of the Gospel, a weapon that should have been kept out of their hands at any cost.

To his everlasting credit, Pope Innocent III saw things otherwise, realizing perhaps that the Holy Spirit has a notorious disregard for proper channels. Instead of condemning the work of Francis and Dominic, Innocent blessed it and so brought a vital new force into the Church. A more Christ-like Church emerged from a crisis that could have left it devastated. Three centuries later, the popes of the Reformation were not as enlightened, and seven centuries later John Paul II's views on liberation theology remain obscure and contradictory.

Begin's views on the reigning pontiff were quite measured, at least for a Rebel Priest. Prior to the last papal election, he said, an analysis had been conducted by Andrew Greeley, the priest-sociologist-novelist-you-name-it, who marshaled a group equipped with all the appropriate hardware and software. They ran all their data through the computer and came up with Karol Wojtyla, the archbishop of Cracow, as the most likely successor. Greeley's group had proceeded on the assumption that the cardinal electors were looking for somebody who would project a "holy man" image. "They wanted somebody who would get out of his plane and kiss the ground. And that's who they elected. John Paul II spends a lot of time and money and energy doing just that. And he understands Eastern Europe. He carries the same scars that its people do. When he talks about communism, he always means Stalinism. I don't think he's ever going to take on the system."

I thought so, too, but we had forgotten about the capriciousness of the Holy Spirit. John Paul II would prove us wrong to some extent with his encyclicals "Social Concerns" and "Centesimus Annus" (to mark the centennial of Leo III's epochal "Rerum Novarum," a Magna Carta for the labor movement). As John XXIII had with "Mater et Magistra" thirty years earlier, John Paul II's "Social Concerns" would stir indignation and dismay in what was still called the free world by withholding his benediction from capitalism. John Paul II would in fact go beyond his beloved predecessor and speak of "sinful structures," East and West, that exploited the poor. But, as usual, there would be little or no follow-up. Liberals would cheer (though much less enthusiastically than they had for John), and William F. Buckley, Jr., who thirty years before had punned "Mater, sí; Magistra, no," would tut-tut a bit in the *National Review,* and that would be that. At best, only echoes of this discord would reach the ears of Catholics like the patriotic, tax-paying wedding guest, posing no threat whatsoever to his tranquil conscience. He was more likely to run into Madonna in the supermarket than to hear a sermon on social justice.

When I had asked Dan Berrigan the same question about the Church, I told Begin, he had said that he expected nothing whatsoever from those in authority. Nothing whatsoever. Begin laughed. "When the Jesuits bailed Dan out after the FBI finally caught up with him, he told reporters that the Jesuits were a group of men vowed to poverty who could come up with two hundred thousand dollars in a couple of hours."

It wasn't an especially gracious thing to say, especially under the circumstances, but Dan Berrigan was a poet, and Plato had warned rulers about poets.

Despite his lack of expectations, Begin took a keen interest in where the Church was going. "I'll make a prediction: they're going to insist on a male celibate clergy for so long that they'll destroy people's belief in the need for an ordained priesthood. They can't find native Bolivian priests to be bishops because they all have wives and children. Nuns and lay workers baptize babies and marry people and distribute preconsecrated hosts. The people know that priests marry, and they don't care. They expect them to. Once you start changing rules, like no meat on Friday, they start to see that these are just laws, and laws can change. This kind of demythologizing is going on all over, and I think it's a real good thing for the Church."

All this was happening, he stressed, without any by-your-leave from Rome. It was not a revolution, however, but an evolution, one that his recent experience with an ecumenical group well illustrated. They had asked Begin to join them a year before. He said that he would be happy to do so as long as they accepted him as just another member and not as their priest.

When it came time to celebrate the liturgy with the group, Begin wore a stole at first but soon dispensed with vestments entirely and sat with everybody else instead of having a special place. Everyone participated in the prayers, and after a few months they began passing around the Eucharistic prayer; each would read portions of it or they would all read it together, even the words of consecration, those awesome syllables that epitomized priestly power and had appeared in large type in the old Roman missal to signify their sacred character: "Hoc est enim Corpus meum. . . . Hic est enim Calix Sanguinis mei."

So egalitarian did things become that a visitor remarked after a liturgy that he hadn't had a clue as to the identity of the priest. One Sunday, Begin wasn't able to attend, but three former priests, now married, were members of the group, and they went on with the liturgy as before. "Tu es sacerdos in aeternum" the Roman liturgy insisted, laicization to the contrary notwithstanding, and so even the most hostile of curial functionaries would have to declare such a Mass valid if illicit. But then on a later Sunday, as it happened, neither Begin nor any of the three defrocked priests was present.

Begin asked one of the group what they had done. "He told me: 'Oh, we just went on as usual,'" said Begin with a laugh. It seemed, however, that some members were uneasy. Was Jesus really present? they wondered. And so the group selected that as the topic for discussion the next Sunday. Begin hadn't been sure just what he himself would say.

He had dinner with some nuns the night before, one of whom was studying theology, and he asked her advice: "'What will I tell these people?' I said. 'Was Jesus there?' 'You don't actually believe that Jesus is present,' she said, 'because you're an ordained priest and you say magic words?' I said, 'Yes, I guess I do.' 'Jesus is present,' she said, 'because there's a worshiping community performing a sacred rite.' And she's right."

Perhaps she was, but I would have preferred a touch of fear and trembling or at least humility. The nun wanted to be a theologian, and I have little patience with theologians. Had the theologians somehow preceded the martyrs, there would have been no sacred rite for the theologians to theologize about. Besides, too many memories lay claim to my feelings. As a thirteen-year-old I had knelt at the altar of St. Philomena's Church on dark winter mornings, and to the priest's "Introibo ad altare Dei" ("I will go unto the altar of God"), I had answered: "Ad deum qui laetificat juventutem meam" ("to God who gives joy to my youth"), words that David himself might have composed nearly three millennia before. How wonderfully awesome it had been in contrast to the rest of life in East Cleveland in the forties. Movies and books had opened me up to a wider world, but the Church had gone much further. The promise it held out was infinite. But now, I realized, the infinite and the sacred were passé to the nun-theologian and her teachers. It would probably be in bad taste, for example, to bring up the subject of life after death with them.

Begin himself wasn't sure what he thought about it. "I don't know," he said. "When it's time to die I'll probably be angry because I'll have something unfinished. I don't know. My wildest thought is that somehow there is a way for the love that bonds us here to keep on growing. The whole thing defies the imagination. I certainly believe there is something after this. I don't know how you figure in the reward and punishment. Maybe it has to do with the capacities you develop. If there is an afterlife, I look upon it as a pure gift. This life, too, is a gift. I really believe that. Heaven will have to go some to beat this. I'm having a good time.

"I need to see it as a process. I have to see myself as part of it. What Gandhi did. What my mother did. What my teacher did. I hope to hand it on to others."

But for those who die horribly and senselessly, I said, there is no process. The mothers and children who perish in famines, the victims of psychopaths, the victims of natural and manmade catastrophes.

"No, no. There's nothing for them personally. I come from two different places. I'm Thomistic. I know all the things you know I must know. But, on the other hand, I know God exists because I experience God. I know from that that all being is participatory being. Close to pantheism. So I'm pretty sure my life will continue, but I don't know in what state, or even if it will be in a conscious state. But I don't even speculate on that. I trust God. He will take care of it." He laughed. "She will take care of it.

"I'm pretty much convinced from anything I can figure out empirically that there was definitely some experience of Jesus as alive after death. That does console me, but it doesn't motivate me. I would do exactly the same thing I do now whether I believed there was an afterlife or not."

How, then, I asked, did he differ from mere humanists?

"We differ from humanists because we believe in the Resurrection. We know victory is now. In Nicaragua, they're always quoting the passage 'I thank you, Father, because you have concealed it from the wise and revealed the mysteries of the kingdom to the little ones.' I'll keep doing what I'm doing as long as there is hope of getting something across to people.

"I went to the fiftieth anniversary celebration of a priest, a man who wouldn't let me perform the wedding of my sister in his parish, and a priest a few years older than I came up and said: 'When I see all that you've done, I feel as though my priesthood has been wasted.' I told him that if he feels that way, he should invite me out to talk to his people. He hasn't yet, but he might."

———————

I walked back to my car. My feelings toward Begin were intermingled with a host of others. I was leaving Clinton Street behind again. Things had changed since my father had grown to manhood on this street. But in some ways they hadn't. In 1914 my grandfather, for whom I was named, had died of pneumonia just a few blocks away. When he confronted the ultimate reality of life, had it really been any easier for him to have faith than it was for me or for Bob Begin?

Dorothy Day's Children

Marcia Timmel
and Paul Magno

Washington, D.C., January 22, 1988. It was the anniversary of *Roe vs. Wade*, the Supreme Court decision that struck down all state anti-abortion laws, a day invariably marked by a massive outpouring of anti-abortion demonstrators. Today, the fifteenth anniversary, the turnout was larger than ever.

The day was gray and overcast but warm for January as contingents from all over the country marshaled on the Ellipse between the White House and the Washington Monument. I was one of their number, having ridden down from Ridgewood, New Jersey, on a bus chartered by the Knights of Columbus. A few years before, Michael Harrington, the gallant old socialist, who like Jesus was more admired than imitated, had provoked consternation at a Planned Parenthood conference honoring the one-hundredth anniversary of Margaret Sanger's birth by observing that he was convinced that the right-to-life movement represented "one of the few genuine social movements" of the time. However one felt about Harrington's assertion, the outpouring today gave it a corroboration hard to dismiss.

Like all popular movements, the right-to-life movement was rife with contradiction. Nellie Gray, one of its leaders, read a cordial declaration of moral support from Ronald Reagan, who was wholly taken up just then with giving immoral support, the Constitution and the law of the land be damned, to the Contras, whose modus operandi included blowing up buses carrying women and children. Then, after hearing speeches from pro-life champions such as Jack Kemp, who had once described gun control as a steady arm and clear eye, we debouched from the Ellipse in a ragged but enthusiastic parade that wound its way up Pennsylvania Avenue and Constitution Avenue and then took a sharp right turn behind the Capitol so as to pass in defiant review before the Court itself before breaking up.

Most of the groups that marched by, including the ultraright Tradition, Family, and Property contingent, with its scarlet sashes and its scarlet banners held high on pike-like poles a good twenty feet long, chanted "Abort the Court!" in tones hostile enough to give even the warmest sympathizer pause: What sort of love could express itself in so hateful a fashion?

Though their lyrics were aggressive, the demonstrators' choreography was not. They were careful to stay well clear of the grim-faced Washington police who stood shoulder to shoulder along the steps that gave access to the plaza in front of the Supreme Court.

One of the few exceptions was Marcia Timmel, a member of the Olive Branch Catholic Worker house, where I was going to stay that night. We had arranged to meet in front of the Court, but Marcia had something else to attend to first. A tall woman with strong features, she hadn't taken part in the parade because she had been working in a soup kitchen all morning. She wore a scarf on her head, and she had fastened a poster that said "Abortion Exploits Women" to the back of her cheap rust-brown raincoat. She wasted no time in finding an opening in the police ranks, and once she had darted through and reached the steps of the Court, she knelt down and took out a rosary.

In due time, three officers with blank expressions walked up to her and warned her that she would be arrested if she didn't leave at once. Marcia kept on praying, and the police handcuffed her wrists behind her back and hauled her away, her legs dragging behind her.

Just as did its founder and guiding spirit, the indomitable Dorothy Day, the Catholic Worker movement, which espoused solidarity with the poor and renounced violence in any form, resisted definition and much else besides. There were two Catholic Worker houses on the bleak northeast side of Washington, D.C., an area where, in the first weeks of 1988, nobody was in the least surprised to learn that the capital of the free world was, thanks to the inroads of crack, well on its way to setting a new homicide record. Besides the Olive Branch House there was the Dorothy Day House, a huge, rambling old mansion well suited to the primary mission of its community, giving shelter to homeless families. The Olive Branch House was actually the upper floor of a row house about a mile and a half away. The members of the Olive Branch community ran a soup kitchen, but their main work lay elsewhere. Theirs was a "resistance community," and they maintained a constant nonviolent witness against the militarism for which the Pentagon, the mighty fortress that is our god, provided so apt and convenient a symbol.

Things were not as clear-cut when it came to abortion, however. The Catholic Worker movement was indeed opposed to abortion, but the conduct of Marcia and two other members of the Olive Branch community who were also arrested on January 22 was the exception, not the rule. Doctrinaire, all-or-nothing feminism had affected the Catholic Worker movement as it had the rest of the Church, and its relative silence on abortion was a source of pain to older Catholic Workers such as Gordon Zahn and Eileen Egan, as it would have been to Dorothy Day.

Something else also confused the issue, not just for the Catholic Worker movement but for the whole American Catholic Church. In 1984, Cardinal Joseph Bernardin of Chicago had used the metaphor of the seamless garment (Jesus' robe, which was "woven in one piece" according to St. John's Gospel) to describe the consistency of the pro-life ethic and its opposition not only to abortion but to capital punishment and war as well. It was a nice image, but it might have been better had it never occurred to the cardinal or to his speech writer. For the seamless garment, beside provoking endless argument — Catholics opposed to war and Catholics opposed to abortion constantly berate each other with it — proved to be an apt covering for a multitude of sins of inaction. The American Catholic hierarchy seized upon it at once, and their consistency on abortion, capital punishment, and war has been impeccable ever since. They deplore all three, and they invoke the seamless garment whenever anyone is rude enough to suggest that something more is in order on one issue or another at any given moment.

What the bishops preached, Marcia and her husband, Paul Magno, lived. They were the parents, moreover, of an infant daughter, Sarah, the kind of responsibility that lies beyond most episcopal imaginations. Before coming to the Olive Branch House, they had spent three years caring for the homeless as members of the Dorothy Day community. Each, at different times, had served a sentence in federal prison: Marcia for five months, Paul for a year and a half.

Paul was an Italian-American, short and wiry, and the vigor of his convictions didn't preclude a relaxed charm. Marcia was quite a bit taller than Paul. She was also more intense in manner than her husband, more likely to burst into laughter than to smile, a woman capable of disconcerting even those who agreed with her. With her flashing dark eyes and prominent jaw, it was easy enough, despite Marcia's espousal of nonviolence, to visualize her holding the Tricolor aloft and urging the *citoyens* forward in a latter-day "Liberty Leading the People."

Marcia was born in Wisconsin, but her family moved to Florida when she was six and finally settled in Fort Lawton Beach, near Pensacola. It was, Marcia said, a typical Catholic family. Her father was German. Her mother was Irish. Catholicism was taken for granted, never questioned, as the arrival of eight children in as many years suggested.

The children went to a Catholic grade school, but Marcia left the Church shortly after entering high school. The school happened to be public, but her defection had much more to do with family than with school. Her father's behavior had become abusive years before. The unfortunate man was, in fact, schizophrenic, but the family would suffer for a decade before his condition was properly diagnosed.

As time went by, he became more and more violent, starting with verbal abuse and then striking Marcia's mother and the children. Her mother sought the help of a priest the family was close to, but all he could do for her was urge her to pray. To be fair, no one had any idea her father was in the grip of a serious disorder. In public he was very gentle, the sort of person people liked instinctively. No one would have dreamed he was capable of inflicting such cruelty on his family.

At the time, however, the priest's inability to respond angered Marcia. The Church, as she saw it, was unable to help her family; how could such a religion be true if it was so ineffectual? At fourteen Marcia thought a priest and Christ should be the same. If the priest failed, then Christ failed.

Marcia started running away from home. Once she took the bus to Mobile, Alabama, and called a priest with whom she thought she had a rapport who had been assigned to the cathedral there. It was two in the morning when she called from the bus station. The priest refused to see her. That was the end, Marcia decided. Any church served by a priest who had no word of comfort for a fourteen-year-old girl desperate enough to be calling from a bus station in the dead of night wasn't a church that had any claim on her.

In the late sixties, Marcia started to run with an older crowd and to dabble in drugs. Chastened by the bad experiences some of her friends had with LSD, she was cautious enough not to go much beyond the abuse of standard prescription drugs. At sixteen, she had no trouble obtaining her own Valium prescription, a coup she followed by getting several more from other doctors and doing the same with codeine.

The young people in her crowd were mainly from the middle class. Many, in fact, were military dependents. Despite her wildness, despite her getting thrown out of her house, Marcia did not drop out of high school. She got a job working at a newsstand and rented a room in a rooming house, going to classes all the while. Then, with several of her friends, she rented a two-bedroom apartment. The result was a kind of haphazard commune, with the others far more dependent on drugs than Marcia was. As it turned out, only she came through; for the others it was a story of ruined lives or death from overdoses.

An event that happened just before she graduated from high school may have been what saved her. She was in an auto accident, and though she escaped uninjured, her car, an old Volkswagen, was demolished. The other driver was at fault, and the adjuster for his company turned out to be her father, whom she had not seen in more than a year. He offered to disqualify himself, but his company told him to go ahead. The transaction was quite straightforward; Marcia got the book value of the car, which was $600.

In 1969 that sum was enough to pay for a semester at a Pensacola community college. Marcia's idea was to excel in that first semester and earn a scholarship. Besides working hard on her studies, she joined every organization that she thought would impress those who held the academic purse strings. All this activity topped off with working till 4:00 A.M. as a waitress at a truck stop brought the unlooked-for benefit of cutting herself off from the lethal street culture she had been part of. She did continue to use drugs for a time, but this did not prevent her from winning the school's leadership scholarship at the end of the semester. She could now continue her education.

The debate coach, a man named Lee Cain, had taken notice of Marcia's abilities even though debate was one of the few activities that she had avoided. What contact she had had with Cain through her involvement with forensics had not endeared him to her. Cain had been quite frank in expressing his disapproval of the way Marcia lived, but when he offered her a debate scholarship, she promptly accepted.

Marcia's father had failed her. Her church had failed her. But Lee Cain did not fail her. It was a remarkable re-creation of the parable of the Good Samaritan. For, like the Samaritan, Cain, a homosexual, belonged to an outcast tribe, and, unlike the priest in Mobile, he didn't pass by when he encountered a victim lying by the roadside. "Lee was a wonderful person," said Marcia. "He loved his work. He loved his students. They were his family. He saw as his great purpose in life to challenge people to do greater things than they had." Lee Cain got Marcia off her dependence on drugs and alcohol. His friendship broke the pattern of abusive romantic relationships in which she had become entangled. It was Lee she'd go to when she had a problem. It was Lee who'd scold her when it was necessary. "Lee was the greatest Christian I ever met. He told me candidly that he had no problems with Christianity, just with the Christian churches."

Marcia went on to a four-year Florida college, Stetson, but despite Lee Cain's support, despite her reconciliation with her family, her inner turmoil was far from over. She was unable to free herself entirely from the kinds of relationships that had almost destroyed her before. She was still promiscuous at Stetson, became pregnant, and had an abortion.

"I wanted to believe it wasn't a baby," she said, "but there was no doubt in my mind that it was. The nurse had to assemble the fetus afterward to make sure that no 'debris' remained, which could cause peritonitis. I felt the grace to ask her if it had been a boy or a girl, and she said it was a girl." Marcia knew she had been a mother, and it was this realization that caused a breakdown six months later. In retrospect, Marcia was glad that she had not succumbed to a state of denial, something that she believed would have stood in the way of a return to full mental health.

In the midst of the anguish of her breakdown, Marcia got into her car and drove for three days until she was at last back in Pensacola. Once there, Marcia walked unannounced into Lee Cain's office. He happened to be holding a seminar at the time, but he took one look at her face and dismissed his students. "I can believe that Christ can love us unconditionally," said Marcia, "because I experienced that kind of love in Lee Cain."

Marcia was able to return to Stetson and finish her studies with honors, winning a graduate scholarship to Wake Forest. There she did brilliantly and coached nationally ranked debate teams. Everything seemed to be going well. Drugs were behind her save for a bit of pot smoked socially at parties, and it was the same with alcohol. Her achievements and her relative control masked a deep unhappiness, however, which expressed itself in a stronger and stronger urge to commit suicide.

One December night, Marcia walked into her bedroom resolved to kill herself. She got two bottles of gin and gathered together a formidable array of drugs gained through her prescription collection. Everything was set. She felt a weight that had been pressing down on her for a long time, a seemingly irresistible force that demanded that she do away with herself.

"But then," she said, "I had what I can only describe as a mystical experience of Christ. I thought I had put Christ behind me. I had searched around in Buddhism, in Judaism, and other religions. Then I had given up on faith altogether. I was in the grip of an overwhelming sense of evil, like an actual physical sensation. But then in the midst of all this, I experienced a sense of light and of a voice saying: 'I love you. There is nothing to forgive. I just want you to come back.' Everything within me told me this was Christ. I had the experience of having this Christ whom I didn't believe in, who I thought didn't care for me being right there with me. And it terrified me. At the same time, it was as though evil had its own voice, too, and this voice said: 'Don't believe him. It's a lie. He knows the worst punishment is to go on living.'

"I was keenly aware of a real battle, a real combat for my soul taking place that night. Any way I describe it would be true and yet not true. It was taking place inside me, it seemed, but I also had a vivid awareness of light and darkness and an actual confrontation of two forces. I had a real sense of my soul hanging in the balance. The prospect of either outcome terrified me. I couldn't tell which scared me more, the light or the darkness." Through it all, her pills and her gin stood ready and waiting. But then, about four or five in the morning as she remembers, she surrendered to the voice of light and its simple message of love.

After her surrender, Marcia got up and walked into the living room. She picked up the phone book and turned to the yellow pages to find the nearest Catholic church. There was one just three blocks away, and it had a 6:00 A.M. Mass. She walked the three blocks to the church and sat on the steps waiting for its doors to open. She was still fearful, however. The voice of darkness hadn't given up.

As she sat there, she suddenly realized, traditional Catholic that she had been, that it was the first Friday of the month. Keeping the "first Fridays" — going to Mass and Communion on the first Fridays of nine consecutive months — was a major part of the Sacred Heart devotion, a form of piety immensely popular in the pre–Vatican II Church that focused on Jesus' love for humanity, symbolized by a heart emanating tongues of flame. Though its popularity had waned in the sixties, when the more florid forms of piety fell into disfavor, the Sacred Heart devotion had been central to Marcia's faith as a child and even as a teenager. Until she had turned her back on the Church in high school, she had never missed Mass on a first Friday.

That morning, the priest who said the six o'clock Mass chose the Sacred Heart as the theme for his homily, something that Marcia could not recall happening before or since. As she listened to the priest talk about the promise that Jesus was supposed to have made to the seventeenth-century visionary St. Margaret Mary Alacoque that he would never forget those who were faithful to his Sacred Heart, Marcia began to sob. No sin was too great, said the priest. Christ would never permit those who had been faithful to his Heart to die out of his grace. Up to that moment, Marcia hadn't shed a tear. She had still been in the grip of abject fear. She hadn't believed that

God could forgive her. The evil voice had still insisted that God was out to trick her.

Marcia decided to go to Communion, a decision totally unexpected given the circumstances, one contrary to all the caveats of her religious formation. If a person had committed serious sin, going to Communion without prior confession was simply unthinkable. But Marcia went. She trusted the voice that urged her to. As soon as she had received Communion, she felt a desire to confess.

Her confessor was the priest who had said the Mass. As Catholics do, she began by specifying how long it had been since her last confession. The interval was nine years, and she spent much of the rest of the morning pouring out the events of those nine years.

"For me," said Marcia, "this event, this mystical experience, is my Christian foundation. Everything else I learn or experience must go back to this." The priest told her that she had received a great grace. God had espoused her, he said. Up to then, she had been thinking of her return to the Church as something that would cost her dearly in terms of penance, but now she discovered that the Church in 1975 was a different Church in many ways from the Church she had left in 1966. It had become a more open and human Church.

A big influence in deepening Marcia's awareness of what the new Church was like came from the Glenmary Home Missioners, a congregation of nuns and priests who worked in Appalachia. Oddly enough, it was something as unspiritual as summer stock theater that brought her into contact with Glenmary. While at Wake Forest she had joined a repertory company that each summer put on historical drama called "Unto These Hills" at a theater in Cherokee, North Carolina. The theater was adjacent to a reservation where Glenmary priests and sisters lived among the Indians. Her admiration for the Glenmary congregation grew to such an extent in the years that followed that she considered joining them several times, but each time events would take a different course.

After finishing her graduate work at Wake Forest in 1976, Marcia taught forensic debate at Morehead State University in Kentucky. Her stay at Morehead, in the heart of Appalachia, was short but eventful. As usual, she threw herself into things — not only her regular work but also activities at the local parish, including teaching religion classes on Sundays. Then something happened, another of those seemingly chance events that so affected her life.

She was out walking one snowy day when she came upon two teenage girls living in a miserable shed. It was, in fact, an abandoned dog kennel.

The girls, she discovered, were sisters, and each had a child: one a baby girl, the other a five-year-old boy. Both children were born of incest, the girls having been abused and raped by their own father. One of the sisters, moreover, was suffering from appendicitis. There was only one thing to do. Housing was cheap in Kentucky, and Marcia was living by herself in a three-bedroom apartment. Without wasting any regrets over lost privacy, she promptly converted her apartment into a shelter for battered women.

It was at this time that Marcia committed her first act of civil disobedience, though she didn't think of it in those terms. One of her Glenmary friends, a nun, told her about all the families who were too poor to buy a Christmas tree, and Marcia, ax in hand, went into a federal forest preserve, chopped down a few trees, and presented the nun with the spoils of her foray.

"Appalachia was a mind blower for me," Marcia recalled. Despite the irregularities of her personal life, she had remained a political conservative. "I knew we had lost the war in Vietnam, but nobody told me we had lost the war on poverty, too. The Glenmary priests and nuns were very gentle with me, opening up my mind bit by bit."

Marcia felt herself called to do something. She wasn't happy about the call, which like all such calls came collect, and she didn't know what it might entail. "I made a bargain with Christ," she said. "I told him, 'I'll do everything you want, but please let me not give up teaching.' Every time I make a bargain like that, I know down deep I might as well give up. Because I know that what I'm doing is resisting grace."

In 1978, Marcia was back at Pensacola Junior College. Lee Cain, with retirement in mind, had decided to cut back on his workload, and when he offered her a job teaching his more demanding classes, she jumped at the chance. Cain also persuaded her to help out at a local mental health center where he was a volunteer. The experience of being on call one night a week on the center's hot line made her realize quite soon that there was just as much suffering, just as much pain and poverty in the place she had been raised as there had been in Appalachia. Life had become a series of revelations to Marcia. She had thought that she would be able to sort things out better on home ground, but now she felt the need to get away from all that was familiar and to be able to focus in a more deliberate way on her life and what God might want her to do with it.

Like Bob Begin, Bernie Meyer, and the Corrigans a decade earlier, Marcia decided that what she needed was a retreat, that staple of traditional Catholic spirituality that, unlike some other traditions, had survived Vatican II more vigorous than ever.

She made the retreat at Christmas at a Jesuit retreat house in Milford, Ohio, just outside Cincinnati. Two decades earlier a flourishing novitiate had been the main Jesuit presence in Milford, but by the time Marcia came for her retreat, the novitiate where I had spent three years after leaving the army was but a memory. The Jesuits were as hard hit as anyone else by the lack of vocations, but *vocation* means "call," and perhaps God was broadcasting on a new frequency, one that Marcia was tuned to.

The Spiritual Exercises of St. Ignatius, the basis for Jesuit retreats, are oriented toward helping a person to make a choice, to weigh his or her feelings and conviction to determine if a change might be in order. Marcia decided that the answer was yes. She had spent a wonderful year as a teacher at Pensacola Junior College, but she felt that God was asking her to give that role up in favor of something that represented a more direct expression of love of neighbor. She wrote a letter to the Jesuit Volunteer Association, a kind of domestic Peace Corps run by the order, and handed in her resignation to the college. Marcia is not one to do things by halves.

The directors of the Jesuit Volunteers were happy to get her application since she was older and had managerial experience. There was an opening in Akron, Ohio. She would be the executive director of a program that offered alternatives to abortion. It would, that is, if Marcia got it going. It was her responsibility to set things up and to train counselors.

"There was nothing at that moment I could have wanted to do more," said Marcia. "I felt I had something to offer women who had abortions." Besides the personal experience that had had so profound an effect on her, she had been developing new insights into facing the experience of pain and loss by her readings of Elisabeth Kübler-Ross's work, including her landmark *On Death and Dying.*

Marcia spent two years in Akron. It was to be a crucial period for her. Events were to come together in such a way as to complete in more measured fashion the transformation that had begun so dramatically with her surrender to the light and her first Friday Communion five years before. She was the only one of the five-person Jesuit Volunteer community who remained for the full two-year period, and after the last of her companions had left, she went to live with a community of nuns, the Sisters of St. Joseph, an experience that she found congenial. She began to think seriously of becoming a nun once her Jesuit Volunteer commitment was completed in the spring of 1981 and of joining her friends in the Glenmary congregation. Glenmary, as it happened, was in a state of disarray after a confrontation with the archbishop of Cincinnati, Karl J. Alter, one of those doughty prelates who saw themselves as damage-control officers on the

Bark of Peter after its Vatican II collision with the modern world. Perhaps a streak of ambition might have insinuated itself into her attraction to Glenmary now that it was in crisis. She could, she admitted, see herself becoming its superior in a few years and turning things around despite the see of Cincinnati. Liberty leading the people.

Living with the Sisters of St. Joseph, however, though it may have initially turned Marcia in the direction of a religious vocation, had other effects as well. It made her aware as nothing else would have of the ferment of activity that had transformed the Church since Vatican II and the prominent part of the laity in it. The nuns were on everybody's mailing list, and Marcia began to read and learn. One flyer, signed by Dan Berrigan and Juli Loesch, was from Pro-lifers for Survival, a group opposed to both abortion and nuclear weapons. (Juli Loesch, frustrated at the temporizing of her fellow Catholic feminists, had created the organization on the spur of the moment, and it's still going strong.) Marcia thought about their position, and it made sense to her. How could one be opposed to killing a baby in the womb of an American woman by an abortion and indifferent to killing a baby in the womb of a Russian woman with a nuclear missile? Politically aware by now, she saw the pro-life protestations of the incoming Reagan administration for the cant that they were, and she sensed that administration posturing would lead to an era of moral bankruptcy in the public sphere. She also read the letters the nuns received from members of their order working in El Salvador. The letters frequently mentioned Jean Donovan, a laywoman, and Ursuline Sister Dorothy Kazel, two members of a mission team from the diocese of Cleveland who worked with refugees. Before the year was out, Jean and Dorothy were dead along with Ita Ford and Maura Clarke; and Jeane Kirkpatrick, Reagan's favorite intellectual, was calling them political activists.

Three months before the deaths of the four churchwomen, the year saw another event, one less publicized, but, like the martyrdom itself, an event of the deepest significance: On September 9, 1980, Daniel and Philip Berrigan and six others entered a General Electric plant, the Nuclear Missile Reentry Division, in King of Prussia, Pennsylvania, and hammered on two nose cones for the Mark 12A nuclear missile and poured blood over blueprints for it. This was the first of a series of acts of civil disobedience that came to be called Plowshares disarmament actions, after the celebrated verse from Isaiah (2:4): "They shall beat their swords into plowshares and their spears into pruning hooks." The Bible was indeed a dangerous book if the wrong sort of people got hold of it.

Everything was falling into place for Marcia. In the weeks that followed, she felt more and more angry at Reagan not only because of what his minions were saying about the four murdered women but because of the havoc his administration's budget cuts were wreaking on the work she was trying to do. "Once we persuaded a woman to have her baby instead of aborting it," she said, "we incurred a long-term obligation. We had to see to it that the woman really did have the option to raise her child in suitable circumstances. But the funds that could have helped her to do this were instead going into the arms race." Marcia's personal experience as well as her moral logic confirmed the arguments made by Juli Loesch and Daniel Berrigan. She was seeing causal links that she had never seen before.

To realize and not to act was foreign to Marcia's nature. Around Ash Wednesday of 1981, she began to feel that she had to do something, something quite clear and specific. "I felt I had to get to Washington," she said. "I had to go to the Pentagon and say no — no to the arms race, no to intervention in Central America." Women and children were suffering in both Akron and El Salvador because of what was being done in the Pentagon. She decided that what she wanted to do was to pour blood on the steps of the Pentagon.

Despite her own Operation Christmas Tree in Kentucky, Marcia was no activist. She had probably heard the term "civil disobedience" at one time or another, but it certainly wasn't part of her active vocabulary. She knew none of the jargon. Her decision came from the concepts and feelings that she had been wrestling with in the course of her prayers. Its inspiration was not liberal rhetoric but the Lenten liturgy, which seemed to reverberate with the anguished cries of those who suffered and those who mourned.

She confided her plan to her spiritual adviser, a priest at her parish. He was a bit taken aback — it wasn't every day that someone came in with so sanguinary a proposal — but, to his great credit, he confessed that neither he nor anyone else could say that God didn't in fact want her to pour blood on the steps of the Pentagon. If she was meant to do it, said the priest, two things would happen: all the doors would open for her, and God wouldn't ask her to go into it alone but would give her a community to support her. And, he assured her, it was all right to be afraid.

Things turned out as the priest said. Marcia ran into some immediate logistical difficulties. How, for example, was she to get proper access to her own blood? "I just couldn't figure out how I was going to do it," she said, bursting into laughter. She had been calling Akron blood banks. She'd be happy to donate a pint, she told them, but would they be kind enough to draw another that she could have in a bag to go? It seemed a reasonable enough proposition, but it invariably provoked a moment of shocked silence on the other end of the line.

"They thought I was a bit of a sicko, I guess," said Marcia, again laughing her full-throated laugh.

Then in the middle of Lent, two weeks before Holy Week, a St. Joseph nun who was a campus minister at the University of Akron's Newman Center brought home a newsletter called *Year One*. "She told me," said Marcia, "that there were actually people who seemed to be doing the same kind of crazy stuff I had been talking about." Marcia eagerly read the inelegantly printed newsletter. *Year One* was put out by a community in Baltimore called Jonah House. Marcia had never heard of Jonah House, but Philip Berrigan, who had participated in the Plowshares disarmament action, was one of its members. The Plowshares Eight, as his group was called, had just been convicted, and its participants had received five- to ten-year sentences. (The lengths of the sentences but not the convictions would be successfully appealed, and the case would remain in the Pennsylvania courts for years, a sword of Damocles over the heads of the Plowshares Eight.) The Jonah House community, protesting the arms race in general and the sentencing in particular, was planning a continuous presence at the Pentagon throughout Holy Week.

Marcia telephoned Jonah House, and a woman who identified herself as Liz McAlister answered. The name was somehow familiar to Marcia, but she couldn't place it, a failing that showed just how far removed Marcia's life had been from political protest. She couldn't identify Liz McAlister, the former nun who had married Philip Berrigan a decade earlier. Liz McAlister was the heroine of a Catholic left romance that had hit the front pages together with an alleged plot to kidnap Henry Kissinger and blow up heating tunnels beneath the Capitol, a chimera that was one of the more fabulous growths sprung from the fertile soil of Nixon era paranoia.

"I told her," said Marcia, "that I was thinking of pouring blood on the steps of the Pentagon. 'What do you think of that?' I said." Whenever she had announced her intent before, she had met stunned disbelief, but Liz McAlister took it quite calmly. "She said: 'Well, yes, we usually have a couple of people do that each year.' 'You do?' I said, flabbergasted. 'Are all of you Catholics?' And she said, 'Yes, we are.' She told me that nurses drew the blood, and when I asked if there was any chance of getting a ride to Washington, she said that someone from Cleveland was coming down and he could drive me. After I hung up, I turned to the others. 'Does anybody recognize the name Liz McAlister?' I asked them. They just stared at me, open-mouthed."

The protesters met in a Washington church for a prayer meeting that to Marcia's delight was solidly grounded on scriptural texts. She became caught up in the spirit of the enterprise, overjoyed to find that there were people making the same kind of connections that she was making. The probable maximum sentence for the planned action, she was told, was a year in jail, and she was ready for a year in jail. She had arranged for volunteers to take over the counseling service back in Akron.

When it came to the actual event on Good Friday, however, Marcia was frightened. She didn't sleep the night before, and she threw up before she left for the Pentagon. She would never take getting arrested lightly and would always be afraid. "Even yesterday," she said, referring to her arrest in front of the Supreme Court in 1988, "I was on edge, short-tempered all morning when I was working in the soup kitchen."

The Jonah House group, about sixty or seventy people, including Philip Berrigan and Liz McAlister, gathered at the River Entrance of the Pentagon to pray aloud and sing. The white pillars to either side of it were adorned with brass plaques, one of which said "Department of Defense." Marcia was talking casually with a security guard. Since she was a new face, the man didn't expect her to do anything. But at an appropriate point in the liturgy, Marcia took out the plastic baby bottle that contained her blood, opened it, and poured it out, not on the steps, but on one of the white pillars. The blood dripped over the gleaming brass plate inscribed "Department of Defense."

The reaction from the startled guard was immediate and brutal. He grabbed Marcia, knocked her down, and, his knee in the small of her back, handcuffed her hands behind her. Then he took her by the ankles and dragged her inside the doors as her back bounced against the steps. "At that point," said Marcia, "I was really scared, and I was crying. As soon I was left alone, I got myself up on my knees and started to pray." After a few minutes, the guard, a black man named Jones, came over and spoke to her for the first time. "I'm sorry," he said. "I shouldn't have been so rough. I guess I freaked out." The handcuffs were on much too tight, and since they were the plastic kind that couldn't be loosened, Jones called over another guard to cut them off. "You'll have to recuff her," said the other man. "No," said Jones. "She's not going to do anything."

That was the start of a wary friendship of sorts between Marcia and Jones. In demonstrations to come, after Marcia had joined the Catholic

Worker movement in Washington, Jones, if he was anywhere in the vicinity, would see to it that he was her arresting officer and keep her from getting roughed up. He would talk with Marcia and her companions in the course of their regular Monday vigils. Formality was maintained, however. She called him "Officer Jones" and he avoided calling her by name — probably, Marcia thought, because he wasn't sure just how to address her. He certainly knew her name, having booked her often enough.

Jones was an archconservative, dead set against freeloaders of whatever race. Though less gifted and less fortunate, he was a man cut from the same cloth as Clarence Thomas. He had been born in poverty and raised in poverty, and he didn't see why other black people couldn't get a job as he had done and make something of themselves.

"I'll never forget the first time I came to the Pentagon carrying Sarah," said Marcia. "He looked at Sarah and shook his head. 'I just don't understand you people,' he said." When Marcia asked why not, Jones answered: "With all you know about nuclear war, I don't see how you can bring a child into this world."

If that was the way he felt, said Marcia, why did he keep on working at the Pentagon. "I'm not working here because I have any hope," said Officer Jones. "And I don't see how you can have any hope either."

After her Good Friday arrest, Marcia asked for an immediate trial. She was found guilty, and she served thirty days in the Washington municipal jail. She spent her time in prison sorting out motives. She wrote to her Glenmary friends, and they sent her warm letters of support. After her release, she visited the motherhouse of the sisters, Glenmary, still thinking she might want to join the congregation. The level of comfort she saw there, however, contrasted sharply with the kind of life she had recently been leading and the kind of poverty she had seen in both Appalachia and Pensacola. If she became a nun, she'd be living in far more comfortable circumstances. She'd be doubling her monthly income immediately. She'd probably pick up another graduate degree. And she could put aside all worries about health insurance for the rest of her life.

The young Augustine came to Carthage burning, burning; young Marcia came back to Washington searching, searching. In the early summer of 1981, she took part in an action cosponsored by the Community for Creative Non-Violence, a call for prayer and civil disobedience at the White House. She found she did not see eye to eye, however, with CCNV's dynamic founder, Mitch Snyder, who had been converted to Christianity and social action by Philip and Dan Berrigan while all three were serving time in a federal prison. Snyder's life would end tragically nine years later when he committed suicide, but in 1981 he was well on his way to be-coming famous as a champion of the poor and homeless; and his celebrity would even include a television movie starring Martin Sheen.

Snyder's ideas of faith and of community, it turned out, were not the same as Marcia's. "I needed a place," she said, "where my very traditional Catholicism would be more respected." Jonah House was the other co-sponsor of the action, and so it was that she went to Baltimore to live at Jonah House for a year. Her one reservation about the Jonah House community was that they didn't work directly with the poor, but she decided nonetheless to go to Baltimore because she realized that she needed a thorough grounding in what it meant to live in a "resistance" community. The term itself was a new one for Marcia. She was like an immigrant who, besides adapting in other ways, has to learn a new language.

The years 1981 and 1982 were to be eventful for Marcia. She would meet her husband, Paul Magno, a man who shared her ideals fully. Her religious conversion in Pensacola and her political awakening in Akron had altered the course of her life. Her passionately held beliefs compelled her to sail into the wind, and her marriage to Paul would confirm her determina-tion to do so. This, in turn, would lead to actions that were incompatible with the kind of safe, comfortable life that most of us aspire to, no matter how idealistic we like to think we are.

Paul and Marcia met, appropriately enough, in court. While still living at Jonah House, she went to Washington in September 1981 to participate in an action at the famed "arms bazaar," the merchants of death's annual hoe-down at which they hyped their wares in a luxury hotel ballroom to their good old buddies in Congress and the Pentagon. It was a surrealistic affair, perhaps beyond parody, at which lovely young women posed seduc-tively beside heat-seeking missiles, and you could go around filling your goody bag with Trident paperweights and Peacekeeper pens. A Catholic Worker named John Shields had also taken part in the action, which involved blocking an entrance. When their trial at the end of December stretched out to four days, Marcia accepted an invitation to stay at the St. Francis Catholic Worker house on M Street, the community to which John and Paul Magno belonged.

It happened that most of the St. Francis community were going out to Ohio over Christmas to attend a wedding, and Paul asked Marcia if she was willing to help out while they were shorthanded. She agreed to stay a little longer.

So it was that Marcia was in Washington when she got the news that Lee Cain died on Christmas Eve. Her dear friend, the most important person in her life until then, died just when she no longer needed him. Marcia would never have put it in those terms, and it might strike the humanist as cruel to do so, but there is no such thing as a random event, faith insists, and the Spirit speaks to us through one another.

In the spring of 1982, Marcia left Jonah House to become a Catholic Worker in Washington. Since she had always wanted to incorporate her resistance work with some form of direct service to the poor, the Catholic Worker movement represented an ideal choice. She and Paul made another choice the following August: they became engaged. The day after they announced their engagement, Marcia was invited to join a Plowshares group. She laughed as she remembered: "I said, well that's very nice, but I just got engaged, and I'll have to talk it over with my fiancé. So I said to Paul that this seemed like a crazy way to start out an engagement, but if we were serious about taking risks in our future together, this might be a valuable experience."

Paul agreed, so much so that he too joined the nascent Plowshares group. Its members were drawn from all over the Northeast, and for the next three months they met at various places almost every other weekend for an intensive series of retreats lasting three or four days.

Marcia became certain quite early in the course of these weekends of prayer and reflection that she was meant to participate in the group's action. Paul decided against it. He came from a close-knit Italian family from Boston, and he hadn't done enough, he thought, to prepare them for what was to come. His father worked for the government, with the Environmental Protection Agency — the family now lived in Rockville, Maryland, just outside Washington — and his particular expertise, ironically, had to do with the effect of nuclear radiation on the environment. Marcia and Paul, moreover, had just taken over the management of the Dorothy Day House, set up a year before as a shelter for homeless families, and the loss of both of them would have presented a problem to the house's programs.

Six others besides Marcia from the group meeting in the fall of 1982 decided to go through with the action, which came to be called Plowshares Number Four. They were John Grady, an auto mechanic and pizza deliverer from Ithaca, New York; his sister Ellen Grady, also from Ithaca, an aide to an elderly woman; Peter DeMott, a Vietnam veteran and member of Jonah House; Jean Holladay, a grandmother and nurse from Massachusetts; Roger Ludwig, a poet and musician who worked with the poor in Washington, D.C.; and Elmer Maas, a musician and teacher from New York City. (There are no CEOs in the Catholic Worker movement. As a French theologian once put it — perhaps too harshly, perhaps not — even a bit of true faith makes worldly success impossible.) Two years earlier, DeMott had single-handedly carried out Plowshares Number Two at the General Dynamics Electric Boat Shipyard in Groton, Connecticut, by getting into a security van and ramming it again and again into the Trident submarine *Florida*, which was in drydock. Maas was a veteran of Plowshares Eight in King of Prussia, the action that had started it all.

Again the target was the electric boat shipyard in Groton, the scene not only of DeMott's action but also of the Trident Nein (German for "no"), carried out just four months earlier, on Independence Day 1982. On November 14, 1982, five days after the Trident Nein group received sentences ranging up to a year in prison for, among other things, painting "U.S.S. Auschwitz" on the conning tower of the *Florida*, the Plowshares Number Four team invaded the Groton shipyard. They divided into two groups. Four people hammered on Trident components in a storage yard and poured blood on them. The other three, Marcia among them, boarded the Trident submarine *Georgia* and hammered its missile hatches and poured blood on them.

In her essay "I Am So Small: One Woman Responds to Nuclear War," Marcia would describe the moment vividly:

> I stand on the deck of a nearly finished Trident submarine, a household hammer in my hand. I tremble, my knees weaken. What am I doing here? This is the most deadly weapon in the world; more than 2000 Hiroshimas are under my feet. I feel weak, powerless. What can I do? With my sisters and brothers, I, an ordinary woman, can hammer this nuclear sword into a biblical plowshare. In faith I hammer.*

On May 6, 1983, Marcia Timmel and Paul Magno were married. Two weeks later the Plowshares Number Four team received sentences ranging from two months to a year; Marcia herself would spend five months in prison.

So it was that married life for Marcia and Paul began under circumstances that even those who shared their vision most fervently might hesitate to call ideal. Marcia went to prison for five months two weeks after their wedding, and Paul would spend his first and second wedding anniversaries in prison.

Paul, in contrast to Marcia, had had a warm and secure childhood. He had gone to Georgetown University, an expensive school, which, despite being

*Marcia Timmel, "I Am So Small," *Swords into Plowshares*, ed. Arthur J. Laffin and Anne Montgomery (San Francisco: Harper & Row, 1987), p. 87.

founded like all Catholic universities to better proclaim the Gospel, had become a content and docile handmaid of the federal establishment, with its prestigious School of Foreign Service and its exuberantly chauvinistic Institute for Strategic and International Studies. Its environment was one in which people like Jeane Kirkpatrick flourished.

For all that, however, it was still possible to pick up dangerous ideas at Georgetown. The Jesuit reputation for deviousness is not altogether unearned. One can never trust Jesuits completely, no matter how eager to please they seem to be. Thus it was that lurking in the corridors of Georgetown was Richard McSorley, a gaunt priest in his sixties with unruly Gaelic eyebrows. McSorley was a veteran pacifist whose writings had influenced Archbishop Raymond G. Hunthausen of Seattle and Auxiliary Bishop Thomas J. Gumbleton of Detroit, the two members of the American hierarchy best known for their opposition to nuclear weapons. Nuclear weapons are the taproot of violence in our society, McSorley had written; even to build one is a sin. McSorley's use of the distasteful three-letter word *sin* (the active vocabulary of even suburban matrons these days is much more likely to include *fuck* than *sin*) revealed him as the crusty traditionalist that he was.

Paul came under the influence of McSorley's ideas about what it meant to be a Christian in the twentieth century. While still an undergraduate, he went to work for the Zaccheus Soup Kitchen, the same one that the Olive Branch House would later assume responsibility for, and he also took part in protests directed at ROTC (Reserve Officers Training Corps, a campus military training program), an institution that a placard-bearing McSorley campaigned against in season and out. After his graduation in 1977, Paul spent six months or so wondering whether he should become a priest, living much of the time at the Catholic Worker house founded by Dorothy Day in lower Manhattan.

Paul came back to Washington to join the community of the St. Francis Catholic Worker house, which, thanks to the efforts of Fr. McSorley, had opened its doors on M Street a short time before. It was there, a year and a half later, that he met Marcia when she came to Washington for the arms bazaar.

On Easter Sunday, April 22, 1984, less than a year after Marcia had wielded her household hammer against the massive bulk of the *Georgia*, Paul took part in the Pershing Plowshares, an action directed against Martin Marietta in Orlando, Florida. Martin Marietta made components for the Pershing missile, whose deployment in Europe the previous December had provoked a storm of protest and, according to the *Bulletin of Atomic*

Scientists, had set the doomsday clock ahead to three minutes before midnight.

Though a Plowshares protest is certainly a political act, it is also much more than that. It flows from faith, and its political significance, though important, is secondary. Most of those who took part in Plowshares actions belonged to the Atlantic Life Community, a loosely organized East Coast federation whose inspiration was profoundly scriptural. Plowshares activists had to conduct themselves, not just during their action but throughout their trial and imprisonment, in a manner that left absolutely no doubt as to the religious nature of their motives. Each Plowshares group within the Atlantic Life Community was itself a community — a believing community, a praying community.

It was this support, this trust in God, this trust in his community, that enabled Paul, reunited with Marcia at Dorothy Day House after her release from prison seven months before, to turn his back on normal happiness and commit himself to the Pershing Plowshares.

The Pershing Plowshares was unusual in that all those who went into the preparation, including Anne Montgomery, a serene, rail-thin nun in her fifties who was a veteran of Plowshares Eight and of Trident Nein, actually followed through. They spent Holy Saturday night at a house near Orlando, celebrating a liturgy together. Then they went to bed around 10:30 and got up at 2:00. They arrived at the Martin Marietta plant at four o'clock on Easter morning.

As was the usual experience of Plowshares activists, they had no trouble getting in. They simply cut a hole in a wire fence. Then they enacted the by now familiar rituals. They wielded their hammers and poured their blood. This time the Isaian imperative fell upon Pershing II missile components and a launcher for a Patriot missile, the weapon that would go on to glory in the Persian Gulf seven years later. They also served Martin Marietta with an indictment for engaging in the sinful and criminal activity of building nuclear weapons and displayed a banner that read "Violence Ends Where Love Begins."

The actual disarmament action, as they called it, took no more than fifteen minutes, and since Martin Marietta's alert and highly trained security personnel needed about an hour to detect an incursion, the group had some forty-five minutes to pray and to share food, the basic elements of worship. They had poured blood over the weaponry and over a table of blueprints they had found in a warehouse. They had made bloody handprints over the lettering "Pershing" on the door of the warehouse, an unplanned, spontaneous evocation of Passover.

As they prayed and ate together on Easter morning, the sun suddenly broke through the clouds, and brilliant sunshine poured down on them. Paul would remember this as one perfect moment, a memory that would help sustain him throughout his prison term.

Martin Marietta was the biggest employer in the county, a fact the local sheriff was well aware of. An officer named McCleary made every effort to gain the group members' confidence after they were taken into custody, telling them that he was their friend and that he alone understood their motivation. But they gave their names, addresses, and birth dates, nothing more. Nor were they any more cooperative with a subsequent FBI interrogation. (The FBI became involved, a Martin Marietta official explained, because the property they had defaced had already passed into the possession of the military.) The Plowshares participants were saving what they had to say for their trial in federal court, when they hoped to be able to speak at length, a vain hope as it turned out.

They were arraigned next day, Easter Monday, in county court. The arraignment was open to the public, but the public was obliged to watch justice being done through a chicken wire screen that lent a covert air to the proceedings.

The county prosecutor, a young woman, was obviously inexperienced, and when Patrick Reilly, one of the accused, respectfully urged the judge to make sure that the county didn't attempt to suppress any of the evidence against them, she looked nonplussed. It wasn't the kind of behavior she had been led to expect from the accused. The eight of them, all in blue prison garb, were handcuffed together, Paul said, like sausages. To acknowledge their supporters, fifty or sixty of them, who filled the courtroom behind the chicken wire, they had to coordinate their efforts so that they all turned together.

Marcia, formidable as ever, was there organizing their support and explaining what the group was about to the media and whoever else cared to listen.

The bail was $100,000 each, a sum that provoked general amusement among the defendants. Eventually, after a month in jail, they were freed on their own recognizance until their trial two months later.

During their stay at Orange County jail, they were treated like other prisoners, which meant none too well. The food, passed in on trays through a slot in the bars, was tasteless. The jail was overcrowded, with at least thirty men assigned to each twenty-four-bunk section. Their jailers took care to assign each of the seven male Plowshares prisoners — Sister Anne Montgomery was the lone woman — to a separate section; nor were two of them allowed out for recreation at the same time. The sheriff's office was well aware of the political implications of the situation, but this was the first Plowshares action in Florida, and their jailers really didn't know how to cope with their quixotic charges. As a result, there were some remarkable lapses.

Paul was able to use the pay phone in his section anytime it was free, and Marcia arranged for him to participate in a local radio talk show. He had, of course, to persuade his thirty section mates to relinquish the phone at the proper time, but this proved to be surprisingly easy. The other prisoners, who were mostly black, enjoyed having a celebrity in their midst. The biggest of them, contrary to the media stereotypes of racial animosity and brutality behind bars, became Paul's enthusiastic ally. And so it was that Paul participated in the live talk show for more than an hour and a half. He expected a guard to appear at any moment to order him off the phone, but evidently the good old boys and gals in the sheriff's office didn't much favor talk radio, and nobody tumbled to what was going on. As might be expected, most of the listeners who called in were vehement, even profane, in their denunciations, but, again contrary to stereotypes, others said that they understood what Paul and his companions were doing and sympathized with them. More than one said, "God bless you."

After their release, the Pershing Plowshares group spent much of the summer of 1984 with the prospect of ten-year sentences hanging over their heads. They were convicted that August of destroying government property and of conspiracy, and they each received three years in federal prison along with a five-year suspended sentence with probation. Each was also ordered to pay $2,900 in restitution.

As was invariably the case with Plowshares defendants, the court denied them the necessity defense — the argument that what one does is legitimate even though it involves breaking the law since it is the only means to forestall an imminent danger to the common good. Thus during their week-long jury trial, they were forbidden to speak of their motivation or to utter a single word that happened to be on a forbidden list drawn up by the court, lest the jurors' ears be affronted by "nuclear weapons," "New Testament," "disarmament," or "Jesus." The federal prosecutor, perhaps inspired by *Catch-22*, did indicate that he would be receptive to an insanity defense, but no one took him up on it.

Surprisingly, the response of Bishop Thomas J. Grady of Orlando to the Pershing Plowshares was rather favorable. Writing in his column in the local Catholic paper, the bishop said that however much one might disagree with the methods involved, the Plowshares activists were, in fact, raising important questions that Catholics had to think about. When his failure to condemn the Pershing Plowshares provoked violent reactions from some of his flock, Bishop Grady wrote a second column in which he reminded everybody of the fundamental Christian concept that it is wrong to hate.

Since many of the angry Orlando Catholics had invoked that ultimate deterrent to ecclesiastical authority, the threat to stop putting money into the collection basket, Bishop Grady deserved great credit for his pastoral courage and integrity, especially compared with the action of Cardinal John Krol of Philadelphia, who two years later would promptly suspend two of his priests when they took part in a Plowshares action.

Still, just a year before the Pershing Plowshares, in May 1983, the American hierarchy had in fact endorsed by an overwhelming margin "The Challenge of Peace," the pastoral letter that put Cardinal Joseph Bernardin of Chicago on the cover of *Time*. Despite being weakened by compromise, the peace pastoral denounced as "a crime against God and man" the kind of warfare that the United States was prepared to wage. And since it was against just this readiness to commit nuclear massacre that the Plowshares activists had been fighting the good fight since 1980 while the bishops, perhaps exhausted by the force of their rhetoric, had been resting on their laurels, it seems fair to contend that Paul and his companions deserved more from the hierarchy than a temperate defense by a single bishop.

Paul served twenty months in federal prison in Allenwood, Pennsylvania, a minimum-security prison sometimes referred to as "Club Fed." Despite its nickname, it was still a prison; but as prisons went, it was much better than most. Its inmates were mostly middle class, many of them well-educated, sophisticated people. Some were prosperous. Though there were some drug dealers and representatives of organized crime, there were no prisoners doing ten or twenty years for violent crimes, and so the environment wasn't one of tension and fear.

Paul had his own six-by-eight-foot cubicle with a desk, locker, and shelf. He had books and time to read and write. He worked on a grounds crew, cutting grass, shoveling snow, and planting trees. If one had a suitable outlook, and Paul did, the atmosphere of Allenwood was almost monastic. Working within its restraints, he was able to fashion a personal regime of work, prayer, and recreation. About sixty of the six hundred inmates went to Mass on Sunday, and Paul took a leading role in this very special faith community, organizing a daily rosary, passing around religious books, arranging for Mass servers, and the like.

He had to endure the hardship, of course, of being separated from his wife, his family, and his friends, even those with whom he had been arrested.

The government had taken care to send each of them to a different prison.

There were, however, two other political prisoners at Allenwood, Puerto Ricans involved in the independence movement who were serving three-year sentences for contempt of court. Their politics were different from Paul's, and the conversations he had with them proved mutually educational. "You waited for the cops?" they said. "Why did you do that, man?" The Puerto Ricans laughed at him for the first three months. "There goes the terrorist," they'd say. "Only he doesn't make bombs, he takes them apart!" Paul would go back to his cubicle and think once more about what he stood for. So it was that he developed an ever deeper insight into what it meant to be a Catholic, a peace activist, and a political prisoner. "The four hundred fiftieth time you get asked if it's worth it," he said, "you have a better answer than you had the first time."

Paul came home to Marcia in the spring of 1986. For a second time they were reunited after a long separation. Marcia became pregnant and Sarah was born a year later. They were now a family, a happy family, but the struggle to which they had committed their lives not only had made them ex-convicts and brought them to a bleak and dangerous corner of the nation's capital but posed a direct threat to the stability that seems essential to family life. What if either of them were arrested again? Olive Branch House, which Paul and Marcia founded in the summer of 1987, was a house of resistance, and all who lived there had to be willing to risk arrest.

"My God, I have you until 1992!" Paul's parole officer had said when he opened his file. The threat of the five-year suspended sentence hung over his head and the heads of his companions. An even stronger threat hadn't deterred one of them, the indomitable Sister Anne, from participating in both the Pershing and Trident Nein Plowshares actions while her sentence as one of the 1980 Plowshares Eight was still under advisement by the appeals panel of the Pennsylvania superior court. Anne Montgomery was a nun, however. Paul was married. As we talked, Sarah, a blond-haired toddler, was playing with her toys in front of us, sometimes leaving them aside to make an unsteady progress from chair to table to couch and back again. "I'll do whatever I feel I should do," Paul said. "It remains to be seen whether or not that means challenging the law again."

Most of us would consider their struggle an unbearably forlorn one, but Paul and Marcia didn't see it that way, despite the lack of support from a Catholic Church whose teaching they subscribed to so wholeheartedly and from a Catholic press that, with the exception of the *National Catholic Reporter*, usually followed the example of the Jesuit magazine *America*. With its characteristic dispassion, that journal touched on the nuclear issue from time to time but remained as determinedly centrist as the unfortunate ass who perished of hunger and thirst between the bale of hay and the bucket of water.

"Sure," said Paul, "it's frustrating to me as a Catholic that neither the hierarchy nor the Catholic press acknowledges what we're doing. The rank and file of American Catholics, the folks in the pews, have no idea that we even exist. On the other hand, you can't depend upon how much people like you and support you. Your inspiration has to come from something more profound. We do what we do out of faith. Jesus loved us enough to die for us. We have to learn to live out the same kind of love."

Officer Jones, Marcia's friend at the Pentagon, may have had no hope for the future, but Paul and Marcia did have hope. There was Sarah. And there was the Olive Branch House itself. Their choice of northeastern Washington was, in the Catholic Worker tradition, meant to show solidarity with the poor. His prison experience had made Paul more keenly aware that prison and oppression were the norm in the early Church, with so many of its leaders, beginning with Peter and Paul, enduring repeated imprisonment and, finally, martyrdom.

How foreign such things were to triumphalism, that arrogant complacency pretending to be faith made perfect, which despite Vatican II remained the ordinary style of Rome. The pomp and circumstances that Rome did with such dazzling flair, a showmanship perfected over the centuries, may have stirred universal acclaim, but I couldn't help thinking of the French general who coolly observed as he watched the charge of the Light Brigade: "C'est magnifique, mais ce n'est pas la guerre." So with triumphalism: it was splendid, but it had little to do with faith.

Paul explained the finances of the Dorothy Day and Olive Branch houses, a brief recital since few words were needed. The benefactor who had established Zaccheus Soup Kitchen sixteen years before pays them $350 a month to run it. The food that sustains Zaccheus and the three Catholic Worker houses in Washington is all donated. There is a food run every Wednesday morning to the city's wholesale market, using an old van that belongs to Dorothy Day House. Merchants are quite willing to give away food that is edible but unsalable because it is past its prime or blemished in some way. The Olive Branch community is responsible for the soup kitchen four days a week, serving one meal a day from 9:30 to 11:30 in the morning, to two hundred to four hundred people.

The rent for the upper floor of the row house that shelters the Olive Branch community is $650 a month. Where does the money come from to pay it? Paul smiled. "Peter Maurin," he said, referring to the French peasant who had been Dorothy Day's friend and mentor, "said people who beg give others the opportunity to do good." No one has any medical insurance, needless to say. A local Catholic hospital provides a sliding-scale prenatal care and delivery program for low-income families, and so Sarah had come into the world for $450. There is also a pediatrician at the neighborhood clinic. The vision that Paul, Marcia, and the others share is that they must trust God in all things, allowing for no exceptions, not even for medical care. "If we're sick, if we're injured," said Paul, "we present ourselves at the hospital or clinic and say we need care even though we don't have the money to pay for it, and we hope that they'll respond in a human way. If they don't — well, then, we have to suffer as do so many others in the world. If there is something particular someone needs — glasses, for example — we check our finances, and if we can afford it, we get it."

Some people come to a Catholic Worker house, stay for a while, and then leave. This makes forming a stable community difficult at times. Considered another way, however, it helps promote the kind of spirit that the Catholic Worker movement is striving to foster. Each sojourner takes away an awareness of what it means to be poor that he or she probably would never get otherwise. Most of them also carry away a realization that disarmament is something to be achieved not by the thrusting and parrying of politicians but by ordinary people living out their faith. Everything comes back to faith. Catholic Workers join so readily in Plowshares actions because their symbolism — the hammers, the blood, the Isaian context — is grounded in faith.

The world in general, including some who profess to be sympathizers, finds the blood and hammers unnerving. But the hammers are ordinary household tools, said Paul, useful and sensible things. Why be upset with hammers and not with nuclear missiles, things that are in no way useful or sensible, things that have no other purpose but to destroy? Why be upset with the pouring of blood when the spilled blood, like a flash of lightning, reveals the doomsday machines for what they are, hideous monstrosities that never should have been built, things that pervert the genius of their builders.

If Plowshares disarmament actions disturb some peace activists, said Paul, perhaps this shows how deeply ingrained our society's regard for property is. There is a need, therefore, to confront not just the immorality of nuclear weapons but the immorality of a value system that would protect itself with such weapons. There is a need to ask if property still deserves the protection of law when its *raison d'être* is its ability to massacre millions of human beings.

As is the pro-life movement, the peace movement is divided on the issue of breaking the law. The major Catholic peace organization, Pax Christi, though many of its members participate in Plowshares actions, shows no enthusiasm for the Plowshares movement. The universally respected Gordon Zahn, a pacifist during World War II and a man who has labored through the heat of the day in the cause of peace, is quite explicit in his disagreement with the Plowshares movement. Zahn disagrees in terms of strategy, not morality. He himself has no qualms about dented nose cones and blood stains, but he argues that Plowshares actions harden rather than soften hearts and that the effort spent on them could be better channeled into the educational methods he favors. The Plowshares actions also have the effect, he said, of removing some of the most dedicated members of the peace movement by consigning them to prison cells.

Paul disagrees with Zahn, a man for whom he has great respect. There can be no better use of resources, he believes, than in direct, nonviolent challenges to the massive structure of violence. Followers of Christ have a clear obligation to make every effort to dismantle this structure, to put their bodies in the way of the planned slaughter of half the globe and absorb the wrath of the government — especially since the grand plan for slaughter was authorized in their names. As for prison swallowing up the most dedicated, prison witness might perhaps be the most effective witness of all, a sentiment that the example of anti-abortion activist Joan Andrews, then serving a five-year term in Florida, and its effect on the pro-life movement seemed to corroborate. At the time of my interview with Paul and Marcia there were fifteen Plowshares activists in prison. Their example had to have an effect on their brothers and sisters.

The government, of course, meant for it to have an effect, an inhibiting effect. Thus the sentences meted out could be severe, especially for Plowshares actions in the heartland, where there was less public sympathy for protest than on the East Coast. Helen Woodson, for example, was serving a twelve-year sentence and Carl Kabat, an Oblate priest, a ten-year sentence. The Plowshares actions have gone on nevertheless, averaging three a year since 1980, and there are usually a dozen or more Plowshares activists in prison. Some, especially Helen Woodson, carry on the struggle behind bars, refusing to cooperate with their jailers — the same kind of behavior that was making Joan Andrews a thorn in the side of the Florida prison authorities. "We said that we were willing to give up our freedom and our lives," said the courageous Woodson. "So we have to decide whether we mean it or not."

"I believe," said Paul, "that ordinary people have a capacity to be moved by what we do and that we'll come closer to a just and peaceful world, closer to the kingdom of God. For Catholics, the sacraments are very important. They sustain us. We should think more seriously, then, about what baptism really means. In the early Church, baptism precluded involvement in anything that involved violence. We have a lot of people being born again today, but the link between baptism and nonviolence has been lost in most Christian traditions, though for the Amish, the Mennonites, and the Quakers it's second nature. Anyway, I consider myself a quite ordinary person, and if I can do this, anyone can. The concern has to be with being true, with being faithful. Effectiveness is something that will follow from that."

A cold January rain was falling the morning after my final conversations with Marcia and Paul at Olive Branch House. Marcia was on her way to Philadelphia to take part in a study session on the Gospel of St. Mark led by a Protestant theologian who insists on the revolutionary nature of Mark's message. It would last most of the week. Paul and Marcia had eaten at a small and quite cheap Italian restaurant the night before, a rare treat.

Sarah had had a bad night, and Paul was afraid that she had an ear infection. The neighborhood clinic was more than a mile away. He was going to take her there in her stroller, trusting its plastic cover to shelter her from the rain. Sarah was a pretty, bright-eyed little girl, laughing even now despite her earache. She could have been living in a nice house in the suburbs with affluent parents who, though nominal Christians, practiced the child worship that was the dominant creed in such environs. Perhaps, even this early, Mom and Dad would have been weighing the merits of various nursery schools. Instead Sarah was playing in the midst of second-hand furniture in a decaying row house. In the desolate streets outside, more forbidding than ever beneath the winter rain, the twin epidemics of crack and AIDS raged, and murder was so familiar a figure that it could hardly be thought of as an intruder.

An eminent Jesuit theologian, Avery Dulles, the son of John Foster Dulles, writing in the pages of *Commonweal,* had recently praised a book by George Weigel called *Tranquillitas Ordinis,* an exposition of muscular Christianity at its brawniest. Dulles had praised Weigel for breaking new ground in the theology of the use of force, a theology, Dulles lamented, that had lately been reduced to "abstract discussions on the morality of nuclear weapons."

There seemed, indeed, to be more things between heaven and earth than were dreamed of in Weigel's theology or Dulles's. There was nothing abstract in the theology that had led Helen Woodson to a twelve-year prison sentence or in the theology that had led Paul and Marcia to bear the risk — to Sarah as well as to themselves — posed not just by vindictive judges but by the place in which they chose to live.

What about Sarah, really? Paul answered by quoting Liz McAlister before she took part in the Plowshares action at Griffiss Air Base in Rome, New York, five years before, an action for which she, the mother of three children, one of them only two, would serve eighteen months in federal prison: "We are going into this," she said, "filled with hope for our children." Christian hope is not the same as optimism, said Paul. Christian hope is bound up with suffering. It is hard for many to grasp that.

No wonder.

All Happy Families
Are Not Alike

The Berrigans of Baltimore

On a warm day in early May of 1988,
I got off the train in Baltimore. I had passed through Baltimore often
enough on the way to Washington, but this was the first time I had gotten
off. The view from the train had never been especially enticing. All that had
ever caught my eye was street after street of drab brownish-yellow row
houses, a cityscape that made me think of a Civil War–era diorama. And
now that I was getting off, chances were, I knew, that I wasn't going to
have the occasion to experience a sleeker and more modern Baltimore. I
hung out with the wrong sort of people.

There was no one inside the station, which I was surprised to find so
small, but a young woman was waiting for me outside, and with her was
a little girl. The girl was seven-year-old Katy Berrigan, the youngest of Philip
Berrigan and Liz McAlister's three children; the young woman introduced
herself as Dale Ashera-Davis. Ashera, I wondered at once — was it a family
name or a feminist deity, as in Astarte and Ishtar? But I didn't have the nerve
to go into it with her just then. Or even later.

Dale was very pleasant, but she had the daunting self-assurance of so
many peace activists — daunting at least to those of us whose moral reach
exceeds our grasp. The following September, she and three companions
would chain themselves to the gate of the American embassy in Guatemala
City and fast for nine days in protest against the campaign of extirpation that
the army, American trained and equipped, was waging against the Indian
population under cover of the democratic facade of the Cerezo regime. One
of her companions would be John Schuchardt, a former Marine, who had
been with the Berrigans at King of Prussia and who would, three years later,

disrupt a church service in Kennebunkport, Maine, attended by George and Barbara Bush by speaking against the Gulf War. Another would be Charles Liteky, the man I was going to visit the next day in Washington.

I was taken aback to see that Dale was driving a Volvo. Back home in Ridgewood, New Jersey, they were more common than Chevrolets and Fords, but a Volvo in connection with Jonah House? A second look, however, allayed any sense of scandal. It was a very old Volvo and, whatever the virtues of Swedish steel, it had its share of dents.

Two weeks before, Philip Berrigan had called me from jail in Yorktown, Virginia. It was an odd sensation, exhilarating yet unsettling, to be sitting in my cozy little kitchen talking with a man who for the past twenty years had been one of my heroes. And he was calling from jail, a place not much less familiar to him than my kitchen to me. Dan Berrigan, who had arranged the call, had urged me to go to Baltimore to visit Phil and Liz, but before I could do so, something had intervened.

On Easter Sunday afternoon, a month before I got off the train in Baltimore, Philip Berrigan, accompanied by Sister Margaret McKenna of Philadelphia and Greg Boertje and Andrew Lawrence, two young men who lived at Jonah House, slipped away from a tour group on the battleship *Iowa*. They made their way undetected to an upper deck and gained access to two of the launchers for the thirty-five Tomahawk cruise missiles with which the *Iowa* was armed, weapons that when equipped with nuclear warheads represent destructive power enough to obliterate hundreds of Hiroshimas. Before the astounded sailors and Marines on guard could arrest them, the four poured their own blood on the launchers, pounded them with hammers, and unfurled two banners that read: "Seek the Disarmed Christ" and "Tomahawks into Plowshares."

Our phone conversation was brief. I expressed my admiration for all that Phil had done and the example he had set, and he responded by praising my articles, none of which, needless to say, had ever landed me in jail. He then told me how to arrange for an interview with him and Boertje and Lawrence. (McKenna was being held elsewhere.) I would follow through on my intention to talk with the Jonah House community, but now I would have to go to Yorktown to see three of its members — three revolutionaries imprisoned at the place where revolution had triumphed two centuries before.

As Dale was driving back to Jonah House, Katy suddenly pointed gleefully at a blue Volkswagen that appeared around a corner. "Punch-bug blue!" shouted Katy. It was a game my own children played. (When you saw a Volkswagen before anybody else did, you got to punch whoever was within reach. It made no sense, but no matter.)

Jonah House turned out to be one of the row houses I had seen from the train. The buildings were more impressive close up, at least in this neighborhood. (The Berrigans lived on Park Avenue, like the Volvo an incongruous touch.) There was no lawn as there had been in front of Olive Branch House in Washington. Here the front doors opened right onto the street, but the street itself seemed a lot cleaner. The houses were three stories high, and their architecture gave an impression of ample space and solid craftsmanship, quite different from the dreadful places we build today with the poor specifically in mind. These, of course, hadn't been built to house the poor. The poor had no need of ten-foot ceilings. I thought of the row house in Dublin in which Sean O'Casey, then a day laborer, had written *The Plough and the Stars*. It had a fine wooden door with a brass knocker.

The first floor of Jonah House was spacious, but it was essentially one long room, with little to divide the living room in front from the dining room and kitchen in the rear. The atmosphere was one of cheerful purposefulness, even gaiety. Even silliness at times. Frida and Jerry, Katy's siblings, ages fourteen and thirteen, were in charge of dinner, and they decreed that everything was to be served in reverse order, starting with dessert. The meal was otherwise unremarkable. I hadn't encountered a memorable meal during my stay at the Catholic Worker houses in Washington, and I had been right in not expecting to do so at Jonah House. Tonight's bland casserole was the classic dish, all the blander because some of the community, like many peace activists, were vegetarians.

Dinner conversation involved ordinary topics. Sometimes Phil, Greg, and Andrew would be mentioned, usually in terms of something they had said or done recently, with no melancholy overtones. John Heid, a slim young man who was a former Franciscan seminarian, smiled quietly but said not a word. Jerry more than made up for John's silence. At one point, male teenager that he was, he came up with an untoward pun on the word *hormone*, which earned a stern reproof from his mother: "Jerry!"

After the dishes were done and everyone else went off to do other things, Frida and I sat down at the dining room table to talk. Jerry was presumably deeply involved with his homework in the living room, but, as we'd soon learn, he was well within earshot.

Frida was, I knew, named for her paternal grandmother, to whom her Uncle Dan had paid such tribute in his recently published autobiography

To Dwell in Peace. Full-faced like Jerry, she was a cheerful girl, though, unlike Jerry, there was a trace of shyness in her manner. She wore braces, and she had on a *Far Side* T-shirt depicting two bespectacled sharks of cheery, hapless mien captioned "Nerd Sharks." She may have looked like a typical teenager, but, as the daughter of Phil Berrigan and Elizabeth McAlister, her heritage was anything but typical.

I had recently seen a tape of a four-year-old *60 Minutes* segment about Dan and Phil narrated by Mike Wallace. In one extremely moving scene, Phil and his three children, Katy only three at the time, paid a visit to the federal prison in West Virginia where Liz was serving a term for the 1983 Plowshares action at Griffiss Air Force Base in Rome, New York.

Though Frida couldn't remember much about the Griffiss action since it was, as she said, so long ago, she was well aware why her mother and father and those who lived with her at Jonah House thought and acted the way they did.

"What we're all trying to do," she said, "is make people aware of what's going on, what's going to happen. What we're doing are mostly symbolic actions. We never do a lot of damage, nothing irreversible. What we do makes people think. It's supposed to make them think, anyway."

She thought that more and more people were becoming aware of the danger they were in. Her classmates at school were not happy about the possibility that they might never get a chance to grow up, except, that is, for one "very weird boy" who was looking forward to nuclear war.

Her parentage had not attracted any undue attention at school. One social studies teacher had been very aware of how crucial the nuclear issue was but had never asked Frida about her parents. Her social studies teacher this year had in fact done so, but then she had said she would like to have Frida's father and mother come to talk to her classes, but she couldn't do that. Most of the teachers realized who her parents were, Frida thought, but they didn't say anything about it.

She herself was never asked to talk, something that she was quite happy about. "I wouldn't like that kind of thing," she said. "How do you feel about this or that since Philip Berrigan is your father?"

Jerry, who had shouted something that we had ignored earlier, now wanted to know if Frida had told me about *60 Minutes.*

Frida laughed. "In the sixth grade last year, Jerry had to write about it in the school newspaper. He had to talk to his class. Right, Jerry?"

"Actually, all the sixth-grade classes," said Jerry from the living room. "It was embarrassing." Somehow it didn't sound all that embarrassing.

Though she wasn't the outgoing type like Jerry, Frida was interested in many things. She liked to read. Madeleine L'Engle was a favorite writer of hers, and she identified with the young heroines of *A Wrinkle in Time* and *A Swiftly Tilting Planet.* She also liked Ellen Conford and Paula Danzinger, who she thought were very funny. The book she was currently reading, however, Upton Sinclair's classic exposé of the meat-packing industry, *The Jungle,* was not typical fare even for bright teenagers. "Just reading it's enough to make you a vegetarian," she said. Frida, in fact, already was a vegetarian, as were John Heid and Dale Ashera-Davis. Six months before, Jerry had made the mistake of betting her that she couldn't do it for a month.

Frida didn't get to the movies as much as she would have liked, but the family saw movies together on their VCR on weekends, and she sometimes went to see some with friends. She had seen *Beetlejuice,* which was "good, if kind of stupid."

"I saw *For Keeps,*" she said, "with Molly whatever-her-name-is. Then I saw her in *The Pick-Up Artist.* I liked *Moonstruck* a lot. Then John and I and Dale and a bunch of others saw *Hairspray.* Oh, that was a really good movie! At the theater where we saw it, Divine and John Waters had written their names in the cement of the sidewalk in front." The late Divine, a hulking female impersonator of unfailingly sweet disposition, had been the put-upon heroine of most of Waters's films. Baltimore had other local heroes besides Frida's parents.

The VCR family fare turned out to be sterner stuff, as might be expected. Together the Berrigans had watched *Matewan,* John Sayles's film about a coal mine strike in West Virginia, and Roland Joffé's *The Killing Fields,* about genocide in Cambodia.

Her Uncle Dan had had a symbolic bit part in Joffé's later film *The Mission,* about the eighteenth-century Bourbon suppression of the Reductions, the mission settlements that the Jesuits had begun two centuries earlier in South America to protect the Indians from Portuguese and Spanish slavers. The Reductions were an enterprise that Voltaire, by no means an uncritical admirer of his old teachers, had called a "triumph of humanity." Thanks to the family connection, Frida had attended a gala screening in New York, though I had to learn this later from her mother. Apparently Divine's and John Waters's signatures in cement had been more memorable.

James Herriot's *All Things Bright and Beautiful,* read to her by her father, had made Frida think of a career as a veterinarian. She also thought she might like to study architecture. An aptitude test at school had pointed her in the direction of science, and though mathematics was not a favorite subject, chemistry was. Whatever she did, she said, she thought that she might first like to spend some time in the Peace Corps even though she didn't like studying foreign languages that much. John Heid had been teaching her sign language, but she had given it up because there had been no deaf people around to practice on. I told her that I knew some Chinese characters, and this prompted another intervention from the living room.

"I learned some cuss words in Chinese from a friend," said Jerry.

"Quiet," said Frida good-naturedly. "I'm interviewing."

Everyone had assigned jobs at Jonah House. Frida and Jerry cooked on weekends. They made lasagna a lot, and pizza. Frida was good at pizza, she said. She put fried vegetables on top. Most of the time everything turned out fine, but sometimes it didn't, Frida confessed. The latter was the case the previous Friday. "We had baked potatoes," she said. "I took them out of the skins and mashed them, putting in sour cream and salt and pepper. Then I fried the skins. It took two hours, and when it was time to eat, I had nothing done but the potatoes."

Frida was going to Syracuse in the summer to stay with her uncle's family for two weeks. She was going to be a volunteer at a day care center there. She was also going to spend another two weeks working in a soup kitchen in Providence, Rhode Island. She was looking forward to the summer.

"Usually in the summer I have to work with Mom and Dad painting houses," she said. Painting houses was the major source of income for Jonah House and Plowshares activists in general. There was no major funding available from corporate or private foundations or from state or federal agencies. "I hate it. It's hot and boring. It took us two years once just to paint one little house."

She might have hated painting houses, but that most children her age had a different outlook on life didn't seem to bother Frida in the least. After all, she said, who knew what they were thinking in their hearts. Shy as she was, having to deal with new people all the time, as life at Jonah House required, wasn't easy for her, but once she got to know them, it was fine, she said.

One thing that did bother her was that there were no girls her own age in the neighborhood even though there were plenty of children around, and Katy and Jerry had friends in the neighborhood. She did have friends at school, however, especially the one other white girl in her class. Aside from a Peruvian girl who was Indian, the rest of her class were black. The Berrigans were radicals, not liberals, and the educational and social environment of their children was, accordingly, light-years removed from that of the children of white liberals.

The Berrigan family didn't go to church, said Frida, but they had a home liturgy on Sunday with the breaking of bread and the celebration of the Eucharist. "Every week somebody else does it," said Frida. "Sometimes it's Dad. Sometimes it's Mom. Or this teacher at Jerry's school whose son is Jerry's friend. We read the Bible a lot too. We're going through this book on Mark right now. They discuss it and then go on to all kinds of different things." There was also a prayer service on Wednesday night at which anyone could read whatever he or she liked from Scripture, but Frida usually passed it up.

We came at last to her father, who had been in the Yorktown jail for a month awaiting trial and who, since she was six years old, had had the threat of a long prison term hanging over his head because of the original Plowshares action.

"Yeah," said Frida, "it's very hard." Her eyes filled up, but her voice was steady. "We're going to see him Sunday. When Mom went to jail, it was Dad who was with us. Mom was away for a long time, and Dad was both Mom and Dad. It seems like a long time ago, but Mom hasn't been home that long. It's hard to make a total reverse. First you've got a dad who has to be a mom and dad. Then you've got a mom who has to be a mom and dad. It'll be good to have a mom and dad again."

It was easier for her now, she said, since she was older and understood more. "I know all about the training and stuff," she said. "And the stupid code names they use. They say I have rabbit ears because I pick up everything."

It was different when her mother went into the Griffiss Plowshares five years before. Frida hadn't known until the day before. "I take back what I said just now," said Frida. "It's easier not knowing. This time [Phil's action on the *Iowa*] I knew just what was going to happen. Just before he did it, I made Mom tell me everything. I was really scared. What if something happened? I thought. On Easter Sunday I was going crazy." Frida expelled her breath sharply to show how tense she had felt. "Where are they now? I thought. What's happening? Before I didn't know all that. Anyway, when we got the news about them being arrested, I was really glad to hear that nothing had happened. I was happy."

Shortly after Frida's little talk with her mother, her father had called the three children together and told them that an action was imminent. "He told us," said Frida, "he told us very, very briefly. I mean, he didn't go into depth. He told us . . ."

Jerry spoke up again from the living room. He was quite willing to help Frida out, but we ignored him.

"Well," said Frida, "he told us . . . sometime in the near future a couple of us are going to do something. He talked to Katy more in depth because he had to explain to her why he was doing this. Jerry and I know why. She had been too young to understand what happened with Mom."

All Things Bright and Beautiful, it turned out, was but one of the books her father had read to her. "We read lots and lots of books together," said Frida, "ever since we were little. Dad would read to Jerry and me in the evening after dinner, when Mom was putting Katy to bed." Their most recent books had been *The Hobbit* and *Ivanhoe*, but the preparations for the *Iowa* action had forced her father to stop reading to them a few weeks before, and they hadn't finished *Ivanhoe*.

Had she ever heard the story of Antigone? I asked. She hadn't, and so I told her. I had told it to children many times before, my own included, but never under circumstances quite like this. When I got to the part where Creon, putting national security above the law of the gods, orders Polyneices's body to be left unburied, food for carrion birds, Frida was taken aback. "Gee!" she said.

Jerry Berrigan was a big boy for thirteen, quite husky. Frida had had to search for the right words now and then, but words were no problem for Jerry, even words like *metaphor*.

"It's sort of like this truck has gone out of control," he said, explaining why resistance was necessary. "The truck is our government. Some people have decided to stop the truck. Some have decided to help those hurt by the truck. Other people are doing both, trying to stop it and to help people too."

I found it striking that Jerry's metaphor hadn't come out of any indoctrination session. He had been listening in, rather, when John Heid was talking to a reporter. Then, fearful of embarrassing him frightfully, I ventured to ask about *60 Minutes*.

Many of the teachers at summer school had seen the episode, he said, handling his discomfiture quite well and not bothering to enlighten me on why he was in summer school. Nor did he go into one of the lighter moments of the visit to his mother, when Liz asked him how he was doing in school and he answered that everything was fine, only to have his father observe that further explanation was in order. "They came in next morning," he said, "and they're talking about Jerry Berrigan being on *60 Minutes*. I had done a social studies project before this on nuclear war, and I got a 97 on it, which was pretty good." He had a social studies teacher whom he described as a "really great woman, opposed to America's doing this, to America's doing that." The teacher then asked the new-minted celebrity to give a presentation of his project to the whole sixth grade. "It was sort of humiliating in a way," said Jerry. "You don't want your friends to know about all that. But I was surprised. Nobody called me a Communist or anything. So it was pretty good, actually." I couldn't help wondering if Jerry would have fared as well in a white suburban school.

Jerry remembered his mother going to prison as a painful experience. Besides missing his mother for all the reasons an eight-year-old boy would, his mother's absence made his relationship to the rest of the community more difficult. A long-time member had gotten married, and he and his bride had spent their honeymoon at Liz's trial. Jerry had known the woman since he was four, but, as he put it so well, you don't really get to know people until you live with them. He didn't get on well with the couple, and he felt that things would have been better if his mother had been there. "You need a mother and a dad," said Jerry. "During all that time, I had a lot of people in the house who were acting like moms and dads, but it's not the same thing."

Liz, by way of preparation, had taken Frida and Jerry aside one day to tell them what she was going to do. The consequences didn't come home to Jerry at once. "I thought, oh wow, she's going to block a gate or something," said Jerry. "And then she goes, 'I'm thinking of a Plowshares action,' and it hit me like a bucket of cold water. I knew about them because my dad had been in the first one and all."

Jerry was five at the time of the King of Prussia action, at that place so aptly named for a symbolic gesture against violence cloaked in legitimacy. The Berrigans had been on their way to visit relatives in Syracuse when their father left them in Pennsylvania. "I remember him saying," said Jerry, " 'Kids, now I'm going to get arrested.' " The news wasn't upsetting to Jerry and Frida because their father's getting arrested had become a familiar thing to them, and they didn't realize that this time would be different. "We saw it on television," he said, "and our reaction was, 'Oh wow! There's Dad,' you know."

Though King of Prussia didn't mean much to Jerry at the time, he came to realize as he grew older that it marked the beginning of something new and more threatening. His first reaction to his mother's announcement about considering a Plowshares action, then, was that he didn't want her to do it. But a few days later, *The Day After,* the television movie on the aftermath of nuclear war, was shown in prime time, and the Berrigan family watched it together, with a degree of attention, one might well imagine, unmatched anywhere else. After seeing *The Day After,* which Jerry pronounced "a very fine movie," he decided that it was right that his mother do what she was going to do. But it was hard, he said, and he did wish that somebody would volunteer to take her place, but no one did.

Their father took the children to Alderson, West Virginia, every month to see their mother. Jerry remembered how beautiful the countryside had been on the way to Alderson. The trip had taken six hours, five, he said, if his father drove all the way.

Alderson, at the time the only federal prison for women, had become a second alma mater to most of the women in the Plowshares movement, among them such indomitable spirits as Anne Montgomery and Helen Woodson. Phil and the children would visit them all when they came to see Liz. Helen Woodson, still at Alderson in the fourth year of a twelve-year sentence for pouring blood on the hatch of a missile silo in Missouri, was a favorite of Jerry. He had seen her pour blood on a pillar at the White House when he was only six, and, besides, she was very funny.

"At first it was hard to leave," said Jerry. "But after a while, I realized that this was going to end, that my mother was going to come home. So it wasn't bad. Well, it was bad. But it wasn't bad in a sense."

Five years after Liz had her serious talk with Jerry and Frida, a similar conference took place at Jonah House. This time it was with their father instead of their mother, and Katy, only two at the time of the Griffiss Plowshares action, was there too. "Dad sat us down one night after dinner," said Jerry. "Just us kids and Dad. 'Kids,' he said, 'I know that you've been worrying about some action going on. Four of us are going to go someplace and do something, and I'm going to leave the rest up to your imagination.' That's what he said, very general. But we all knew just what was involved. Frida had asked Mom and gotten it out of her, and Frida had told me. But I was like saying, 'Dad, we probably have bugs in our house. Why are you saying this?' And he said, 'Well, I'm not saying anything specific.' I knew, though."

Jerry had in fact known for three months that something was in the wind. Greg Boertje had told him one day when they were alone during a family picnic at a state park. "He was like," said Jerry, " 'You know, I'm probably going underground before my sentencing and then do something to get arrested. And your dad is also considering some sort of heavy action.' Now people don't usually trust me with that kind of thing, but, you see, Greg is the trustful type. He always believed in you and he always had faith in you. Greg is a wonderful person. Really good."

Greg Boertje, a quiet young man from Louisiana who had once been an army officer, had taken part with three companions in the Epiphany Plowshares on January 6, 1987, at Willow Grove Naval Air Station in Pennsylvania. The government had finally convicted him and one codefendant, Lin Romano, on its fourth attempt; its first three had ended in two hung juries and a mistrial. Two other defendants, priests from the archdiocese of Philadelphia — who had incurred the severe displeasure of Cardinal Krol, who had once told a congressional committee that nuclear war was immoral — had accepted a deal from the government after the second trial.

Lin Romano received a sentence of two years and one hundred days at the sentencing, which Boertje had declined to attend. He had instead sent a letter to the court in which he explained his absence: "Although resistance can continue in prison, going underground is a direct way to say no to the criminal courts which safeguard the bloody crimes of our government. In a short while, I hope to witness by non-violent direct action and will wait to be arrested."

And so he had, a month before my visit to Jonah House. The *Iowa* action, the Nuclear Navy Plowshares, was Boertje's third.

I had asked Frida how she liked having to live in the same house with so many different people, and now I put the same question to Jerry. His response was somewhat less edifying. "It's pretty good. Most of them are very nice. Some are not very nice. I mean, some are very nice, but I don't get along with them." He had a sudden thought. "You know what? Everybody I really get along with, they go off to jail and, usually, the people I don't really like don't go to jail but stay here. I have a real problem there."

Holden Caulfield couldn't have put it better.

Liz McAlister Berrigan has a throaty voice, its accents unmistakably eastern urban, and she is what in the golden age of male chauvinism we would have called pleasingly plump. Her features are unmistakably Irish. Her thick hair is white like her husband's. She is fifteen years younger than Phil and a few years younger than I. In our youth, we had all three known a Catholic Church of neatly ordered certainties, none of which ever changed.

"My family always thought that we would settle down. I'd do an action at the White House, and Mom would call up here: 'Why'd you do it?' 'Mom, you know why I did it. We've been through all this before.' 'I know, but why'd you do it?' That was my mother's approach. If Dad had been alive, he would have held on and pursued it more. She was a good woman. She really loved us and loved her kids and wanted to keep peace.

"She hoped we'd settle down. And we didn't. And we started having kids. And now they're going to settle down, she'd say. We didn't. We actually went to jail, and we were all right, and the kids were all right. But she wanted us to settle down now and leave it to somebody else."

All happy families may not be alike. But what happens to family life for the happy family that doesn't settle down? The two-year separation that followed the Griffiss Plowshares had been hard on everybody, Liz acknowledged, especially the children. "But their dad was home," she said. "There were others in the community who were here. And it was hard. One doesn't minimize that. But their lives were not that disrupted. I was in prison with women whose children were scattered all over, who never saw them or who saw them once a year. Their children were going through all kinds of things. They were paralyzed. They couldn't do anything. They couldn't reach out to them."

Liz laughed a throaty laugh when I asked about the effect of prison life on her outlook. "Oh, that's a loaded one," she said. "I don't think we could cover that even in a few days. One has to start with the human dimension. What it means to experience some great differences in people. There are many women I was in jail with that I would rather be in jail with than meet on the streets. Yet there's the discovery of common humanity and even common struggle with people who are very different. We get ourselves in boxes sometimes, the way we think. It's good to get out of them."

She had met some great people in prison, she said, some special people who had marked her life. You shared something so extraordinary, and you came through it. You were better people for it, she thought, or at least she hoped you were.

She had just given a talk about her prison experiences at an organizational rally in New York against the long-term maximum-control prison for women that the government had set up in Lexington, Kentucky, and the one it planned for Florida. These prisons, she said, showed where the government was headed. It could now decide what women were suited for such prisons, and, if needed, it would set up more. Helen Woodson, she thought, would be one of those selected. She had walked out the front gate at Alderson a short time before, and she made it clear to the authorities that if they gave her the chance she would do it again. When Helen Woodson made up her mind about something, as she had on noncooperation, she went with it all the way.

The long table at which we sat in the high-ceilinged dining room was covered with envelopes and with flyers that announced a commemoration of the twentieth anniversary of the Catonsville Nine action, in which Dan and Phil and seven companions seized draft board records in the Baltimore suburb of Catonsville and burned them publicly, much as Gandhi and his first companions had burned their registration cards in South Africa sixty years earlier. Throughout the afternoon, people had come and gone, sitting for a time at the table and talking with Liz and Dale as they helped put the flyers into the envelopes. And now, in the evening, Liz and I continued to stuff envelopes as we talked.

Frida came in from the store and put a bag down on the counter. "I need gratification for all I did today," she said to her mother.

"Not gratification," her mother answered. "Something less. After that you and Katy should get a bath and hair wash. And, by the way, could I have my change?"

"What change?" said Frida. "I don't got no change." Liz frowned, and Frida rephrased it: "I don't have any change. I just got two quarters." She put the fifty cents on the table with an air of injured innocence.

"Don't forget to take some glue to school tomorrow," said Liz. "Prepare your arsenal." The metaphor was unexpected, given the family business.

Inevitably, we began talking about children. The Berrigan children didn't fit in with most of their peers. My own didn't either, but the environment in which mine lived, prosperous Ridgewood, was far more seductive. As parents, Liz and I both had to contend with dangers to our children. The world readily acknowledged the dangers that hers faced, and that's why most middle-class parents who could do so had fled the inner city. But if one had faith, if one was rash enough to believe that Jesus had gotten the numbers right about the price of one's soul, then the dangers mine faced were far deadlier. If one had faith.

She and Phil, she said, felt very strongly that their children had to see the poverty in which most of the world lived. This was the reason that Frida was going to spend two weeks that summer living with a Catholic Worker community in Providence, where a cousin, a daughter of her Uncle Jerry, ran a soup kitchen, and then two weeks in Syracuse, where another of Jerry's daughters managed a program for very poor children. (There are in fact six brothers Berrigan, not just two. As with another large blue-collar Catholic family of the same era, the DiMaggios of San Francisco, it was the three youngest who brought fame to the family — and two of them much more than the third. Jerry was the Vince DiMaggio of the Berrigans.)

Liz thought that the Maryknoll lay missionary program, which had brought the martyred Jean Donovan to El Salvador, would be ideal for her son once he was old enough. "It would be great," she said, "for Jerry, a youngster coming out of his culture, to experience firsthand the poverty in which people live and the strength and courage that they have."

Liz was making it sound as though it were her children, not mine, who lived in Ridgewood, but the neighborhood just outside the door, as I wasn't at all surprised to learn, also provided a fair share of firsthand experience of poverty. Some twenty to thirty-five people lived in the row house across the street, with uncles, aunts, lovers, grandchildren all together, their respective relationships too complex for an outsider to sort out. This household represented a pattern that was becoming dominant throughout the neighborhood. Two houses down from Jonah House was a group home for retarded adults. Some of them showed a real interest in becoming part of the neighborhood community, but the few middle-class people who remained would have no part of them.

Liz smiled. "There's one woman in the group home," she said, "who has a voice that can shatter glass. And she uses it. It's all she has left, and what a variety of foul language! It's fascinating. The woman next door, who has a house the size of this all to herself — she owns it — she gets into fights with this woman, and they stand there screaming at each other."

Whites in Baltimore send their children to private schools if they can afford to. In some of the advanced academic classes in middle school and high school, there might be a white majority, but in the lower grades, there are usually no more than a handful of white children.

Jerry had been going to the same school as Frida, both in the same grade though Frida was a year older, but it hadn't worked out. Jerry had been enjoying life too much, and Frida had kept up a steady stream of reports on her unfortunate brother's sins of commission and omission. Now Jerry was riding the bus (there were no school buses as such, but children got free passes for the municipal transit system) to a city school outside the inner city, and he was at last passing algebra.

"Many kids have their moms and dads take them to school and pick them up," said Liz. "We said no dice."

I asked about the 60 Minutes segment and what it was about Jerry's schoolwork that had required further explanation. Liz smiled ruefully. "Jerry had failed two subjects," she said, "but only one was marked on the card. Phil went down to school to check with the teacher of the subject marked, and, on some inspiration, he decided to talk with the other teacher. It turned out Jerry had altered the card. So he was in hot water." A scriptural reference came to mind, and she laughed: "His last state was worse than the first."

Children and the duties that come with having children. Sometimes what you have to do is hard, sometimes it is easy, sometimes it is agonizing, sometimes it is amusing, sometimes it is all of the above or none of the above, but there is always something. How much care children need! How heavy a responsibility they represent! No wonder Liz's mother had thought for sure that her daughter and son-in-law would settle down once they started having children. They hadn't, but each time one of them considered taking part in a Plowshares action, separation from their children was an inevitable factor, the weight of which no one who had never been a mother or father could fully comprehend. And for Phil, anything he did might well trigger a court decision on the still-unresolved King of Prussia sentencing.

"You can't let things like that rule your life," said Liz. She and Phil had said no to all of that long ago, but not without pain. "I think we were mainly concerned with the effect on the little one," she said, referring to Katy at the time of the Griffiss Plowshares, "because she was so young then. So I went into my participation in a very tentative way — depending upon my ability, depending upon how Katy fared." A series of six weekend retreats preceded the Griffiss action, and Liz had three months to gauge Katy's reactions to her mother's involvement. "Actually, in a sense, I think it was easier for her than for the older ones. She was little and she got a lot of attention. Kids live pretty much in the now, and the now was okay for her."

As Jerry had related, *The Day After* played a major role in preparing the older children. "Their reaction," said Liz, "was that we should do all that we could to prevent that from happening. So I told them that there was a community with the serious intention of doing something and that I wanted to act with them. I didn't go into specifics. We never do. There were things about the Nuclear Navy Plowshares that I didn't know about and wouldn't ask."

As we talked and stuffed envelopes, we could hear Frida and Katy giggling and splashing in the tub. The bathroom was off the kitchen.

"We explained to the children that what we're doing in Plowshares is to carry out a disarmament action. That's something that requires a lot of thought. You go back to what is the beginning point for me, the symbolic form." Liz had once been an art teacher. "The idea is not just to disarm this weapon or that weapon but, by actually disarming, to achieve the spirit of disarmament. What you're trying to do, beginning with the Plowshares Eight, is to take the responsibility for these weapons and the responsibility to disarm them and to begin to build the spirit of disarmament — which includes one's own spirit. I think that the question for us today in the spirit of nonviolence is how do we live a sound life."

There was a loud splash in the bathroom, and Katy squealed.

"That's something we've been exploring lo these many years. And I think we will be exploring it for a long time. What I've learned from the process is that the weapons that are out there came from somewhere. And the somewhere is us. Before we made them, before we detonated them, their source was somewhere in us. The question is, How do we learn to live without them?

"Anytime we build a we-they situation, we construct a wall — a wall we fortify with whatever weapons are at hand. Prison was extraordinary in showing me that. All the we-theys that operate there! We've got to break down such walls. We-they thinking can't survive without walls. That's what Helen Woodson is doing, breaking down walls. She said, I'm not going to acknowledge the wall. I'm going to take being here as an invitation to go through it. She just walked through it. Went right out the gate." Liz laughed. "Helen's a character."

Liz paused to address her younger daughter, who was still in the bathroom. "Katy, I think it's time you stopped this nonsense and went to bed."

"Un-huh," said Katy. "I'm going to the bathroom, okay."

Liz turned back to me. "This is the kid who was so sick this morning."

Katy, I said, had told me all about how she had thrown up.

"They love the yucky details. They love them, they do."

Liz went on to tell me more about Helen Woodson. She had twelve children, most of whom she adopted and five of whom have Down syndrome. "One little kid, I don't know how he was classified. He had been born after a twelve-month pregnancy to a twelve-year-old girl, and things had never worked right for him. When Helen took him, they told her he had too much brain damage and he'd be like a vegetable all his life. But the little guy is walking and running and talking. I remember her saying at the time, 'He's not going to be a vegetable.'

"Her kids understand what she did, even the Down syndrome kids. She explained to them that she was kicking the bomb. 'Mommy's going to kick the bomb,' she told them. What that means to them, I don't know, but it certainly means something to them, something very important. And they know the difference between serious and nonserious punishments. Ten days, thirty days, they know is not serious."

Twelve years, of course, is very serious. Three women were now taking care of Helen Woodson's children. She had arranged everything, knowing that her relation to them would never again be as it had been. But as extraordinary as Helen Woodson is in so many ways, she isn't unique among women Plowshares activists in being a mother. More than half of them are.

"Kids are bright enough and honest enough," said Liz, "to know that there is something wrong with the way the world is. So you should ask something of them. We've made it clear to our kids about college. Start now, we said. It will be scholarships or work."

Jerry walked in from the front room.

"You want to do stamps?" his mother asked him.

"Okay," said Jerry. "Could I have some cookies or chips or something?"

"All right, some cookies."

"You know, Mom, I'm sure I really did get a hundred on that last test."

"Did you really?" said Liz, hope contending with incredulity.

"Did you doubt what I told you?"

"Well, Jerry, sometimes you . . ."

"I come home all confident, and then I fail, huh?"

"Your perception of how you do is not always exactly on target. By the way, I think we've found an algebra program for the computer. And no more than four of those cookies, all right?"

We talked on. Eventually, the Catonsville envelopes were all stuffed and stamped, Jerry and Frida had followed Katy to bed, and Dale and John had retired to their rooms. It was nearly eleven, and Liz and I were sitting alone in the dining room.

I picked up one of the extra flyers, which were printed on one side of thick, dark green paper. The tone was brisk and matter of fact. Only the heading and the first paragraph actually paid tribute to the events of twenty years before. The Catonsville Nine had made a "quantum leap," but the heading that followed in large block letters read: "What Today's Events Call For," and a list and dates followed. The first was indeed an anniversary vigil in Catonsville on May 17, but it was meant to be as much continuation as commemoration. The others were the Festival of Hope, a program in Norfolk on May 19, the night before the trial of Phil and his companions in the *Iowa* action; a party at Jonah House and another pretrial vigil at the end of May for the protesters arrested at a demonstration at Johns Hopkins's Applied Physics Laboratory; a demonstration the following day at Johns Hopkins's graduation ceremonies; and, in June, yet another demonstration at the Applied Physics Laboratory. (Mis-Applied Physics, they called it.) Catholic radicals have no time for nostalgia, it seemed. Nor do they take themselves too seriously. A cartoon figure of the archetypal protester, bearded and sandaled, carried a sign that read: "Ban whatever they come up with next."

The legions of hirsute young radicals of the sixties who had idolized the Berrigans had long since melted away. The young rebels had faded back into

American society and had grown middle-aged, too many of them quite comfortable with the moral twilight of the Reagan era and the opportunities it offered. But the Berrigans themselves went on, still believing, still not taking themselves too seriously.

"What happened toward the end of the Vietnam War," said Liz, "was typical of something that has happened again and again — large peace groups attracting people out of self-interest. So the great rallying cry became 'Bring our boys home.' " She smiled. "So what do you do then when your dream comes true? Nixon won that round. There was no more self-interest to motivate people. When an organization becomes oriented toward effectiveness instead of being faithful, its goals become narrow."

And being faithful, as she had need to tell a fellow Catholic, meant that you had to go on forever. It seemed terribly daunting, however, even to a fellow Catholic.

"There's a fine film by Paul Jacobs, *The Nuclear Gang*. While he was making it, Jacobs contracted cancer from a hot spot in the desert. He had to take painkillers to continue, and when he was being interviewed on television you could see the pain on his face. The reporter asked him: 'How do you keep going when you're working against such odds?' And Jacobs quoted the . . ." Liz stopped. "I can never get the pronunciation right. It's the Hindu epic about the oneness of humanity. The Bhaga . . ."

I know, I said. I gave it a try but couldn't manage it. There was a bottle of wine on the table, but even without the wine, the Bhagavad-Gita would probably have proved to be too much for us.

"But, anyway, what Jacobs quoted was: 'It is not our task to finish the work. Nor should we confuse our task with the work.' He saw his role, and his duty was to complete that role."

She and Phil began Jonah House in 1973, she said, after they had finally been acquitted of the charge of plotting to kidnap Henry Kissinger and do other untoward things. Its founding was an event, I'd learn the next day from Charlie Liteky, that Howard Zinn had deemed important enough to record in his *People's History*.

"Our idea was community development," Liz explained. "We did a lot of that the first four or five years, meeting with small groups almost every night of the week. We still do it, but in quite a different way." The Atlantic Life Community grew out of this and brought things into better focus. The ALC had sessions in Washington, and people came from all over the country. The idea was to reflect together and evaluate. Liz and Phil insisted that reflection always had to precede action. "And we'd tell people," she said, "that it's great you've come to Washington. But you really need to look in your own backyard and see what's going on there. They did, and they began resisting at home."

Jonah House got its name by chance, it turned out, though faith, of course, leaves no room for chance, and Jonah, the reluctant prophet, was certainly an appropriate patron. "Jonah's there in the living room," said Liz. "Didn't you see him?" The little statue on a shelf by the door had caught my eye, but I didn't know who he was. He looked a lot like pot-bellied Hotei, one of the seven gods of good fortune, a little ivory statue of whom I had brought home to my parents from Japan years before. Dan Berrigan had given them Jonah when they moved in, and when they later realized that they needed a checking account and nobody wanted it in his or her name, somebody suggested giving the house a name, and they hit upon "Jonah."

The neighbors were curious when the Berrigans and their extended family moved in, but they accepted them readily enough. The Jonah House community began a food program right from the start, and when I had arrived with Dale and Katy that afternoon, Liz, John, Frida, and Jerry were unloading food from a battered pickup truck. Every Tuesday morning, they drove the truck to a wholesale market and filled it up with food. They drove it back to Park Avenue where, depending on the time of the month, twenty to thirty people would be waiting. The rule, heeded by all, was that nobody took anything until the truck was completely unloaded.

I asked Liz about crime in the neighborhood. Was there a lot of it?

"Uh-huh," she answered laconically. Pressed to say more, Liz began an unsettling recital. "The guy right across the street has been busted for selling drugs. We knew he was into drugs. You don't have to be too sharp to know. The guy in the top floor of the same house was knifed to death in a family squabble. We got involved because one of the little kids — he was about nine — came to our door to call the cops when the fight was going on. He came in, and then his mom came and fetched him and took off. Then somebody else came over and said; 'Call the ambulance. He's bleeding all over the place.'

"Then there was an old couple that lived four doors down. Last fall people got worried about the fact that they hadn't been seen for a while. Someone climbed in the window to take a look, and he found that they had been knifed to death in their own house.

"There's a nine-year-old boy missing in the neighborhood now. Last February there was an eleven-year-old child named Lisa who lived just up the street. There's a branch library close by, and the kids like to go there. Frida was up there doing research one afternoon, and then she came home. Two days later, we learned that the girl, who had been there with Frida, hadn't come home. They found her raped and knifed to death. The police came here and talked with Frida." Liz sighed. "Heavy stuff! Heavy stuff!"

Liz had a long talk with Frida after the murder, and then, shortly afterward, another opportunity arose when she had to go to New York to give a talk. She left Jerry and Katy with her brother's family in Montclair, New Jersey, and drove into the city with Frida. After Liz had given her talk, they decided to visit Frida's Uncle Dan, who lived in the Jesuits' Woodstock community, which was housed post–Vatican II style in an old apartment building at Broadway and 95th, a far cry from the tranquillity of rural Maryland, its former home.

"It was a Saturday night in New York City," said Liz. "I had to park seven or eight blocks away on Amsterdam Avenue. It wasn't too nice an area. I had lived in that neighborhood for five years, though. So I was pretty familiar with how one has to walk on city streets. I was trying to communicate this to Frida when we were going back to the car, walking along Broadway by Columbia University. It was about ten o'clock, and these guys were heading toward us. 'Come on, Frida, take my arm,' I said. 'Walk with your head up and looking straight ahead.'

" 'You mean you don't turn around,' she said after we passed them." Liz laughed. "I said, 'No, you keep your ears open, but you don't ever turn around and look.' "

When they had gotten back into the car, Liz explained that by locking arms they made it a little harder for somebody intent on grabbing a purse or doing some other harm. They made potential attackers think twice about bothering them. "Frida took this in," said Liz and then she said: 'You know when that happened to Lisa — I knew before why you wanted me to be careful and not go out and run around — but when that happened, I really knew it. Before I knew it in my head. And it wasn't real. But that made it real.' And then she said: 'It really makes me mad. Jerry can do what he wants and go where he wants because he's a guy and he's big. But because I'm a girl, I can't.'

"I said, 'Well, it's true. You should be mad. Dale has that T-shirt, you know, that says: "Women unite! Take back the night." That's what that's all about.' I said: 'It's maddening, Frida, but it's real.' "

Liz had then explained that Jerry, too, had to be careful, and there were certain times when she would be more worried about Jerry than about

Frida. They had been in Washington during Holy Week and were staying at Mitch Snyder's Community for Creative Non-Violence, which sheltered more than fifteen hundred homeless men. Jerry had been about to run off somewhere when Liz took him aside to impart a few words of wisdom. "I said to him: 'Jerry, you really need to watch yourself. The word is that there's a male prostitution ring going on right here in the shelter.' 'How could that be?' he said. 'Easy,' I said."

Many of the volunteers working at the shelter, Liz explained, simply didn't know what to look for, and they were dealing with survivors of the streets. "These guys are really sharp," she said. "They know how to get by. How to get what they want, and so they can pull the wool right over the eyes of some of the CCNV volunteers. What our kids have got going for them is that they know the dangers, and they've learned to cope with them over the years.

"But still . . . what happened to little Lisa is a mother's nightmare — it's anybody's nightmare. It has to be the most terrible thing. I sensed that with her parents. My original sense of it — it was a Thursday morning that her body was found — my original sense was that she had been missing since Wednesday. But then when the police came to talk with Frida, I realized that she had been missing since Tuesday." She spoke slowly, her words measured. "I can't imagine the terror of her parents."

I felt a chill. It was very late by now. When we're children we scare one another by telling ghost stories. When we're adults we have far more frightening stories to relate. And they're true.

The police patrolled the neighborhood all the time, Liz said, but they were like an army of occupation. "You might hear the helicopter tonight. I've seen that helicopter come right down into this intersection, and I've seen them focus right in on the alleyway." The house had been broken into several times, though only once when they were home. The Berrigans had become more convinced in recent years that it was the FBI putting people up to it. They were convinced that the FBI had pulled dirty tricks to harass them, such as sugar in the gas tank of the old pickup truck. Nobody in the neighborhood would do something like that, Liz said. People respected the truck. It was a lifeline for them, and they knew it.

"We had a flat tire on it one day and we started to change the tire and the thing began to roll. I just instinctively moved against it to push it back, and before we knew it there were a dozen people pushing it back so we could get it into position where it could hold itself. That's not the spirit of people who would put sugar in your gas tank. The back window of the old

Volvo was just smashed to pieces. Tires have been slashed. Things like that. It's not the kind of stuff you see in this neighborhood. The stuff you see is stealing for the sake of money."

There were neighborhoods much worse than this, Liz said, ones in which she would have great difficulty living. One of them was a mere two blocks away. The young people living there had no chance. Their lives were wasted. Liz and the children had to go there from time to time to their dentist. The dentist worked in a clinic run by a Franciscan priest named Tommy Composto.

Sometimes Composto would take time off to sit with Liz on his little front porch and give her a running commentary on life in the street outside. He would point out everybody who was on drugs. He would explain how the man wheeling the carriage and giving his baby some fresh air was actually a dealer who had rented baby and carriage from the mother for thirty dollars an hour. Customers would come up, bend over to look at the baby, and then slip money beneath the baby's bedding on one side and take their purchase out from the other.

"And the baby's mother is pregnant again," said Liz. "And they go on like this. It's a beehive of activity, an absolute beehive of activity." A few of the matriarchs worked somewhere, but no one else did. Unemployment among blacks in Baltimore must have been about 60 percent, she thought, especially among black males. "So you go down this street on a nice day, and you see them spending the day on the stoop. Nothing to do, nothing to do."

People came to the door of Jonah House at all hours asking for food. " 'I need something to give my kids to eat,' they say. We went through a period in this house when we could do nothing because we were forever running to the door and meeting the needs of people. It had gotten so bad — just in the past year — that we said to people: 'We will distribute packaged goods and canned goods on Thursday morning from the truck. And fruits and vegetables on Tuesday morning. Do not come otherwise.' "

Some kept coming every day. Some were so drunk that they had forgotten they had come before. One morning when Liz was home alone working, a man came to the door three times. "I finally said to him: 'If you ring this doorbell once more today, I'm not giving you anything ever again.' He was drunk as a lord, and he kept forgetting. It got so you couldn't have a meeting, you couldn't have a meal, you couldn't pray together."

The people in the neighborhood conformed pretty well, however, to the new distribution policy. The exception was the household across the street in which the man had been stabbed to death. They felt free to come at any time. "Like this guy this afternoon," said Liz. "He said: 'I want a stamp or some sugar.' And I said to him: 'Either one?' And he said: 'Yeah.' A stamp or some sugar! Another time he'll ask for four stamps.

"Then sometimes we have the people who come and say: 'I know you want us to come on Thursday morning, but I need something to feed my kids tonight.' So you give them what you've got. But it had gotten to the point that the person who was preparing the evening meal would go to find what they wanted to cook, and it wasn't there. It was gone." She laughed. "There just wasn't any food there to prepare. We're all right now, but for weeks and weeks on end we kept getting down to the point of having nothing."

There was no need, it seemed, for the Berrigans to read the *New York Times* and subscribe to the proper journals of opinion to realize that the gap between rich and poor had widened and that life in the inner city had grown still more desperate under the malign neglect of the Reagan administration. But was such firsthand knowledge really necessary? Couldn't they carry on the struggle just as well without incurring so many risks for themselves and their children?

"I think that our neighbors keep the connections very strong for us," Liz said. "We see how they're the first victims, the ones who can be wasted and killed and nobody cares. We see that, despite all the rhetoric, nobody really cares about these people. They're the waste product. The stench of alcohol when they come to the door and out there on the corner will knock you over sometimes. Just knock you over." That, indeed, was an experience you wouldn't get from reading the *Times* or *Commonweal*.

"It's much, much harder, I think, to be aware that something is terribly wrong when you're living in some beautiful place. Here you're always aware of it — unless you've killed something inside of you. You see it in the kids running around and what becomes of them."

When they were younger, Jerry and Frida had two friends who were in the house all the time. Their mother was gone most of the time, but their grandfather did what he could for the children. An uncle was also part of the extended family, all of whom lived in one apartment, and he took everything he could lay his hands on for himself and his girlfriend, who also lived there. After a while, the boy and girl kept showing up in the evenings asking for granola bars or Popsicles or whatever the Berrigans had. Liz asked them if they had had any lunch. They hadn't. They hadn't had any breakfast either. By the middle of the month, there was no food in their house, and the two children, nine-year-olds, had to go out and forage for themselves. Liz began putting together packages of food for them, and their grandfather promised that he would hide them from the uncle and his girlfriend.

The children eventually moved away. They lived in another part of the city with their father for a while, but Liz had no idea of what finally became of them. "The little guy," said Liz, "he's maybe a year or a year and a half older than Jerry, had already been busted twice by the cops for breaking and entering with older boys. You know where this kid is going."

This was the kind of thing we called an urban tragedy and thus gave it a place in the scheme of things so that it didn't hurt us too much.

Then there was the story of Sid. Sid was one of Sally's boys. Sally was a divorced white woman who lived on the street and was a good friend of the Berrigans. She opened her house to the neighborhood children every day between four and six, a practice she had begun nine years before. She was wonderful with children, said Liz. Of her original group, however, all but one was either in prison or dead.

One of them, Sid, had been a frequent visitor at Jonah House after he'd grown up. "Sid would come to the door," said Liz, "and say: 'Whatever you've got.' One of us came down one night and gave him a tomato. Sid said: 'What have you got to go with the tomato? Do you have any peppers?' So he got him a couple of peppers. 'Any onions?' said Sid. So he got him an onion. Then Sid asked: 'Have you got a bag?' " Liz laughed. "The guy was incorrigible.

Incorrigible Sid happened to see a dealer stash some heroin in the alley one day. He sold the heroin, and a few days later he was sitting on the steps across the street from Jonah House when the dealer walked up and shot him dead. "So that was the end of one of Sally's kids. She stays faithful to them. She doesn't excuse what some of them do, but she's learned over the years how high the odds are against these kids amounting to anything in life or in their own esteem."

They have no regard for their own lives, I said, and they have no regard for anyone else's. The story had affected me, and I hadn't meant to accuse, but Liz bristled. "No one regards them," she said with some heat. "How can they get a sense of regard when no one regards them? That's how they can get a sense of regard. That would be the starting point. No one but Sally respected those kids, and that did mean something to them. Though it wasn't enough with all they had going against them. You know what our culture is about? You know what Reaganomics is about — what it has done to the inner city? When we stayed in the CCNV shelter in D.C., it was like living in a war zone, I kid you not."

Liz spoke of a presentation by a health care worker named Kurt who had spent a great deal of time in Guatemala. Kurt was an extraordinary person, she said, a very gentle human being. He told the story of a little thirteen-year-old boy who was brought in suffering from the last stages of dehydration from malnutrition and unable to hold anything down. They gave him a shot and other medication and, finally, nursing him through the night, they were able to get him to retain something with nutritional value. The boy made it, Kurt had said, but eighty-three out of a hundred children in Guatemala suffer from malnutrition, fifty of them severely.

What was the government of the United States doing for Guatemala? We were helping the repressive Cerezo regime to set up a model village as a means of combating guerrillas, a strategy obviously inspired by the notorious Strategic Hamlet program in Vietnam. Kurt showed the group some pictures he had taken of the children in these model villages. They were, he said, nothing but concentration camps.

Liz left before Kurt had finished because she had to take part in a vigil at the Pentagon. "I sat for four hours over at the Pentagon — sitting and looking and feeling. And this was the thought that came to me: What's really happening in some of these so-called Third World countries is almost an experiment for something to be put into practice here. And it's already well on its way. You don't even have to talk about the new maximum-security prisons. You just need to talk about what's happening to the poor. This neighborhood, as I said, sometimes feels like occupied territory, with that helicopter."

Though the Berrigans lived in the inner city, Liz readily admitted that in most ways there were some significant differences between the way they lived and the way their neighbors lived. "We really live very well. We eat very well," she said. "We have enough heat so that the house in winter is livable. We scrounge the wood for the stove like we scrounge the food. You can live well off the waste of this culture, but you have to know how to do that."

Despite everything, many of their neighbors still believed in the dream world that they saw on television. One black man who worked with the Berrigans painting houses went out and spent seven hundred dollars to outfit his little girl for school in September. He did it because he thought that that was the way you had to do it. "We take the kids to the Goodwill store," said Liz, "and turn them loose there for a while. You need clothes? You need books and a backpack? We have a fifty-dollar budget for the whole thing. And that's your paper and your pencils and your new books and your backpack, if that's what you need. And whatever else you need. And you operate within that. And they do, and they do very well. They aren't the best-dressed people in the world, but they're decent."

I remembered Frida's "Nerd Sharks" T-shirt. I had asked her if she liked

Gary Larson's *The Far Side*, and she said that she did. Whenever she was in a bookstore, she'd page through one of his collections. We had four at home. My daughter, the same age as Frida, had given me one for my last birthday.

There was no tension, Liz said, when the children visited her brother and his family in Montclair. "The kids have a good time — a good time. Bill and his wife are wonderful, very welcoming people, and they love the kids. And they know we love them and care about them. We don't go up there with a judgmental attitude. We care about one another. Our lives are different, that's all."

I told her about a couple I talked with in Detroit, Bill and Mary Carry. Bill had been a high-ranking executive at Chrysler. They had been conservative Republicans, enthusiastic about Barry Goldwater. But then they had gotten to know Bishop Thomas Gumbleton, the Detroit auxiliary bishop who for years had been the most prominent advocate of nonviolence among the American Catholic hierarchy. Gradually their thinking changed, and so did their lives. Bill quit his job with Chrysler. They moved out of their palatial home in Bloomfield Hills and into a more modest one in a less fashionable suburb. They apologized for how nice the house looked. And it did look nice. They wanted to live more like the poor, but they admitted they still had a long way to go.

Liz was quite sympathetic to the Carrys' dilemma. "You keep trying," she said. "We're critical of the fact that we have this big TV set. A friend was here and he said, 'I've got a TV we're not using,' and that afternoon he came over with this thing, and it had a VCR with it."

The children had been putting pressure on their parents to allow them to watch television on Friday nights. Instead they started getting movies on Friday nights to play on the VCR, either just for the children or for the whole family together.

"One they liked was *Amazing Grace and Chuck*, I think it was called," Liz said. I knew about it. A little boy teams up with a pro basketball star to rid the world of nuclear weapons. "I didn't see it, but the kids did. They loved it. At least it creates the idea that people can make a difference. I enjoy the things with the kids that are your basic classics, children's classics. Then we saw *The White Rose*, the German movie about resistance to Hitler by some young college students. It was extraordinary. They loved that. Then they enjoyed the documentary about the Chicago conspiracy trial. Frida's got the thing memorized. And we just got *The Killing Fields*, a great film."

I told Liz about interviewing the director Roland Joffé in New York just before *The Mission* opened. He confirmed what I had surmised: his casting of Dan Berrigan in a bit role had not been incidental. He intended the suppression of the Reductions in eighteenth-century Latin America to be a metaphor for the struggle between liberation theology and secular and ecclesiastical reaction in twentieth-century Latin America. Joffé, a slim, intense man, professed himself to be "an old atheist." He wasn't at all old and the noun, too, might have been tinged with irony. At any rate, the central question posed by *The Mission,* Joffé said, had to do with the sacrifice of Christ. Did the sacrifice of Christ mean that Christians were supposed to sacrifice themselves for others or to sacrifice others to protect Christianity? Maybe atheism sharpened one's vision. If you didn't take Jesus' ideas for granted, for example, then maybe their absurd and outrageous nature became quite apparent. Joffé's insight was, at any rate, one that had eluded many bishops, especially the bishops of France and Germany, who a few years earlier had issued a pastoral letter blessing nuclear weapons as an indispensable means for protecting the Christian West from Communist aggression. Nor did the American hierarchy seem to have grasped it fully when, in their own more courageous peace pastoral, they wove their net of structures loose enough to let a fleet of Tridents slip through.

Liz was less than enthusiastic about the peace pastoral. "I think it's been a tool," she said, "but that's as far as it's gone. It's helped us to a degree. But nothing was ever done with it, especially among the bishops. It's real cowardice. It's hard not to tear your hair out." Liz laughed.

The bishops would have a meeting in Washington the following month, June 1988, and one of the topics would be nuclear deterrence. Five years before, after coming out with so much that was stern and commendable, they had pronounced a "conditional acceptance" of nuclear deterrence as long as it was a stage toward a progressive disarmament and not a permanent condition, a weak and disheartening dénouement. They had compounded their failure in nerve by showing no zeal whatsoever for any follow-up. The Pentagon flourished in the Reagan years, with bigger and better and more numerous weapons of all kinds, nuclear and conventional, but the hierarchy took no notice. They were so gratified, apparently, by Cardinal Joseph Bernardin's celebrity that their cup runneth over. Why not quit while you're ahead?

The June meeting would set the seal on the hierarchy's capitulation to the Pentagon. The bishops would approve a lackluster and rambling document that, while admitting that the United States had made no progress whatsoever toward nuclear disarmament, would conclude that "the condemnation of deterrence would be too drastic a solution." In their desire to patch up the marriage of Cross and Flag, the bishops would forget, it seemed, that their corporate logo was the Cross, the symbol of a solution drastic in the extreme. Three years later, Cardinal Bernardin would extend "conditional acceptance" to the Gulf War, but it wouldn't get him back on the cover of *Time*. That's show business for you.

It was now very, very late. It was a time when one could ask foolish questions and attribute them to fatigue — or perhaps the wine. Liz smiled and shook her head when I mentioned the institutional Church. Her voice was soft and perhaps a trifle wistful. "We just have so little to do with it," said Liz McAlister Berrigan.

I had a big room all to myself on the top floor of Jonah House. There was a bookcase against one wall. On it, among other books, lay a hardcover version of a symposium on the Brothers Berrigan published in the late sixties by the College of the Holy Cross, Phil's alma mater. On the cover was a picture of Dan and Phil in their Roman collars.

I had read the symposium in its original form. When I picked it up and glanced over the introduction, I noted with a certain malicious amusement that Andrew Greeley had refused permission to reprint his essay, a savage attack on the Berrigans. Father Andy believed that nuclear weapons were necessary to make the world safe for good sex, Chicago Catholic style. (Tinkle, tinkle go the entwined scapular medals.)

Then something else caught my attention.

Taped to the wall were some children's pictures drawn in bright crayon and signed "Frida" and "Jerry." The artistic merit was slight — I remembered that Frida had said that her art classes bored her — but the subject matter was arresting. In more ways than one. Men and women were hammering and pouring blood on airplanes marked with air force insignia. A sign said, "Griffiss AFB."

I didn't hear the helicopter that night.

An Ordinary
Reaction

Charlie Liteky

When I got off the train in Washing-
ton the day after my visit to Jonah House, it was much warmer than it had
been in Baltimore, to the point of being uncomfortable, in fact, since it was
sultry and overcast. The weather had been quite different six months before,
the day I had last talked with Charlie Liteky.

The sun had shone bright upon that bitterly cold January morning,
about as cold as it gets in Washington. The day before a wet snow had
fallen, immediately turning to slush underfoot, and the mercury had
plunged overnight, freezing the slush to clusters of ice crystals that glinted
on the walks and drives that curved around the Capitol.

"Didn't expect it to get this cold," Charlie Liteky had said.

He said it as though it wasn't a matter of much interest to him one way
or the other. You wouldn't have thought from his tone that he intended to
spend the next two hours there on the broad steps leading up to the rear
entrance of the Capitol. Nor could you have guessed that he hadn't eaten
anything for two days and wouldn't for another seven. Liteky, along with
two dozen or so other demonstrators, was there to protest the Contra aid
that the president of the United States had called for with such fervor in his
1988 State of the Union Address the night before.

Charlie Liteky was a man of determination, but he expressed it quietly.
A lean six-footer with rugged features, Liteky at fifty-six fit the Hollywood
image of a field-grade officer, an impression heightened by his laconic
manner and the slight drawl that went so naturally with the uniform. The
drawl came from his Jacksonville birth and a boyhood spent on naval bases
as the son of a career enlisted man. The rugged features, however, weren't

the Anglo-Saxon of central casting but a blend of Slavic and Celtic. Liteky's father had been Slovak and his mother Irish, and though his manner may have been like John Wayne's, Charlie Liteky's exploits were quite real. They were such, in fact, that a grateful nation had awarded him the Medal of Honor.

Like Gettysburg, Waterloo, and other battles that history makes much of, the fierce, anonymous clash that took place seventy miles northeast of Saigon twenty years before began in haphazard, piecemeal fashion. In December of 1967, a platoon of the 199th Light Infantry Brigade blundered into the base camp of a large North Vietnamese Army unit marshaling for the fateful Tet Offensive. Liteky, a Catholic priest and regiment chaplain, was with the platoon.

"Intelligence reported a large concentration twenty miles northeast of Phuoc-Lac in Ben Hoa Province," Liteky had explained the previous afternoon in his Washington home, a small, neatly furnished row house he shared with his wife, Judy. "So a battalion was airlifted in by helicopter. Five hundred people were in there by midmorning, and by nightfall we had set up a perimeter a mile around, sandbagged in. After dark, ten mortars came in. They walked right in, as though they had started with a high elevation and just lowered the tube a notch at a time. Nobody was hurt, but the next morning Alpha Company sent out a platoon to try to discover the mortar site."

Liteky went along with the platoon, as did the company commander. It was something, he said, that chaplains did to show moral support and to be there in the case of casualties.

"We were out about a mile, traveling on an azimuth from the line of mortar rounds, when the point men called out that they had seen what they termed two or three VC. So we double-timed up to where they had disappeared into the woods."

Up to then the brigade had never encountered any North Vietnamese soldiers. "All we had ever run into was indigenous VC. So we thought we were just chasing some more VC, and they always ran away before." It was a costly misapprehension.

The company commander ordered fifteen men, half of the platoon, into the grove. They were no more than ten yards into the trees when machine gun fire and exploding mines shattered the silence, followed by the screams of the wounded and shouts of "Medic!" "It was really quite a surprise," said Liteky.

Liteky asked the company commander if there was anything specific he could do, but the man was too busy trying to make radio contact with the base camp to answer. "So then," said Liteky, "I went in looking for people who had been wounded. I found some. Some of them were dead. Some wounded badly. Some not so badly. So I began to take them out — crawling around in there trying to get them out. It was an ordinary reaction."

It wasn't quite so ordinary, according to the Congressional Medal of Honor citation. The citation describes, for example, how at one point Liteky moved "to within 15 meters of an enemy machine gun position." Nor was getting the wounded out exactly all in a day's work. "When I got a hold of one. . . ." He paused, reflecting. "You couldn't stand up. There was no way to stand up in that." (Again the citation disagreed: "In a magnificent display of courage and leadership, Chaplain Liteky began moving upright through the enemy fire.") "I rolled over on my back and got them on top of me. I asked them to help to push with their feet if they could — to get us back to where the others were." The company commander ordered another assault and more men were wounded. Then he called for an air strike and the helicopters arrived in no time. He called for reinforcements and a company was landed on both sides of the woods. The brigade commander had decided that the platoon had run into a large NVA base camp, and he was determined to overrun it. A four-hour battle ensued. "In the course of that time, before darkness came, we lost twenty-five killed and eighty wounded," Liteky recalled. "That was very serious."

We were sitting by a window. Throughout Liteky's account of futile slaughter beneath a tropic sun two decades before — an apt metaphor for the whole war — heavy, wet snow fell silently from a dark sky, muffling the street noises of Washington, the Imperial City, whose elders had sent to their deaths the boy soldiers who fell that day in Ben Hoa Province on the mainland of Asia.

Liteky continued his story. More reinforcements arrived, including armored personnel carriers. "They were not really ominous weapons," said Liteky, showing his fondness for the occasional unexpected word. "APCs could be easily stopped. They were armed with a .50-caliber, and I guess that was supposed to make them menacing. But, anyway, my action essentially there was to get people back out of the line of fire and back to the landing zone."

According to the citation, the landing zone itself wasn't all that secure. "On several occasions," it read, "when the landing zone was under small arms and rocket fire, Chaplain Liteky stood up in the face of hostile fire and personally directed the medivac helicopters into and out of the area. With the wounded safely evacuated, Chaplain Liteky returned to the perimeter, constantly encouraging and inspiring the men."

When I asked him how many he had saved, Charlie Liteky paused before answering, a glint of wry amusement in his eye. Obviously, he had been asked the question before and, obviously, he hadn't counted. "The citation says twenty," he said. (Actually, it said "over twenty.") "That's somebody's estimate. But it went on. The fighting went on for four hours."

The helicopter strikes the company commander called in took place while the wounded, and Liteky himself, were still in the woods, though it wasn't intentional, he explained. "I really thought I was going to get hit when the helicopters made their passes."

All this time, fortunately, the North Vietnamese did not move forward. They were very much aware of American firepower, and they knew that reinforcements were on the way. "Their plan was immediate withdrawal," said Liteky. "They got all their stuff ready, and when darkness came they moved out. What we did was put a ring of steel around them and ourselves with artillery fire, but they were getting away all through the night." Incredibly enough, Liteky escaped with minor wounds. He still carried in his foot what he thought was a piece of American shrapnel from a helicopter rocket. The citation mentioned a neck wound, too, but Liteky said that was nothing but scratches from the vines and brush he crawled through.

The brigade had been in action for about eight months. "We had been fired at before," said Liteky, "but that was our first big encounter. And they were very tough."

The Medal of Honor was gone now. Liteky had laid it down in front of the Vietnam Veterans Memorial two years before, a gesture of protest against aid to the Contras that was unprecedented enough to land him on page 2 of the *New York Times*. Today on the Capitol steps, instead of the Medal of Honor he wore a large button, just above the peak of his cap. "Peace is possible," it said, "because love is possible." The source was Pope Paul VI.

Poor, tortured Paul VI, John XXIII's Hamlet, seemed an unlikely inspiration for Liteky, the man of action, whose personal odyssey had taken him very far from the simple certainties of his seminary days. And though he had called his leaving the priesthood "traumatic" the day before, he now told me with uncharacteristic vehemence that whether the Church as an institution survived was a question that didn't even interest him.

Charlie Liteky believed that support for the Contras in their savage incursions into Nicaragua was immoral, pure and simple. Many of us did, but few of us felt so strongly about it that we'd give up a Medal of Honor to show our opposition. But Liteky did. Nor would most of us undertake a water-only fast for the nine days preceding the vote and demonstrate every day from eleven to one on the Capitol steps. But Liteky was doing just that, and so were his fellow members of Citizens Fast for Peace.

There had been a press conference the day before. Besides Liteky and Brian Willson, who had lost his lower legs to an armament train in California four months earlier, the speakers had included Martin Sheen, Daniel Ellsberg, and former CIA man John Stockwell. The chair of the group was Philip C. Roettinger, a tall, courtly former CIA man in his seventies who had been directly involved in the overthrow of the democratically elected Arbenz regime in Guatemala during the Eisenhower administration.

All the speakers were eloquent, but Ellsberg, whose daughter was a health worker in Nicaragua and therefore a prime Contra target, had probably made the strongest impression. He had held up a blond doll whose body had been shredded by a Contra grenade thrown through the window of a *campesino* cabin. The same grenade had severely wounded the child whose doll it was and her brother and sister as well. Her mother and father and two other children died in the attack. The mother died instantly, blown through the floor by the grenade, but the father remained conscious while life seeped out of him. Throughout the night, as he lay dying on the floor of his home, he talked to his surviving children, telling them to be good people when they grew up.

Not a line about all this had appeared in the *Washington Post,* the paper that, as movie fans well know, did so much to preserve freedom as we know it during the Watergate crisis. The *Post* was currently in favor of Contra aid because, for the moment at least, killing and maiming *campesinos* was, it deemed, in the national interest. God help those who got in the way of the national interest.

Martin Sheen had had to go back to New York to rehearse for a play, but most of the others were here on the Capitol steps. Ellsberg wore a cap with fur ear flaps. He was eager to talk with me about his son, Daniel Jr., who had become a Catholic and was an editor at Orbis Books, run by the Maryknoll order. Phil Roettinger, a Marine colonel before he joined the CIA, sported the Corps's classic olive green fatigue cap. Dr. Margaret Brenman-Gibson of Harvard Medical School, fresh from a jail near the nuclear test site in Nevada, had bundled herself up in a shawl against the cold. She wore a scarf around her head, as did actress Shirley Knight.

All in all there were about thirty people gathered on the steps with banners and posters protesting Contra aid, including Linda Bohlke and Louie De Benedette, whom I had met at the Olive Branch Catholic Worker house. Louie would be arrested at the Mexican border a year later as a member of a veterans' group that organized a truck convoy to bring food and medical supplies to Nicaragua. Linda, a fragile teenager wrapped in a blanket, seemed to have come via time warp from the sixties, a lone flower child blooming where once thousands had flourished. She had gone with Marcia Timmel to the Supreme Court on the *Roe vs. Wade* anniversary, but "all those fascists freaking out" had upset her, and she had sought out a Native American exhibit at a nearby museum to recover her tranquillity. According to Paul Magno, Linda had never seen an arrest she didn't like. Another participant in the anti-Contra protest was a Japanese Buddhist monk, who was happy for the chance to talk in his native tongue. He now lived on a Navaho reservation in Arizona. He prayed by chanting and by beating a stick against what looked like a large paddle, leather stretched tight over a frame. Around the edge of it, "Hail the Wondrous Lotus Sutra" was written in Chinese ideograms, some almost worn off by the fervor of his blows. The American Catholic hierarchy had come out — quietly, to be sure — against Contra aid two years before, but no bishop was there on the bleak, windswept steps to mingle Gregorian chant with the monk's praise of the Lotus Sutra.

Liteky's renunciation of the Medal of Honor may have made the *New York Times,* and the Pentagon Papers may have been one of the major stories of the Vietnam era, but, perhaps because, as F. Scott Fitzgerald observed, American lives weren't supposed to have second acts, at least none fit to print, nobody was there from the *Times* today. The only media representatives on hand, in fact, were a television crew from London. A handsome blond woman with a Scandinavian accent held up a microphone as she asked Brian Willson if it was true that the crew of the train that ran over him was suing him for the mental anguish he had caused them. When he said that that was correct, she looked incredulous.

"Well, what do you make of that?" she asked.

Willson smiled faintly. A burly man and, like his friend Charlie Liteky, a star athlete in his youth, he moved with incredible ease on his artificial limbs despite the short time that had passed since he had been maimed. A few moments later, in fact, he would do an impromptu dance with Dr. Brenman-Gibson while singer Mark Levy played "This Train Ain't Moving" on his guitar, a ballad he had composed in Willson's honor.

"I don't think they're doing it of their own volition," said Willson.

The choice of the Capitol steps for the demonstration was symbolic rather than practical. In an enterprise like this the only way to be practical was to be symbolic. No one was really going into the Capitol via these steps. Our chosen leaders and their aides with the clever faces, warm and unseen, were passing beneath us through the underground passageways that lead from the House office buildings just across Independence Avenue to the south, and the cold kept the occasional passers-by from doing much more than cast a curious glance in our direction.

This was Liteky's second fast. Two years before, in September and October of 1986, right after he had laid down his Medal of Honor, he had fasted for forty-nine days in protest against Contra aid.

"During a demonstration like this," I asked, "do you ever tell people that you won the Medal of Honor?"

Liteky looked embarrassed. "Nah," he said, shaking his head. "Well, just once I did. Some smart kid was giving me a hard time about what kind of veteran are you, and I lost my temper and told him."

Just then, as we were standing on the second or third step, a group of seven or eight high school youngsters, all of them neatly dressed and wearing plastic-encased name tags with "Close-Up" printed on them in large block letters, began to edge warily in our direction. They were shepherded by a tall, genial young man.

"Come on, come on," he said to his charges. "These people are human just like you." Then he smiled at Charlie Liteky. "My young people here are shy. They'd like to ask you what you're doing, but they're afraid to."

"Well," said Liteky just as genially, "we're here because we're against aid to the Contras. All of us are fasting until the vote comes up. Many of us are veterans and some are ex–CIA men. Personally, this is not the kind of thing I much enjoy. I'd rather be sitting around drinking a beer and watching a football game or something. But we feel very strongly that it's wrong to aid the Contras, and so as patriotic Americans we're doing this to let people know how we feel."

"We're from Texas," said the young man. "The idea of Close-Up is to bring young people like this to Washington and show them how the government works. We've just come from Congressman Delay's office."

"He doesn't agree with us, does he?" said Liteky.

The young man laughed. "Indeed he doesn't. He showed that Ollie North videocassette all over his district."

The mention of North set me off. In the name of Hunter J. Thompson and the sacred tradition of gonzo journalism, I had to speak out. "I'm not part of this demonstration," I said, "but let me tell you this. Oliver North might have won the Silver Star in Vietnam, but this man here won the Congressional Medal of Honor."

I had their full attention at once, and I then went on to describe just how Liteky had won it and how he had laid it down in front of the Vietnam Memorial on a hot July day two summers before.

There was a moment's pause, and then the young man from Close-Up spoke again, his voice quite earnest now. "You see," he said to the students, "some people try to tell you that people who protest aren't patriotic Americans, but you see it just isn't so."

"You're young and you're learning things," said Liteky to the boys and girls standing in front of him, "and I'm in my fifties, and I'm still learning things. I read all the time. I found out there isn't any Santa Claus. This country of ours has been treating people badly for a long time — starting with Columbus and the Indians."

A boy in front, a Hispanic with a crewcut who was wearing a neat gray sport jacket, nodded his head earnestly as he looked up at Liteky. "I guess if people don't start protesting like you're doing," he said, "things are just going to go on that way."

It was one o'clock. Time to pack up the signs and banners and the sound system and store them in the nearby United Methodist building until eleven the next morning. I helped Liteky carry some of the posters.

"What are you reading now?" I asked.

"Howard Zinn's *People's History*. I took a job on the front desk of a high-rise to give me a chance to read. I work from six in the evening till two in the morning, and there's hardly anything to interrupt me. The only problem during the fast is that I'll have to find some other way of staying awake than drinking coffee."

Later, on the train back to New York, I thought about a fasting Charlie Liteky reading through the night at his post in the lobby of a high-rise. A forlorn vigil, most would say, especially in a city where power was the end-all and the be-all. What took more courage? To go down into the valley of death time after time in the course of a long afternoon or to turn your back on everything that American society prized, security included?

Charlie Liteky was much more at ease with me during my second visit. He liked the article I had done for the *National Catholic Reporter* on the fast and the Capitol vigil. "I almost never look at the paper," he said, "so I just took it out of the mailbox and put it on the table. But then when Judy went to work, the sisters there showed it to her."

His wife worked for Network, an organization of nuns devoted to lobbying for social justice. Network was held in high esteem in liberal circles, but I had mixed feelings about them, and I'm sure they would have returned the favor. The regard they enjoyed with liberals came at the price of their silence on abortion.

Liteky had quit his job at the high-rise, and he was doing some painting around the house. Since my visit in January, he had been arrested twice in connection with demonstrations against sending troops to Honduras. One case had been dismissed, but the other was pending. I told him that I was on my way to Norfolk to cover the trial of Philip Berrigan and his companions and that I had spent the previous day at Jonah House. He was very interested. As to his own future, he was plainly at loose ends.

He picked up Zinn's *People's History*. "Listen to this," he said. "This is what Zinn has to say about heroes":

The treatment of heroes (Columbus) and their victims (the Arawaks) — the quiet acceptance of conquest and murder in the name of progress — is only one aspect of a certain approach to history in which the past is told from the point of view of governments, conquerors, diplomats, leaders. It is as if they, like Columbus, deserve universal acceptance, as if they — the Founding Fathers, Jackson, Lincoln, Wilson, Roosevelt, Kennedy, the leading members of Congress, the famous Justices of the Supreme Court — represent the nation as a whole. The pretense is that there really is such a thing as "the United States," subject to occasional conflicts and quarrels, but fundamentally a community of people with common interests. It is as if there really is a "national interest" represented in the Constitution, in territorial expansion, in the laws passed by Congress, the decisions of the courts, the development of capitalism, the culture of education and the mass media.*

Liteky, burning with indignation, shut the book and laid it down. It was like the old joke about the Lone Ranger turning to his faithful Indian companion when they find themselves surrounded by Apaches and saying: "Well, Tonto, it looks like we've reached the end of the trail." Tonto replies: "What do you mean 'we,' white man?" We assume so many things to be true that simply are not true, and the history books they gave us in school and the old Hollywood movies we saw when we were young have

*Howard Zinn, *A People's History of the United States* (New York: Harper & Row, 1980), p. 9.

had much to do with fostering our illusions. But truth, like murder, has a way of willing out, especially truths about murder. How could Zinn, I wondered, at his most sanguine, ever have imagined that his words would be read with such stern conviction by one of the very heroes he denounced, a man around whose neck Lyndon B. Johnson — who, for all his cynicism, firmly believed that he was president of all the people and had a title to the universal love and gratitude of every last one — had once hung the Congressional Medal of Honor?

When, finally, over a lunch of Japanese noodles — the kitchen was separated from the living room by a counter — we took up where we had left off four months before and began talking about why Liteky had finally changed his mind about the Vietnam War.

"I never went against it while I was there," he said. He had lived on bases all of his life, and he felt very comfortable with the military. He was familiar with its culture, its class structure. Being a chaplain was something that fit easily into this. When the Vietnam War came along, he had accepted it as right and proper, a decision bolstered by the just war theory he had learned in the seminary. He laughed. "There was very little I learned in the seminary that I didn't accept," he said. "It wasn't an age when people were encouraged to question or think. It always was *de fide*, or whatever."

"Or whatever" was a favorite expression. It wasn't a throw-away phrase. He pronounced it with a harsh edge, like the final blow of an ax.

"I did get turned off, though, by the way the war was being fought, especially during my second tour of duty. I thought we weren't using proper tactics. I wasn't too impressed with the quality of the leadership. I always thought there was a lot of carelessness. A lot of nonchalance. I'm not a military man, but it didn't take much to see that in jungle war, with them hitting you whenever they wanted on their terms, the best way was to break up into small units and have everything covered, all over. So they could hardly move without running into an ambush. We did set up ambushes, but they could come out from a central base camp. They could see our people going out to the ambush sites.

"After I got out of the service, it was rather sad, I thought, to see us pulling out without accomplishing our mission. I thought we were letting those people down. It was only as time went by that I began to change."

Liteky was thirty-seven when he came home to stay from Vietnam in 1968. He wasn't sure what he wanted to do, and his unsettled state of mind came to the attention of his superiors under rather embarrassing circumstances. For them, not for him. Liteky belonged to the Trinitarians, a small congregation founded in the United States to work with African Americans.

The Trinitarians were naturally overjoyed at the fame that had come to one of their own. On the day that Lyndon Johnson placed the Medal of Honor around Charlie Liteky's neck on the White House lawn, there was a gala banquet at the Trinitarian house in the capital, with an array of honored guests, including the archbishop of Washington and the apostolic delegate. One by one, dignitaries rose to praise the priest-hero in their midst. The superior of the Trinitarians said that Father Liteky reminded him of the congregation's saintly founder. Finally, the man upon whom these encomia had been heaped got to his feet. It would be difficult to say anything memorable under such circumstances, one would think, since the occasion itself was so overwhelming, but Charlie Liteky did so with ease. What he said, in fact, remained quite vivid twenty years later in the memory of the Trinitarian priest who told me the story, one of Liteky's classmates, who also remembered him well from touch football games. ("Many a time Charlie knocked me on my ass.")

After thanking everybody, Liteky said that just before he left Vietnam for home, he had pretty much decided that he didn't want to be a priest anymore. If he hadn't had everybody's attention before, he certainly got it then. Against a backdrop of hushed silence, he went on to tell how he had stopped in Hawaii on the way back and rented a car. He got out of the car in an outlying neighborhood of Honolulu to walk a little. Some boys were kicking around a soccer ball, and it bounced in Liteky's direction. "I kicked it back to them," he told his rapt audience, "and then we started talking about one thing or another. After I got back in the car, I started to think. If I could talk to those kids like that and get a response, well, maybe I ought to stay with the priesthood and see what I could do."

Once the pomp and circumstances of his homecoming, however chilled by his candor, were behind him, Charlie Liteky had to decide what to do with himself. Giving the priesthood another try was not the same as plunging into apostolic activity. He wasn't in the mood for that. He had to have some time to think, so he decided to get a car and tour the country. He wanted to see what was going on. The Church, once so serene and above the fray, now seemed itself to have succumbed to the chaos around it. The campus demonstrations against the war, moreover, made a strong impression on Liteky, mostly unfavorable. He felt that most students had no contact with reality, no sense of patriotism, but were out to save their own skins. But Charlie Liteky was open to new ideas. He really wanted to find out what was going on. And he was, of course, a man of determination.

Before Liteky's odyssey could get well under way, however, his mother had a heart attack, and he went home to Jacksonville to stay with her. His father, the navy petty officer, had died of a heart attack in 1966, just before Charlie had become a chaplain. Ten months after his return to Jacksonville, his mother, too, was dead, after open heart surgery. The only surviving member of the family was a younger brother. A second younger brother had drowned at twenty-one. At age thirty-eight, Charlie Liteky had more reason than most to have a keen sense of mortality, an awareness that came out again and again as one talked with him.

Liteky didn't function as a priest during the ten months he stayed with his mother. He took a job in drug rehabilitation for the Veterans Administration. "I did that," he said, "for the specific purpose of supporting her. The salary was about fourteen thousand dollars, which was a substantial sum at the time."

He stayed with the VA after his mother's death, but he wasn't happy at the way the program was being run. Addicts who were cooperating well were being thrown out of the program, and others were playing the system for all it was worth with no intention of breaking their habit. "So I said: 'Look, if you guys want to help yourselves out, I can provide the place. You know what drugs are about. I know a little about human nature.' " So in Cleveland, Ohio, as it turned out, he set up a sort of rehabilitation house for drug users.

In Cleveland he met Bob Begin and also Begin's sister Laura, a Dominican nun. He found himself very much drawn to Laura and, though he held back, the experience had a strong effect on him. "It was after that," he said, "that I decided to leave."

It wasn't easy to leave the priesthood, something I well understood from my own experience in leaving the Jesuits after thirteen years. "In 1974, I finally succeeded in doing it," said Liteky, "a couple of days before Christmas. It was a traumatic thing. I had been in the order close to nineteen years, and I had this mindset about my sacred, wonderful vocation and about the Church itself being the way to salvation — though I'm still pretty much into that — and that was why I wasn't the sort of guy who could just walk out. I wanted it done according to the rules and all that. I had to have the approbation of the Church."

Those nineteen years of celibacy had been unhappy ones. The paternal nature of religious life, moreover, tended to make a man very immature. "You had your superior," Liteky said. "Everything was taken care of. And if you should take it into your head to do something that had no precedent, your superior tended to look askance. Who knows, you might be on the verge of bolting. You might be poised to throw obedience to the winds. That kind of environment got to be a little heavy for me."

In early 1975, Charlie Liteky began a new life in San Diego. His brother Patrick, a former seminarian, was one of the county supervisors of Santa Cruz County. This turned out to be a problem. Charlie didn't want his identity tied up being somebody's brother. "I needed to go to a place where no one knew me. I wanted to begin to develop new relationships on the basis of just being a person and have people respond to me." He laughed. "Because I think my identity really got lost in the priesthood."

At first, he thought about going into psychology since he had already done so much counseling without formal training. He liked it, too. But as he began to take courses and saw all that lay ahead of him, he had second thoughts. He imagined himself five years down the line with a Ph.D. and an office of his own. "I asked myself if this was what I wanted to do, and I said no because it was too much like what I had been doing." Liteky expressed strong feelings quite effectively by simply raising his voice slightly. "So at the same time I was taking a creative writing course as sort of an aside, and I got enamored of it."

He started to write in earnest, he said, trying one method or another, going from first person to third to first to fiction to fact. But he felt that there wasn't enough passion in what he was writing. He came to realize that he wasn't in touch with his own feelings, with the human side of life. Perhaps because of his years in a religious order, perhaps because of his childhood experiences, his way was to distance himself emotionally from the events around him. In dangerous situations, in heart-rending situations, he remembered, he would simply cut off his emotions and size things up in a cool, logical manner.

"I began to realize this in Vietnam," he said. "I've really become a hard human being, I said to myself then, and that was bothering me. I mean, when I could see little children killed and burned, when I could see old people uprooted and see young American boys torn to pieces, and I could just go calmly about my business of anointing the dead and then go up and have lunch at the hospital. I said, Jesus, what's happening to me? I'm getting used to this stuff. So I knew I had to get out of it then."

Writing appealed to Liteky because it seemed to offer a means of finding himself. He felt he needed some direction, however, so, dropping out of his psychology studies, he decided to go back to school to study writing. He was accepted into a special program at Santa Cruz University.

He was "thrilled" to be accepted, this winner of the Medal of Honor. By the time he was notified, however, Liteky's GI Bill benefits had run out, and he could no longer afford to go to school. He decided to go to San Francisco and do his writing on his own while living on the pension from his Medal of Honor and the disability benefits that came from the shrapnel in his foot. This amounted to somewhat less than $300 a month, but Liteky lived at the YMCA and his life as a religious had taught him frugality.

He would have gotten on just fine, he thought, but his teeth began bothering him, and to pay for the dental work he took a job as a counselor with the Veterans Administration. Going from just about nothing an hour to eight or nine dollars was a heady change, and in the three months it took to get his teeth into shape, he got used to working again. He laughed. "So I said, I'll stick with this for a while. I'll also look for a lady in my life, I said. And I kept looking around."

There were a lot of nice ladies at work but Liteky had enough experience by then to know what kind of woman he wanted and what kind of values he wanted his future wife to have. He met Judy through a friend, a member of St. John of God's Parish in San Francisco, who suggested they get together. Judy was from Los Angeles, but she had been a member of St. John of God's for seven years. Liteky himself took to the parish as soon as he started going to Mass there. The people were great, he said, and the parish priest, Fr. Mickey McCormack, was at once extremely liberal and extremely faithful to the traditional Church. So it was that Liteky became a happy married man very much involved in a vibrant community. Life was opening up for him. Liteky paused in his account. "Then along came Central America."

It wasn't until 1984 that Charlie Liteky became aware that there was something amiss in Central America — something, he would come to see, for which he bore a measure of responsibility.

According to his own indictment, he had been a typical middle-class American who would come home tired at midnight after eight or ten hours' work, sit down and have a drink, and watch a little TV. Most of his reading was limited to the book on his nightstand, which, though he might not have thought so, probably put him ahead of most Americans. Then he'd go to bed, always looking forward to the weekend. But one night Judy suggested going to the home of a friend of hers to meet some Salvadoran refugees.

Charlie Liteky did not bring an open mind to the encounter. "I'd heard something about them coming up. When I went and heard this little girl's story, I didn't believe it. I thought a lot of it was made up. The girl — and a boy, too — talked about people getting slaughtered, about torture, about the dangerous journey up here. I thought, If it was so bad, why didn't these kids stay there and join the guerrillas? I was skeptical and a bit hard on them."

That was the beginning. He went to other meetings, and he listened to some priests. One who had a particularly strong influence on him was Jim Curtin, who had been in Guatemala for nineteen years. He presented a slide show that had a devastating effect on Charlie Liteky. "It was a Saturday, I remember. The next day I stood up in church and said, 'Yesterday I saw the most terrible things I've seen since I was in Vietnam.' I asked that everybody pray that I be given the strength and the courage to go on looking. I didn't want to go on looking."

What most affected Liteky was the priest's saying that there was good reason to believe that an American adviser had been present at a torture session in El Salvador. "That really infuriated me," said Liteky.

He started reading. He read former *New York Times* correspondent Raymond Bonner's *Weakness and Deceit,* a critical assessment of the American effort in El Salvador. He read Air Force Academy graduate Charles Clements's *Witness to War,* an account of Clements's work as a doctor in guerrilla-controlled territory in El Salvador. He also heard Clements speak. He was still working for the Veterans Administration, and his wife was also working.

Liteky decided that he needed to go down and see for himself what the situation was. He and Judy decided that he should quit his job at the VA and go. He tried to go with a group sponsored by Witnesses for Peace, but he kept getting bumped off for one reason or another. "Finally, I said, To hell with it. I'll get some veterans and go on my own."

Just then, however, Charles Clements called offering a paid trip to El Salvador with eight other Vietnam veterans. "So I went — to El Salvador, to Nicaragua, to Honduras — and when I came back I was emotionally decimated. I said, What am I going to do?"

He had met with the Mothers of the Disappeared in El Salvador. They showed him their books and their records. They showed him pictures of mutilated bodies they had sorted through in an attempt to find their vanished loved ones. He met with refugees who were in sanctuary in the cathedral in San Salvador, nearly five hundred people jammed into an interior the size of a small gym. Some told him that they had been there for four years, afraid to leave. They were *campesinos* who had come down from the hills to escape the army's heedless and murderous sweeps. They were afraid they'd be treated as guerrilla supporters. "I saw all these people," said Charlie Liteky, "women and children and old men — all victims of a regime we were supporting."

He spent about four days making an individual retreat after he returned. "I walked the beaches of Florida by myself, saying, God, what am I going to do? And before I left, I got an answer. I put my fingers on the keyboard of my typewriter and began typing. What came out was: 'Are you willing to be led?' " He looked down at what he had written and then thought about it. "Am I willing to be led, I said? Well, I said, I guess I'm willing to be led by the spirit of love. And that's what I've been doing ever since."

There was a bill pending in Congress for $100 million in aid to the Contras, who had been trying to overthrow the Sandinista government of Nicaragua for some five years. It was the product of compromise. The Democrats were opposed to giving any aid to the Contras, but, unlike Reagan, they were not, for the most part, true believers, and so they lacked the moral courage to deny an immensely popular president everything that he wanted for his beloved freedom fighters. This despite the outrageous and lawless nature of open support for an armed insurgency directed against a government with whom we had diplomatic relations, an insurgency, moreover, whose principal victims were innocent peasants for the very good reason that the Contras didn't dare take on the Nicaraguan army. Contra aid was an enormity almost without parallel in American history, but few people seemed to notice.

Charlie Liteky was one of those who noticed. The spirit of love, he was quite sure, did not accord with slaughtering women and children to achieve diplomatic ends. "I said, Well, I'm going to have to give this medal back and start fasting." It was as simple as that for Liteky. He wanted to get as much press coverage as possible, so he renounced his Medal of Honor in connection with a Campaign of Conscience organized by Witnesses for Peace. The theme could hardly have been more appropriate.

Brian Willson was one of the Witnesses for Peace gathered in Washington. He and Liteky had already met in Nicaragua and later they worked together to form a veterans' coalition for peace. Two others involved in the coalition were Bud Murphy and George Misener. "I told Brian and the others that I was going to fast. Brian said he was thinking of the same thing. And Bud and George said they'd go along with us on it." So, right after Liteky laid down the Medal of Honor, he began the water-only fast that lasted for forty-nine days.

Later, after Reagan had had his way with a supine Congress and the Contra aid bill had passed, the success of Sylvester Stallone's macho box office smash *Rambo* prompted Charlie Clements and Liteky to put together a counter-Rambo presentation, which they presented on college campuses to try to convey to students what war is really like.

"We got good reactions for the most part," said Liteky. "Charlie had impeccable credentials, and I had pretty good ones. I started by saying that I'm a person who did a complete one hundred eighty degrees. I was as hawkish as some of the people I now regard as hawks. I said some outlandish things back in those days, but I've changed and here's why, I told them. I just tried to take people through my own journey. I'd say, 'If there is anybody here who can prove me wrong, I'll be very grateful because then I don't have to do this. I can go back to San Francisco where I want to be and plan for my retirement and my sailboat on the bay. That's what I want to do. My life's practically over. But yours is just beginning.' "

The students' reactions might have been good, but their numbers were not impressive. All too often, only a handful showed up. "I said: 'Well, where are you? Where are you people?' It just confirmed what I had thought about Vietnam. If it's yourself, you get concerned, but if it's somebody else, you don't. The killing going on now in Nicaragua and El Salvador is every bit as bad as what went on in Vietnam, if not worse. But life goes on here as usual."

The renunciation of the Medal of Honor had received far less attention than it merited, not only in the regular press but in the liberal Catholic press as well. The only follow-up piece I had seen on the fast in the *National Catholic Reporter* had been an essay by a woman who belonged to the St. John of God community in San Francisco, and her focus was not Liteky or the issues involved but the turmoil that his decision had created in the community.

Liteky was quick to come to the woman's defense. It was a shock to the community, he said. They had never known anyone who intended to fast even to death if need be. Nor did he talk it over with any of them or ask their advice. He just told them he was going to do it. They were very much attached to Judy, more so than to him, because they had known her a long time. The people in the St. John of God community really cared about one another. After Liteky lost the pension that went with the Medal of Honor, they raised an amount of money equivalent to a year of the lost pension, and they kept in contact with the Litekys even after they moved to Washington.

"What I did presented them with a challenge, and nobody likes to be challenged. One guy said: 'Who the hell do you think you are, Jesus Christ?' And I said: 'No, but isn't that what we're all called to aspire to?' 'Are you going to save the world?' he said. 'No,' I said, 'but this is my reaction to what's going on.' "

It was Central America that started it all for Charlie Liteky. It was Central America that brought back Vietnam for him. He had wanted to forget Vietnam, and, in fact, he thought he had. He had certainly been no bleeding heart when it came to the travail of his fellow veterans. "My attitude toward Vietnam vets was, well, okay, you've been through something bad, but get on with your life. Don't keep moaning over something that's past. If you did something wrong, forgive yourself and move on. I had very little sympathy for the vets suffering from posttraumatic stress." He raised his voice. "Because I wasn't suffering from it." Then he laughed. "I didn't think I was, anyway. But I was in my own way."

Whatever the case, when the reality of what was going on in Central America hit Liteky, his thoughts turned at once to Vietnam. "I picked up Stanley Karnow's book *Vietnam*. In the front I wrote: 'I don't want to go back. I don't want to look back. This is behind me, and I don't want to look back, but I have to.' I read other books after that. Then it dawned on me: Jesus Christ, this thing never had to happen! Lyndon Johnson, the president of the United States, lied to people, lied to Congress. There was no Gulf of Tonkin incident."

He became an avid reader of history. A passion to understand took hold of him. "I saw that the Vietnam War was one of a long line of incidents in which the U.S. government has behaved in an egregiously inhumane fashion. And when it hits you that you're a part of a very oppressive society and culture and when you see how ignorant you've been about what's been going on in the rest of the world! And when you realize how they can use my tax money to support oppression because of my idealism and trust! Just like Ollie North. I think I was every bit as much the kind of patriot at one time as he is now."

He had defended the war publicly at Manhattan College in 1969. He was the only one there willing to speak in favor of it except for the colonel in charge of the ROTC unit. "There were a couple of theologians and a professor who taught a peace class. They listened to me, and I listened to them, and some of the students got a little bit snotty, and I got emotionally angry over it. But, you know, no one speaking against the war talked back to me about the history of the U.S. involvement in Vietnam, and since this was 1969, there was plenty to be said."

Seventeen years later Liteky's single-minded desire to say something about that involvement and all similar involvements brought him to Washington to lay down the Medal of Honor and, eventually, to live in the row house in which we now were talking. His wife had finished her job and had come from San Francisco after he and his companions had progressed twenty days into the fast. When the forty-nine-day fast ended on October 17, 1986, he and Judy decided that they would stay in Washington and, along with others, continue to maintain a presence on the steps of the

Capitol as a symbol of dissent. They bought the house they live in, in fact, because it was within walking distance of the Capitol.

We had spoken earlier about the dangers of inner-city life in terms of the Catholic Worker houses I had visited in Washington and of Jonah House in Baltimore, and now we returned to the subject of risk — not the risk that comes of confronting a powerful government but the risk that comes of refusing to avail oneself of the privileges that go with being white, middle-class, and well educated.

"Our neighborhood isn't so bad," said Liteky, "but we live on the edge of one that is. The whole time we've been here there've been only two incidents. But it's here. You don't walk around this neighborhood at night without taking a chance. The store, a Safeway, is a block away, but Judy takes the car if she goes after dark."

I told him about my late-night walk from the Olive Branch House to the Dorothy Day House with Paul Magno in the midst of an epidemic of crack-related murders. The streets hadn't seemed dangerous, and I was so bemused by Paul's nonchalance that I hadn't been nearly as apprehensive as I should have been.

Liteky nodded his head. "But you take a chance when you do that, no doubt about it. That's what the Berrigan family does in Baltimore, I guess. And if you're nonviolent, you have to put yourself in the hands of God."

He frowned and shook his head. "Part of my problem here is that I didn't come here to live. I came here to do something, and now it's done." He and his companions had continued their presence on the steps for a year, and now it was time to decide what to do next. He told his wife he felt that it was time for him to go to jail. If that was true, Judy had answered, she wanted to keep on living in their house, even if she had to live there alone.

Going to jail was, as Charlie Liteky no doubt saw it, just an ordinary reaction to a situation that had gone terribly wrong, as had been crawling into a grove torn by machine gun fire and exploding mines that afternoon in Ben Hoa Province twenty years before. No matter that he was now a married man. Going to jail, he was convinced, was the only way to get people to pay attention.

"What we have to do," he said, "is get as many people in prison because of civil disobedience as there are because of drugs. This would be a very serious problem. Then somebody might say: 'What are these people there for?' And the answer would be: 'Well, they're there because they're objecting to what's going on in the system.' "

He paused for a moment to reflect. "But there again, I'm not going to say that everybody should do this. Gordon Zahn is very definite in saying that nobody should do it. But I don't know anybody who has wisdom enough to be sure one way or the other. What I do know is how much I admire people like Helen Woodson, the Berrigans, and so many others like them. I just have so much respect for them. I hope to get there before I die. I'd like to be that sensitive. I'd like to be sensitive enough to be like Helen Woodson and say the place for me to spend the rest of my life is in jail if necessary. To make that strong a statement! That's a lot harder for me to do than to go in and fast and then check out. To live that kind of life on a daily basis! Though I'm beginning to see that one of the positive aspects of being in jail is internal peace.

"I'm not at peace out here, of course. I'm in a state of constant turmoil — about what's going on and what I can do about it. And part of that is because I'm free to do something. If I had children, or if I had parents who needed to be taken care of, there'd be no problem. That would take precedence. But if you don't do what you feel you can do and should do — either to go to jail or to risk your life for the sake of truth and love and peace — it's going to drive you crazy."

I told him that Joan Andrews said the same thing: when you're in jail, you know you're doing the right thing, and you can sleep at night — despite the noise. I recalled a poster we were both familiar with, which I had seen at Jonah House: a photo by Jim Harney of a sad-eyed Salvadoran child and the caption "When they come for the innocent, if they don't come over your dead body, cursed be you and your religion."

"But you know," said Liteky, "one of the things I've come to accept about myself and other people is my cowardice and their cowardice. Because, you know, I don't think saints or courageous people just happen. I think that most of us grow in things. And you can grow in nonviolence. I've only been embracing nonviolence for a couple of years. It's the hardest thing I've ever tried to do. I'm a lot more fearful than I was, because I'm committing myself to the nonviolence of other people. Whereas before I did that, I committed myself to be ready. If I weren't nonviolent, I would have a weapon in this house, you know. There's a comfort that goes with knowing how to take care of yourself, knowing how to defend yourself. A certain security. But once you give that up in the name of love, you have to live your daily life without it."

I mentioned Archbishop Raymond Hunthausen's saying that those who rejected deterrence were forced to rethink their faith, whereas those who accepted it had no need to.

"That's the way I see it. You have to turn yourself over to God," Liteky said. "And then when you think of it, look what God did to his own son.

His permissive will allowed it to happen so that the Scriptures would be fulfilled. His own son! So, you know, you can look forward to a crucifixion of your own. There's a real embracing of the Cross involved, I think. I'm intellectually convinced that that is the best way to God. I'm convinced, but, boy, emotionally do I want to pull back!"

Liteky began to talk about his father, a fearless man whose reaction to danger was to get in the first punch. His father wasn't given to mediation or discussion. He might not have gone around looking for a fight, but he was always more than ready when one came his way. This was Charlie Liteky's legacy, and he was still working to distance himself from it. In the process, he had obviously thought a great deal about the question of violence and religious faith.

Liteky was quite sure that the early Church had gone wrong in moving away from nonviolence and diluting the social justice message of the Gospel. Only the saints, he said — people like the Curé d'Ars, Francis of Assisi, and Dorothy Day — had held fast to the truth. The Church has always balked at declaring it a sin to pile up wealth while others are in need. This despite Christ's quite clear words on the subject. "Christ himself said it would be as difficult for a rich man to enter heaven as for a camel to pass through the eye of a needle, but the Catholic Church honors the richest and the most powerful men by making them Knights of Malta. It's really amazing now that I think about it. I got sucked into it as much as anybody else did. I'm happy now that I'm free of that. I'm free to decide how to divest myself of what I have."

He had been exploring ways of doing just that, not a quest that most of us would think of pursuing. When American soldiers had been sent to Honduras, he had joined hands with other demonstrators on several occasions over two weeks to stretch a banner across Pennsylvania Avenue in front of the White House. They were arrested for "incommoding." Most of the demonstrators paid a fifty-dollar fine and left, but a few, Liteky among them, decided to stand trial. One charge was dismissed because the arresting officer couldn't explain to the judge exactly where Liteky had been standing in the line, as though that would have made any difference. "To tell the truth, I think the judge was just looking for a way to dismiss our cases. He was very much in sympathy with what we were doing. He got very emotionally involved with us. You could just see it. He was doing everything he could to get us off. When one guy came right out and pleaded guilty, the judge almost begged him not to." The next time, however, Liteky faced a different judge, a man who evidently didn't want a dismissal of a civil disobedience case to go on his record. This was the case still pending. He had also been arrested in front of CIA headquarters, and one time in Florida, near a clandestine Contra training camp. In Florida, the demonstrators trespassed on government property and blocked a gate. They were released the same day on their own recognizance and given the choice of paying a $100 fine or coming back in thirty days.

"I wasn't ready to go to jail then. So I paid. But when you're ready to go, you get this sense of freedom. I was really looking forward to it last time. So when the prosecution witness didn't show up, and the judge said I could ask for a dismissal, I said to myself, I don't want it to be dismissed."

All of these arrests, together with some that went back to San Francisco, were reactions to specific government actions. They were incidental, not part of a deliberate way of life such as he was now seriously contemplating. As he saw it, the evil that confronted him was so great that it called for just such a response.

"I believe that right now the U.S. citizen is the victim of the psychological warfare that is part of the low-intensity warfare being carried on in Central America. It seeks to placate the taxpayers who support it. If they had massacre after massacre down there, if they bombed it and just obliterated it, then the public would react just as it did when the troops were sent to Honduras. The ghost of Vietnam hangs over things. This much anyway has come out of the war. It's left us with raw nerves. Those wounds are not healed yet. Maybe in another generation or two they will be. Then the government will be able to get away with a lot more stuff."

The day that Liteky envisaged as ten or twenty years in the future would, unfortunately, come much sooner than even the Pentagon would have dared to hope in May of 1988.

Low-intensity warfare, said Liteky, could be conducted in such a way that most Americans wouldn't even be aware that much of anything was going on. Liteky pointed to its being a nonissue in the election campaigns then under way. We were supporting terrorism in Guatemala, El Salvador, and Nicaragua, but no candidate bothered to bring up the subject. They played instead to what they saw as the electorate's self-interest — preserving the status quo, preserving the American lifestyle. Jesse Jackson was an exception, Liteky thought, but even Jesse Jackson did not dare condemn too strongly our crimes in Central America.

"So what do we do? This is the question I ask myself. What do I do as a victim of low-intensity warfare? And I'm a victim of either no information or of disinformation. My government and the State Department, with the help of the media, which are part of the establishment, are trying to keep me ignorant and ill informed."

Liteky's response was to inform himself — by any means possible. He talks with people who have just returned from Central America, reads outside of the mainstream press. "If I were in Nazi Germany — and I like to draw this analogy — and I wake up in the morning and the wind is blowing in the right direction from Dachau, I say: 'My God, that smells like flesh burning! Can it really be true, these rumors I've heard? It must be true.' So once you establish that it's true and that it's horrible, what do you do? My awakening is that I've been duped. It is true. It is horrible. We've been doing horrible things."

It infuriates Liteky that so few Americans knew about what was happening south of their border, that the country is just too busy to notice. There were all sorts of things that people could do. For himself, Liteky felt that he needed to find some way of dealing with the root cause.

"So what do you do?" he asked again. "This is for me where opening oneself up to the spirit altogether comes in. This goes back, I think, to what came to me after prayer: 'Are you willing to be led?' Where? It doesn't make any difference where. But by whom, by what? It's the spirit of love that's calling you. Taking the concept of God as love, I don't believe that God is going to call us to become involved in something until our motivation is relatively pure.

"I think about Pius XI and Gandhi. Pius XI wrote a beautiful encyclical about social justice, 'Quadragesimo Anno,' but it just came and went. But Gandhi lived with the poor. He acted with the poor. I was happy to see John Paul II criticize both East and West in 'Social Concerns' and talk about the importance of solidarity and development. Paul VI said the same kinds of things, very good things, using other words, in 'The Progress of Peoples.' But if all you do is write about these things . . . what good does it do in the long run?"

A good way to distance yourself from something is to publish articles about it in respected journals. Who could be less passionate about God than our theologians? Charlie Liteky was one of those troublesome people who thought that action had to follow knowledge. "I want to be able to understand the nature of our system and how it affects the world," said Liteky. "I want to understand how the way we live — how we participate in the system — affects other people, people in the Third World. To be able to pinpoint that!" He insisted that one had to relate the big questions to everyday life. "As simple as saying, 'Look, in this day and age' — this is a down-home example, but it's the only one I can think of — 'you simply don't buy Saran Wrap. You don't buy Styrofoam. It's a sin. It's a sin against the planet. The toxins they cause pollute the air, cause acid rain.' Something else very simple but much more difficult is to say: 'If you're a single person, you don't make over fifteen thousand dollars a year or eighteen thousand a year or whatever — because that's all a person really needs to live a normal life.'

"Decide for yourself what your level is to be and stick to that as your moral standard. Decide for yourself, but put some limits on yourself. People have to be told: 'Folks, possessions are an area in which you can sin.'

"The Catholic Church has been so goddamned obsessed with sex, and I'm convinced that's relevant to celibacy. I've never known any group of people more hung up on sex than the celibates in the priesthood. And then there's all the surrogate sexual activity that we involve ourselves in. You should hear the jokes at Forty Hours celebrations," he said referring to a pre–Vatican II devotion honoring the Eucharist which gave parish priests an opportunity to get together and have a bit of fun. "And this preoccupation carries over into the doctrine, ignoring everything else."

Others were asking the same kinds of questions as he, I said, and agonizing in the same way over what to do. I had talked with some of them, and no one had come up with any easy answers. It was like a variation on the old joke you can't get there from here. In this case, you couldn't get there without suffering.

"I think," said Charlie Liteky, "it goes back to the Scripture verse that we are never tempted beyond our strength. God does not lead us into temptation — does not put us into situations before we're ready for them. Only a very poor teacher or poor coach would do that kind of thing. When I think about what some people have gone through and suffered, I think, My God, do I have the strength to do that? The answer always seems to be: When you're ready, when you're ready."

Brian Willson, he said, was an example of somebody who was ready. Despite being afraid of lightning, despite being afraid of flying, Brian Willson was able to sit there and watch a train coming right at him. "There were two people right with Brian that day. One was David Duncan, a minister. The other was Duncan Murphy. David was able to jump off the track, and Duncan jumped onto the train, the cowcatcher. He injured his leg. He rode the train to where it stopped, a hundred fifty yards or so. But, anyway, Brian was ready for what happened."

Until you're ready, you have to wait, of course, and waiting is not easy, especially for somebody like Charlie Liteky. He found it very hard to limit himself to his books. "I've never wanted to understand anything so badly as I want to understand this system of ours — from the time when it was conceived to the present time."

He had to cope with things that bothered him as a proud, independent person. It irked him, he confessed, to have to depend on his wife. "I've been offered a couple of jobs recently, and the temptation is to reach out and take something, but I don't want to do that. I want to stay on this direction as long as I can. Unless, you know, I see that this is not what I should be doing."

The support of a community would be of tremendous help, he said, in the struggle against the system. If, that is, they could find the right one. They had found one in San Francisco in St. John of God's, but they hadn't been able to do so in Washington. "What we've been doing is going out to Takoma Park. There's a group out there called the Pilgrim Community. They're a combination of Methodist and Presbyterian, but there's not much emphasis on the doctrinaire side of it. We have potluck suppers. We're going to have a retreat in June. What they ask of you is to be a Christian.

"We don't go to a Catholic church now," he said, speaking more softly than before. "One of the things I still really have a lot of trouble with is the male-dominated Church. And there's so much centering on the priest. And so I guess if I were in a community, I'd want people, very simply, to take the New Testament seriously and just take the two laws of the New Testament about loving God and loving your neighbor — that's all. Everything that we do with one another, to one another, as a community or as individuals should be put up against that scale. If it's a loving act, well then, do it."

He spoke about the retreat he planned to take part in if he wasn't in jail. Its theme was discerning the will of God, both for oneself and for a community. For him, he thought, that meant discerning just how God wanted him to love in a world and in a culture so desperate for love. You loved God by loving God in creation. "Everything is God," he said. "Everything is the body of Christ because Christ has identified himself with matter."

The Word was made flesh and dwelt amongst us. It was a bit disconcerting when you thought about it.

"So that's how I'd like to see people come into communities. And that would mean sharing, really sharing our daily bread. And, just think, the greatest one of all in the New Testament made himself one who served others — an act whose significance is so often lost on people. The more talent we have, the brighter we are, all these things that are just given to us — all they think of in our society is how you can market it. But that's not why we were given what we were given. The idea is the better to serve others with. Not the better to serve me with. And there lies happiness. But we don't teach that in the Church. Instead of changing the world, the Church has been co-opted by the spirit of the world. In this country it's been the Protestant church that's formed the culture. In Latin America it's been the Catholic Church. Neither one of them has done a very good job of it."

He realized that not everybody was called upon to do the same thing, but he did believe most profoundly that we were all obliged in our own way to carry the Cross. "And I believe the more truthful we become, the more uncompromising we get with regard to truth, with regard to love, the more we're followers of Christ, the more we're going to be persecuted. He predicted it. The world is going to hate you. Following him is antithetical to what the world wants. The more men persecute you, the more they insult you, the more certain you can be that you're doing the right thing."

So they persecuted the prophets before you, Jesus had said. Liteky was right, of course. But the game plan for most Christians has usually been to settle for being a good example and let the prophets take the flak.

Liteky laughed abruptly. "I get a kick out of Brian Willson because he gets pretty upset about these things. People calling him up and cussing him out and calling him a Communist. Really vicious attacks. I tell him, 'You're doing the right thing, Brian.' "

There was enough work around to give gainful employment to myriad prophets. So much that most Americans believed to be true simply was not true.

"Before I went down to Central America," said Liteky, "I sat down and read two or three books. When I got back, I realized how little I knew, and I said, What am I going to do? And one of the things I knew I had to do was to talk to people. But before that I didn't go anywhere for three months. I quit my job. I laid up in my room and read. Read all day long. As fast as I could read and comprehend. I just devoured the stuff. When I went out, I didn't want to be at a loss. The first time I got called upon to talk about Central America — I thought I wasn't ready — I had to fill in for Charlie Clements, who couldn't make it that night. And there I was. They brought me in off the bench.

"I said to the people, Jesus, this is very difficult for me, and I don't know. . . . Well, I talked for an hour and forty-five minutes straight." He laughed. "I stopped after an hour, and I said, Look I've been talking for an hour straight. Would you like me to stop? Do you have some questions? They said continue.

"It's like I had discovered a truth, and I was sharing it with these people. This whole thing was devastating for me. I think we do have the potential for change, however. I think it is possible to change the system by making the decision to live a lifestyle that is contrary to the system and to work at that."

We shook hands at the door of the little row house that Charlie and Judy Liteky had bought, not because it was the house of their dreams but because it was within walking distance of the Capitol.

A sudden thought struck him. He grinned. "Say," he said, "did you ever see *The Life of Brian*?"

I nodded. *The Life of Brian* is a Monty Python satire in which an ordinary, hapless soul, born at the same time and in the same place as Jesus, keeps getting hailed as the Messiah. The satire had been directed at biblical movies, not at Jesus, but the Catholic Church in the United States had pronounced it "morally offensive."

"Do you remember when that guy was standing up on top of a platform and all those people down below were yelling: 'Save us, save us! You're our Savior!'?" And he yelled back: 'I can't save you. Save yourselves!' " Charlie Liteky laughed. " 'Save yourselves! Save yourselves!' "

I laughed.

"Near Phuoc-Lac, Bien Hoa Province, Republic of Vietnam," read the citation, its flatness not without a certain incantatory power, "6 December 1967. . . . Noticing another trapped and seriously wounded man, Chaplain Liteky crawled to his aid. Realizing that the wounded man was too heavy to carry, he rolled on his back, placed the man on his chest and through sheer determination and fortitude crawled back to the landing zone using his elbows and heels to push himself along. Pausing for breath momentarily, he returned to the action and came upon a man entangled in the dense, thorny underbrush. Once more intense enemy fire was directed at him, but Chaplain Liteky stood his ground and calmly broke the vines and carried the man to the landing zone for evacuation."

Judgment at Norfolk

The Trial of Philip Berrigan, Greg Boertje, Andrew Lawrence, and Sister Margaret McKenna

$\mathbf{M}$ary Grace — how Catholic a name!
— knocked on my door at 7:00 A.M. as I had asked, but I was already
awake. I got up and looked out the window. The lovely house in which I
had spent the night stood beside a river, I discovered. A big backyard
extended to the very bank, which was lined with tall, graceful willows. A tire
swing hung from a lower limb of a tree farther in from the water. On this
morning in mid-May, from this window at least, Virginia looked as one
imagined it should.

I was in Norfolk for the trial of Philip Berrigan, Greg Boertje, Andrew
Lawrence, and Sister Margaret McKenna. The night before, I had been fully
resolved to sleep on the floor of the Episcopal church where the pretrial
rally, A Festival of Hope, had been held. After the rally, however, Dan
Berrigan asked me where I was staying, and when I told him nowhere
special, he called over Mary Grace, who was busy helping to put away chairs.
Mary was short and perky, and she wore a T-shirt embodying a revisionist
version of the famous "I Want You" recruiting poster. Her version read,
"Not me, Sam." Her lawyer-husband, I learned later, had defended Dan
and Phil at the first Plowshares trial. Mary immediately volunteered to take
me with her. She and her little boy, seven-year-old Nicholas, were staying
at the home of a local supporter.

I had spent all the previous day traveling by train and bus through several
states, and the prospect of sleeping in a bed was too enticing to resist.
Besides, Catholic moral theology focuses on the intention above all else —
one of the reasons why nuclear deterrence should be anathema — and so,

since I had *intended* to sleep on the church floor, I had already gotten credit for doing so.

When Mary and Nicholas turned up about 11:30 that night with me in tow, I think that Mary's hostess, Donna Spockenburg, was a little taken aback. Well she might be, since her husband wasn't home. I was a little taken aback myself. Donna Spockenburg was the most striking looking peace activist I had met since Dr. Helen Caldicott, whose hug I still cherished.

Southern hospitality and solidarity in the cause of peace made for a potent combination. Donna was graciousness personified, even though she had to evict her young son, already asleep, from his room. The quilt of the boy's bed was covered with dinosaurs — tyrannosauri reges rampant, lumbering brontosauri, and, my own four-year-old son's favorite, spiny-backed stegosauri.

The three of us — Mary, Nicholas, and I — had just a bowl of cereal for breakfast. I couldn't imagine that there wasn't orange juice around somewhere, but if Mary hadn't foraged on Nicholas's behalf, I certainly wasn't going to betray my own bondage to a consumerist culture by looking for it. We carefully rinsed our dishes and placed them and the silverware in Donna's dishwasher. As I had seen the night before when she had pitched in with such zest on the chairs, Mary Grace was a team player. I was thankful that I had made the bed.

As we made our way quietly out of the house, Mary carried a shopping bag loaded with odds and ends. Besides the peanut butter and jelly sandwiches that she had just made, there was a board game or two, a copy of the magazine *Highlights for Children,* and candy and potato chips. Nicholas carried some posters he had drawn celebrating peace and ecology. He wore shorts and a T-shirt and a baseball cap over his sunglasses. Both shorts and cap seemed much too big for him. Nicholas hadn't gotten the sleep that was a seven-year-old's due, but, little boy though he was, he seemed formed in the same intrepid mold as his mother and just as fit for the day's adventures. No whining, no complaints.

We piled into Mary's tiny, cluttered car, which was plastered with provocative bumper stickers, and were off. The vigil outside the federal district court in Norfolk was to begin at eight. We had gotten lost the night before on our way to Donna's, and this morning we did again. Mary had scribbled the directions up and down both sides of an old envelope, and the only map she had was much too cryptic for our purposes. After we had made a U-turn, our second, and his mother had gotten out to ask directions at a real estate office, Nicholas and I got to talking about summer vacations, and he took the opportunity to confide that his grandparents were rich. Very rich.

One last U-turn, and we were on our way once more. We got to the courthouse at about 8:15. For no good reason, I had envisaged a tranquil, small-town setting, but Norfolk turned out to be urban and bustling, with glittering high-rises, wide streets, and heavy traffic. The navy's ubiquitous presence made it quite apparent just how much our tax dollar had contributed to local prosperity. There was even a Military Highway.

There was nothing quaint or regional about the federal district courthouse. It was the familiar rectangle of gray stone cloaked in the portentous anonymity of civic buildings put up since World War II. No hint of the pseudo-classical exuberance of a more innocent and hopeful America, an era that had endured even into the Depression. No breasts, no buttocks, no muscular thighs, no discreet hint of genitalia. The fun had gone out of things. And the humanity.

This morning, however, humanity at its most motley had made a comeback and was in full possession of the sidewalk outside the courthouse. Our friends had apparently gotten better directions. Two demonstrators among the thirty or so were holding a huge banner declaring that "Armaments Kill the Poor." One of those holding it was Joe Byrne, a tall Chicagoan in a Cubs cap whose room I had shared for a few days in January at the Dorothy Day Catholic Worker house in Washington. Byrne had a court day of his own coming up in less than a week in Baltimore. He was one of sixteen demonstrators arrested in February for blocking the entrance to Johns Hopkins University's Applied Physics Laboratory, an institution that ranked first nationally among academic recipients of Pentagon largesse.

A frail old woman with a crucifix around her neck, a nun most likely, was, along with some other older demonstrators, sitting on a low concrete barrier that enclosed a parking lot. A stocky, handsome young man with blond hair and decidedly Teutonic features was wearing a pair of wooden shoes just like those worn by the woman hell-bent after dirt on Dutch Cleanser containers. His name was Karl, as I would learn that night when we got a ride back to Manhattan together, and he was a Catholic Worker from West Germany. A bearded young man whom I didn't recognize was carrying a sign that read: "Tomahawks into Plowshares." Two other demonstrators were holding the big poster that had served as a backdrop for last night's rally at the Episcopal church, the Isaian text illustrated by the figure of a naked man beating a sword into a plowshare. The blacksmith's right leg was extended and bent so as to preclude anything that would distract from the seriousness of the concept, but the thigh and buttock, even if noticeably overdone, were fully in the spirit of the sensibility whose passing I had been lamenting.

Oddly enough, there wasn't a policeman in sight. Nor a single wooden barrier, the kind that New York's finest routinely used to pen up even striking librarians.

Mary had pulled up to the curb to ask where we could park. A woman pointed to the next corner, saying something about a parking garage, but before she could give further directions, the shrill whoop of a siren right on our tail prompted Mary to tramp down on the gas pedal. Around the corner we went and then around the next corner, where she stopped to ask directions of some demonstrators on the other side of the building. Another irritated siren blast, however, made it all too clear that we were still not alone. Before Mary could react this time, the car behind us abruptly pulled around us with a screech of tires and careened around the corner. As it did we caught a glimpse of Sister Margaret McKenna. She was grinning and waving out the back window.

"I guess they thought we were going to grab her," said Mary, exhilarated at our close encounter with the Feds. "We'd block them, and then the others would move in." For somebody so committed to nonviolence, she seemed to find the idea awfully appealing. A few months later, Mary would in fact be arrested for a federal offense, a nonviolent one to be sure and of so delicate a nature as to severely tax the rhetoric of the editors of the Jonah House newsletter, *Year One.* They would finally hit upon "peeing in the Pentagon parking lot."

After circling the courthouse, we at last found the parking garage, but Mary was dubious about going in. "I don't have any money," she said. "It's okay, I do," I answered. My publisher's advance had been such to preclude most indulgences, but a parking garage I could manage. Still, I was happy to see that the price was $2.00 for all day, another contrast with Manhattan. After we parked, Mary pulled out the shopping bag and a couple of quilts from the back of the car. She gave Nicholas a toy electronic keyboard to carry, and I took the quilts and the posters.

People were already lining up to go inside when we reached the courthouse, and since I had heard that the courtroom was small I decided to go in at once, leaving Mary to settle Nicholas down on the sidewalk with some other children.

There was an electronic scanning device at the entrance, and after having heard a chilling talk on radiation at the rally, I felt a qualm on behalf of the two federal marshals manning it with such unconcern. The marshals, beefy, cheerful men, knew where we were headed, of course, and they must have realized that the rangy Marine sergeant in our midst was the exception that proved the rule. They were cordial, however. Again, I was reminded that I wasn't in New York.

The courtroom, on the first floor, was indeed small, seating fewer than a hundred. I sat next to a short, bald man about sixty, neatly dressed in a suit and tie. His name was Bernstein, he said, and he was from Philadelphia.

Federal marshals escorted in the Nuclear Navy Plowshares four promptly at nine. Their supporters — the whole courtroom, it seemed, save for the marshals and the witnesses for the prosecution — jumped to their feet to cheer and applaud. Andrew Lawrence was in the lead. He had managed to grow a bushy black beard since I had talked with him two weeks before in the Yorktown jail. Once the cheers and applause died down, a female voice, soon joined by those of all the other supporters, began to sing "Happy Birthday." This was for Greg Boertje, who was thirty-two that day. Max Obuszewski, who handled media relations for the four, followed up with the Polish version. No one joined in.

The Marine sergeant who had come in when I did had been joined by other servicemen: two sailors, two other Marines, and a young man in a denim jacket and jeans whose haircut identified him as a Marine. They were seated on a row of chairs against the wall on the right side of the courtroom, and in their midst sat a fat navy officer in whites wearing a submarine badge. The only officer present, he was obviously their mentor.

On the other side of the courtroom, Sister Margaret McKenna, wearing a nondescript dress, sat on the far left of the defendants' table. Next to her sat Philip Berrigan in a navy blue nylon jacket that he had probably bought at Goodwill. Under it he wore a plain white shirt open at the collar. Greg Boertje had on a mottled sport shirt of indeterminate colors. Andrew Lawrence at the end wore a faded blue work shirt.

All rose as the U.S. Magistrate Tommy E. Miller entered. About forty, with a full head of neatly styled dark brown hair, Judge Miller was somewhat below middle height and a bit heavier than he should have been. His full face was as pleasant and unthreatening as his name. His voice, too, was pleasant as he explained to the defendants that while, strictly speaking, those who conducted their own defense, if they chose to take the stand, had to put questions to themselves and then answer, he was willing to dispense with this cumbersome procedure and let the defendants testify straightaway, as long as they didn't wander too far afield. The first of many signs that the government was determined to be very, very indulgent.

Philip Berrigan rose to say that Sister Margaret McKenna would make an opening statement on behalf of all four. Berrigan was polite enough, but there were no "Your Honors" and not the least hint of ingratiation.

Judge Miller explained that they could do as they wished but that he would have to take Sister Margaret's statement as being offered on her behalf alone. Then the nun walked over to a podium immediately in front of the judge's bench.

"I'm not here to defend myself," she said, her voice calm, her manner wholly undramatic, "but to defend life — life on this planet." She knew all about Robert Emmet in the dock ("Let no man write my epitaph until Ireland be free"), but she wasn't Robert Emmet in the dock. She was Sister Margaret in the classroom. "The four of us had no desire whatsoever of trying to conceal what we did. On the contrary, we meant it to be an act of public witness. We did hammer upon two of the *Iowa*'s armored box launchers on Easter Sunday and pour blood on them. We did this in the spirit of the prophetic command of Isaiah 2:4: 'They shall beat their swords into plowshares and their spears into pruning hooks.' Our action had a religious, nonviolent nature just as the messages on our banners proclaimed — one reading 'Tomahawks into Plowshares' and the other 'Seek the Disarmed Christ.' We believe that our purpose was lawful, and we believe that every element of our action and its motivation is altogether pertinent to our defense. Speaking for myself, I acted on strong moral and religious convictions grounded in the Scriptures, based on the love embodied in Jesus. I broke a positive law, true, but so did Jesus, time after time. He broke the law of the Sabbath. And he didn't break it for the sake of an ox or an ass that had fallen into a pit but for the sake of someone who was suffering. My concern, the concern of my companions, was for all people."

The plump nun, something girlish about her face despite her fifty-seven years, was very much in control as she stood before her judge, so confident of her authority that she had no need to press. No one could guess from looking at her that her legs were bothering her, painful symptoms of the Lyme disease that would remain undetected for another three weeks and then would put her on crutches. Despite her secular garb, she stood there at the podium every inch the serene, formidable figure whom anybody who ever went to a parochial school would have recognized. The Honorable Tommy E. Miller, I ventured to guess, had never encounted a representation of this archetype of American Catholic folklore, but now, with all of us poised on the brink of annihilation, he was getting his chance. A good boy, Tommy, but a boy who had much to learn and many missed assignments to make up. The situation called for clarity and firmness. Sister Margaret would explain everything, and Tommy Miller had better listen. It was a pity that playwright Christopher Durang wasn't here to appreciate this. The real Sister Margaret McKenna would probably outrage the pious faithful even more than had his fictional Sister Mary Ignatius.

"We asked ourselves and we ask the court the question that Jesus put to us: 'What is lawful? To take a life or to save a life?' We believe that if and when all the elements that constitute our action and its motivation are presented here in court that it will be clear that what we did was protected by the First Amendment. We will argue that our government has, in effect, established nuclearism as a civil religion and this religion, established in violation of the Constitution, is inherently idolatrous, and as such must be rejected by every Christian.

"It's self-evident that we were not guilty of any criminal intent. On the contrary, our concern was the public good. We acted to prevent crime and catastrophe. We acted to uphold the law of God. International law, more-over, supports civil disobedience in cases like these. For these cruise missiles are first strike weapons, and their deployment runs contrary to international agreements forbidding offensive warfare."

"Sister Margaret," said the judge, interrupting politely, "I must warn you that in trial after trial of this sort, the appeal to necessity has not been allowed because the defendants were never able to show that all the conditions essential to such a defense were fulfilled. As for international law, the offense involved here is the simple one of trespassing, and there is no need whatsoever to bring in any other kind of law."

"We've made a thorough study of the pertinent international laws, Judge Miller," said Sister Margaret, unruffled, "and we believe that they do apply. We trespassed to perform the symbolic disarmament of Tomahawk missiles, which are part of the navy's Maritime Strategy. And this Maritime Strategy, which is explicitly aggressive and offensive in nature, is a violation not only of international law but of the navy's own field book, which calls for limiting conflicts and forbids direct assaults on civilians."

The strategy that this Catholic nun was excoriating was the very strategy then being pushed with unqualified enthusiasm by a Catholic secretary of the navy, John Lehman. Lehman had been one of the bitterest Catholic critics of the American bishops' 1983 peace pastoral (and Catholic critics were the bitterest of all), and in his official capacity he had cooperated wholeheartedly with Paramount Pictures in making the jingoistic 1986 movie *Top Gun*. The film's hero, played by Tom Cruise, is a sexually promiscuous hot pilot whose exploits in a climactic dogfight with Russian jets are celebrated like a football victory over an archrival. As though the world did not stand at the edge of the nuclear abyss.

"According to international law, moreover," said Sister Margaret, "instruments of genocide are not protected. The common law of the United States, itself, moreover, sanctions breaking laws under certain circumstances — trespassing and breaking and entering, for example, to save a child in a burning house.

"We considered ourselves privileged to be able to act as we did. We did intend to do damage, yes, but doing damage was not the overriding purpose of our action. Our action was symbolic, and because it was symbolic, nothing that bears upon it should be irrelevant to this court. Everything should be brought out, especially since the recent obsession of our government to conceal things in the name of national security constitutes a more dangerous threat to American democracy than any external enemy.

"Is the government to be the sole critic of itself? Isn't that the mark of the totalitarian state? We believe that the U.S. Maritime Strategy constitutes a grave offense against the Judeo-Christian tradition. Like the prophets before us, we were compelled to do what we did." Sister Margaret paused for the briefest of moments before concluding. "We are not, therefore, guilty as charged," she said, her tone of voice still quite calm. "Ours was a religious witness made to redress grave wrongs."

"Sister Margaret," said the judge, as pleasant as ever, "just for the general knowledge of you and your fellow defendants, let me just go over the conditions that have to obtain if a necessity defense is to be allowed." He looked down and read from his notes. "First, there has to be a reasonable belief on the part of the one acting that he is acting to avoid a danger that represents an imminent threat to self. Secondly, he has no other means. Thirdly, there is a direct connection between his action and avoiding the threat."

The four defendants exchanged glances, but since no one seemed to feel the need to respond, Judge Miller directed the prosecution to present its case.

The prosecutor, U.S. Attorney John S. Martin, a man about forty, of properly sober mien in his gray suit, had, significantly, forgone the opportunity to make an opening statement. He didn't seem at all happy with the task ahead, and he probably wasn't. With the accused so eager to convict themselves, there was no glory to be gained by winning. It was likely, however, that Martin's uninflected tone of voice and his detached manner stemmed not from mood alone but from judicious choice. Nuclear war was at issue here. Patriotism was at issue here. Morality was at issue here. This was the stuff of passion, but passion was something that the government of the United States could just as well do without at the moment. A narrow focus was essential. If Martin insinuated the barest trace of moral condemnation into his voice, it would be an indulgence that could cost him dearly. The floodgates could burst open. Martin was outgunned morally, and Martin — and Martin's superiors — knew it. Morality, passion, patriotism — these were the natural element of the accused. This gray, anonymous agent of federal power was bound to win, but winning wasn't what counted when you were up against beautiful losers. You must at all costs convey that there wasn't much at stake here.

The prosecutor gave a dry recital of the substance of his case before calling his first witness. Marine Lance Corporal Jimmy Ray Solomon, Jr., looked like he should still be in high school. He was slender and wore glasses, and he had the thin, sensitive face of a boy you were surprised to hear had joined the Marines. The kind of boy who wanted to see if he had what it takes. I had been just such a boy, as had many of my comrades at jump school at Fort Benning long, long ago.

After telling the court that he was a member of the Marine detachment on board the *Iowa,* Corporal Solomon described the kind of Sunday tour that had given the accused their opportunity. The prosecutor, intent though he was on making everything as dull as possible, made the error of asking Solomon if the purpose of the tours was to promote "goodwill for the navy." The courtroom erupted in laughter, prompting a warning from Judge Miller.

The Easter Sunday tour had gained precious little goodwill for the navy, especially since a quick-thinking and profit-minded tourist had caught much of the action with a video camera and sold it to a local television station, which had shown it repeatedly. According to the account both Phil Berrigan and Greg Boertje had given me two weeks before, the other prisoners in the Yorktown jail had greeted them as local heroes. They had seen the whole thing on television, they said, and had been cheering for them. Even the Yorktown sheriff, a cheerful, heavyset man, had seemed delighted to have celebrities in his jail. He had been most accommodating when I had phoned to make arrangements for a visit. I had been able to talk with the three as long as I wanted, and he had stopped by once or twice to ask me if everything was going okay.

When the prosecutor asked Corporal Solomon to identify the four, he pointed them out and described what each was wearing. Greg Boertje's shirt threw him off, understandably, but he finally came out with "pink." No one disputed him.

In the cross-examination, Philip Berrigan gently asked Solomon if he knew that the weapons he was protecting violated the laws of war. The prosecutor objected, and Judge Miller sustained him. Then Berrigan asked the boy if he had ever had any classes in the laws of war, and Solomon answered that he had.

I had, in the meantime, given my seat to a cheerful young woman with a baby, Ellen Grady, who had served fourteen months in prison as a result of a Plowshares action at the Trident base in Groton, Connecticut. Standing next to me in the aisle was a stern-looking older woman, who was watching the proceedings intently. She wore a button that read: "Question Authority."

The second prosecution witness, Geoffrey Crawford, was the tall sergeant whom I had noticed at the courthouse entrance. Despite his rank, he seemed scarcely older than the first witness. Crawford, who testified that he was on the scene of the crime before Solomon, described Phil Berrigan as "pounding on the blowout pad on the back of an ABL," prompting Judge Miller to intervene on the side of clarity, and the prosecutor drew out the information from the sergeant that an ABL was an armored box launcher and that the blowout pad absorbed the recoil when a missile was launched. And while Berrigan was doing this, said Crawford, Andrew Lawrence was starting to hang up a banner.

"Did you notice any red liquid on the launchers?" asked the prosecutor, and again Tommy Miller intervened smoothly. "I think we can call it blood," he said, "since it's been established that it was blood."

"Call it blood because it was blood," said Philip Berrigan without looking up from his notes. He was out of order and not at all gracious, but Tommy Miller let it pass. He was a liberal, Carlotta Bright, a local black activist, had said the night before and was in favor of the nuclear freeze.

When Berrigan cross-examined the sergeant, he pressed him politely, as he had Solomon, on the nuclear capability of cruise missiles.

"I don't know a thing about nuclear weapons being on board the *Iowa*," Crawford answered confidently. This was but a homier version of the navy's official "neither confirm nor deny" policy. The warriors of old, the Pattons and MacArthurs, loved rhetoric, but the martial bureaucrats who had taken their place preferred semantics. Since they weren't leaders of men, their pressing need was not to inspire but to conceal.

When Berrigan persisted, the judge intervened to say that he thought Crawford had answered the question as well as he could.

"I don't think the defendant has," said Berrigan. "He's fully aware of the nuclear capability of the Tomahawk."

"Mr. Berrigan," said Tommy Miller very gently. "Sergeant Crawford is a witness. You're the defendant." Berrigan shrugged off the correction. He knew who was on trial.

The fat officer with the submarine badge sat slumped in his chair over on the right, his stomach thrust forward and his chin almost touching his chest. Despite myself, I felt embarrassed for the navy. Embarrassed and a little sad. This was evidently one of the new breed of submarine officer, the technician. There was nothing about the man that recalled Mush Morton, the legendary captain of the *Wahoo,* who coolly gave commands to maneuver and fire as a Japanese destroyer, hot for revenge, bore down on his submarine at full steam, the most difficult and dangerous target imaginable. It wasn't the same thing as pushing a button and obliterating Leningrad.

Greg Boertje, the birthday boy, rose to ask Crawford if he was aware that a missile fired from the launcher could destroy a whole city. Whatever happened today, Boertje, like Phil Berrigan, would still have a lengthy prison sentence hanging over his head since he had been a fugitive from justice when he joined in the Nuclear Navy Plowshares action.

In our conversation in the Yorktown jail, I had asked Boertje, who was of slight build, how he felt about the well-publicized dangers of prison life. "If you're nonviolent, God is with you," he said. "Dangerous situations sometimes occur. I've never been assaulted. I've felt the need to intervene when others were fighting, and things always worked out. You take the risk and you trust. You know that you're living with these guys, many of whom are in for murder and other serious crimes. But everybody has good in them. You take one day at a time, and you begin to feel more strongly that you have to treat everybody as a brother. And you'll find that there are others who want to do the same thing and who are interested in talking about the Bible."

"Do you know," he asked Crawford, "that the nuclear warhead of the cruise missile is powerful enough to destroy a Hiroshima ten times over? Do you know that such a weapon violates international law since its use means the massacre of millions of civilians?"

"It's not my job to know about them," said Crawford. "I guard them. I don't shoot them."

When the prosecutor called yet another witness to establish that the defendants had actually committed the crime, Berrigan objected mildly. "We admit we did it," he said. "There's no need for a stream of witnesses to establish that we did." It was to no avail.

The next witness identified himself as Lance Corporal Clifford Andrew Marshall. Unlike the others, Marshall was husky as well as tall, burly in fact.

His accent, moreover, was northern and urban, quite different from the softer southern tones of Solomon and Clifford.

Marshall, it turned out, had been the first Marine to confront the intruders. He heard a bang, he said, and then he came running to discover Berrigan hammering on the box launcher. Then he went on to corroborate the evidence that the others had given.

When it was time for the cross-examination, Philip Berrigan rose to his feet, a tall and commanding figure with his rugged, seamed face and his pure white hair. He had the power to inspire people, but it was a power that carried with it a terrible responsibility. How many people were in prison because of Philip Berrigan? Were it not for Philip Berrigan, Helen Woodson would be at home with her children instead of in solitary confinement in Alderson.

"She wrote me after King of Prussia," Phil had told me in Yorktown. "I thought it was a particularly intelligent letter. Helen is the best natural writer I've ever seen. So even though we were swamped with mail, I felt I had to answer this one. She said that she had these nine handicapped children to take care of. So I wrote: 'What are you doing to protect them? The government is threatening them. The whole question revolves around whether or not they have a future.' She wrote back furious. She practically cursed me out in her letter. 'Here I am going eighteen, nineteen hours a day! Come off it, Jack.' But Helen thought about it. Then it was a matter of along about a year or so before she was coming to the Pentagon all the way from Wisconsin."

Lance Corporal Marshall could hardly have encountered many Marine officers who were as soldierly looking as this pacifist, a man old enough to be his grandfather but with no trace of the weaknesses of age. Berrigan looked scarcely different, in fact, than he had in the famous photo of him and Dan burning draft records with homemade napalm in Catonsville, Maryland, twenty years before almost to the day.

"Do you remember what I said to you?" he asked Marshall.

"You said: 'I'm doing it for the people, and I'm doing it for you.' " The answer came without hesitation. It would be a long time, it seemed, before Lance Corporal Clifford Andrew Marshall forgot that moment.

"What did you think when I said that?"

"Well," said the young Marine, "I don't encounter 'I'm doing it for you, and I'm doing it for the people' every day. So I thought I had two loonies on my hands."

The fat submarine officer chuckled. The boy was hanging tough, but according to what an FBI man had told Berrigan the night of their arrest, the experience had so unnerved Marshall that he was still shaking an hour afterward. Parris Island hadn't prepared him for radical Christians.

"Don't you understand," asked Berrigan, "that if those missiles are ever fired, we'll all die?"

"I wasn't up there to understand anything," said Marshall, raising his voice slightly. "I was up there to do my job. I do my job, I'm done. That's it."

After two more Marines had testified, Judge Miller asked if the defendants wanted to recall any of the witnesses. Otherwise he would dismiss them. He pointed out that one, evidently the boy in the denim jacket, was on leave, and he would like to release them as soon as possible. After the briefest consultation, however, Philip Berrigan said that they wanted the witnesses to stay. They might want to recall some of them, he said, but one would have to know almost nothing about these four not to realize that they probably had a deeper purpose in mind. Education played a large role in their committing the crime that they did the way that they did it. And what better subject for education than these clean-cut young men so vital to the functioning of the monstrous evil that they opposed?

The next government witness was Stephen Shiner of the FBI, a man whom Philip Berrigan had told me about in some detail. He had described Shiner as a "nasty guy" who had been furious and insulting on Easter Sunday evening in the master of arms' quarters on the *Iowa*, trying his best to get a rise out of Berrigan.

"What's the matter with you, Berrigan?" Shiner had said. "As old as you are and still acting like an adolescent!"

It was a different Shiner who now took the stand. He was quite composed. Wiry, of medium height, he had wavy blond hair and a mustache. The FBI had gotten away from sober dress codes, I had read, and Shiner's appearance corroborated this. He had on a somewhat garish blue-green suit, and his light blue tie had a bright silver streak winding through it. Shiner looked more like a salesman than an FBI agent, but nonetheless he seemed tough and competent. If he had indeed been furious with Berrigan and his companions, he was nobody's fool. He realized the significance of the blow they had struck.

Shiner testified that he had arrived at the master of arms' station on the *Iowa* at eight o'clock on the evening of April 3. The prosecutor asked him nothing about any exchange with the accused, and Shiner volunteered nothing. He then went on to give the familiar description, with some more details, of the damage done to the missile launchers. On the deck beside the launchers, he said, were four plastic baby bottles with traces of blood in them. Also found, said Shiner, was a three-page indictment directed at the entire chain of command, beginning with the president of the United States and ending with the base commander, Admiral James Pappas.

Three little boys, one of them Nicholas, were sitting on the floor in front of me intent on a game of tic-tac-toe.

The prosecutor offered as evidence a one-page declaration that had accompanied the indictment and asked Shiner to read aloud a single phrase from it. Shiner complied. " 'And so we come to Norfolk,' " he read, " 'bearing blood and hammers.' " Prosecutor Martin had been intent on establishing the facts of the case beyond all shadow of a doubt, but, by being so thorough, he had inadvertently presented the defense an opportunity that quick-witted Andrew Lawrence wasted no time in seizing.

"As long as he's read part of it," said Lawrence when the prosecutor had finished with Shiner, "could we have him read the whole thing?"

"Objection, Your Honor," said the prosecutor. "The rest of the document is not pertinent to what's at issue here."

"You've offered it as evidence, Mr. Martin," said Judge Miller, happy, it seemed, for the rare chance to be the good guy. "So I have to grant his request." He turned to Shiner. "Please read it, Mr. Shiner."

Shiner, his face a blank, began to read in a clear, not unpleasant voice. He gave the words and phrases their proper emphasis, but there was no trace of emotion, either proper to the text or reactive. The side he read first was for the most part a straightforward description of the Maritime Strategy that the defendants had been referring to throughout — "the policy represents a clear departure from the Navy's traditional wartime role of keeping sea lanes open and ferrying ground forces" — and of the capabilities of the Tomahawk missile — "Widespread deployment of Tomahawks . . . places hundreds of nuclear weapons at sea to be used at the discretion of naval commanders who face extremely stressful conditions."

The destruction of an Iranian airliner in the Persian Gulf a year later would corroborate this assertion in unmistakable fashion. A commander in a seemingly either/or situation gave an order that cost 290 innocent people their lives. The commander of the *Iowa* or the *New Jersey* or God and the navy know how many other warships, faced with a like dilemma, might take several million lives.

Only the last sentence of the Tomahawk section offered much of a test to Shiner's control, but his voice didn't waver in the least as he read it: " 'Its development and deployment are a national disgrace and a crime against humanity.' "

In the first row on the other side of the courtroom, Frida Berrigan was playing with her mother's abundant hair. Katy sat on the other side of Liz. Jerry was home in Baltimore, something about schoolwork that had to be made up. Next to Katy sat her Uncle Dan in a flowered sport shirt, the traditional garb of choice for Catholic priests when they put aside their Roman collars. The only difference was that Uncle Dan seemed to have put his aside permanently. A framed black and white picture, worthy of a time capsule, hung in a dark corridor of the Jesuit residence that housed *America* on West 56th Street in Manhattan. It showed Berrigan and Mother Madaleva, both celebrities of the American Catholic literary world of the fifties, holding plaques attesting, no doubt, to this celebrity. With them stood a benign and motherly Cardinal Spellman, a skullcap on his head and a shiny cape draped about his rotund frame. Mother Madaleva's face was all but lost in a pleated expanse of white wimple, and a boyish Berrigan was wearing a stiff Roman collar that seemed at least two inches high. Now, three decades later, instead of Mother Madaleva, at Dan Berrigan's right was a moderately exotic blond woman of indeterminate age. She had introduced herself to me as "Marianne from Malibu," and somebody said that she lived in a gypsy cart and that Bob Dylan had once written a song about her. Why not?

Shiner paused after he finished the page and looked up at the judge. Miller nodded for him to continue. Shiner turned the page, his face still betraying no emotion and began to read:

In the beginning, the Spirit moved over the waters, calling forth life from the chaos of the sea. In the fullness of time with a command word, Christ calmed the sea: Peace, be still. Yet in our own day the superpowers seem determined to undo the work of creation and return the seas to chaos and death.

For example: the proliferation of nuclear weapons at sea now number some 15,000, including the deadly family of Tomahawk Cruise Missiles; an aggressive Maritime Strategy that threatens to escalate any conflict with the Soviet Union to the level of global nuclear war; the increasingly prominent role played by the Navy in our military interventions through-out the Third World — in Lebanon, Grenada, Nicaragua, Libya, and now in the Persian Gulf.

The USS *Iowa* is not only a component, but a symbol, of this superstate madness. Armed with 16 inch guns and nuclear-capable Cruise Missiles, this battleship epitomizes the Big Stick with which the U.S. enforces oppression by its client states (Israel, El Salvador . . .) and exacts revenge upon those resisting its imperial designs (Iran, Nicaragua . . .).

And so we come to Norfolk bearing blood and hammers, symbols of another kind. They are symbols of repentance and re-creation, most appropriate to this season of resurrection and rebirth. These offerings express a hopeful desire — the desire to expose a national illusion that peace begins with superpower summits that leave intact the threat of nuclear annihilation rather than with conversion to compassion and justice. To resist a national addiction to violence that, in the nuclear age, has become criminal, insane, and threatening to the world's future. To act, finally, in the spirit of the God who "will judge between nations / And will render decisions for many peoples; / And they will hammer their swords into plowshares / and their spears into pruning hooks. / Nation will not lift up sword against nation, and never again will they learn war.

Shiner then read the names of the four signers: Philip Berrigan, Gregory Boertje, Andrew Lawrence, and Sister Margaret McKenna, M.M.S., the initials standing for Medical Missionary Sister.

"Thank you," said Andrew Lawrence.

"You're welcome," said Shiner.

The prosecution called two more witnesses: another FBI man, who corroborated Shiner's account, and a boyish seaman in summer whites who testified that he had seen Philip Berrigan in a tour group the previous day and that Berrigan had asked some questions about the *Iowa*. Much to the boy's mortification, Berrigan brusquely told the court he must be mistaken. "If I'd been there, I'd admit it," said Berrigan, and it was obvious to everybody in the room that the matter was closed. Whatever crimes the Berrigan brothers committed, everybody knew that they never lied.

It was now the turn of the defense to present its case. Judge Miller, before calling a brief recess, cautioned Berrigan and his companions once more about the difficulties of trying to argue the necessity defense. He alluded to a case in which blood and ashes had been poured at an entrance to the Pentagon. There the necessity argument had been disallowed because the defendants could not establish that the three essential conditions had been fulfilled. "I'm bound by the precedent set here," said Tommy Miller, and there seemed to be genuine regret in his voice. The pain, however, seemed to be the sort one could live with. Not a severe toothache but more like a stiff calf muscle.

Philip Berrigan asked Miller to allow him to call expert witnesses who would testify with regard to the religious motivations of the defendants, the devastation that would result from nuclear war, the ever-increasing danger of its occurring, and the pertinence of international law.

"I'll have to consider your request, Mr. Berrigan," said Tommy Miller carefully, "but I have to tell you right now that the role of expert witnesses is to testify with regard to some special sphere of knowledge not generally known that pertains to the case at hand. You're accused of trespassing, and it's hard to see how expert testimony of the kind you mention would have any bearing upon a simple offense of that sort."

"It's not a simple offense. The motivation behind it puts it into a different category entirely."

"As I said, I'll have to consider it, Mr. Berrigan," said Tommy Miller.

There was little reason to wonder about the outcome of Miller's hermeneutics. Shiner, according to Phil Berrigan, had "pretty well let the cat out of the bag" Easter Sunday night in the master of arms' quarters on the *Iowa*. "We know what you want, Berrigan," Shiner had said. "You want felony charges. You want a showcase trial. You want publicity. You want a long jail term. We know what you want, but we're not going to give it to you."

In keeping with this game plan, the prosecution's presentation was relatively brief as well as dispassionate, and when the court reconvened to hear the defense, it was only about eleven o'clock.

Philip Berrigan got to his feet and walked to the podium in front of the judge's bench to make his opening statement. "We all know," Berrigan began, "that the Constitution of the United States forbids any law that restricts freedom of religion. We all know that the Constitution provides for the separation of church and state and that any kind of established religion is contrary to the spirit and letter of the Constitution. Yet, as we'll argue here, the military-industrial complex have established a state religion in this country, the religion of nuclearism, a religion that compels us to worship gods of metal instead of the true God. It's a religion of death rather than of life, a religion that threatens the existence of every man, woman, and child on this planet. It's our contention that when we performed our disarmament action on the *Iowa* on Easter Sunday, we were doing something that had to be done to uphold the Constitution. We had no other recourse but to act as we did."

When the prosecutor objected that Berrigan's argument was extraneous to a simple trespassing charge, Judge Miller upheld him. "I would advise you once again, Mr. Berrigan," he said, "in line with Mr. Martin's objection, that I'm obliged by precedent to give a very strict interpretation to the three conditions that have to be met to argue a necessity defense." He glanced and began to read the prescriptions yet again. These three were fast becoming Tommy Miller's Jesus Prayer. They would keep him safe through every toil and peril.

Berrigan nodded curtly. Then, knowing that he intended to take the stand, the judge read him the standard caveats. He need not testify, but if he chose to, he would be subject to cross-examination and all the consequences that flowed therefrom. "And as I said before," Miller continued, "you may give your testimony directly without putting questions to yourself — as long as you keep to the subject."

"I understand," said Berrigan. He left the podium and walked over to the witness stand, which was right in front of the table where his companions were sitting.

Berrigan looked around the courtroom briefly after sitting down, taking in the young Marines and sailors sitting along the opposite wall but not bothering to look up at the bench. There were souls to be saved, but Christ had enjoined against throwing pearls before swine. Forty years before, Berrigan had been a party boy at Holy Cross — his yearbook photo shows a strikingly handsome young man — but the thought had come to him one day that there must be more to life than chasing girls and drinking beer, the same thought that had spoiled the fun for so many Catholic young men in the immediate postwar era. Now he may have thought of himself as an ex-priest, he may even have come to believe that the very idea of a consecrated priesthood was an abuse, but Phil Berrigan, sitting there in his Goodwill jacket and white shirt, would never in his heart of hearts be anything but a priest.

"I was raised on a farm during the Depression, the youngest of six brothers," said Berrigan. "My family and I were familiar with poverty. Poor people tramped the roads in those days. When they stopped at our door, my mother always gave them whatever she could spare." Phil Berrigan's was an All-American voice. A heartland voice in which there was no guile. It was a familiar kind of voice, like the voice of Jimmy Stewart, Clark Gable, and — yes, yes — Ronald Reagan. It was a voice that men and women listened to and trusted, and the young Marines and sailors directly across from him were listening. Their faces showed it. The words themselves were hard to take, however. Frank Capra wasn't the director anymore, and God no longer seemed to be on our side.

"The Vatican says the nuclear arms race is a crime against the poor," said Berrigan. "It's true that Christ did say, 'The poor you have always with you,' but he meant it not as a reason to be complacent but as an indictment. I have various degrees and many, many years of education, but nothing in my education really prepared me to work for peace — except insofar as it exposed me to the Scriptures. I've written five books and a sixth with my wife."

Elizabeth McAlister, wearing a plaid shirt and blue slacks with jumpsuit-style pockets halfway down the legs, was now standing at the back of the courtroom. Last week in Baltimore, she had been wearing overalls and a painter's cap when she, John Heid, and Dale Ashera-Davis had dropped me off at the train station. The children of Jonah House had already gone to school, and the adults were on their way to a house painting job.

Now as Liz watched her husband testify, she wore a calm, cheerful expression. Had she not fallen in love with Phil Berrigan some twenty years before, had the world not become a quite different place from what it had been in her youth, she might have been the principal of a school, the president of a college, or a reverend mother superior — one of those calm, steadying presences that used to hold the world together for us Catholics. Instead she was standing in a federal courtroom, an ex-convict and the wife of an ex-convict. But she was still the same Liz McAlister, and, for some of us at least, she was still holding the world together.

"Three older brothers went into the service ahead of me in World War II," said Berrigan. "One of them was wounded on D Day, though not seriously. I was a sergeant in the artillery. I experienced such things as mortar attacks but no close-up action. I received a commission as an infantry officer, but by that time the war in Europe had ended."

In his autobiography, *To Dwell in Peace*, Dan Berrigan recounts a fascinating vignette about Phil carrying the flag in an impromptu VJ Day parade at the Jesuit seminary in Woodstock, Maryland. I had asked Phil about it in Yorktown.

Phil's expression had turned rueful. "We were supposed to take part in the invasion of the Japanese home islands," he said, speaking into a phone from the other side of the glass partition that separated us, "and we got thirty days' leave once we got back to the States. I was visiting Dan at Woodstock on VJ Day, and somebody organized a parade to celebrate. There were a lot of military visitors, but I was the only officer, and somebody stuck the flag in my hand. So, like an idiot, I led the parade around the circle in front. It was an awful thing to do, but neither Dan nor I knew any better. Harry Truman said that dropping the bomb saved millions of lives, and I believed it at the time."

Though it was only later that he would come to a different conclusion on the bombing of Hiroshima and Nagasaki, events remote from his experience, Phil Berrigan's thinking on the morality of war, even as he played his ironic part in the Woodstock celebration, had already evolved far beyond the simple certainties that he had embraced as an eighteen-year-old recruit. As an artilleryman, he told the court, he had a providential opportunity to experience the horrors of war as a "kind of spectator," though most of us, I think, would consider ourselves bona fide participants if mortar rounds were dropping in our laps. "And there was horror," he said. "Fifty million people died in World War II. Twenty-two million of them were Russians. Am I now supposed to hate a people who suffered twenty-two million dead? Who suffered four major invasions in the course of a century? My country dropped nuclear bombs on Hiroshima and Nagasaki. We opened the era of nuclearism. A new era of manifest destiny under the sanction of the bomb."

Next to Elizabeth Berrigan, but apparently unaware of her, stood a lanky young woman in shorts who seemed scarcely out of her teens. Hers was the sort of face you'd see on a girl riding a horse or playing field hockey in the pages of *Life* in the forties and fifties, an image of privilege to inspire and edify the middle class, but she was wearing a black T-shirt with "Brigade of Young Communists" written on it in Spanish and, over her shoulders, a tasseled Palestinian shawl with black and white stripes. The girl was gazing at Philip Berrigan with an expression of rapt innocence on her long face. She was a member of the Revolutionary Communist Party.

"I began early in my career as a priest to work for the poor and oppressed," Berrigan calmly went on with his testimony. "In Anacostia, in Washington, D.C. Then, when I was a teacher in New Orleans, black students I taught were beaten up by whites. I'm on trial today for civil disobedience, but my first act of civil disobedience was at Selma, Alabama. Even earlier than that, however — with the 1962 Cuban missile crisis — I got the sense of the world spinning out of control. Two men, Khrushchev and Kennedy, were debating as to whether hundreds of millions of people should live or die. What gave these two men the right to do that? I thought.

"So I moved logically from civil rights activism to activism against the Vietnam War. It was a war that brought three nuclear powers into confrontation — the U.S., China, and the Soviet Union. Nuclearism is genocidal in all its implications. Four million children are dead who could be alive if we spent on them some of the money we spent on nuclear weapons." Berrigan went on to give a concise account of his life thereafter as a Catholic activist, from the bonfire at Catonsville exactly twenty years before to the first Plowshare action at King of Prussia.

The *Iowa* action could hardly have helped the King of Prussia appeal. If, on the other hand, the government's strategy had been to restrain Philip Berrigan by keeping him in suspense, it had failed.

"I've always admired Phil Berrigan," said the Catonsville Nine prosecutor, Steven Sachs, in a newspaper interview the previous week commemorating the Catonsville anniversary. "Phil Berrigan was a helluva guy. But this country can't take too many Phil Berrigans. Saints don't work in a democracy." Fortunately for him, Sachs was now a Washington lawyer and, presumably, had few saints to contend with.

"Nuclearism has become a civil religion in this country," Berrigan continued. "According to its theology, America is the Promised Land. In our Revolutionary War, however, the elite fought so that they would no longer have to share their wealth with the elite in the mother country. Our Civil War was fought to preserve the Union so that the United States could expand to the Pacific. Freeing the slaves was a secondary consideration. Very secondary. We've established a civil religion with all the trappings of a civil religion. Look how the word 'Trinity' was used at Los Alamos. We worship gods of metal just as the Gentiles were charged with doing in the Bible. Believers must endure sacrifice on behalf of these deities, and it's blasphemy to go against them. Courts have dealt out prison sentences as long as eighteen years against Plowshares activists. Nuclearism is a religion of death, and we are dying of it right at this moment."

The young servicemen were taking all this in, their faces solemn, even that of Lance Corporal Marshall, who had insisted he was free and clear once he had done as he had been told.

"We chose the navy for this Plowshares disarmament action," said Berrigan, "because we believe that the nuclear holocaust is more likely to come from a naval action than from a Third World crisis. The Tomahawk cruise missiles with which the *Iowa* is armed have a fifteen-hundred-mile range and can land within ninety feet of their target. They have, therefore, a 'decapitation' capability. They can destroy not only a first strike force but also a nation's leaders.

"We have all this murderous force deployed against our enemies, but the Bible tells us that 'the enemy' is, in fact, people created like us in God's image and likeness. The religion of nuclearism tells us that we must be ready to kill for the sake of survival, but the religion of the Bible tells us that we must love in order to survive. Our courts, however, support not the Bible but nuclearism. Just as the German courts, which Adolf Hitler Nazified, supported Nazism."

Berrigan had at last pushed Tommy Miller's goodwill a bit too far. "I assure you, Mr. Berrigan," he said, his tone chilly, "that nothing remotely like that has taken place in the United States." Had Miller stopped there, he might have come out ahead, but he chose to push his luck. "Those who appointed me to the federal bench have no idea what my politics are." Who were these paragons of disinterested virtue? one wondered. Somebody should report them to Steven Sachs.

"It's my experience," said Berrigan, unrepentant and unimpressed, "that most federal judges know nothing whatever about international law and its claims. Nor do they understand the role of nonviolent resistance."

Prosecutor Martin cross-examined Berrigan briefly to establish the only facts that suited his purpose, Berrigan's presence on the *Iowa* and the assault on the launchers. But then, tempted perhaps by the prospect of discomfiting, however incidentally, a man who had been on the cover of *Time* magazine, the good gray prosecutor ventured out of his shell for a moment and went a bit further, careful, however, to eschew emotion and to maintain a detached pose.

"You say that the *Iowa* represented an imminent danger to you, Mr. Berrigan," he said. "What was it doing that Sunday afternoon when you walked up to it, firing off missiles?"

"No it wasn't," said Berrigan. "When the warheads fly, it will be too late to do anything. This case might represent the last chance to declare them illegal."

"Did you have any apprehension when you performed your action?" Martin asked.

"No. Other than the possibility of getting shot by one of the guards."

Actually, his feelings had been more complicated than that. "You're always afraid," he had told me in the Yorktown jail. "But you've gone into this business of fear, mostly from the biblical standpoint, thoroughly enough to know that that fear is really an evidence of disbelief struggling with belief. Fear has to be controlled. You go up against a hellish monster like the *Iowa* — all that power, those guns, that armorplate — and you think: 'What am I doing here? How did I ever get into this bind?' I was first involved seriously in 1967, and now here I am twenty-one years later, and I'm still asking the same questions. But you know that they're false questions, and you know that, with the help of others and the help of grace, you have to learn to control your fear and your uncertainty."

How much the existence of a wife and very young children must have intensified that fear and uncertainty, I thought, as one who was in a similar position. Liz and Phil had been married since 1969, and their prison terms had kept them apart for nearly nine years, much of the separation occurring after their children were born. He and Liz took these risks, he said, because the state of the nation throughout this entire era had been the moral equivalent of war.

"People think nothing of men going off to war," he told me, "away from their wives. And their wives bear children while their husbands are away fighting. And yet the whole culture rises up to support this kind of sacrifice. We've had a whole lot of experience in this. It's painful for everybody. Liz and I are very close. We love each other very deeply, and we love the children. But we understand that we can do it and we understand that we have to do it. And our children are not harmed by it because we have our community and because they've been schooled in this all the way through. So we can give ourselves a hundred reasons why we should continue. So we'll go on being nonviolent like this as long as we can without making extravagant claims.

"Meanwhile, we miss each other a great deal. I write her every day. She writes me every day. She was down here last Sunday, and we had no more than twenty minutes together in this booth, talking by phone. But that's part of it."

I had gone on to ask him about the "ordinary" risks of their way of living, the risks of living in an inner-city neighborhood, the risks that come of turning one's back on the good life and the security that Americans prize.

"You come to a slow awakening of faith in that area as in any other," Berrigan had answered. "The Psalms say that you go from grace to grace. What you try for with the help of Scripture and the help of community is an overall consistency. As you get deeper and deeper into the causes of the arms race, you see that we're protecting our loot."

Sympathetic to his position as I was, "loot" came as a mild shock. Wasn't he overstating it? When the Gulf War came two and a half years later, however, the accuracy of Berrigan's word choice became painfully apparent.

"War is about who controls the resources and the people. You'll find that what's behind this, by way of systematizing the whole structure, has to do with conspicuous consumption and making every person into a producer so that he can conspicuously consume what he produces and what others produce, mainly the poor in the Third World. This is the whole structure."

Within a year, John Paul II would cause a stir by saying precisely the same thing about "sinful structures" in the encyclical "Social Concerns." The American Catholic right expected the Brothers Berrigan to say such things, but "Et tu, Joanni Paule!"

"So you realize that you can't conform to that if you're going to be faithful. And then you read the Gospels and you see that the Lord himself didn't have a place to lay his head. You've got to believe that if God is going to take care of the sparrows, he's going to take care of you."

Faith was the theme that Philip Berrigan kept returning to that afternoon in the Yorktown jail. "What we have now is a crisis of faith," he said, "and faith is absolutely fundamental. We have to redefine faith in terms of events and in terms of world realities. I think that this crisis with war and weaponry puts things pretty much on an either/or basis. I believe with Gandhi and King that it's a case of nonviolence or nonexistence. And if the American bishops are going to think themselves legitimate as pastors or shepherds or anything resembling that, they're going to have to come to grips with this, and it can't be in solidarity with the bureaucratic Church. They're going to have to start acting like individual Christians who have a conscience."

But now, two weeks later in Norfolk, Prosecutor Martin had more pragmatic things in mind than either faith or the kind of fear that faith confronts. "Suppose there had been a missile armed with a nuclear warhead in there, Mr. Berrigan," said Martin, "and you set it off. Wouldn't you have regretted that?"

"Yes, I'd regret it. If I survived, I'd regret it. But it was our understanding that nuclear missiles are removed from a ship when it comes into port and stored onshore."

Martin could have pressed ahead here — suppose Berrigan's presumption had been incorrect? — but he thought better of it. It was obvious that he stood not the least chance of provoking Berrigan, whose responses were casual, almost offhand. He did try another tack, however.

"Are you opposed, Mr. Berrigan," he asked, "to all nuclear weapons or just American ones?"

"I'm opposed to all of them," said Berrigan.

"Have you ever protested Soviet missiles?"

"No."

"Have you ever traveled to the Soviet Union?"

"No, I haven't. I've been to Europe, including Britain and West Germany."

"Have you staged any protests there?"

"Yes."

"When was your most recent trip?"

"1985."

"How long have you been protesting against nuclear weapons?" A good lawyer never asks a question in court that he doesn't know the answer to, and Martin was a good lawyer. He had no idea, however, how well prepared Philip Berrigan was for this line of questioning.

"For more than twenty years."

"Your efforts don't seem to have had much effect, have they? Do you really think that you could affect American policy by hammering on the side of that missile launcher?"

"If it weren't for protests," Berrigan answered, "nuclear weapons might have already been used."

There was a murmur of approval from the spectators. Especially loud in approbation was a tall middle-aged man, bald and with a neat beard, who wore a T-shirt with the slogan "Resist Trident with Love and Life." He was John Linnehan, a former priest and the founder of the Metanoia Community in St. Mary's, Georgia, the site of a Trident base. Judge Miller felt obliged to warn the spectators that he had the power to clear the courtroom. But, as it turned out, the murmuring subsided when Phil Berrigan stepped down after a half hour on the stand, and Greg Boertje took his place.

Boertje, young Jerry Berrigan's good friend and a former student of Dan Berrigan's at Loyola University in New Orleans, had a thin, sensitive face with a prominent nose and high forehead. He was born in Iowa, but his family had moved to Louisiana and his voice had a trace of a southern accent. While Boertje's manner was gentle and soft-spoken, a steely determination lay just beneath it. Not for nothing was he the descendant of Dutch Calvinists. Not for nothing had it been the writings of Dorothy Day that had turned him in the direction he was now going.

This was Boertje's third Plowshares action. On April 18, 1985, he and John Heid and five others had entered the Electric Boat Quonset Point facility in North Kingston, Rhode Island, boarded a Trident submarine, and hammered and poured blood on three missile hatches. Along with the others, he received a three-year sentence, but he was released after a few months in the summer of 1986. Then on January 6, 1987, on the Feast of the Epiphany, he, along with Lin Romano and two priests of the archdiocese of Philadelphia, had taken part in an action at the Willow Grove Naval Air Station in Horsham, Pennsylvania. It was after this Epiphany Plowshares and four attempts on the government's part to convict him that Boertje, already intent on a third Plowshares action, decided not to appear for sentencing and became a fugitive.

"I want to explain something about my background in terms of its shedding light on my actions," Boertje began. "I was in ROTC in college, and at graduation I was commissioned a lieutenant in the medical corps. In the military I was taught the distinction between a lawful and an unlawful order. And I believed that no military order that conflicted with a law of the

Church could be lawful. As a medical officer, I found myself involved in training that was a preparation for nuclear war. The enemy was dehumanized, objectified, hated. It came to me gradually that this was all wrong. I also came to realize that we had a first strike nuclear strategy, something that international law said was illegal. According to international law, only defensive wars are legal.

"I was, at the same time, studying the Bible more and more. I came to realize that laws that exploit people must be broken. Jesus broke such laws a lot. The Sabbath law, for example. He let his disciples pick grain on the Sabbath. Then he ate with sinners, something that the law also forbade."

Judge Miller interrupted. "Mr. Boertje, our concern today is some very specific recent events, not something that happened two thousand years ago."

Tommy Miller thus consigned the Christian tradition to the dustbin of history. And on the home ground of Jerry Falwell and Pat Robertson.

Faith was the key thing for him, Boertje had told me in the Yorktown jail. "Liz says we grow in faith as we practice it," he said. "When we put our faith into real-life situations, then we get more faith. We have to keep on making leaps of faith."

But how did he feel about turning his back on the American dream, I had asked, another question that lay outside of Judge Miller's purview.

"My approach there is to take the Gospel seriously, to take seriously what Jesus said to the rich young man, who I once was. But community is essential, as in the Acts of the Apostles. I don't see how one person could stand against the culture, against all its temptations without community. It's especially true with regard to resistance. This is where Jesus promised he would be — wherever two or three were gathered together in his name."

Like Philip Berrigan ahead of him, Greg Boertje showed a serene disregard for Judge Miller's views on what was pertinent.

"Laws that protect weapons like this," he said, going on in the same vein despite the judge's warning, "are laws of death, and Christians are obliged to disobey laws of death. And when they do it, they're not criminals. When Jesus overturned the tables on the Temple grounds, he wasn't the criminal. The merchants who were dishonoring the laws of God were the criminals."

Once more the long-suffering Tommy Miller intervened, again admonishing Boertje not to wander so far afield.

"Nuclear weapons," said Boertje, unperturbed, "are a sin of blasphemy. When we build them, when we deploy them, when we guard them, we are violating God's sovereignty. An American judge in a state court ruled that the threatened use of nuclear weapons was a war crime. In West Germany, five hundred judges and prosecutors have demonstrated against nuclear weapons. So, you see, while most courts protect death, there are some who protect life."

After Greg Boertje had finished his testimony, which took about twenty minutes, Philip Berrigan requested that his brother Daniel be permitted to testify as an expert witness. Judge Miller glanced down at the prosecutor, who after his brief surge of aggression while cross-examining Berrigan had lapsed once more into a Zen-like detachment. "I would have expected the government to have some thoughts on that," said the judge, a slight edge to his voice. Tommy Miller, it seemed, was getting a little piqued at having to do all the dirty work himself. Under Miller's prodding, Prosecutor Martin summoned up enough indignation to object.

It was then up to Miller — after explaining that an expert witness must be somebody who possesses a special expertise in technology or whatever discipline has a direct bearing on the facts of the case — to rule that the Reverend Daniel Berrigan, S.J., would not be permitted to testify because nothing he could possibly say would have any bearing on the sole aspect of the defendants' intentions that was relative to the case being tried: their intention to violate specific laws.

Philip Berrigan objected to this line of reasoning. The government was insisting that there was nothing at issue here but a simple case of trespassing, ignoring even the incidental but no doubt expensive damage done to some prized hardware. But what sort of law court would refuse to consider the question of motive? "My brother, with his knowledge of moral theology," said Philip Berrigan, "could offer the kind of testimony that would make it inescapably clear to the court just what was in our minds when we did what we did — everything that went into our intention besides the resolve to break these laws you speak of."

Miller insisted, however, on defining intention narrowly. The accused had confessed that they intended to do something that was contrary to law, and by law Miller meant American law, no other. Stephen Shiner had indeed "let the cat out of the bag," but there was no need for Tommy Miller to have received specific marching orders. He hadn't attained his present eminence without intuiting how to keep in step.

Sister Margaret McKenna also objected. "Your Honor," she said, in a show of deference untypical of the defendants, "according to the precedent set in *Berrigan vs. United States*, the defense need only prove that the intention was reasonable even if it happened to be mistaken."

Tommy Miller would have none of it, however. He had already shown immense largesse in letting the defendants talk freely about their motivation, and he seemed to be growing more and more pained at their giving no hint of appreciation but, on the contrary, demanding more. The best of fathers, after all, gets impatient with greedy, thoughtless children. Thus in short order Miller ruled against hearing testimony not only from Dan Berrigan but also from Paul Walker, a weapons analyst from the Institute for Peace and International Security in Cambridge, Massachusetts, and John Linnehan of the Metanoia Community.

During the fifteen-minute break that followed, curious about the Revolutionary Communist Party, I talked with a second young member who was attending the trial. Pleasant and quite poised, she introduced herself as Sally Wilson and said she was from New Hampshire. She also took the opportunity to sell me a copy of the RCP organ, *Revolution*, for $1.50. The RCP made a point of selling its message rather than giving it away, I had been told, though a former Jesuit who was a member of RCP had given me a copy in Seattle, perhaps out of solidarity with a fellow former Jesuit and prospective convert.

Two of her comrades were at the trial, she said. She pointed out the third: Phil Farnum, a slim middle-aged man with piercing eyes and a black beard heavily streaked with gray who had been a Presbyterian minister. Like the young woman I had first noticed, Phil Farnum and Sally Wilson were also wearing Palestinian shawls.

I asked her if she really believed that violence was necessary. My tone was hesitant though it certainly wasn't as though I were ferreting out incriminating evidence. For Sally Wilson wore a huge button with a picture of Mao and the slogan "Revolution in the 80s." Less threatening, even verging on Benetton chic, were her black beret and the yellow T-shirt she wore beneath her tasseled shawl and an unbuttoned yellow shirt. On the T-shirt a panther was sketched in bold black strokes, and, even as Sally Wilson smiled up at me, the beast, poised to spring, glared with red cut-glass eyes.

"Yes," she said. "We feel that nonviolence is a noble ideal, but sometimes you have to use violence." Despite this fundamental difference, she went on to say, the RCP admired the courage and dedication of the Plowshares activists immensely, especially since Catholic radicals seemed to be the only people whom they saw eye to eye with on most of the issues of the day.

I had to smile. Fervent Catholics and fervent Communists had always been the best of enemies. We understood each other quite well long before Jerry Falwell could define dialectical materialism, if, indeed, he could now.

We both prized morality. We revered martyrs. We despised pragmatism. It had been only a matter of time before areas of common agreement emerged.

The trial resumed at about 12:15 with the testimony of Andrew Lawrence. Like Berrigan and Boertje, Lawrence began with an account of his life and the elements that formed his outlook. "I was born in 1960 and raised in Washington, D.C.," he said. "My family wasn't at all religious. On the contrary, it was rather irreligious. I received a degree in political science from the University of Maryland. Then I spent two years in Morocco with the Peace Corps and then a year in France before coming back to the States. All I did in France was study French.

"I do not identify myself with any particular faith. But I work with that. I struggle with that. I found that my contact with the Christian tradition at Jonah House was fruitful. Only they and the people I met at the Community for Creative Non-Violence in Washington have made sense of the Christian tradition for me.

"I joined the Peace Corps because I had been studying Third World development in school, and I was sick of dealing with things in the abstract. I wanted to touch, smell, and feel these things. I wanted to help people as much as I could, though I knew I would for the most part be learning. As a matter of fact, Morocco certainly did make things concrete for me. Faces, names, sights, and smells — these are my memories, fond memories. All these I got as a high school teacher. Morocco is a place, unfortunately, where the people are very much afraid of their ruler. King Hassan is our boy. We support him in logistics and intelligence so that he can carry on his dirty little war down in the Sahara.

"I wasn't sure what to do when I came home. I went to work for a co-op restaurant. At that time I met Lin Romano, who took part in the Epiphany Plowshares with Gregory and is now serving two and a third years out in Lexington, Kentucky. She had been with the Community for Creative Non-Violence for about nine years.

"Lin Romano was the first Christian I ever met." Lawrence was obviously capable of irony, but there was none of it in his simple declaration. Oh, maybe just a trace. He was no less earnest than Greg Boertje and Phil Berrigan had been, but there was a lighter touch to his presentation, as though he took a certain detached pleasure in laying out the incidents and concepts involved. "So I went down to Washington to work with CCNV. After five or six months of exposure to Lin, I decided that I was moving in the direction that was right for me. I spent some time helping care for the homeless with medical problems. I didn't get paid for it. What happened was comparable to my experiences in Morocco. My abstractions had been torn way. I realized that I had been living a privileged, comfortable life."

Lawrence then urged the necessity defense. "The actions we took were legal," he said, "because there was no other way open to us to prevent an immense evil from occurring."

Once more Judge Miller had recourse to his Jesus Prayer. He reminded Lawrence that the harm that threatened may not be some hypothetical future harm that may or may not happen but one that was imminent and threatened great personal harm to the one who acts. Per omnia saecula saeculorum. Amen.

"We were facing imminent personal harm on Easter Sunday," Lawrence insisted.

"There also has to be a connection, Mr. Lawrence, between the action committed," said Miller, "and the prevention of the imminent harm, in this case nuclear war."

"But there is more than just the threat of nuclear war," said Lawrence calmly. "There is the actual danger of radiation caused by the manufacture of nuclear weapons and the research done on them. Then there is the psychological harm wreaked by the threat of nuclear war and the danger of a reactor accident. I believe that the nuclear sword of Damocles hanging over all our heads will eventually drop. The danger is imminent. It comes from the nature of the weapons themselves. It comes from the nature of the navy's Maritime Strategy."

"If you believe as you do, Mr. Lawrence," said the judge, "then I would think that you'd want to persuade people. And the best way of changing minds and hearts over the long run is to work within the political process. Look at Jesse Jackson, for example. Four years ago he had little success as a political candidate. This year he carried Virginia, the capital of the Confederacy. Things change. But he didn't go beating on the deck of the *Iowa*. He used alternate means."

Indeed he had, alternate means that had made him as much as possible like any other liberal Democrat, even to his stance on abortion, which he had once opposed. This is what had made America great, Tommy Miller would insist, people working within the system. He was right, of course. There was a large element of truth in all those Norman Rockwell *Saturday Evening Post* covers. It wasn't the whole truth, however, and it never had been. And now there was a frightening catch: only drastic measures could save us, but drastic measures were the one thing that no electable candidate dared promise. So it was that the Berrigans and their friends expected nothing from the great ones of this world, whether secular or ecclesiastic. Tommy Miller still did. Or so he said.

"We came to the conclusion long ago," Phil had said in Yorktown, "that only the Catholic laity, the Christian laity, will have a significant voice in this whole horrid mess." He referred to his and Dan's experience with the bishops over the years on Vietnam and on nuclear arms. "We know the ethics of the club. The bishops are essentially managerial types. They're ill informed. They have no knowledge of history. Old Archbishop Thomas Roberts of England, a dear friend of Dan and mine, used to call them 'biblically illiterate.' "

In 1978 he and Carl Kabat and three others imprisoned in Allenwood, Pennsylvania, had sent a letter to every bishop in the country explaining why they were there. They had gotten just five replies, in three of which the bishop had assured them that he would remember them in his prayers. It was a sorry performance, but, despite everything, there was always hope, Phil had insisted. "Because Dan and I and most of the Plowshares people come from the Catholic tradition, we'll keep on trying with the American bishops, though our real hope lies with the hierarchies of the Third World or at least those bishops among them who have made common cause with the poor."

Now in Norfolk, Andrew Lawrence responded moderately to Tommy Miller's call for moderation. "All we're contending," he said, "is that our action offers a reasonable hope for a good effect. We don't presume that we can put an end to the arms race with our magic hammers."

"It's too bad you can't." Tommy Miller was wholly sincere now, but his sincerity gave Lawrence's wit an opening.

"But we did the best we could in three minutes." Laughter erupted. Lawrence let it subside before going on. "When Rosa Parks decided that she wasn't going to get up from her seat and move in that bus in Montgomery, did she have any idea what she was starting?"

Miller stared at Lawrence. For a moment he seemed vulnerable up there on his high bench. Then the moment passed. He could presume that the question was rhetorical. It was a reasonable presumption. There was no cause for the well-oiled machinery that the government had set in motion to falter.

"What we're doing," said Lawrence, "we're not doing in isolation. Two thousand people have been arrested at the test site in Nevada. What we did on Easter Sunday was make a significant contribution to a much larger political process. There was no adequate, reasonable alternative open to us. Civil disobedience stimulates the peace process just as it stimulated the movement for civil rights. Doing it is no more culpable than breaking into a burning house to save a child's life."

Lawrence concluded his testimony by challenging the "alternative methods" clause of Tommy Miller's Jesus Prayer. "We would indeed have less drastic alternatives available to us if our democratic institutions functioned as they should. But with regard to foreign policy and to nuclear weapons, they've too often been subverted by secrecy and the abuse of executive privilege. We've seen the rise of the military-industrial complex. We've seen the government's obvious contempt for international laws. We've seen the scorn of top administration officials for the wishes of the majority of the American people, who want a freeze in nuclear weapons and who want us out of Central America."

The prosecutor, as he had with Greg Boertje, declined the opportunity for cross-examination, and Sister Margaret McKenna, the last of the four to testify, walked purposefully to the stand after waiving her right not to testify.

After leaving Yorktown two weeks before, I had driven down to Chesapeake to talk to Sister Margaret in the county jail. I had found her in excellent spirits. Whatever the pious faithful might have thought of her adventures, she was evidently making a lot of new friends for the Church of Rome behind bars.

The other women prisoners were quite sympathetic, she said, and though the area was very conservative, everyone seemed to realize that she and her companions had had the best of intentions. "One of the guards told me," she said, laughing, "that if he had some other job, he would have been congratulating me. Then I met the Baptist chaplain in the library, and he told me that he was convinced about the truth of nonviolence and that he had explained to the women volunteers who worked with him that my breaking the law was an act based on Scripture." She also had had a long conversation with the sheriff. "He told me at the end that if we followed the Bible, we'd all be nonviolent, and if Jesus were here in our time, he'd be in jail, too."

Judge Tommy Miller, whatever his sympathies, could not be as candid in expressing them as had Sister Margaret's friends in Chesapeake. Now the weight of office lay heavily upon him as he leaned forward slightly to listen to her testimony.

"The motive behind our actions," Sister Margaret told the court, "was our regard for the law of God and for international law as well. The spirit in which our action was done was the spirit of love. How would we have any criminal intent when we acted out of love for the whole world? We acted out of necessity. We acted to prevent a crime. What we did was part of mounting a campaign of nonviolent opposition to nuclear weapons."

If Andrew Lawrence had taken an intellectual pleasure in presenting his arguments, Sister Margaret brought a warm enthusiasm to hers. She had let out a whoop of laughter when I had asked her how she'd react if six or seven bishops showed up at her trial. "That would be a miracle!" she had exclaimed. And it would have been.

When she had been arrested, she experienced, it seemed, the same kind of exhilaration that Paul Magno had described to me, the kind of near rapture that had overtaken him four Easters before at the Martin Marietta facility in Orlando, Florida.

"I was left lying on the deck, my arms out, face down," Sister Margaret said. "It was a tremendous time for me spiritually." She recalled being very happy in those moments. And then when a woman officer helped her to her feet, she said to her: "Happy Easter," and the woman replied: "Happy Easter to you too."

I thought of Saul Bellow's hero Charlie Citrine, who observed in *Humboldt's Gift:* "People are really far more naive and simple-hearted than we commonly suppose." But Tommy Miller, needless to say, had to suppress his naiveté and simple-heartedness. "But what you have to show me, Sister Margaret," he told the nun, "is how this danger you speak of was so imminent that no other course was open to you but civil disobedience."

"We see it, Your Honor, not as civil disobedience but rather as divine obedience," said Sister Margaret, tranquilly ignoring Miller's pointed inquiry. Sister will get to that, Tommy. Just be patient. "How many divisions has the pope?" Stalin had once asked mockingly, but Mikhail Gorbachev would probably be delighted to have even a regiment of post–Vatican II nuns deployed on his behalf.

"We chose the *Iowa* to dramatize the fact that thirty-seven percent of American nuclear missiles were deployed at sea. We chose it because this battleship seems to embody big stick diplomacy at its worst. The *Iowa* was off Nicaragua. It was in the Persian Gulf. Its presence in all these areas of crisis shows just how perilous is this country's Maritime Strategy. Our nation's laws forbid carrying out acts of war against a nation with whom the United States is at peace, but what is a strategy so aggressive, a strategy so dependent upon nuclear arms, but an act of war? The navy's policy is neither to confirm nor deny the presence of nuclear weapons, but the sea-launched cruise missiles the *Iowa* carries are intended to replace the missiles removed in Europe under the INF treaty.

"Hammers like the ones we used are universally understood to be tools. They're simple and ordinary. The blood we poured, too, is well understood as a symbol. It's a symbol of the lives that a Tomahawk missile could destroy. In daring to perform our disarmament action, we were following the example of Peter who, coward though he was, dared to leave the security of the boat and step out onto the water to meet Jesus, who was coming to him. Easter itself, of course, is richly symbolic. It's symbolic of God's determination to give life. Christ poured out his blood for us on Good Friday, making a tremendous claim in behalf of life."

I looked around the courtroom. Sally Wilson with her Mao button, the girl whose name I didn't get, and Phil Farnum were listening with rapt attention. The Honorable Tommy Miller and the government of the United States didn't consider the blood of Christ relevant to today's proceedings, but the Revolutionary Communist Party seemed receptive enough.

"Now, as my friends have done, I'd like to say something about my background in terms of how it influenced me," said Sister Margaret. "The biggest influences on me have been my family, my religious community, my peace work community, and my education.

"There were two children in our family. My sister and I. My father was a big influence on me. Although he was anticlerical, he knew all about the papal encyclicals on labor and social justice. He was a socialist, and he had me read all kinds of things, including socialist novels."

The socialist novels drew a broad smile from Sally Wilson, but it was a kindly smile, with no trace of condescension.

"My father had a passionate concern for justice," said Sister Margaret. "He was an organizer for the AFL-CIO, and he eventually became one of its vice presidents. My mother, too, was quite liberal. She was a teacher, and she taught in Harlem, commuting every day from Teaneck, New Jersey, where we lived. Then after she retired at seventy, she taught in Catholic schools." Her mother was now ninety-three, Sister Margaret had told me, and she fully supported what her daughter was doing. "My sister, who is married, is also active in peace work.

"I entered the convent at eighteen. I felt strong religious sentiments and, like the rest of my family, a concern for social justice. I became a Medical Missionary Sister, the order established by Mother Dengel in Philadelphia. It was an international order, alive and vital, and its broad perspective appealed to me. The international factor was very important. It helped to bring home a lot of truths. It was becoming clear to more and more of our sisters at the time that many of the health problems that they were confronting in various parts of the world had their roots in the sociopolitical order. Because of this I came to realize quite early that my own country was a major factor in creating disorders of this kind. I saw quite early, then, that peacemaking was intrinsically related to healing."

She described how she had gone for further study after a decade of teaching. She enrolled at the École Biblique in Israel, where she studied the Bible and archeology. "My study of the Bible had a very important effect on my thoughts on war and peace. I saw the need to relate the Bible to the world as it is, and this I tried to do in all my work, whether as a mistress of novices or as a worker among the poor of the inner city.

"I also studied international law prior to this action, and I came to see that the current policies of the United States were violations of it as well as of biblical morality.

"With this action on the *Iowa*, I've put to rest all my doubts with regard to the validity of Plowshares disarmament actions. They are altogether nonviolent even though they do upset people, even those opposed to nuclear arms. They are acts that are meant to be understood as symbolic. They are not acts of sabotage."

After Sister Margaret stepped down from the stand, Andrew Lawrence, perhaps inspired by her, got up once more, this time to speak about the role personal integrity played in his decision to participate. His parents, irreligious though they were, had inculcated it in him, he said. They had told him to practice personal integrity and good judgment and to listen to the small, still voice inside. "If the clerk at the Seven-Eleven let you buy something even though you're a couple of pennies short," he said, "you don't let it go at that, but you return and give him the pennies. And if we saw a broken public phone, we were to report it, not make as many free long-distance calls as we could. We were taught that you don't rip off Ma Bell no matter what Ma Bell herself did.

"All those people walking around on board the *Iowa* on Easter Sunday — it was as though they were taking a stroll beside a swimming pool. They thought everything was okay, but that didn't mean that everything was okay. A lot of people thought Auschwitz was just fine, too."

The spectators listened, intent on every word. Many of them had extraordinary stories of their own to tell. Elmer Maas, a middle-aged man with a full face, who combed his thinning black hair straight across his head, was a musician and teacher from New York City. Maas had been with Philip and

Daniel Berrigan in the first Plowshares action in King of Prussia, and he had also boarded the Trident submarine *Georgia* in 1982, carrying a symbolic hammer and plastic bottle of blood. Boyish, curly-headed Tom Lewis, an artist from Worcester, Massachusetts, went back even further as a peace activist. He had been one of the Catonsville Nine. And on August 6, 1986, Hiroshima Day and the Feast of the Transfiguration, he, Dan Ethier and Margaret Brodhead, all from Worcester, carried out the Transfiguration Plowshares action against two naval aircraft at a base near Boston.

————————

A story in the *Virginian-Pilot* the next day would describe the sympathizers who crowded the courtroom in terms of "ponytails and tie-dyed shirts," but I didn't notice any of the latter, and the only ponytail I noticed was John Heid's. And, indeed, John did make the paper. A picture showed him and Nicholas sitting on the sidewalk in front of the courthouse, John holding one of Nicholas's posters, and Nicholas, in sunglasses and cap, looking through *Highlights for Children*. Catholic radicals and their allies — with the notable exception of the contingent from the Revolutionary Communist Party — showed little concern for style, quite in contrast to the young rebels of the sixties. If there was anything that set them apart, it was that none of them seemed to give much thought to clothes, which, admittedly, would have made them seem idiosyncratic enough back home in Ridgewood. In that suburb of New York City, filled with Catholics from Brooklyn and Queens who had made good, the hot item of the moment was Guess jeans.

All four defendants had pretty much avoided deliberate eloquence, so confident in the rightness of their cause, perhaps, that they felt no need for it. Now, however, in his summation, Andrew Lawrence called upon it at last. "We believe," he said, "that the threat is imminent and that we had no reasonable alternative but to act as we did. I don't know if the system is redeemable, but I do know that human beings are redeemable. And I do know that if these weapons are not evil, then nothing is. If these weapons are not illegal, our laws are worse than meaningless. And if the decision of this court is in favor of such laws, then there could be no greater vindication for what we've done."

Once again the defense asked to be permitted to have expert witnesses testify — Eric Markuson of Old Dominion University on the psychological and social aspects of the nuclear threat and Ramsey Clark on international law — and once again Tommy Miller invoked his Jesus Prayer.

Elmer Maas protested, voicing the frustration of many. "But you won't let the experts who could establish all this testify," he said. Maas earned a reprimand from the judge and the stern attention of two federal marshals, but he was not ejected, not then at least.

"We'll have an hour lunch break now," said Judge Miller, "before the defense and the prosecution present their closing arguments. The government assured me that this wouldn't take any time at all." He glanced down ironically at Martin. "As it happens," he continued, "I have another engagement at 2:30. So I wonder if the defense and prosecution might be kind enough to give me some idea how long they intend to take with their final remarks."

"I'll be quite brief, Your Honor," said Martin.

Miller looked over to the defense table. Berrigan, Boertje, Lawrence, and Sister Margaret conferred for a moment, then Phil Berrigan looked up. "We'll make just a very short statement," he said, "and that will be it."

It was a bright, sunny day outside, pleasantly cool. Daniel Berrigan was standing in front of a television camera, and Ramsey Clark was talking to two reporters.

"Civil disobedience is essential if you're going to have any kind of change," said Clark. "When I was attorney general, black people in the South were being killed for trying to vote. The defendants in there don't deny the facts of the case by any means. They celebrate them. The construction of first strike weapons and the preparation for a first strike are acts contrary to the Nuremberg principles and international law. First strike strategy, moreover, violates the Constitution. By its very nature, it violates the separation of powers."

I couldn't help but notice that the former attorney general of the United States, though dressed in a quite respectable sport coat and a tie, was wearing a faded khaki army belt with the same kind of smoothed-faced brass buckle generations of recruits had labored over with blitz cloths.

"But," said the reporter, a very serious-looking young man with a beard that two decades earlier would have tagged him as a radical, "doesn't this case have to be tried according to the specific laws involved, such as those against trespassing and the violation of public property?"

"This case," said Clark quietly, "has to be tried according to the Constitution of the United States."

"I know that they wanted to defend themselves," said the reporter, taking another tack, "but wouldn't they be doing better if you were defending them?"

"Well," said Clark, "let's look at it this way. If you have to go and pay some fellow five hundred dollars an hour to tell you what rights you have, you really don't have those rights, do you? With regard to the things that are at issue in this case, a couple of those people in there know as much as any lawyer in the country."

The small corner restaurant across the street — a lunch counter and a few tables presided over in relaxed fashion by three pleasant gray-haired women who could have voted for Franklin D. Roosevelt — was filled with Plowshares supporters. There was no sign of Mary and Nicholas. They were probably eating their peanut butter sandwiches somewhere. Nor did I see Liz McAlister and Frida and Katy. Daniel Berrigan was sitting at a table with Tom Lewis and George Bernstein, the man I had met when I came into the courtroom. Marianne of Malibu was at another table.

Peter DeMott, a tall red-haired man in his late thirties, sat next to me at the counter with his wife and their infant son. A former seminarian and a Vietnam veteran, DeMott was the one who had carried out the second Plowshares action all by himself, ramming into the rudder of the Trident submarine *Florida* with a security van.

The trial resumed at 2:30. Tommy Miller would be late for his previous engagement, but not terribly late.

True to his word, the prosecutor limited his closing argument to a few sentences, a dry recital of the facts. Philip Berrigan, speaking for all the defendants, then rose one last time. He remained behind the table and didn't go to the podium. "In the light of the court's unwillingness to allow us sufficient time to meet together to prepare our defense," he said, "and of its siding with the Reagan administration in not allowing the truth to be spoken by keeping from the stand expert witnesses who would have testified to the guilt of the United States in violating innumerable laws, we conclude that this court reinforces the fallacy that the government is a law unto itself. Therefore we turn our backs on this court in which we have no hope and face our friends in whom we have hope."

Good as his word, Berrigan turned his back, and his three companions got to their feet and did the same. A roar of approval and a burst of applause filled the courtroom. Supporters — practically everybody except for the hapless marshals, the press, and the military — got to their feet and turned their backs, too. The marshals, who had moved forward to get the defendants back into their seats, stopped in their tracks, uncertain, and looked to the bench for guidance.

They weren't going to get any from Tommy Miller. Instead of trying to regain control of his courtroom in the face of what amounted to open revolt, even if it meant clearing the court, Miller bent his head and began to plow doggedly through the text of his judgment. It was not one for the ages.

"The court did not lightly choose to limit the testimony the defense could offer," Miller read. "The court let them testify widely. They have chosen not to reciprocate, however, and follow the accepted courtroom decorum." This last, with a perceptible note of grievance, was probably an ad-lib. The courtroom was becoming a little quieter now as some Plowshares supporters turned back around to catch what Miller was saying.

"The defendants brought forth no evidence that the *Iowa* posed imminent harm to them. They could, therefore, have used other means available to them within the framework of law. They could have passed out leaflets. They could have taken part in election campaigns in favor of candidates who believed as they did." Laughter and other derisive sounds greeted these last, but Tommy Miller read on, picking up speed now that it was all too apparent how little chance he had of winning minds and hearts that day. "Nor did they show how their action could have achieved the disarmament that they sought.

"Our system of laws simply cannot condone their acting as they did. Otherwise, those who believed the opposite of them — people who believed that the government was not building enough nuclear weapons — could go into the office of a senator who opposed further spending on nuclear arms and pour blood on his files.

"The defendants claim that they acted in the name of religion, but some of the bloodiest wars in history have been fought in the name of religion."

This was one of those things that everybody knew simply wasn't true. What wars of religion could compare to the wars of Genghis Khan, of Napoleon, the Civil War, World War I, World War II, Korea, Vietnam?

"We live in a society governed by law," Miller read. "What the defendants did promotes anarchy. They are not as radical in their thinking, but their reasoning is the same as that of somebody who, because he felt that our tax laws were unjust, would kill an IRS official."

This time Tommy Miller provoked not derision but gasps and groans of incredulity and dismay. But he read on, heedless of the droplets that heralded a downpour. "Judge Silberman ruled in the Catonsville Nine case — of which Father Daniel Berrigan was one of the defendants — "

"Thank God!" said Dan Berrigan, and a marshal escorted him out of the courtroom. Outside, he told Berrigan that he regretted having to do it because he was a Catholic himself.

"Judge Silberman," said Tommy Miller, his voice a bit strained, "ruled that sincerity of intention was not an acceptable defense."

"Your laws are like the laws of Nazi Germany," shouted John Linnehan, the ex-priest who wanted to fight the Trident with love and life. A marshal moved in, and Linnehan was on his way to join Dan Berrigan. Others, including Elmer Maas, quickly followed, but the crowd was still on its feet, and Philip Berrigan, Greg Boertje, Andrew Lawrence, and Sister Margaret were still standing, their backs turned defiantly to the bench.

"I find the defendants . . .," said Miller, but just as he was coming out with his "guilty," a female voice, loud and clear from the rear of the courtroom, shouted, "Innocent!"

"The state is guilty. The state is guilty," chanted Phil Farnum, former minister and present Communist, in his Palestinian shawl, and the crowd took it up.

Such was the turmoil that most didn't hear Miller's announcement setting sentencing for July 14. Tommy Miller, the victor of record but an obvious loser, got to his feet and, head down, descended from the bench, turned on his heel, and abandoned the field with no attempt to preserve his dignity.

Philip Berrigan, Greg Boertje, Andrew Lawrence, and Sister Margaret McKenna smiled and waved to their wildly applauding friends as the marshals led them away.

Somebody began to sing "They Shall Beat Their Swords into Plowshares," and everybody joined in: "Nations shall learn war no more. / They shall beat their swords into plowshares. . . ." Liz Berrigan, a calm and radiant smile on her face, walked down the center aisle with Katy on her shoulders and Frida beside her as the singing continued:

And all alike 'neath their vine and fig tree,
Shall live in peace and unafraid
And into plowshares turn their swords.
Nations shall learn war no more.

The Church wasn't what it had been a generation earlier, but, despite all the changes, some things remained the same. In Catholic monasteries and convents throughout the world that day, the martyrology ended as it had for centuries: "And in sundry other places, many other martyrs, confessors, and virgins, to whose intercession we commend ourselves. Amen."

We Must See
the Faces of the Babies

Joan Andrews

The Women's Correctional Institute in Claymont, Delaware, could hardly have been a prepossessing sight under the most favorable of circumstances, but it probably wasn't at its best the somber February day that Susan Brindle dropped me off just inside the gate. It was a bit before noon, and a light drizzle was falling. I had never been to a prison before, and I had been bracing myself for something disturbing. But Claymont, whatever its effect on those coming to stay, was more likely to depress than to threaten the visitor.

The prison wasn't a single structure but a collection of nondescript one-story buildings. The exception stood farthest from the gate, a large Victorian house whose bold architecture and blocks of carved stone, black with grime, made the interlopers' cheap cinder block anonymity all the more apparent. Claymont, I thought, might have been a rich man's estate at the turn of the century. The house evoked in me the same thoughts as had the bell tower of St. Agnes's in Cleveland. Here in this place of failure, the sad parable it embodied was all too appropriate.

Susan Brindle, full-faced and cheerful, was the sister of Joan Andrews, whom I had come to see. It was Susan's second trip to the prison that morning. She had picked me up at the railroad station in Wilmington, about fifteen miles away, two hours earlier and dropped me at a Roy Rogers in Claymont while she kept a ten o'clock appointment with the warden. The warden had asked to see her and Joan together, and Susan had been in high spirits when she met me, three-month-old William, the youngest of her six children, in her arms. Maybe today would be the day Joan was released, she said with a bright smile, and we could all go home and celebrate. The interview hadn't produced anything, however, and Susan's long-cherished hopes for her sister's freedom were frustrated once again.

Following Susan's directions, I walked up the path to a flat-roofed building designated "Administration" and stepped inside. Two sets of doors were separated by a minuscule foyer, with a bench on either wall. A guard with a pistol at her hip opened the locked inner door and asked me whom I wanted to see. She was young and black and had a very nice smile. Inside was a narrow corridor that ran the width of the building and a counter. Behind the counter, a fat middle-aged white woman in civilian clothes sat at a desk typing something in desultory fashion. Beyond her were the doors of two small offices. The place had the air of middling neglect and cluttered inefficiency that invariably prevailed when government and governed confront each other and the former has no need to please the latter. But the atmosphere was no worse and in some respects better than that of a social security or unemployment office, both of which I was familiar with. The guard did have a nice smile, and there wasn't a line.

I surrendered my billfold and keys after putting them into a plastic bag. The guard hung the bag on a numbered hook and gave me a check. She didn't ask to see the letter I had brought from Tom Fox, editor of the *National Catholic Reporter,* and she didn't object to my camera and tape recorder, all of which, I was to learn during a second visit, I didn't appreciate as much as I should have. Finally, she led me into a medium-sized, rectangular room just off the entrance. It had a table, and a dozen or so molded plastic chairs, their colors faded, lined the walls. A soft drink machine stood at one corner. A dash of more vivid color came from the garishly patterned drapes at the windows. It could have been the laundry room of an apartment house. Even the heavy grilles that covered the windows fit the image, no matter if they had a contrary purpose here.

I hadn't yet sat down when I turned to see Joan Andrews standing in the doorway, a shy smile on her face.

Joan Andrews, in February of 1988, was just a month shy of her fortieth birthday. She had been in prison for nearly two years, most of it in solitary confinement in Broward Correctional Institute in Florida, a maximum-security prison. Like her sister Susan, Joan had prominent features. She was of medium height, and, as expected of an accomplished horsewoman, she seemed wiry and strong. Prison life had obviously taken its toll, however. Her drab green uniform hung loosely on her body, and she looked older than she had in the pictures I had seen of her. In the pictures, her face had a girlish fullness, but now it was much thinner, somewhat haggard, in fact. Her eyes were gray-blue. She had lost the right one to cancer years before, and the glass eye in its place not only had an unnerving cast to it but threw her face off balance. The lid of her good eye crinkled when she smiled, which she did frequently, but that other stayed fixed in place. Her light brown hair, flecked with gray and parted in the middle, hung straight down over her chest nearly reaching her waist.

Though we had never met or even talked on the phone, to embrace seemed the natural thing to do, and so we did. This meeting had been in the works for more than half a year, and neither of us had thought it was going to be so long delayed. I had phoned Broward again and again for an interview, only to get the runaround from the warden's secretary. "Would you please give me your name again. . . ."

Joan and I knew quite a bit about each other. She, a faithful daughter of the Roman Catholic Church, knew that I, though faithful in my fashion, had written some things sharply critical of bishops and even of popes, but she was still quite willing to talk with me. She also knew that I, unlike most of her admirers, was opposed to nuclear weapons, and I knew that she not only wholeheartedly agreed on this but went far beyond me in her opposition to violence. I also knew that she had saved a cousin from drowning when she was a teenager even though she was a bad swimmer herself. She had kept the boy's head above water by making him stand on her shoulders. And I knew the general sequence of events that had brought this shy, gentle woman to Claymont Women's Correctional Institute — Joan Andrews who had once wanted only to marry a nice Catholic man and have a big family and perhaps write children's books.

She had been raised on a farm near Nashville, Tennessee, a member of a warm and loving family, two boys and three girls, with Joan the second oldest after her brother Bill. Her mother, who came from a wealthy Irish-Catholic family in Detroit, had dropped out of the University of Detroit during World War II to become an army nurse. It was in the army that she met Joan's father, a southern Protestant who would convert to Catholicism and become a schoolteacher. There never was much money to spare in the Andrews family, but there were all those acres to roam around in and horses, even thoroughbreds, to ride, a sport that Joan and her sisters came to love.

While still a preteen, Joan developed a love of history. She took all sorts of books out of the library, and so it was that she learned at a tender age about the Nazi slaughter of six million Jews.

Susan couldn't bear to look at some of the pictures in the books Joan brought home. "Joannie," she'd protest, "I don't see how you can look at those terrible pictures." But Joan would answer: "Susan, I have to look at them. Germany was a Christian country, and they killed millions of innocent people. And the only reason that the bad Germans were able to do it is because the good Germans looked the other way."

Joan Andrews was already making people feel uncomfortable at age eleven; and she was still at it nearly three decades later when, in March of 1986, she entered an abortion clinic in Pensacola, Florida, through the back door in broad daylight — accompanied, in fact, by two policemen — and disconnected a suction machine used in performing abortions. Then, as she was trying to tear the cord from the machine, one of the policemen seized her, and, when they arrested her, she went limp.

This hardly qualifies as a rampage, one would think, but for her actions she was charged with burglary, criminal mischief, and resisting arrest. In the nonjury trial that followed, Judge William H. Anderson, calling Joan "a danger to the community," gave her a five-year prison term even though the prosecuting attorney had asked for no more than a year.

The severity came as a result of Joan's refusal to say she was sorry for what she had done and her declaration, freely given, that she would do it again. There was also abundant evidence that she meant what she said: in the course of the previous eight years, Joan had traveled around the country participating in what she called "rescue missions" ("spewing hatred rather than doing anything constructive" was the way the Honorable William H. Anderson put it) and incurring more than one hundred arrests, some of which resulted in jail terms. All the while she lived out the kind of selfless dedication that most of us would expect to find only within the most austere of cloisters. Her wardrobe was by Goodwill, and it took dozens of coats to get her through a single winter because she was always giving the current one away to somebody she deemed more in need.

"Won't you say you're sorry and promise not to do it again?" asked Judge Anderson. "I can't promise not to save babies," said Joan Andrews.

Much more tractable, much less a menace to the community, it seemed, were the two men who rode in the paddy wagon with Joan to the court-house on the day of her sentencing. They had been convicted of being accomplices to murder, but, obviously moved by the fervor of their contrition, Judge Anderson, perhaps brushing aside an errant tear, gave them four years.

Joan's protest didn't end with her arrest. Because she believed that the laws that permitted abortion were immoral and because she believed herself to be a prisoner of conscience and not a common criminal, Joan Andrews felt obliged to refuse to cooperate. For if she cooperated, she would, as she saw it, be acknowledging the legitimacy of a process that was immoral from first to last.

Her refusal to admit that she was a criminal and that the laws under which she was convicted were just would cost her dearly. It brought her to a maximum-security prison in which she sat in solitary confinement for up to thirty days at a time, all privileges suspended, including attendance at Mass. Then she was given a few days to rethink her position, after which, inevitably, she went back into solitary. Getting to see her was difficult under such circumstances; her mother was turned away on one occasion after making a thousand-mile trip.

Pro-life groups — though not the national leadership, which disowned her because of her espousal of direct action — were outraged by the treatment given Joan Andrews. Their indignation was so intense, in fact, that the consequent uproar and its embarrassing implications — some pro-lifers were talking about boycotting Disney World, for God's sake! — came at length to the attention of the Catholic hierarchy of Florida, an extraordinary occurrence considering the layers of insulation that intervened. The bishops' wonted tranquillity had been disturbed.

The Florida bishops appointed a lay bureaucrat in the employ of the Florida Catholic Conference to investigate the case. Like many lay people in service to Holy Mother Church, the man seemed to have been well schooled in how to devise the kind of response that his employers preferred to hear. Nobody, after all, who works for bishops wants them to get disturbed or, once disturbed, to long remain so.

"[I]t appears to me that the actions of the court and the prison system are appropriate and, in fact, compelled by the actions of Miss Andrews," he wrote soothingly in a memorandum of December 10, 1986, that, among other faults, presented a wildly inaccurate account of what actually happened in Pensacola. (Joan, according to the memo, had been convicted of "breaking into" an abortion clinic and "injuring some people.") "She has the key to her maximum security cell. One can admire her zeal and her faith, but the state has to enforce its laws. She has chosen to violate them, albeit for a good cause, and the consequences have been freely chosen by her."

He was right, of course. Joan Andrews's whole bearing verified his claims, including her refusal to allow money to be spent in her defense that could be better used, she thought, to support families whose breadwinners were in prison because they had broken the law to save the unborn.

The man was a Catholic, one presumes, and so, when he concocted this tranquilizer for the Florida hierarchy, he believed, one also presumes, that abortion was a grievous offense against the sacredness of life. But nowhere in his letter is there a hint of any agony of soul over what was, at the very least, a painful dilemma. Or, if agony of soul is a little too much to ask of the Florida Catholic Conference, there is not the least indication in his memo that the men to whom he was giving this advice — men on record as declaring abortion to be the slaughter of the innocent — might possibly search their own souls a little before deciding what to do or not do with regard to Joan Andrews, a woman whose actions and demeanor manifested the kind of faith and selfless devotion that bishops praise so unreservedly in the saints, who, of course, are no longer around to embarrass anybody. One seeks in vain for any hint that the bishops might consider taking a bit of risk themselves. The memo, on the contrary, gave them permission to do nothing, and they graciously accepted.

At the end of January 1988, Joan, a thorn in the side of Governor Bob Martinez of Florida — a Republican elected with the support of pro-life groups and now overwhelmed by thousands of pro-Joan letters — was transferred from Florida to Claymont, which was near Susan's home in Newark, Delaware. It was here that I was at last able to get permission to see her.

Once we got through the usual things people say at a first encounter and started to talk about what really mattered, Joan Andrews's manner, quiet and reserved, immediately changed. She didn't raise her voice, but it became stronger, and the words rushed out of her like a long pent-up stream, her eyes fixed on mine. Her phrasing was as clear as her words were passionate, and, as she talked, she emphasized her words by gesturing forcefully with hands strengthened by years of gripping a bridle and guiding spirited and powerful thoroughbreds.

"I've always been against violence of any sort. The values of Our Lord Jesus Christ and Francis of Assisi were inculcated into my brothers and sisters and me right from the beginning. So whenever anything was read to me or I heard anything, I always thought about it in terms of how Jesus would respond to it."

How Jesus would respond to it. I had labored for a decade in a central bureaucracy set up by the American hierarchy, and I had never once heard anybody wonder what Jesus might think of a proposal under consideration. To be fair, it was sometimes a difficult question to answer, as Joan would be the first to admit. When she was very young, she confessed, she often got it wrong. She'd become angry in grade school whenever she ran into instances of injustice, and she was a fierce, not always nonviolent defender of smaller children against bullies, a failing that some distant day in Rome a devil's advocate might seize upon, but not one that anyone else was likely to hold against her.

Her Catholic high school was the only integrated school in Nashville in the early sixties. It was the antiwar movement, however, not the civil rights movement, that provoked the first significant expression of the activism to which her faith and her temperament would inevitably compel her.

"I was totally against war even in high school. I wrote and prayed and thought about war," she said. "I didn't believe that killing should be a response to injustice. I could understand having a just cause to protect yourself, but I couldn't see killing. I can see giving my life to protect somebody else. And if somebody broke into my house and tried to kill my children, for example, I would do all I could to protect them, even injuring the attacker, but I wouldn't kill anybody. I was very disturbed about our government being involved in the overthrow and murder of Diem, even if his government had been corrupt."

But it was not until the late sixties, when she was a freshman at St. Louis University, that she became involved in the antiwar movement. She was so upset when her younger brother, John, was drafted that she dropped out of school.

John, as it turned out, didn't go to Vietnam. Joan's older brother, Bill, who was already in the army but was stationed in the States, went to Senator Fulbright and asked if he could go to Vietnam instead of his brother, and the senator arranged it. This relieved Joan's mind to some extent, since Bill was a clerk and, unlike John, who was an infantryman, was less likely to kill someone or be killed himself.

Despite her fierce opposition to the war, Joan was put off by the hostility of the antiwar movement on campus. So she prayed, she took part in demonstrations, but she avoided any sort of leadership role.

Then came the event that irrevocably changed Joan Andrews's life. "The 1973 Supreme Court decision legalizing the killing of little babies came like a stab in the heart to me, and I became fully involved in pro-life work."

A stab in the heart. Charlie Liteky may not have used the same words, but what had happened to him when he learned about what was going on in Central America had had much the same intensity. There are those who take things too much to heart. That which, for want of a better term, we call "normal life" becomes impossible for them. Joan Andrews's pro-life work would eventually entail breaking the law, a decision that would involve great risk and even alienate her from the pro-life establishment.

It was a step that she would begin taking in 1979. She was, at the time, living in Delaware with Susan and her family when Miriam, the youngest of the three sisters, who was a freshman at St. Louis University, told them about the work that had begun in St. Louis.

"It was wonderful. They were actually intervening and saving babies. I'm a person who doesn't do things easily. I need a diagram. But when I heard how they were blocking the doors of these killing centers, I realized at once that doing that was certainly the most natural thing in the world." Like Charlie Liteky's "ordinary reaction" when he saw American boys lying wounded under heavy enemy fire in a grove in Ben Hoa Province.

A keen sense of logic was obviously part and parcel of Joan Andrews's purity of heart. She realized the power of language. She never said "abortion clinic." "Clinic" had to do with healing, and she was unwilling to concede so precious a nuance. She said "abortion mill" or "killing center."

She decided to do a rescue mission in Delaware, and she got eight other pro-lifers interested. On the day scheduled for the rescue, however, she found herself standing alone in front of the targeted clinic.

"Today, of course, I would just go in and do it on my own, but I couldn't then. One of the pro-lifers who really regretted not participating — he was the last to drop out — was a Third Order Franciscan. His superior wouldn't allow him. He told him it was morally wrong to get involved. I decided I had to learn to be a better leader, and so I went to St. Louis."

She grinned broadly when I asked her if she had been scared standing there all alone. "You hit the nail on the head there. I was scared all right. I'm a very shy person. I hate to cause a fuss, and I want to hang back. Susan and Miriam always took the lead in things."

But once she got to St. Louis and saw rescues in operation, her fears vanished, and performing rescues became second nature to her. Now that she had moved out of safe harbor of legally sanctioned activity and into the open sea, Joan Andrews found a peace of mind she had not known for some time. It was a transformation that recalled that of Oscar Romero, a worrier afflicted with bad health, who began to manifest vigor and unfailing good humor as soon as he took up the cause of the poor and oppressed as the new archbishop of San Salvador and the death threats began to pile up at his door.

"Before I went to St. Louis, I had been going through a crisis that had lasted for a long time. I remember traveling in a car in '73 and being tormented by thoughts of the abortion holocaust. I had taken a day off to go on a one-day retreat. I wasn't thinking about thanking God for anything.

Then I noticed that the trees were gorgeous along the road, and then I felt still worse. The babies who were being killed wouldn't be able to enjoy the trees. They weren't able to run away as I was doing. I realized that I should thank God for the trees. I knew that I should appreciate them for the babies who couldn't. Even in the midst of the killing, God gives us these things. But my life was unhappy. I felt helpless. I felt unworthy to be working for the Lord because of my own weaknesses."

There was something more to it, too, than a feeling of futility, something else that, again, a future devil's advocate might draw upon. Joan Andrews had started to feel bitter toward the clergy, the very men whom she had always so revered.

At the time, she was doing pro-life educational work — lobbying, offering women alternatives to abortion, getting pregnant women into homes. She began to realize that it was much easier to get into Protestant churches than Catholic and to talk to their congregations. "I remember one priest — and he was a good man in other respects, against the Vietnam War and working for the poor — who made an announcement from the pulpit about our being in the church that Sunday as we had asked him. But this is the way he put it: 'There's someone here who wants you to sign something against abortion. You can do it if you want, but I wouldn't.'

"This was an attitude we ran into frequently — actual hostility. It struck me to the heart. We had to be as humble as we could be, as sweet as we could be, and grovel — all so that we could be allowed to ask people to save babies. It made me bitter that we had to do this constantly and play these games constantly." It was easy to imagine the indignation that she must have had to suppress — and the fury with which she had confronted grade school bullies.

The hostility wore her down. She became very bitter and eventually suffered what she thought was a nervous breakdown. But then Joan experienced a kind of epiphany: "It was at this point that a saying of Mother Teresa finally came home to me: 'We're not called to be successful,' she said. 'We're called to be faithful.' That saved my life." Mother Teresa, it seemed, knew her Bhagavad-Gita as well as her New Testament. And why shouldn't she?

———————

Joan's cancer was discovered in the fall of 1979 after she had gone to St. Louis and was living with Miriam and Susan. She was given just a month to live, and she thanked God that this trial had come when she was at peace rather than a year earlier. Far from killing her, however, the cancer didn't even slow her down. She had her eye out on a Thursday, and she was helping to blockade an abortion clinic the following Saturday.

The rescue movement flourished in St. Louis. Most of the rescuers were working people, many of them parents, both older parents and parents of young children. There were few students, though the movement itself had begun at St. Louis University. At first, the tactics had involved stealth — going in quietly and hiding in bathrooms.

"Then we publicly announced an operation ahead of time. Up to then we had only a small number of people involved with at most five getting arrested," Joan recalled. "This time we had ten or fifteen counselors, the ones who try to persuade women not to have an abortion, and over one hundred and fifty pickets. We had appointed marshals, but at that time they didn't have much experience in controlling crowds. And then the police overreacted because of the numbers involved."

In the course of one of the struggles that ensued, Joan got her hand caught in the handle of a door, and she passed out for a few moments. Her finger was broken. "A police captain offered to take me to the hospital, and I agreed on condition that he bring me back. It turned out that his own son was taking part in the rescue."

A second publicly announced rescue operation went off much better. The pickets remained outside the building, and there were counselors on the sidewalk to meet the women coming in. "This time we got the method down right, and it was beautiful. That day we saved seven babies. These women just didn't turn away. They said: 'I want to save my baby.' "

The St. Louis abortion clinic they had been focusing on, which normally performed thirty to forty abortions every Saturday, lost most of its business. This success, entailing as it did a major loss in revenue for the abortionists, prompted the clinic to seek an injunction.

Joan firmly believed that they should have stood their ground. The injunctions would have piled up, and the pro-lifers' credibility would have increased accordingly. The lawyers who were advising them, however, counseled prudence. They suggested the tactic of moving on to another abortion mill when one got an injunction and then another after that until there was just one left. Then, the lawyers assured them, everyone would join in, themselves included, to defy the injunction.

It was a mistake. Caution, like anything else, can become habitual with enough practice. When the moment of truth finally came, only a handful were willing to take the risk, no lawyers among them, apparently. Joan Andrews was quite matter-of-fact in placing a major portion of the blame.

"What broke the movement in St. Louis was the bishop," she said, referring to Archbishop John L. May, who went on to become chairman of the United States Conference of Bishops. "We had more than three hundred people willing to picket when he came out with a statement calling the rescues 'counterproductive and ill advised.' We had about thirty rescuers ready to get arrested and about twenty-five counselors. The only ones who stayed after that were the rescuers and some of the counselors.

"We shouldn't do anything illegal, said Archbishop May. He himself had sat in at a lunch counter during the Civil Rights struggle. He said that was different, but he wouldn't say how it was different. Actually, it was different in that here lives were at stake right there and then. We thought it was a terrible injustice."

Four people, including Joan Andrews, went to jail for breaking injunctions. She stayed there for four months. Ironically enough, after their own shepherd had abandoned them to the wolf in his zeal to render to Caesar what was Caesar's, Caesar himself, in the person of the St. Louis City Council, voted to commend them for what they had done. Big-city politics being what is, it's not likely that the council was made up solely of daily communicants and devotees of the Little Way of Thérèse of Lisieux, but nonetheless the secular authorities of St. Louis, unlike its most visible spiritual authority, were willing to go on record as acknowledging the claims of a moral realm whose laws sometimes contradicted human decrees — a gracious gesture that honored the civilized traditions of a city identified with Louis of France, Josephine Baker, and T. S. Eliot.

Generally speaking, women coming for abortions reacted in three different ways when pro-lifers approached them. Some were very hostile, some broke into tears, and some laughed coldly, showing no sign of emotion. There was little or no chance of influencing the latter, Joan said, but, surprisingly enough, there was a fair chance of having some effect with the very hostile. Their screams and curses often masked deep misgivings about what they were about to do, and sometimes the pro-lifers could dissuade them.

With those who were crying, of course, there was the best hope of success. Often these women were being coerced into having abortions — by circumstances, friends who insisted they were being selfish to have a baby, or irate boyfriends or husbands.

"Once a woman who looked like she was still in her teens came in a car driven by an older man about forty. He started cursing us. She was very quiet. We had a counselor on both sides of the car. Then when the man tried to get violent, she jumped out and ran away from him."

The young woman showed them her back. It was covered with scars, some fresh, some old. Later the same day, the woman came back and joined the pickets. She told reporters that she didn't know there was anybody out there who cared. She went to live with a pro-life family, and she had her baby.

"In another case, one of our sidewalk counselors who had a maternity home tried to talk with a woman who was one of the cold type who showed no emotion. But after this woman had gone in and lain down on the operating table, she started thinking. It must be a baby, she thought. Nobody would go to that trouble if it wasn't a baby. Nobody would risk getting arrested. Then she got up off the table and went out the back door. Since her mother wouldn't let her come back home, a girlfriend brought her to a place she had heard of. It turned out to be a maternity house run by the counselor who had tried to stop her."

———————

Joan Andrews was no leader. Though her admirers were quick to compare her with her namesake from Lorraine, she was like her only in her courage and unswerving faith. But despite her lack of flair and her apparent simplicity, Joan Andrews was a woman keenly aware of the cruel and vicious paradoxes of the twentieth century and the fallibility of heroes. It was a time, she knew, that demanded more faith than ever before. It was not a time for charisma but for humility and self-effacement. Like Charlie Liteky, a man who also distrusted heroes, she put no trust in her abilities but let herself be led by the Spirit. And the Spirit had led her to Pensacola and to confrontation in a region of America notoriously unreceptive to "outside agitators."

She happened to be in the Washington office of a pro-life leader named John Byrne when a call came from John Burt, a Protestant minister who ran a home for pregnant women in Pensacola. Joan was willing to go anywhere at any time for the sake of the pro-life movement, and she told Burt that she would be happy to come to Pensacola, if he wished, run a workshop on rescues, and then, together with local volunteers, close down an abortion mill. She would have to do it right away, however, she said, because she had two court dates pending, one in Annapolis and one in Pittsburgh. The latter was the more serious since the judge there, Raymond Novak, had already given her good friend and codefendant Joe Wall six months to a year, and he had told her attorney that he was going to give her six years.

John Ryan and Joe Sheidler, pro-life leaders from St. Louis and Chicago respectively, came down to Pensacola and talked to the group John Burt had assembled. When it came time for the rescue, however, Joan Andrews was the only nonlocal person to participate. "John and Joe were the heads of their local pro-life groups," Joan explained. "They were needed. I wasn't. I was more available to put myself in the position of getting arrested. I usually do. Unless I absolutely have a commitment to be somewhere else, I'll participate in the rescue. And if I see that there's a door that has to be blocked, I'll forget the commitment and go ahead and perform the rescue."

Supported by about 150 pickets, five rescuers, with Joan in the lead, walked toward the rear entrance of the abortion clinic under the watchful eyes of the police. John Burt and his daughter Sarah were right behind Joan, followed by two other women. Four of them got inside, but the police pounced on the fifth before she could get through the door, and in their enthusiasm they also arrested the pro-lifers' lawyer in the parking lot, ordering him to leave and then seizing him before he had a chance to comply.

In fairness to Pensacola, an abortion clinic had been bombed a few months before, an event that without a doubt greatly aggravated the hostility that Joan and her companions faced. A November 30, 1986, editorial in the *Pensacola News Journal* applauding the five-year sentence Judge Anderson gave Joan had condemned "out-of-town troublemakers." "This is a city of enlightened, tolerant, peace-loving people," said the editorial, "who respect law and order as well as the right to peacefully protest. But when professional rabblerousers and demagogues deliberately besmirch this city's good name and show their callous contempt for its laws, its police officers and its judiciary, then the time has come to enforce the law to its fullest and punish those who deserve punishment." A week later, the *News Journal* warmed to the same theme with even more ardor, generating such velocity in the course of it, in fact, that it shattered the reason barrier and broke through to a warp zone beyond parody: "They ought to take out every fanatic in the world," wrote editor Paul Jasper, appealing to his tolerant and peace-loving readership, "and shoot him down like a dog."

"Every time they played a tape of the rescue on television," said Joan, "they showed the bombing, too. Once a new prisoner came in, and when they told her about me, she said: 'Oh yeah, I know. She's that bomber.' "

John Cavanaugh-O'Keefe, a pro-life leader whom Joan admired very much, was unreservedly opposed to such extreme tactics. Joan described him as a great thinker and a bridge to the antiwar movement. He was the founder of Pro-life Nonviolent Action, and Joan credited him and Juli Loesch with developing the philosophy of the rescues. He had, in fact, been fired by National Right to Life because of his rescue work. Cavanaugh-

O'Keefe, however, looked askance at even some of the tactics that Joan used, such as her unplugging the suction machine. "He realizes that that kind of thing is not violent, but it could put the idea of violence into people's heads," Joan explained. "He agrees in principle that because babies are being killed, every nonviolent means is permissible, but he's concerned about the harm done by misperceptions." Bombings, needless to say, were anathema to Cavanaugh-O'Keefe. They could so easily be exploited by the pro-abortion forces as acts of terror pure and simple.

With all respect to her friend Cavanaugh-O'Keefe, Joan differed from him on this issue. Characteristically, she showed no concern whatsoever for political consequences. "I'll tell you very honestly how I feel. I believe that bombings are altogether moral if the proper safeguards are used and the bomb can't endanger anyone. It has to be done out of love, not to terrorize anybody. And it has to be the killing center itself, nothing else, at a time when abortions are imminent."

Bombing out of love! How dangerously close she seemed for a moment to the caricature of the fanatical anti-abortionist. How evident were Cavanaugh-O'Keefe's fears. Joan, however, had logic on her side.

"If you agree that abortion is the direct, premeditated killing of babies, what's wrong with damaging the killing center so that it's put out of use for six months? And if you agree that it would have been morally permissible to have bombed Auschwitz without injuring any guards or inmates so that the camps would be put out of commission. . . . You have to be practical, though. You have to balance the harmful effect of the bombing against the time gained and the lives possibly saved. I think a better way is to put your own body on the line and change people's hearts that way."

What about those who said that Joan Andrews had gone too far and, in her noncooperation, was still going too far — those who said that she was harming the movement? She was ready for the question. It was the crucial one, after all, since it was long-standing, and it came not from abortionists but from pro-life people — an objection that called into question everything for which she had sacrificed so much. As with the peace movement, there was a deep division in pro-life ranks over the issue of direct action. Joan, in a pro-life journal in sympathy with her, had written an eloquent plea for unity and cooperation despite this difference. She wrote that she thought rescues were "probably a moral imperative" but she understood how other pro-lifers didn't see it that way.

"I believe wholeheartedly," she told me, "in non-cooperation with the abortion holocaust. I don't believe that there is any other way that you can stop it. Even if we overturn *Roe vs. Wade* and legislate a human life amendment, the right to kill — this so-called right to kill — has become so ingrained in our society, that the killing would go on behind closed doors. State officials would look the other way. In Canada, where abortion is illegal, the pro-lifers are arrested and the abortion clinics are protected. We have to change not just the law but the minds and hearts of people, and the best way to do this is to put our own bodies on the line to show the world that we really believe that murder is going on — that we believe that these are babies and that we totally love them.

"Then we can work on legislation. If there's a famine in India, the first thing you think of doing is rescuing the people who are dying of hunger. Yes, you should have a long term plan to see that there is no famine again, but in the meantime you have to take immediate action.

"We have to challenge the indoctrination that people have gotten. We've come so far down the road with killing simply because people have accepted killing. Back in the 70s, once you got someone to see that it was a real baby, they usually wouldn't go through with the abortion. But now they say okay it's a baby. So what? No wonder child abuse has skyrocketed! And look at the killing of handicapped babies and euthanasia for the elderly. This is the direction we're going. It's only natural that it would happen once people got the idea that babies were just things that you can dispose of if you want.

"And that's why we can cooperate no further. We have to make it so that the abortionists can't continue doing the killing without disrupting society as a whole."

Disrupting society as a whole! Catholic schools had taught generations of Catholic children that they were to take their place in American society as good citizens. No, American society wasn't perfect by any means, the nuns had taught, but all we had to do to make it better was to be *good examples.* We were to admire the saints but we were by no means to emulate the extravagances of the more flamboyant of them. We lived in the good old U.S.A. in the twentieth century and there was no need for that kind of thing. The message had seemed quite simple and straightforward and unimpeachably patriotic. But was it really? Could Paul Blanshard, whose *American Freedom and Catholic Power* had provoked hot and righteous indignation in Catholic circles in the fifties, have been right after all? Had Blanshard been onto something that sincere Catholic apologists had missed? Had there really been a subversive cast to what the nuns had taught despite our protests to the contrary? Why bring up saintly excesses to begin with in front of impressionable boys and girls? Especially since saintly excesses were far more compelling than good examples.

Whatever the case, the conversation that morning between Joan and

Susan and the warden at Claymont well illustrated how much Joan the schoolgirl had taken the extravagances of the saints to heart. Susan had described the meeting to me as she was driving me to the prison, and now Joan gave me her own account of it. The warden had been quite sympathetic, she said. She had told Joan that she understood that she wasn't a criminal and that she was acting out of religious principles. Delaware, moreover, hadn't done anything to Joan. Delaware had agreed to take her for humanitarian reasons. Why, then, the woman wanted to know, did Joan continue to refuse to cooperate? "I told the warden that Claymont was the best prison I had ever been in and that I understood her good intentions towards me. But I said to her: 'Even though you are a secondary structure in the abortion holocaust and even though it's not your decision to put me here, still, you are cooperating, and I feel morally obliged to burden you and this prison.' "

The warden had shaken her head and smiled. "Joan," she said, "you're just one person. The system can handle you without any difficulty." It was an objection that Joan was quite ready for. She answered with Charlie Liteky's argument that if enough like-minded people joined her, together they would overtax the resources of the system.

"Prison authorities hate it when a prisoner doesn't cooperate," Joan explained. "In jail you have to have a security system. It's a bad influence on others if anybody doesn't go along with it. I'll cooperate if there's a fire alarm or a drill. I'd never do anything to endanger others. But in all other cases, no. Even if I have to go back to Florida. I don't want to go back to Florida. I've been dumped on them here, and so they have to put up with me. As just one person, of course, I'm not that much of a burden. If there were more, however, they couldn't take it. They'd have to build more jails."

Though she might not have been charismatic in the usual sense, Joan could exert a strong influence on others in personal encounters. It's safe to say that the wardens at Claymont would never forget her, and she also brought this same kind of influence to bear upon her fellow prisoners, whom she described as very sympathetic for the most part. Most of them were also quick to assure her that they too were against abortion. Maybe they did this only to ingratiate themselves with her — something that in itself testified to her appeal — but, as it happened, an opportunity had recently come up to judge the sincerity of such protestations.

Joan had been in solitary confinement in Florida and should have been at Claymont, but because the Delaware prison was so crowded she was put into a cell with two other women when she arrived. Both of them told her they agreed with her one hundred percent, but, as it happened, they had a radio, and the next day a guard came to take it away. Joan could have no privileges because of her refusal to cooperate, the guard told Joan's companions, and so the radio had to go.

"One of the girls got angry," said Joan. "She said to the guard: 'I'm against abortion, but I don't see why I should have my privileges taken away because she's being punished. I want her out of here. I don't care if I have to drag her out myself by the hair of her head.' " Much to Joan's surprise, the guard, who had seemed unfriendly to her, now defended her. "Listen," said the guard, "she's doing it for a good cause. You shouldn't be mad at her."

Joan's cellmate was still far from happy, however, and that night Joan talked over the problem with both women. She told them why she was so much against abortion, and she explained what she was trying to accomplish by refusing to go along with the system. "They were really cute. The girl who hadn't got angry said I must have been sent from heaven." In the days that followed, Joan made every effort to get the radio back. She told the guard that she had never owned a radio and it meant nothing to her, but then one day the woman who had threatened to drag her out by the hair of her head told her to forget about the radio. "She said to me: 'Don't try to get it back anymore. It's a sacrifice we can make. We can participate a little in what you're doing.' "

Later Joan was transferred to another cell at her own request. She had volunteered to take the place of a pregnant woman who had been put with a new prisoner who was reacting violently to drug withdrawal. The guards had double-cuffed the difficult prisoner, and she had broken free three times. She kept threatening to kill the pregnant woman. Joan and another volunteer — who had taken the place of the third woman, who had been close to a breakdown because of lack of sleep — were able to calm the woman down. "She'd threaten us sometimes, but if you were calm with her, if you showed her you loved her, she'd be all right. She had a good heart, but she was twenty-four and she had been on drugs half of her life."

Most of us, even those who might consider Joan seriously misguided, would agree that her behavior was heroic. Joan, herself, however, didn't see it that way. Unnervingly enough, at least to those of us who shared her convictions on abortion, she saw her behavior in quite different terms. Without passing judgment on individuals, something contrary to her nature, Joan firmly believed that what she was doing all pro-lifers should do. The lesson that she felt she had to convey to them was that pro-lifers must go all the way in noncooperation — even to not paying taxes, even to not helping the government do worthwhile things while it was at the same time supporting mass murder.

"I remember a poem I read at St. Louis University. It was an anonymous poem written by a Jew in a death camp. It was summer when the Nazis came to get him, he recalled. People were in shirtsleeves. His neighbors turned and looked the other way. 'It wasn't the executioners who hurt us the most,' he wrote. 'They killed our bodies. It was our friends who turned their backs on us — because they broke our hearts.' "

She raised her voice for the first time, and her look became more intense. "Where are the pro-lifers, those who love these babies? We've been talking all this rhetoric for so long. These children are dying! Aren't we in a way their worst enemies? We've gotten our message across. The media haven't helped us, but we've gotten it across pretty well that these are babies. And society has bought it. John Cavanaugh-O'Keefe puts it this way: society has gotten a double message — our message that these are babies and the abortionists' message that you can kill them."

While striving for the ideal, Joan was willing to settle for less at a given moment, hoping, for example, that pro-lifers would begin by withholding their cooperation as much as they could. But she nevertheless saw this as but a beginning. Direct action could attain real power, she felt, only if those who practiced it refused to cooperate in prison. In this, of course, Joan Andrews was going beyond Gandhi himself, the apostle of nonviolent confrontation. Gandhi had told his disciples to hold off on noncooperation until they were out of prison, but Joan Andrews believed that pro-lifers had to burden the prison system as much as they could.

She believed it was necessary to go beyond Gandhi because she believed that what pro-lifers faced was far worse than what Gandhi and his followers faced, an enormity more akin to Hitler's extermination of the Jews than to England's oppression of the Indians, brutal as it was.

"If only people realized how beautiful noncooperation is! Once the authorities realize they can't push you anymore unless they're willing to keep you in forever, they have to back off. Because you're not going to back off an inch. You're going to be gentle and loving but you're not going to back off an inch. You hate to burden people. You hate to make things difficult for nice officers and others, but there's a war on."

Her argument was the same as Philip Berrigan had given in the Yorktown jail. When there was a war on, sacrifices had to made, including separation from loved ones. Joan recalled her reaction twenty years before when Lyndon Johnson assured Americans that they would still be able to enjoy a high standard of living at home while waging a full-scale war abroad. Johnson saw it as an inducement, but she thought it was horrible to suggest that Americans should enjoy themselves to the full while others, including their fellow Americans, were dying. Why, she thought, should anybody be exempt from suffering? Now it was the same, she said, with the abortion holocaust. "Why shouldn't we all suffer something? It's not that you want to take any satisfaction in making people suffer. It's just that if you're going to bring home to everybody the terrible brutality done to the children, I think that you have to be prepared to make others feel the burden of it. That was hard for me because I hate being a burden on anyone. I felt so bad being a burden on prison officers. But then I realized that they were living in the holocaust, they were living in this society. So they had to suffer, too. Because they were living in a society in which they and we are allowing this to happen. So the burden has to come because of the human condition. We tend to forget those we don't see. We must see the faces of the babies."

She gave the example of John Cavanaugh-O'Keefe's group, who in the early eighties used to pay their fines. Fathers and mothers didn't want to be separated from their families, and if they were released they would be able to take part in another rescue the next week. But then the judges started to raise the fines to such an extent that it took longer and longer to raise the money to pay them, and the rescues began to occur at more widely separated intervals. It was then that Cavanaugh-O'Keefe and his companions decided to stop paying the fines and instead set up communities of support for families whose breadwinners were risking long prison terms. When the pro-lifers stopped paying fines and posting bonds, the judges began to back down, dropping their fines from $500 down to $50 and lower. And when the judges finally realized that they weren't going to pay at all and that they had no more room in their jails for pro-lifers, they backed down entirely. They realized that they could do nothing as long as Cavanaugh-O'Keefe's people were willing to pay the price.

The price did seem a heavy one, however, as Joan's own experience testified. The prison administrators had been hard on her, taking away all of her "good time," the time that counts toward an early release. Had she cooperated, Joan would have been released on January 2, 1988, but now the date had been pushed back to April 19, 1991. They wanted to make an example of her, Joan believed, to frighten other pro-lifers away from direct action. They wanted to make them believe that taking part in a sit-in would cost them five years of freedom. But, Joan insisted, it was only the first ones who had to run such a risk and bear so heavy a burden.

"I don't think people should be scared off because of what has happened to me. They were going to hit me hard, and I knew it. When I made my decision, I was prepared. I was in court waiting for the judge to sentence me when I decided not to cooperate." A picture taken at the sentencing shows her sitting cross-legged on the floor. Guards had to carry her out. "I wasn't thinking in terms of strategy or practical effects at that moment. Rather it just seemed to me in personal terms that this was the only thing I could do.

"After the war, Germans would say how much they were opposed to the Nazis, and that was good, to be opposed to the Nazis, just as it's good to be opposed to abortion. But what had these Germans done? If you don't do anything physically and actually to stop an evil, then you are cooperating with it. We all are, unless we're doing something to undermine it. A holocaust cannot be carried out without cooperation. The government cannot mass-murder people unless the whole society agrees to it. You can oppose it by everyone saying, I'm not going to work anymore. I'm not going to pay taxes anymore."

What she was calling for, some would be quick to say, sounded very much like anarchy, but Joan was quite sure that even massive noncooperation would not have so drastic an effect. Long before that, she said, the government would have to relent and draw back from its legitimization of abortion. "The Supreme Court decision allowing abortion, that was anarchy. Saying that a certain class of human beings was outside the protection of the laws, that was anarchy."

During her stay in prison, a major source of consolation, she said, was the more than 30,000 letters she's received. "Such wonderful letters! Somebody writes: 'I've always been against abortion, but I've never done anything. Now I'm going out to an abortion mill every week. I've got my wife to go or my priest or my minister.' The letters are just gorgeous."

There was indeed evidence that her courage and example, far from frightening off pro-lifers, were inspiring and sustaining them — people like her codefendant in Pittsburgh, Joe Wall, a sixty-year-old Philadelphia accountant who was fired from the city controller's office where he had worked for twenty years when he used his vacation time to serve a jail sentence, and ChristyAnne Collins of Falls Church, Virginia, whose rescue efforts have earned her jail term after jail term and the enmity of the local prosecutor, who invariably demanded the maximum sentence.

"It's been terribly hard in prison. Terribly, terribly hard. Physically, psychologically hard. Spiritually it's been good. When you're doing what you feel God wants you to do, you feel good. You can sleep at night — despite the noise." She laughed, recalling the din of prison nights.

I asked the young guard with the nice smile if she'd take our picture. I focused the camera and she took a picture of us standing by the grilled window with the garish drapes.

That night at the Brindles', Susan and I stayed up late talking after she and her husband, Dave, an engineer, had put all the children to bed. Susan had been picketing the courthouse in Tallahassee with a sign that read: "Free my sister, Joan Andrews." A tall, rugged middle-aged man got out of a jeep and walked toward the entrance. He wore a Stetson hat, but his manner and his expensive clothes led Susan to believe that he was a judge or a lawyer. When he saw Susan's sign, he frowned and said: "Your sister belongs in jail."

Susan was still there when he came out. She saw him leaving by a side door and hurried over to catch him as he got into his jeep. "Excuse me, sir," she said softly, "but if you think my sister belongs in jail, do you think that babies belong in trash cans?"

The man looked at her, Susan said, and to her surprise, tears came into his eyes. "Pray for me," he said, "and my faithlessness."

Another story that Susan told that night — "Joannie always says I talk too much," she confessed — was quite different. It was romantic, but, more significant, it underscored in a very special way just how total was her sister's rejection of violence. A Jesuit seminarian involved in rescue missions had invited Joan to a talk at St. Louis University given by a friend of his, a stalwart and handsome Annapolis graduate who was a Marine officer. The officer's theme that night, as it had been for other lectures he had been giving throughout the country, had been the Christian soldier. A devout Catholic, he accepted the just war theory, but unlike many of its proponents he didn't hesitate about the obligation to refuse to fight if one believes that a war is unjust. The Jesuit introduced Joan afterward, and she was quite impressed with the man's evident faith and the sincerity of his convictions even though she disagreed with some of his conclusions. The Marine officer, for his part, was taken with Joan. They began to date. His younger brother, moreover, also a Naval Academy graduate, began to date Miriam, a relationship that was to culminate in marriage. For Joan and the older brother, however, it was not to be. Much as she cared for him, she found his profession too much of an obstacle.

Eight months after my visit with Joan, on the afternoon of October 18, 1988, I was standing on a corner in Pittsburgh experiencing déjà vu prompted by an ornate and graceful covered stone walkway that arched over the street behind Pittsburgh's Victorian-era courthouse and linked it to the jail. It wasn't déjà vu in the strict sense. I had in reality seen the arch before. If the movies counted as reality, that is. Diane Keaton had crossed it as the eponymous heroine in Australian director Gillian Armstrong's film *Mrs. Soffel,* about a warden's pious wife who fell madly in love with an imprisoned desperado in 1910 and helped him escape. The film was based on a true story, and the picture had ended with Mrs. Soffel's crossing the bridge one last time, not a visitor bearing Bibles for the prisoners but this time a prisoner herself. The somber *Mrs. Soffel* was the kind of film that lingered in the memory even if it was essentially a melodrama. A real drama had taken place in the courthouse that morning, and another unlikely prisoner had crossed the quaint bridge of carved stone. The courthouse itself, an awesome stone pile put up in 1888 with a huge peaked tower several stories high, was built in European fashion around a center courtyard about sixty feet long and forty feet wide. It was the Escorial, writ small but still impressive. Four arched passageways gave access to the courtyard, in the center of which was a fountain. At eight o'clock that morning, Susan Brindle's three older children, Mary, Andrew, and John, had been sitting beside the fountain, empty now in October, while their mother stood nearby talking into a mike held by a black radio reporter with a tape recorder slung over his shoulders. Perhaps twenty or so other people, presumably supporters of Joan Andrews, were standing around the fountain.

Joan Andrews was finally going to have her long-delayed confrontation with Judge Raymond Novak, who three years earlier had told her lawyer that he was going to give her six years. In the middle of July, Joan's relative idyll at Claymont had come to an end. Because of her continued noncooperation, Delaware sent her back to Broward. The Florida authorities made no bones about their intention of breaking her will and making her conform. The homecoming to Broward had been brutal. When she refused a strip search, five guards, including a male, tore off her clothes and subjected her to a painful and humiliating cavity search. Despite Florida's best and worst efforts, however, Joan, true to her word, did not budge an inch. It was, again as she had predicted, Florida that had backed down. Susan had given me the news the previous week over the phone: Florida was releasing Joan to Pennsylvania so she could be sentenced for her conviction for the

May 1985 action in Pittsburgh, and the moment she was sentenced in Pennsylvania her Florida sentence would be commuted.

But what would her Pennsylvania sentence be? If Judge Anderson in Florida had given her five years, it seemed that the Honorable Raymond Novak had ammunition enough to make good his threat of six. The disruption that Joan had wreaked at the Pittsburgh abortion clinic in May 1985 went far beyond what she had done in Pensacola. She and Joe Wall — a kindly grandfather figure with a Santa Claus beard — had barricaded themselves in a room, and the police had had to force their way in to arrest them. They had been convicted of criminal mischief, defiant trespassing, and resisting arrest. Joan had spent a month in jail awaiting trial. She was freed on her own recognizance after she and Joe Wall were convicted, and she still hadn't been sentenced when she pulled the plug on the suction machine in Pensacola.

Doris Grady, a kindly but authoritative-looking blond woman in her forties, who had been arrested with Joan and Joe three years before, gathered the supporters, now about forty, beneath one of the archways leading to the street. It offered welcome shelter from the drizzle that had begun to fall from a dark sky.

"Joan wants us to have a prayer service," she said. "We should always try to remember all that she stands for — humility and a willingness to give of self." A tall, thin priest began the rosary, and everyone joined in. The group was as motley as any collection of Plowshares supporters. There were three priests in clerical black, however, a garb not often seen at Plowshares gatherings. Another difference was that here the religious emphasis, despite strong Protestant support for Joan, was quite specifically Catholic and, save for a couple of anti-Dukakis buttons, nonpolitical, in contrast to the more general Christian cast and more political character of the Plowshares supporters. Both groups favored buttons with sometimes aggressive slogans, but the pro-life people showed a more pronounced fondness for religious medals and other artifacts of popular Catholicism.

Standing next to me was a man with scruffy reddish-brown whiskers wearing an orange and blue Mets hat. His brown corduroy sport jacket was much the worse for wear. With it he wore jeans and dirty running shoes. Pinned to the jacket were the red rose of the pro-life movement and a scapular medal.

After the rosary, someone read a passage from the New Testament, Matthew 25, the Last Judgment. Come you, Blessed of my Father, enter into eternal life. Depart from me, you accursed. Whatever you did to the least of mine brethren, you did to me. The straight stuff. No ambiguity here. The New Testament was indeed a dangerous book. The wonder was the ease with which so long a line of secular and ecclesiastical establishments had been able to get away with pretending to adhere to its message.

The trial was scheduled to begin at 9:30; by 8:45 a modest crowd was already standing outside the closed door to Room 315, which apparently held only about forty people. Several Allegheny County deputies were lined up against the wall. The corridor went all the way around the building, the courtrooms and offices on one side and windows on the other looking down on the courtyard.

The crowd kept growing. By close to trial time, there were about 150 of Joan's supporters filling the corridor. The deputies made periodic forays to try to get people into a single line on the window side, but the most they could manage was one, two, or three deep. The crowd by now extended down the hallway on either side of the courtroom door and around the corners at either end.

The crowd was quite cheerful. People began to sing "Here I Am, Lord," a post–Vatican II song that was more tolerable than many:

Here I am Lord. Is it I, Lord?
I have heard You calling in the night.
I will go, Lord, if You lead me.
I will hold Your people in my heart.

Then Joe Sheidler, a tall burly man from Chicago dressed in black and wearing a black eye patch, started the "Battle Hymn of the Republic." A bit later, Dick Trainor, a handsome gray-haired lawyer and a pro-life leader from New Jersey, urged everybody to be quiet. Earlier the suggestion had been passed down that we maintain silence for Joan, but that didn't last too long. Now, however, I noticed Fr. James Cusack standing by a window, his lips moving in silent prayer. He was the tall, thin priest who had begun the rosary in the courtyard. A long-time supporter of Joan and her spiritual counselor, Cusack was Irish; as a member of the famed Columban missionary order, he had spent years in the Philippines. There the Columbans had run afoul of local authorities because of their courageous support for exploited peasants, and a few of them had gone to jail. Some pro-lifers, Joan had told me, had murmured about Cusack's being a Communist because he had shown a film that depicted just what was going on in the area in which he worked. You could approach a rich landowner, Cusack had said, to ask for money if one of his workers desperately needed medical attention, but you could never persuade him that he had a duty to pay a just wage.

The usual denizens of a big-city courthouse cruised up and down the corridors all the while, lawyers and functionaries of various ilks, the younger ones especially favoring a masculine swagger that evoked the locker room. Sometimes they stopped to engage the deputies, whose numbers had grown, in jovial and occasionally profane exchanges. They were in their element. The group who bore the long wait — it was well past 9:30 by now — with the least equanimity seemed to be the representatives of the media. How young they seemed! Especially the newspaper reporters with their pads and pencils. Joan, the youngest of the Catholic radicals I knew well, had turned forty. The 1960s were a vivid reality to her. How would her idealism and sacrifice strike these youngsters?

One of Joan's lawyers, John Broderick, a burly man with a crewcut who could easily have been a retired NFL lineman, came along to tell Susan and Joe Wall that the delay was due to the judge's studying a motion to dismiss. Finally, at 10:55, the deputies suddenly abandoned their posts by the door of Room 315 and disappeared around the corner. After a moment's hesitation, the crowd followed with a rush. The courtroom had been switched.

Because of my lack of credentials and slowness of foot, I had all but given up hope of getting into the courtroom, especially after I saw the reporters ahead of me presenting their plastic ID cards to the sergeant at the door. When my turn came, I confessed straight out that I had no credentials, but, to my surprise, he let me go in. I found myself sitting in the first row just behind the table where Joan and her lawyers sat. The media had been let in first, and now the less-privileged public was being admitted one by one. First came Susan and the three children, who sat behind me. Finally, after about fifty spectators had been seated, the doors were closed.

The prosecutor entered unattended and took his place at the table on the right, followed by Joan Andrews's four lawyers. Then Joan herself came in. A thrill ran through the courtroom, prompting an officious deputy to warn against demonstrations.

Joan wore blue jeans and a blue denim prison shirt rolled up above her elbows. Her arms were thin and very white. I had seen her briefly a second time at Claymont in May, and she had looked much better than she had during my February visit. In anticipation of a return to Broward, she had cut her long hair. Her face had been fuller and had lost some of the prison pallor of February. Another sign of the more humane regime in Delaware had been the pro-life red rose stitched to her green uniform jacket. Now, however, she was even gaunter and paler than she had been in February, and there was no red rose on her jacket. Joan had come up from Florida just a day or two before. True to her word, she hadn't given an inch, but the struggle had obviously taken its toll.

She glanced around briefly, the usual shy smile on her face, before sitting down with her lawyers.

Judge Raymond J. Novak came in, a tall handsome man in his forties with short, neatly styled brown hair. He looked like a less full-faced Charles Grodin, though without Grodin's mobile features. His confrontation with Joan today had an ironic twist. For Novak was an ex-priest, and, whatever effect that had on his outlook, the record showed that he readily took cases involving pro-life activists and dealt out stringent sentences, taking care to explain that, while he appreciated the defendants' idealism, he had no choice but to uphold the law. On the face of it, it looked bad for Joan, but then much had happened in the three years that had passed since Novak had threatened to give her six years.

The session began with the prosecutor, whose name was Dugan, reading the guidelines that were in effect for the offenses for which Joan had been convicted. Simple criminal trespass was zero to twelve months; aggravated criminal trespass was twelve to eighteen. Then, under special circumstances, the sentence could eschew confinement altogether. Prosecutor Dugan explained that he was quite satisfied with these guidelines as they applied to the present case. The victims, moreover — the directors of the Women's Health Service — had declined the opportunity to be present and offer a statement.

One of Joan's attorneys, Franklin Conflente, then rose to ask Judge Novak if two doctors present could be allowed to give testimony that life began at conception. As he had to, the prosecutor objected, but in a conciliatory fashion. The commonwealth of Pennsylvania, he said, did not consider the question of when life began at all germane to the case, but he did not intend to dispute that the defendant in fact believed that life began at conception when she committed her offense.

Joan's lawyer countered by citing a decision of the Pennsylvania Supreme Court involving insurance payments in a case where a pregnant woman was killed in an auto accident. The court had ruled that the fetus was a person and that compensation had to be paid on its account as well as that of the mother.

Judge Novak answered that, in line with what the district attorney had said, he would, in terms of mitigating circumstances, take into consideration the beliefs of the defendant about when life began but that he was unwilling to go beyond that. Then Novak mentioned something that those close to the case had already heard about: a personal letter from the attorney general of Delaware on Joan's behalf. Novak was taking this too into consideration, he said.

Conflente then introduced John Broderick as a New York lawyer who wished to make a statement on Joan's behalf.

The hulking Broderick got to his feet, amiable and relaxed, and made his way to the bench. "Forty years ago," he said, addressing Novak, "a very special little girl was born in Tennessee. She would grow up to be a woman who loved God, her fellow men, and her country."

Broderick then went on to tell how Joan had saved her cousin by having him stand on her shoulders. "And when people asked her how she could do that," said Broderick, "she answered that it was the only way she could think of to save him, an example of how totally self-sacrificing Joan Andrews was and is." At sixteen, Brodrick said, she volunteered as a cook in a nursing home, and he described how she cared for Vietnamese orphans and how she and her sisters had established maternity homes in St. Louis and Delaware. He told about her habit of giving her winter coats away, something that certainly recalled all the classic stories of the saints familiar to anybody who had ever attended a parochial school, a number that most likely included the Honorable Raymond J. Novak.

There was no way of telling what effect Broderick's eloquence was having, however. Presumably the judge, prosecutor, and lawyers had thrashed everything out in chambers while the rest of us were cooling our heels in the corridor, as the docility of the district attorney seemed to indicate. Perhaps the record demanded rhetoric of this sort. At any rate, Novak sat, head forward, with his fingertips pressed against his shut eyes. Were Broderick's words sinking deep within his soul? Were they boring him? Had he been Charles Grodin, a raised eyebrow or something of the sort would have tipped us off.

Broderick got to *Roe vs. Wade* and its effect on Joan. "Consider," he said to Novak, "what abortion is. What is it that a baby wants, after all? A baby wants love, love, love."

Novak had opened his eyes, and, still not looking at Broderick, he began to scribble something. Chances were slim that it was "love, love, love."

"Someday, as a boy or girl," Broderick went on, "that baby will perhaps want to walk into a church or synagogue and sing a hymn to his or her Creator. But what does abortion offer a baby? Being crushed by pincers, being burnt to death with a saline solution. When abortion became commonplace, we turned a blind eye and a deaf ear. We were all too preoccupied to hear a baby's scream." Novak, eyes downcast, was holding his hand to his mouth. "Joan Andrews did not turn away, however. Joan Andrews took on this battle even though she had nothing to put between the baby and the abortionist but her own body, and we are all in her debt because of it."

Broderick described the arrest in Pensacola and Joan's refusal to cooperate while in prison because of her desire to make things that much more difficult for the system that was supporting abortion on demand. Novak had his eyes open by now, but his hand was still pressed to his mouth. "She spent twenty-one months in solitary confinement," said Broderick. "All she had to do to get out was agree to cooperate. Solitary is a terrible thing. There are two or three things that make life bearable. You get three meals, and you get out for a half hour twice a week. Joan, however, took only one meal, and she wouldn't take advantage of being able to go out since it would smack of cooperation. By doing what she did, Joan Andrews was paying for our sins of indifference and neglect. For I suggest that we are all guilty. When Judgment Day comes, we'll all have a lot of marks, I think, on the left side of the ledger. Today is a day to put something on the right. For ourselves, for the city of Pittsburgh. Set Joan Andrews free. Punishment is for the guilty. Punishment is not for the innocent. The tens of thousands of letters she's received in prison testify to what she is. This angel of mercy has suffered enough."

Broderick had finished. I couldn't see Joan Andrews's expression since she had her back to me, but, like Novak, she had kept her head bowed throughout the presentation. However Broderick's panegyric might have affected the judge, it seemed safe to presume that it provoked significant discomfort in the one being judged.

A third lawyer, Robert Dougherty, got up from the table. He was in his sixties, and his scant blond hair was frizzled in a style that suggested a permanent that hadn't taken. I had noticed Dougherty passing through the crowd in the corridor earlier in the day. He had been walking with his head slightly bent, a faint smirk playing over his features as though he were amused at the fallibility of human nature and the prospects this offered his profession. Until he had sat down at the defense table, there was no way of knowing that he was in fact allied with the forces of light. As I learned later, Dougherty was a veteran Pittsburgh criminal lawyer with a substantial balance in his deposit at the local favor bank.

Dougherty began by saying that he was honored to be able to speak in behalf of the defendant. "I've had to promise her to refrain from praising her. Otherwise, she said, she might go so far as to forget her nonviolent principles and punch me right in the nose." It didn't sound like Joan's kind of joke, but perhaps you had to have been there.

He called for a sentence of nonconfinement on the grounds of the mitigated circumstances that attended the trespassing offense. Joan, he said, had no intention of doing anyone any sort of injury. "I beseech Your

Honor to consider her intentions, not as an excuse for her offense, but as a mitigating circumstance. This was not merely a case of criminal trespass. For Joan Edwards a deeper principle was involved." There was a muted reaction from those around me at Dougherty's slip, but no one at the defense table made any move to correct him. Since Joan's frequent clashes with the law of the land had taken place in a variety of states, she was always being defended by new lawyers. Nor had she ever given any thought to how she was defended as long as no defender dared to ascribe one iota of contrition to her or to promise that she would behave like a good girl.

Dougherty went on to invoke the Dred Scott case. Anyone who aided an escaped slave could have been charged with larceny, but nonetheless the Underground Railroad flourished because enough Americans realized that the laws that protected slavery were clearly immoral and did not have to be obeyed. He cited Rosa Parks, who decided that she would not move to the back of a Montgomery bus, as another example of an individual who had decided that enough was enough and unjust laws were not to be tolerated. He cited the Supreme Court's 1954 decision in *Brown vs. Board of Education*, which declared unconstitutional an unjust set of laws providing for "separate but equal" educational facilities for blacks and whites, no matter that they had been in force for the better part of a century, and declared furthermore that the injustice that they had perpetrated had to be abandoned "with all deliberate speed." And so it was, said Dougherty, that those who broke unjust laws were one day vindicated.

Dougherty, who had been pacing back and forth in front of Novak, now turned and walked behind the defense table, stopping at last behind Joan Andrews and putting his hand on her shoulder.

"In all my years as a lawyer, I've dealt with all sorts of people accused of crimes, but never have I experienced the kind of shock I felt when I first saw Joan Edwards as she was walking out of the bullpen to meet with me. Nor have I ever known anybody who said that she deserved the punishment of solitary confinement — not because of her noncooperation — but because of her failure to save more lives."

Judge Novak was hiding his face in his hands once more. Was he pondering the wisdom of straightening out Dougherty on his client's name?

Coming from behind the table and approaching the bench, Dougherty repeated the request with which he had begun his plea: a sentence of nonconfinement by way of mitigating circumstances. "The law's function is not to rip the conscience out of an individual. The law can acknowledge the motivation behind an offense done in a nonviolent manner. No, we can't ask for credit for the time Joan Edwards spent in prison in Florida, but we can ask that this time spent be considered as another mitigating circumstance. Joe Wall, after all, did not spend two years in solitary confinement. And as I need hardly say, Your Honor, no amount of incarceration will take away Joan Edwards's God-given right to dissent.

"I have one thing left to say." Dougherty paused for effect and then began to intone: " 'The quality of mercy is not strained. / It falleth like the gentle rain from Heaven upon the place beneath.' "

"Oh no!" groaned a young woman reporter sitting next to me without looking up from her pad.

After Dougherty had finished doing Portia, there was some formal business that involved reading various statements into the record. Then it was that Judge Novak addressed Joan Andrews directly for the first time.

"You have, Miss Andrews, the right to address the court on your own behalf, but it is my understanding that you've declined this privilege. I have been further given to understand" — Novak's eyes shifted to Joan's lawyers for a moment — "that you wish to withdraw a statement that you made at the time of your trial. I am obliged, however, to hear that directly from you before acting on it."

There was a brief whispered conference at the defense table. Then Conflente rose to his feet, a strained expression on his face. "Miss Andrews does not wish to withdraw the statement, Your Honor. She would like, in fact, for it to be read into the record at this time."

"Very well," said Novak, his face a blank.

Conflente sat down, and Dougherty got up and approached the bench, a paper in his hand. "Your Honor," he said, his tone ingratiating, "in this statement she made three years ago, Joan Edwards said that she — "

"Joan Andrews," said Novak. His head was up now, but he didn't look at Dougherty as he corrected him.

"Joan Andrews," said Dougherty, unruffled. "Excuse me. Joan Andrews. Joan Andrews said that her actions speak for themselves and that her conscience compelled her to do — "

"No, no, Mr. Dougherty," said Novak, interrupting once more, his voice flat. "Miss Andrews stated that she would like the statement read. So please don't paraphrase it. Let's hear it as she wrote it."

It was an electric moment. Doris Grady, someone later said, sobbed and nearly broke down, sure that now there'd be no hope for clemency.

Dougherty began to read. Joan's declaration, given the highly charged context, could have easily held its own with Portia's speech, but Dougherty, needless to say, did his best to underplay it. It wasn't the time for dramatic effect: " 'My actions speak for themselves,' " he read. " 'Anybody who would have done less in my circumstances would be as worthy of contempt as is this court for condemning me for doing what I did.' " Judge Novak was looking down once more, though probably not out of boredom this time. " 'I hold this court, therefore, in utter contempt. Do your worst. Give me death, if you like. Whatever you do will be small punishment to me for my failures to save babies.' "

There were no further comments from Joan's lawyers. What could they say, after all? Their client had done her best to cut the ground out from under them and herself. Had Joan been willing to withdraw her statement, it would have been possible to dismiss it as an impassioned outburst. But now she had insisted on repeating it despite having had two and a half long years to reflect on its implications. It seemed that Joan had done her worst. But no, not yet.

There was a hush in the courtroom as Judge Novak gathered together his notes.

"In making my judgment in this case," Novak said at last, "I have had to take into consideration a number of diverse factors. First the issue raised by defense counsel on when life begins. The case cited has to do with an infant being injured in the womb. I agree there does seem to be an inconsistency in the law of the commonwealth of Pennsylvania on this point, but after combing through the five opinions given in the case in question, I see no indication that justices had any intention whatsoever of addressing the issues involved in the *Roe vs. Wade* decision.

"Secondly, the governor of Florida has agreed to commute Miss Andrews's five-year sentence to time served, but it is a conditional commutation that does not take effect until she receives a sentence in Allegheny County, Pennsylvania."

"Then it is necessary to consider the circumstances of Miss Andrews's offense. She and Joseph Wall and thirteen others entered the building of Women's Health Service at 7:30 A.M. on November 6, 1985. Their intention was to perform what they called a 'rescue.' Miss Andrews and Joseph Wall blocked the door of Operating Room 6. At that time they removed some sterilized instruments and bandages from a cabinet and rendered them unsterile. The police repeatedly asked them to leave, but Miss Andrews said that they could not leave as long as 'babies are being killed.'

"On November 12, 1985, Miss Andrews and Mr. Wall were convicted of defiant trespassing, criminal mischief, and resisting arrest. At a later date, Mr. Wall was sentenced to six to twelve months in prison and two years' probation. This sentence was confirmed by a superior court, and now Mr.

Wall is free pending an appeal to the Supreme Court of Pennsylvania.

"Finally, we have considered the guidelines applicable to the case. Miss Andrews has been convicted sixty-seven times though, for the most part, not at the level of either a misdemeanor or felony." Novak cited a 1984 Maryland sentence of ninety days with sixty suspended and a Delaware sentence the same year of two years' probation.

Novak paused as he picked up a sheet of paper. "I have here a letter that I received from the attorney general of Delaware. It's a brutally frank letter. He writes that he finds it unbelievable and tragic that a sister state, Florida, should have treated Joan Andrews as it has — trying to exact a pound of flesh from her, trying to break her morally and physically. Each case, the attorney general says, must be judged on its own merits, and even though he by no means agrees with Miss Andrews's position on abortion, he feels that justice demands that she be treated humanely and fairly."

Novak paused again. The courtroom was still. Joan's devout supporters were, it was safe to say, calling down blessings on the head of Charles Oberly III, attorney general of Delaware. He had given them hope.

"I sentenced Joseph Wall to six to twelve months with three years' probation." Novak looked straight at Joan for a second time. "Miss Andrews, I want you to know that I do understand you." (Was it the feel of the black robes that induced such presumption?) "You consider yourself an instrument of God to save lives. I, on the other hand, am an instrument of the law. I sentenced Mr. Wall to six months in prison because his chronic defiance was such that only through incarceration could the law be served. Your counsel is correct, however, in noting that Mr. Wall did not serve two years in solitary confinement and that I therefore have grounds to distinguish between the two of you. It seems fair to presume that any purpose that could be served by incarceration has already been achieved in your case. Everything points to a sentence of probation without incarceration."

I heard a faint gasp from Susan behind me. That was it then. Whatever else, Joan Andrews would go free today. Or so it seemed. I glanced around. Susan was smiling but still tense and distracted. Novak had more to say. And there was no telling what Joan herself might say.

"One of your attorneys has told me that he has made great effort to persuade you to channel your energies into anti-abortion activity that remains within the law." Novak paused. He allowed himself the barest trace of an ironic smile. "He has, I must confess, more faith in his ability to influence you in this regard than do I." Novak paused again, looking Joan full in the face. "Your sentence, then, will be time served and three years' probation." I heard a faint gasp from Susan behind me. Novak's tone became stern. "If you violate probation by deliberately disobeying the law and are convicted of any other crimes, you will also be charged with violating your probation. I will not tolerate defiance."

This neatly coifed instrument of the law, confident in his robes of office, would not tolerate defiance. As a seminarian, Novak must have gotten a classical education, at least of sorts. If he had ever read *Antigone*, there surely must have been a small voice somewhere within him warning him that he was emulating Creon. Perhaps he had heard the voice. Maybe that's why he was so self-righteous.

"In accordance with a legal finding I made in the case of Joseph Wall, I may not exact from you a promise to obey as a condition of probation. I fully expect to meet you again under similar circumstances. I ardently hope that this is not so, however, and that this chalice will pass away from me. But if I must drink it, I will."

Whatever Novak's classical background, as an ex-priest he knew Scripture. But not that well, it seemed. Simple good taste, moreover, should have forestalled the rashness of comparing himself to Christ even if the circumstances had been a hundred times more favorable than they were.

Joan Andrews got to her feet for the first time, prompting, one could imagine, appreciable anxiety in her lawyers. "I can't accept probation with any conditions attached," she said.

Another hush in the courtroom. Another gasp from the long-suffering Susan. I glanced quickly over my shoulder. She was pressing the knuckles of her right hand against her teeth and Mary and Andrew — I couldn't see her son Dan — were doing the same.

Novak smiled faintly. "I'm not asking you to accept it. But I do urge you to listen to the advice of your counsel. Mr. Broderick assures me that he has plans for you."

Joan sat down. Now she had done her worst. A woman two rows behind got to her feet and hurried toward the door. As soon as she was gone, we heard a happy roar from the crowd outside. It was over after nearly an hour and a half.

The Honorable Raymond J. Novak left us. Once more the deputy warned the spectators against a demonstration, and two other deputies hurriedly escorted Joan from the courtroom as she smiled and tried to catch sight of familiar faces.

Reporters crowded around John Broderick. What kinds of plans did he have in mind? "Well," said Broderick genially, "there's a lot she can do. She can give talks, inspire people. A general, after all, doesn't have to go into the trenches with the troops." General Andrews? Novak was right. Broderick had his work cut out for him.

Joan Andrews was sentenced at about 1:30 in the afternon, but her joyful supporters had to wait some three hours before they had their heroine among them once more after two and a half years. They waited in the courtyard for a while, and then some of them made their way down the street that ran behind the courthouse to the jail annex, where Joan was being processed for release. The long wait had been hard on many, especially seventy-nine-year-old Fr. John Dobson, a Jesuit from St. Peter's College in Jersey City, who was bothered by varicose veins. He, too, had been arrested several times at rescue operations.

Since most of Joan's supporters had decided to wait in the courtyard, the cluster of people gathered outside the annex wasn't that large, no more than thirty or so, including a much reduced television and press contingent. In the course of the tedious wait, there was an unexpected diversion. A city bus stopped across the street, and a black woman stuck her head out. "Why don't you people do something to help pregnant women instead of doing all that screaming about abortion?" she shouted. "Any of you people ever thought of adopting a black baby? No!"

Richard Bruno, a big affable man in his forties, got to his feet — he had been sitting on the sidewalk next to Fr. Dobson — and rushed over to the bus and held up to the woman a picture of a handsome black boy of about ten, which he carried in his billfold. "Here's one who has," said Bruno. The woman got off the bus and crossed the street. For about ten minutes, ignoring Bruno's protests, she berated the pro-lifers, while reporters held up microphones and the lone remaining television crew filmed her. "Yeah, you got one here, don't you," she said looking disdainfully at a black teenage girl neatly dressed in a Catholic school uniform. The woman, who was in her thirties, was in no mood to listen. She had obviously been through a lot, and an unlooked-for opportunity to vent her rage and hurt had come her way.

"It's just not fair," said Bruno, shaking his head after the woman had gone. "I adopted this boy as my son. Lots of pro-lifers adopt black children." There were tears in his eyes.

Finally, the word came about 3:30 that Joan Andrews was about to come out. Susan went inside, carrying some clothes she had brought. When Joan did emerge, however, a broad smile on her pale face, she was still wearing her ill-fitting prison uniform. She hadn't wanted to take the time to change.

A shout went up. Susan, after so many disappointments, was beside herself with happiness as her children, Mary, Andrew, and Daniel, clutched the hands of their aunt.

Joan began to hug everybody, beginning with the children and Fr. Dobson, as cameras whirred and clicked. Doris Grady took a "Free Joan Andrews" bumper sticker and stuck it to the front of Joan's blue prison shirt. She had altered it with a marker to read: "Freed Joan Andrews." Laughter and cheers. Somebody gave Joan a bouquet of rosebuds, and she held them up, delighted. Then, without a moment's hesitation, she began to pass the roses out one by one to those around her. As she did, she saw me standing in the background, like one born out of due time, and she held out a rose to me. We hugged each other, her face pressed hard against my shoulder.

The group began to move up the street toward the courthouse, a progress that became a triumphal procession that caused heads to turn. Who was the skinny woman in the ugly, ill-fitting clothes and why all the fuss over her? Those waiting at the courthouse came out to meet us and both groups merged beneath the arched entranceway where the prayer service had been held early that morning.

There were more hugs and shouts of joy. Joan had no roses left to give out. She hadn't even kept one for herself. Somebody starting to sing "Here I Am, Lord," and everybody joined in. Then somebody else began a livelier song, one I had never heard before: a Joan Andrews version of the Davy Crockett song. Its refrain ran something like this:

Joan, Joanie Andrews, Queen of the pro-lifers!

There was more laughter. Still more hugs. Doris Grady announced that there was going to be a Mass in an hour or so — she wasn't sure where yet — and then there would be a party in the evening. Somebody called for Joan to make a speech, and others joined in. Joan made no speech. She had a request, however. Doris conveyed it to the crowd: "The abortion mill Joan and Joe got arrested at is not too far from here," she said. "Joan wants to go over there and say some prayers of thanksgiving."

Two months later, in early December, I drove Joan Andrews from Susan's home in Delaware up through New Jersey to New York City for a talk arranged by Eileen Egan at the St. Joseph's Catholic Worker house on the Lower East Side.

For the first time since Claymont — for the first time ever, in fact — we had the opportunity and leisure to talk about any number of things. When at sixteen, she said, she had heard about the murders of Andrew Goodman, James Chaney, and Michael Schwerner in Mississippi, she had become so angry that she had wanted to go right down there herself and confront the killers. The movie *Mississippi Burning* hadn't come out yet to refocus attention on the martyred civil rights workers, but she had no difficulty recalling the full names of all three.

In the weeks following her release, Joan had been traveling all over the country giving talks to pro-life groups, the kind of blameless activity that John Broderick had envisaged for her. It hadn't ended with that, however, despite Judge Novak's stern warning. Joan was incorrigible. General Andrews persisted in thinking of herself as a private and her place the trenches. There was an ugly black bruise on her left cheek, a souvenir of a rescue operation in Burlington, Vermont, a few days before. Her face had struck the floor of a paddy wagon as she was trying to crawl back out of it. Tomorrow, moreover, she and Joe Wall were going to take part in a rescue mission in Manhattan.

When I parked the car, she left her shabby overcoat inside even though it was rather cold. It seemed that the Burlington police, having no space in their jail, had used a garage to process the sixty pro-lifers they had arrested, and her coat had gotten grease all over it when the police had dragged her across the floor. The concern of most of us who spoke at the Catholic Worker usually lay in the other direction: we took care not to look too well dressed.

Some homeless women were sitting in the front hall when we came in, and Joan stopped to distribute money to them and to ask them to pray for the rescue mission the next day. They all loudly assured her that they would. One of them told her that she had a poodle that had belonged to Zsa Zsa Gabor. The stench that came from one of the women, from at least one, was overpowering, but Joan lingered and talked with them, the usual shy smile on her face.

Joe Wall, who in another month would become a fugitive from justice — Allegheny County justice — came up from Philadelphia in time for Joan's talk, and afterward I drove Joan and him to Co-op City in the Bronx, where they were spending the night at the apartment of Tom Herlihy, an electrical worker who, like Joan and Joe, had given up everything to devote himself to the cause of the unborn. All three would be arrested the next day along with 150 others, two of them Catholic Workers who had been at Joan's talk.

Joan was worried about my having to drive all the way back to New Jersey that night. "You could stay with us," she said. But then she thought for a moment. "Of course, your wife probably wants you to come home. I know if I were married, I'd want my husband to come home every night. . . . Unless he was in jail, of course."

I Want to Be Honest

Archbishop Raymond G. Hunthausen

It's not your standard Washington cocktail party. Nobody's in uniform. Yet everybody's dressed alike. In black. A restless sea of black laps at the walls of the room and eddies into its corners, and black waves, white Roman collars riding their crest, break against the bar. To take a step is to risk spilling an archbishop's Scotch and water or perhaps even a cardinal's. Made much of at home in their own dioceses, prelates and princes of the Church find happy release among equals, relatively speaking, recalling days when they were sometimes told the truth and were even served a bad meal. First names are the rule now, and bluff Irish-American good cheer, the lingua franca of the North American hierarchy, prevails.

There is one prelate, however, whom no one calls by his first name. He is definitely not one of the boys. His hooded eyes ooze craft. His face is an actor's face, the face of the doge's councilor, the king's minister, the emperor's plenipotentiary, or, as it indeed happens, the pope's viceroy, the Apostolic pro nuncio to the United States, His Grace, Pio Laghi, by the Grace of God Archbishop of Mauriana *(in partibus infidelium)*.

During his long sojourn in Washington, Archbishop Laghi has countenanced the appointment of more than a hundred bishops, a quarter of the American hierarchy, including a dozen of its thirty-three archbishops. No wonder, then, that he glides through the black sea trailing a wake of deference. When he draws near, voices modulate, jokes trail off. Some in the room wield spiritual authority over millions of Catholics and oversee vast networks of schools and hospitals and welfare institutions. A few, for good or ill, are major players in the raucous day-to-day dramas of cities so famous that bars and discotheques bear their names in Tokyo, Paris, and Berlin, not to mention Rome. But no matter. They, too, nod and smile ingratiatingly when Archbishop Laghi looks their way. No matter either that barefoot Berber children chase goats through the dusty marketplace of the archbishop's see. The tide of Islam may have engulfed it before Charlemagne was born, but Rome still carries it on the books for purposes of her own. Though they have no flocks, her bureaucrats have no qualms about usurping a shepherd's authority.

Yes, yes, His Holiness will be pleased at the support that the American hierarchy has shown the Holy See. How sad this Hunthausen affair has been! A good man, the Archbishop of Seattle. A holy man, too, I'm sure. But an enthusiastic man, no? Yes, yes. Enthusiasm is commendable . . . a virtue, in fact. But there must be a limit even to virtue, especially in a shepherd of souls. Holy Mother Church has seen much. Her view is the view of the ages.

The blood of martyrs is the seed of Christians, said Tertullian, but if the Roman martyrs had set prudent limits to their enthusiasm, where now would be Pio Laghi's authority? Where now would be the trappings of rank and the dignities of office that set Pio Laghi apart from other men?

How difficult it would be to find two men more different than Raymond G. Hunthausen and Pio Laghi. Both archbishops of the Roman Catholic Church, one of Seattle, one of Mauriana *(in partibus infidelium)*. Oddly enough, however, sports figure in both their stories. For his exploits on the gridiron and basketball court at Carroll College and later as a coach there, the National Association of Intercollegiate Athletics named Raymond "Dutch" Hunthausen to its Hall of Fame. Pio Laghi's like claim to fame is more modest, perhaps, but significant enough given its peculiar context. When the junta reign of terror was at its peak in Argentina in the late seventies — a time when suspected leftists, even pregnant women, were being slaughtered like cattle in clandestine torture chambers awash in blood — Archbishop Laghi, the papal nuncio, played tennis regularly with Admiral Emilio Massera, the chief executioner, who was later given a life sentence for his crimes.

The Vatican investigation of the archbishop of Seattle began in 1983 and didn't end until April 11, 1989, when the papal pro nuncio issued an unobtrusive communiqué to that effect. Thus the Hunthausen affair began with a bang — His Grace of Seattle's going public with the charges against him, to the pro nuncio's chagrin — and ended with a whimper, some pious mumbling about issues being addressed, changes being implemented, remedies being put into effect.

During part of the period of investigation, Rome imposed an auxiliary bishop on Hunthausen, Donald Wuerl (who was rewarded soon after with the see of Pittsburgh), a faithful bureaucrat who had been toiling for many years in the vineyard of the Roman Curia, that ancient and formidable entity respected even by those who don't believe in God. Respected more so, in fact, by those who don't than by those who do. Hunthausen, moreover, was forced to yield some of his episcopal powers to Wuerl, an unprecedented, wholly outrageous démarche, which, to their everlasting shame but no one's great surprise, the American hierarchy later approved by an overwhelming margin, issuing a statement suitably mealy-mouthed. There was, however, a wickedly amusing sidelight to Wuerl's appointment, given that Hunthausen's alleged indulgence toward homosexuals figured so prominently in it. Rumors of homosexual orgies at the Congregation for Religious, Wuerl's bureau, had swept Rome shortly before he was posted to Seattle. One thing about the Vatican, however, is it is not hypocritical. It never claims to be free of sin, just free of error.

Rome's investigation began, coincidentally or not, just after Hunthausen came to national prominence by calling a Trident submarine based in his diocese "the Auschwitz of Puget Sound" and declaring that he was withholding a portion of his income tax as a protest against his country's preparations for nuclear war. The list of charges drawn up two years later by Cardinal Joseph Ratzinger, prefect of the Congregation for the Doctrine of the Faith — better known to simple folk as the Inquisition — made no mention of the archbishop's antinuclear stance. Besides the allegedly too benign ministry to homosexuals, the unexciting bill of particulars included such things as children receiving First Communion without confession (a common practice in many dioceses at the time), some incidental liturgical innovations, certain uses of general absolution rather than individual confession, sterilizations allegedly performed on non-Catholics in Catholic hospitals, and some other matters even less compelling. Not a word about nuclear missiles or Trident submarines or rendering to Caesar the amount specified by the IRS tables. All that had no bearing whatsoever on its concern, Rome insisted.

This was curious indeed, and, subject to even modest scrutiny, it gets curiouser and curiouser. It was, after all, Hunthausen's antinuclear declarations, not his use of general absolution, that had created such a furor among the militant right and gained him the bitter enmity of the *Wanderer*, a far right Catholic paper read religiously, so to speak, by men dressed in soft garments at the Curia. (Not untypical of the *Wanderer*'s style was an article insisting that the reports of devastation at Hiroshima were greatly exaggerated since the streetcars were operating the next day, though what bearing that had on Catholic orthodoxy is anybody's guess.)

Among the more formidable enemies Hunthausen made by daring to question the legitimacy of the marriage of Cross and Flag was Paul Weyrich, later to gain his Warholian fifteen minutes of fame by his hearsay testimony before the Senate Armed Services Committee in 1989, during which he would cast the first stone of the avalanche that buried Senator John G. Tower, whom George Bush had nominated to be secretary of defense. Weyrich, a former Catholic who, traumatized by Vatican II, had abandoned the Roman Church for the more quiescent precincts of Eastern Orthodoxy, a region where Caesar was accustomed to quite a bit more than his due. By the early eighties, the tireless Weyrich had long been busy about many things on the far right. As related by the late Penny Lernoux in *People of God,** Weyrich, buoyed by ample funds from devout brewer Joseph Coors, had helped establish the Heritage Foundation, the most powerful of the far right think tanks, and organized the Free Congress Research and Education Foundation. One of the latter's offshoots was the Catholic Center, whose mission was to make life as difficult as possible for bishops Weyrich deemed unpatriotic. Thus the center held a workshop in Seattle to school local Reaganites, led by a heavy-equipment salesman, on how best to raise their anguished sighs to heaven. The secret, Weyrich's minions counseled, was to heave them by the most direct route: through Rome.

But no, said Laghi, the nuclear issue has nothing to do with the charges against the archbishop of Seattle. Heavens no, said Ratzinger.

But if nothing of great pitch and moment was at issue, why did Rome intervene with such unprecedented rigor and force? Suppose Hunthausen had done something truly scandalous, such as besmirch the reputation of Holy Mother Church by lending her name to a multimillion-dollar fraud that had caused the collapse of a major bank and triggered suicides and murders; what would have happened then? Another American archbishop, Paul Marcinkus, head of the Vatican bank (called the Institute for Good Works, a title that seems to have but limited influence on its operations), had in fact done just that not too long before. Suppose instead of Hunthausen's being one of the most beloved citizens of Seattle, the DA was clamoring for his arrest, as the Italian authorities were for Marcinkus's. Then one could understand Rome intervening in such draconian fashion.

*Penny Lernoux, *People of God* (New York: Penguin, 1989), p. 175.

Rome did, in fact, intervene massively in Marcinkus's case, but it did so to protect one of its own. To be fair, nothing doctrinal was involved — just money, lots of money. Other people's money.

Perhaps Laghi and Ratzinger were telling the truth or, according to their own lights, thought they were. Still, if Hunthausen had not declared that he was withholding a portion of his income tax in protest against the arms race, if he had not called the U.S.S. *Ohio* the Auschwitz of Puget Sound, it seems extremely unlikely — however busily surgeons in Catholic hospitals might have snipped and ligatured in non-Catholic genital areas, however many seven-year-olds might have gone to First Communion with their sins flush upon them, however cordial the archbishop's embrace of homosexuals might have been, however much mimes in whiteface might have cavorted and simpered in the sanctuary — that Rome would have had the effrontery to thus humiliate a successor of the Apostles and vindicate a bulldozer salesman who believed that the Holy Spirit spoke not through his bishop but through a president who never went to church.

I took the airport limo to the hotel in downtown Seattle where I was to meet Richard Carbray, retired professor of classics and adviser at Vatican II to the famous British Jesuit Thomas Roberts, the former archbishop of Bombay and friend of the Berrigans who had pronounced the American hierarchy "biblically illiterate."

Dick Carbray, white-haired, venerable, and irrepressible, was wearing a deerstalker cap, a Don Quixote in Baker Street clothing. As soon as we got into his car — before, in fact — he began to pour into my ear a steady stream detailing the most recent atrocities of the reigning administration and the gallant deeds of the liberal resistance, notably the Christic Institute in Washington, then fighting for its life against a libel suit.

Though we had never met before, we had a mutual friend in Eileen Egan, biographer of Mother Teresa and close friend of Dorothy Day. Eileen had told me how at the Vatican Council in 1961 Dick had translated into Latin a statement expressing the sentiments of Gordon Zahn, Dorothy Day, and some other American Catholic pacifists who had come to Rome. Archbishop Roberts read it on the council floor (they knew, said Eileen, that it would have been useless to approach an American bishop), and it played a crucial role in shaping the strong antiwar statement that finally emerged from the council after heated debate.

Dick, too, had been a friend of Dorothy Day as well as of Gordon Zahn and anybody who was anybody in the Catholic peace movement. Some illustrious predecessors had slept in the bed I would sleep in that night in Dick and Mary Carbray's guest room, including Archbishop Roberts; Dan Berrigan; Phil Berrigan; Hortensia Allende, Salvador Allende's widow; and Danilo Dolce, the Sicilian Gandhi. Dick had once driven Archbishop Roberts from Chicago to Seattle, and one stop on their journey had been a church in North Dakota. There they met a monsignor in his nineties who had known Sitting Bull. "Did you ever shake hands with him, Monsignor?" Roberts asked eagerly. When the monsignor said that he had indeed, many times, Roberts thrust out his hand, and the monsignor took it. From then on, whenever he met someone, the former archbishop of Bombay took great delight in saying: "Shake the hand that shook the hand that shook the hand of Sitting Bull."

It was a Saturday morning, and no one seemed to be on duty at the receptionist's desk in Archbishop Hunthausen's residence, a small rectory beside the cathedral. Not one to hesitate, Dick Carbray knocked at an inner door, and the archbishop of Seattle himself opened it.

Dick was carrying a golf club that had, he said, belonged to Hunthausen, and now he explained to the archbishop, as he had earlier to me, that it was going to be raffled off at a fundraiser for a Seattle peace coalition that afternoon. Hunthausen smiled and nodded, but I got the impression that he had never laid eyes on the club before.

After Dick left, Archbishop Hunthausen led me upstairs to a parlor, the kind of room that Evelyn Waugh had once described as being found only in a Catholic religious house — floors and woodwork polished to a preternatural gloss, walls hung with pious artwork, windows heavily draped, and a table placed in the exact center of the room. There was also a chill in the air, which would eventually compel us to seek a less ornate but warmer setting.

I had wanted very much to interview Archbishop Hunthausen, but I had been dubious about being able to do so because he had not been giving any interviews since the start of his difficulties with Rome. No speeches either. I had written him, but I had gotten no response. But then, the previous summer at the Pax Christi convention in Chicago, Hunthausen had delivered the keynote address, and in it he had quoted at length from an article I had written in *Commonweal* sharply criticizing the lack of follow-up on the 1983 peace pastoral. Drawing on the famous "lust in the heart" passage from St. Matthew, the same one that had gotten Jimmy Carter into such trouble — "I say to you whoever looks at a woman with lust in his heart has already committed adultery with her" (Matthew 5:27–28) — I argued that since nuclear deterrence was meaningless without the real intention to use the weapons (and the overwhelming majority of Catholic moral theologians, though none of them shouted it from the housetops, admitted that actual use was immoral), then deterrence itself was evil because it embodied an evil intention. Jesus may have voiced this stricture in the context of sexual sin, a context so congenial to moral theologians that they rarely venture out of it, but the principle was consistent with his teaching throughout the New Testament: we are judged not by externals but by what's in our hearts.

After that, Hunthausen responded to a second letter with a cordial phone call, and, now several months later — the Church views things *sub aspectum aeternitatis,* as I may have mentioned — we were finally sitting down together.

I never cease to be fascinated by the paths that men and women travel to get to where they are, and so we began at the very beginning.

The future archbishop of Seattle was born in Anaconda, Montana, a small copper-mining town, on August 21, 1921. He was the oldest of six children, three boys and three girls. Three of the children would choose religious vocations, two becoming priests, one a nun. When the idea of a vocation presented itself to Dutch Hunthausen in high school, however, he acknowledged the introduction coolly. Dominican nuns taught at the school, and his geometry teacher, Sister Borromeo, "confused him" by suggesting that someday he might want to become a priest.

"It was an idea that I didn't want to entertain at all," recalled Hunthausen. "But I suppose that that was an indication that it had a hold on me and I was fighting it. I didn't make any positive effort in that direction, and though I ended up at a Catholic college, Carroll, I did so without really meaning to. I had intended to go to Montana State to study chemical engineering, but a priest talked with my father and suggested that I should be going to a Catholic school. I had great respect for my father. He always spoke with me as though I were an adult and would never force me to do anything. I told him: 'Well, I'm sort of decided on Montana State, but I do have some friends who are going to Carroll.' Carroll was very small, a school run by the diocese of Helena, Montana. Its total enrollment was less than two hundred."

Given his father's suggestion, Hunthausen's high regard for the friends who went to Carroll, and who knows what else, he too enrolled there on the eve of World War II and, by so doing, met the man who would have a profound influence on his life, the saintly and brilliant priest Bernard J. Topel, later bishop of Spokane. A graduate of Carroll College, Topel, after his ordination, had been sent to do graduate work in mathematics at Notre Dame and later Harvard. So gifted was he that both schools asked him to stay on and teach, but he returned to Carroll and in 1939 became the spiritual adviser of freshman Raymond Hunthausen.

"It was a time of spiritual growth for me. It was hard, however, and I struggled," Hunthausen recalled. "By the time I got to junior year, I still wasn't sure. I had been majoring in chemistry and math. But I thought, well, I'll add Latin and philosophy to my program and see where it goes."

Hunthausen's inner struggle was itself set in a time of turmoil. He was a sophomore when the Japanese bombed Pearl Harbor and America entered the war, and so a new factor intensified the pressure on him. Not only was he very patriotic, like most idealistic young men of the era, but he felt, he confessed, a strong attraction for some aspects of military life.

"It was very painful. I saw my friends going off to be officers, many of them to flight school, where I wanted to go. I had already been taking flying lessons. But I finally agreed to go into the seminary. Bishop Topel — Fr. Topel then — told me that it was important to find out what God wanted for me. So I went, but I went with the feeling that before the year was out I would make the decision to leave."

He didn't decide to leave that first year, however, nor the second. He went through each subsequent year in the same state of mind, never really certain through most of seminary training.

"I didn't achieve a real degree of certainty until I finally said that I wanted to be ordained a subdeacon, even though I agreed to it only because I couldn't come up with a good reason why I shouldn't. When I was ordained a subdeacon, however, I was completely at peace. It was as though one road had been cut off forever, and I was never in doubt again. It was a great blessing for me."

If not for the Vatican and the Pentagon.

Despite the peace of mind he achieved, Hunthausen never forgot the pain that had preceded it. "I can emphathize with the struggles of the young priests who come to me," he said, "since I myself experienced long years of turmoil in college and in the seminary. I didn't feel really comfortable with myself all that time. I have a great love of children. And I felt a strong need to be a family person."

The archbishop laid great emphasis on Bishop Topel's role in his life. "He had been one of my teachers at Carroll from the beginning as well as my spiritual adviser," he said. "He was a stern man in the eyes of many. He had made up his mind that holiness was his objective, and he didn't hesitate to preach holiness to us students. He always did it with a smile and a laugh, but when it came down to the issues, he didn't beat around the bush."

After Hunthausen was ordained in 1943, he was sent back to Carroll to teach chemistry, and Topel continued to be his mentor. In 1955, Topel became the bishop of Spokane, the same year that Hunthausen was appointed president of Carroll, but they remained close even though they didn't see each other as frequently as before. "He still was the person to whom I turned," said Hunthausen. "When he retired seven or eight years ago, he rejoiced in the freedom it would give him to give retreats to priests, something he loved to do and was very good at. But the Lord had other ideas. He was soon afflicted with Alzheimer's disease. He got progressively worse, and when he died last year he was pretty much unaware of who he was or where he was or anything of that nature."

The sad circumstances of Bishop Topel's demise were the sort of thing that hagiographers pass over in silence, the kind of quite ordinary event that can shake the faith of even the devout. But Hunthausen recounted them in a calm, straightforward fashion. As he saw it, perhaps, Bishop Topel remained God's chosen vessel to the end, imparting a final lesson on the vanity of human endeavor.

I wondered whether Bishop Topel ever had much to say on war and peace and like issues.

"That's a hard one to answer since we never talked a whole lot on that. When I was a seminarian, my friends were in military service, but I don't recall his taking any sort of stand on war at the time. We all accepted it as a reality of the world in which we lived in those early days."

Later, however, the occasion did arise to discuss such issues: the Vatican Council and its Schema 13, "The Church in the Modern World." Pope John XXIII appointed Hunthausen the sixth bishop of Helena, Montana, in 1962, just a few months before the opening of Vatican II. And so he and his long-time friend and guide went to Rome together as fellow bishops. "But even in Rome," said Hunthausen, "my more detailed conversations on war and peace were with other bishops. Bishop Topel and I did take a lot of walks together, however, and when I began to see the need for taking a stand here, he was supportive. I don't recall that he made that many startling statements on current issues, though he always spoke forthrightly on the rights of the poor and came out against right-to-work laws. In his newspaper columns, however, he usually presented a straightforward spiritual approach to life, not often related to the specific concerns of the day. But he always encouraged me in espousing the issues that I felt had to be addressed."

As was true of all American bishops — the minority it acutely distressed as well as the majority, whose hopes it quickened — Vatican II was an overwhelming experience for Hunthausen.

"I didn't consider myself a theologian. I was surprised, in fact, to be accepted into the seminary. Latin and philosophy were a struggle for me. I got good grades, but not without a lot of effort. I was in class with seminarians who started in grade school and had the background I lacked. I went to the council, then, not nearly as well prepared as I should have been. I felt, in fact, that someone had made a mistake in making me a bishop to begin with."

Two decades later, of course, others would come to the same conclusion. Not only about that but about much else that John XXIII had done, especially his summoning of Vatican II.

Hunthausen had gone to the council with great openness and excitement. And despite some initial disappointment, he found much to stimulate him. The press conferences, the gathering of experts were events that made him feel that the Church was grappling with how to be relevant and purposeful in the modern world. "I suppose in some ways what was really exciting for me was that I sensed that the Church — with the freedom of conscience document, for example — was really beginning to head in the direction that I had always felt it should take. The council affirmed me in a sense in what I thought the Church should be saying and doing. And I found that immensely helpful. Though I was ill prepared to speak along those lines, it was a personal moment of support for me. I felt that now as a bishop I could more readily move ahead with what I felt the Church was saying to us through the council — that there was a whole area of shared responsibility, that there was a need for taking one another more seriously. Placing more responsibility on the baptized Christian — to stand up and be before God what we are called to be. All this just resonated with what I thought the Church should be doing, and I guess that some of my difficulty now — the cause of my struggles with the Holy See, if you can call it a struggle — is due to my sense that the Church is going back on all that."

Vatican II would also have a profound effect on Hunthausen's views on war and nuclear weapons and the consequent role demanded of him as a member of the Catholic hierarchy. He had brought to Rome some deeply felt sentiments about the epochal event that ended the most terrible of wars yet seemed to put real peace forever beyond humanity's reach. "My life, personally," he said, "and of course it's true of all of us — and not just in terms of externals, but my own spiritual life, my own attitude toward life and living — all this was radically changed when we dropped that atomic bomb on Japan. I had a deep abiding sense that the world would never be the same again. My mind just couldn't encompass such horrible power.

"I recall thinking, 'Gee, I wish we hadn't done that.' I heard all the arguments in favor of dropping the bomb, but they didn't relieve my sense of distress that we had brought such a thing on the world scene. It frightened me. It left me confused.

"So I paid close attention at the council. I had a lot of discussions with my confreres on nuclear weapons and the arms race then and later. None of this was in the public arena. But I began to assume the positions that I later espoused publicly. I was not always in agreement with my fellow bishops nor they with me. I was carrying things to a point beyond where they stood, but it seemed to me the logical thing to do. Logic alone, if you will, proceeding from the natural law, let alone the Gospel message of universal love."

Logic and faith made for a dangerous mix. How wise the the Vatican was in striving to keep them apart at all costs.

I told the archbishop that once, years before, when I was discussing nuclear war with a Jesuit friend while we were relaxing after dinner and he was playing with my baby daughter, I happened to mention that one of the things that made the danger most real to me was the distinct possibility that the baby girl he was making funny faces at might perish in a nuclear holocaust. My Jesuit friend looked at me amazed, unable to comprehend my entertaining so morbid a thought.

Hunthausen shook his head. "Yes, yes," he said. "That certainly could happen unless we work energetically as the whole human family. But you don't sense that concern among many. They have the idea it will all take care of itself. Or that God won't let it happen. That's the God I love and respect, the God who doesn't want it to happen. But he's left a whole lot in our hands. So I see an awesome responsibility on the part of all of us to recognize that and to do something radical about it. We have to overcome the psychic numbing that Dr. Helen Caldicott talks about, people saying to themselves that it's not real, that it's just something on television."

When Hiroshima and Nagasaki were bombed, Hunthausen was less than a year away from ordination. Despite the profound effect the nuclear massacres had upon him, he didn't at the time voice his feelings to any great extent. When he came back to teach at Carroll after studying chemistry at Notre Dame, there were ICBM silos in Montana and a SAC base at Great Falls. Everyone took it in stride. The country had to be defended, after all. "It struck me, however," Hunthausen recalled, "that this was no way to protect ourselves. I was struggling with it. Asking myself what we were really saying by this. The very nature of the weapon of destruction and our moving to this kind of an extreme were clear evidence to me that we would have no real protection unless we dealt with the reality itself.

"These ideas were forming in my head. I didn't talk about it much because it wasn't a popular subject. After I became bishop of Helena in 1962, I would speak about it occasionally." During his tenure in Helena, he met with several priests in the diocese who expressed concern about more ICBMs being based in Montana. Afterward, he and the priests issued a statement opposing more missiles. Unlike Hunthausen's later statements, this one didn't get much attention.

The ignored statement represented an isolated instance of antinuclear activism on Hunthausen's part. The feeling that there was a need to do something in the public sphere didn't begin to grow on him until after he left Helena in 1975.

"It wasn't a vital part of my awareness when I said yes to the archdiocese of Seattle. There were, I knew, military installations at Bangor and Fort Lewis. Every branch of the service was, in fact, located here. All this made me uncomfortable, but I didn't think about taking issue with this military presence until I was here for nearly a year."

It was then that he met Jim Douglass, the Catholic pacifist and author, who had been one of the lobbyists at Vatican II along with Dorothy Day, Gordon Zahn, and Dick Carbray. Douglass and his wife, Shelley, established Ground Zero, a peace center across Puget Sound from Seattle and cheek by jowl with the Trident base at Bangor.

"Jim came to see me. He introduced himself, and we talked about his background in peace activities. He was a quiet, gentle man, and I found his story fascinating. He and some others, he told me, were going to the White House and fast for thirty days against Carter's first strike policy. I thought it over and said to myself: 'Yeah, by gum, that's putting your life on the line. That's showing people what you believe.' And here I was, feeling the same way and doing nothing."

Hunthausen wrote a letter to the priests of his diocese describing his encounter with Douglass and his ideas. Feeling obliged as the leader of the Church in Seattle to take notice of the nuclear issue, he wrote, he was simply asking them to pray for Douglass's group and its efforts. It was up to them as individuals to decide whether they wanted to present this issue to their congregations. In response, some parishes invited him to come and talk with them, including one that was in the Bremerton area, where the Bangor Navy Base was located.

"The hall was jammed," Hunthausen remembered. "It was a tense evening but a good one. I showed a film, and I talked." In the audience were people whose jobs were on the line and people from the military. After it was all over, there were many who told Hunthausen they didn't agree with him but were glad he came and respected the fact that he was speaking out. People asked if he had considered every facet of the issue and Hunthausen was firm in his stance although he did not at this stage come out with an unqualified no to nuclear deterrence.

"I wasn't that sophisticated. All I did was point out the dangers of the arms race and tell them that we all had to do something, that there was a Christian need to be the voice of the Lord on this issue. I can't imagine, I said, that this is what Jesus wants us to be doing. Jesus wanted us to live for the sake of others, but we're going the opposite way and surrounding ourselves with these idols. We're all going to have to have a deeper faith. Those with jobs at stake said: 'Yeah, but what does that mean to us?' And I'd tell them: 'I'm not asking you to leave your jobs. I'm just asking you to think about it.' "

Hunthausen continued his parish visits, but nothing he said, despite its implications, created much of a stir in the local press. Through his regular attendance at a Thursday morning ecumenical breakfast, however, Hunthausen became a close friend of his Lutheran opposite number in Seattle, Bishop Lowell Knutson. This friendship led to an invitation for Hunthausen to address a synod at Pacific Lutheran University in June 1981. Ironically yet aptly, it was in a Protestant setting that the Catholic archbishop of Seattle made his famous "Auschwitz of Puget Sound" statement.

As was his custom, Hunthausen consulted widely while he was preparing this speech that was to have so profound an effect on his own life and on the direction of the Church in the United States, lending a ready ear to every view. One of those he talked with was Charlie Meconis, a peace activist and the author of *With Clumsy Grace,* an account of the Catholic left in the sixties and early seventies. The circumstances of his conversation with Meconis, an ex-priest, showed just how open Hunthausen was to well-reasoned ideas, however alarming their implications. "After one group discussion just before the Pacific Lutheran talk," he said, "I drove Charlie down to the garage where his car was getting fixed, and I asked him again about his thoughts. I had my speech all ready by that time, but I rewrote it to include Charlie's advocacy of tax resistance. Jim Douglass had a hand in the speech, too, but when I was finished, I said this is what I ought to say. This is what I want to say."

When the speech was finally finished to his satisfaction, Hunthausen showed it to a priest whose opinion he valued. After reading it, his friend was less than enthusiastic.

" 'You're not going to say these things, are you?' he asked me. 'Yeah,'

I said, 'I am.' He went on to warn me of dire consequences. 'But what am I supposed to say?' I answered. 'I want to be honest about the issue.' So I went ahead and gave the speech as is. A lot of people had had a hand in it, as I said, but it represented my own convictions."

Hunthausen began by identifying as "the root of many other terrible events in our country" the "willingness to destroy life everywhere on this earth for the sake of our security as Americans," a concept of Georgetown Jesuit Richard McSorley that had made a deep impression on Hunthausen early in the course of his rethinking the issue of nuclear war. Then he came out with the metaphor destined to dismay or gladden the hearts of many: "And when crimes are being prepared in our name, we must speak plainly. I say with a deep consciousness of these words that Trident is the Auschwitz of Puget Sound." He called for unilateral disarmament:

As followers of Christ, we need to take up our cross in the nuclear age. I believe that one obvious meaning of the cross is unilateral disarmament. Jesus' acceptance of the cross rather than the sword raised in his defense is the Gospel's statement of unilateral disarmament. We are called to follow. Our security as people of faith lies not in demonic weapons which threaten all life on earth. Our security is in a loving, caring God. We must dismantle our weapons of terror and place our reliance on God.

In the same speech Hunthausen mentioned some ways to influence those who make decisions. He mentioned taxes.

We have to refuse to give incense — in our day, tax dollars — to our nuclear idol. On April 15 we can vote for unilateral disarmament with our lives. Form 1040 is the place where the Pentagon enters all our lives and asks our unthinking cooperation with the idol of nuclear destruction. I think the teaching of Jesus tells us to render to a nuclear-armed Caesar what that Caesar deserves — tax resistance.

Hunthausen had thought his Pacific Lutheran speech "might make some sort of splash," and indeed it did. It was, in fact, a media sensation of sorts. And it was more than he had bargained for.

"I found it uncomfortable to be portrayed as a maverick all of a sudden. My thinking, after all, had been evolving for more than a decade. I was even a little annoyed that so much of my time was being taken up with this issue."

Much to his amazement, however, invitations to talk poured in, including one from Notre Dame. This was a daunting turn of events to a shy, self-confessed introvert. But Hunthausen felt that it was important to consider responding, and after praying and discussing the matter with people whom he respected he did respond.

Among other things, the Notre Dame speech, delivered on January 29, 1982, answered the question about what the archbishop of Seattle was going to do about his own Form 1040, a response anticipated by a pastoral letter to the diocese of Seattle dated the previous day. "[A]fter much prayer, thought, and personal struggle," Hunthausen wrote, "I have decided to withhold fifty percent of my income taxes as a means of protesting our nation's continuing involvement in the race for nuclear supremacy."

He went to Notre Dame with a great deal of trepidation. People had been asking him about the tax issue, and now he had made his decision, reached after much thought and prayer, even though he wasn't sure how effective this action would prove to be.

Hunthausen, the reluctant prophet, chose the most incendiary text imaginable to begin his Notre Dame speech: the Beatitudes as rendered in the sixth chapter of St. Luke, the same notorious chapter in which Jesus tells us to love our enemies and do good to those who hate us. Generations of Catholic schoolchildren have dutifully memorized the Beatitudes, and, though the more perceptive among them have been shocked at what was being asked of them, they have rarely found a teacher who would confirm their fears. The Beatitudes are indeed frightening. The Beatitudes should have scared the hell out of us. They were far more terrible in their implications than any words uttered by the prophets of old at their most prophetic. Jeremiah, Isaiah, and Amos condemned what we all piously agree was reprobate behavior. They called for reform. But this man Jesus demanded the impossible. Or so it seemed.

No wonder that both Catholicism and Protestantism had done their best to foist a sweet Jesus image on the young — a sweet Jesus who turns aside and looks the other way whenever the big boys from the Pentagon and the CIA have to step in to do the dirty work needed to keep up international property values. The heresy of muscular Christianity (an unknowledged heresy since, to paraphrase Sir John Harington on treason, if heresy prosper, none dare call it heresy) has been much more congenial over the centuries than have the Beatitudes to the successive aspirations of imperial Rome, Christendom, Spain, the British Empire, the United States of America, and, most recently, the Northern Hemisphere.

The trouble is that new prophets are always turning up in unexpected places to rupture the ordered tranquility that muscular Christians so prize. These disturbers of Pax Romana and Pax Americana alike are inconsiderate enough to apply Jesus' words to what's happening here and now, however awkward the consequences.

This is what the archbishop of Seattle, one of John XXIII's more serious miscalculations, did at Notre Dame. He not only condemned the arms race as immoral — something that even Cardinals John O'Connor of New York and Bernard Law of Boston, give or take a few nuances, were willing to do — he linked it to the Northern Hemisphere's sinful exploitation of the Southern, much as Martin Luther King, Jr.'s quest for racial justice at home had led him to condemn the Vietnam War as racial injustice abroad, a war against the Third World.

Because he himself was well fed, comfortable, and respected, Hunthausen said, he could not presume that Jesus was addressing him as "Blessed." He had more in common, he said, with those to whom Jesus spoke harshly: "Alas for you who are rich. . . . Alas for you who have your fill.":

I hear Jesus speaking out of the experience of deep poverty and suffering to us, the rich, those of whom the world speaks well — not the Third World, which, like Jesus, does not speak well of us — but the world of corporate power. That world of wealth and power usually speaks well of Notre Dame graduates and Catholic archbishops.

In considering a Christian response to nuclear arms, I think we have to begin by recognizing that our country's overwhelming array of nuclear arms has a very precise purpose: it is meant to protect our wealth. The United States is not illogical in amassing the most destructive weapons in history. We need them. We are the richest people in history.

Jesus was addressing that kind of situation when he said: "Alas to you who are rich." He said we would mourn and weep. He said in essence that if we go that way of outrageous wealth and power, we will get the very nuclear war with which we threaten others.

Hunthausen went on to reiterate the metaphor he used in condemning the Trident submarine based in his diocese. It was not just the capacity for mass murder embodied by the U.S.S. *Ohio* that prompted it: "This Trident is the Auschwitz of Puget Sound because of the massive cooperation required in our area — the enormous sinful complicity that is necessary — for the eventual incineration of millions of our brother and sister human beings."

The archbishop followed with another metaphor that would stir almost as much admiration and revulsion:

I say with deep sorrow that our nuclear war preparations are the global crucifixion of Christ. . . .

In saying these words I have no wish to isolate the responsibility for this crucifixion to people working on the Trident base or in the Pentagon. The fact is that everything that goes on in the Trident base and in the Pentagon is paid for by you and me, so long as we pay our income taxes. . . . Our tax dollars are our freely offered incense to a nuclear idol which scientists and physicians tell us may destroy life on earth. You and I, friends, are paying for that crucifixion, at least until we become tax resisters to our nuclear idol.

After once again expressing his advocacy of unilateral disarmament because "the way of nonviolence is the way of Christ," Hunthausen concluded his speech by quoting from his pastoral letter of the previous day expressing the intention to withhold 50 percent of his income tax and explaining why. In taking this action, he stressed that he by no means meant to confront others with a moral imperative to do likewise. Every Catholic had to follow his or her own conscience.

The Notre Dame speech swelled the flood of mail already pouring into Hunthausen's office. Among the correspondents was the secretary of the navy, John Lehman, a Catholic, who took him to task severely. "He put me down by belittling my naiveté, and it was a big story in the newspapers out here. I always tell those who disagree with me: 'I'll respect whatever conclusion you come to provided that you come to it after serious consideration.' "

Of course, it was asking a great deal of a man so taken up with achieving a thousand-ship navy, not to mention functioning to all intents and purposes as producer of *Top Gun*, to divert valuable time and energy to a personal exegesis of the New Testament.

Another Catholic reaction to the archbishop of Seattle's behaving quite unlike an archbishop — evoking the Gospel message in a way meant to afflict the comfortable — was much more nuanced. It came from George Weigel, whose very big book *Tranquillitas Ordinis** Avery Dulles, S.J., had praised so highly. Weigel had risen to the presidency of the James Madison Foundation, one of the new right think tanks suckled by the uberous Weyrich, but he had once been a presumably humble seminary teacher who for several years had written a column on war and peace in the Seattle diocesan paper, one invariably expressing a viewpoint sharply at odds with that of his archbishop.

*George Weigel, *Tranquillitas Ordinis* (New York: Oxford University Press, 1987).

If many liberals of the sixties prospered by enlisting in the war against poverty, so, too, not a few conservatives of the eighties did quite well in joining in the quest for peace. The more prominent among them included Weigel; the supremely nimble Michael Novak, who flourished, love beads and all, as a liberal in the sixties; and William J. O'Brien, one of the Georgetown academics who in the Reagan years tutored Caspar Weinberger like a beauty pageant finalist in the fundamentals of moralspeak. Their influence still seems to be in the ascendancy, moreover, judging from the Bush administration's skillful attempt to seize the moral high ground during the Gulf War and its tagging the incursion into Panama Operation Just Cause. Weigel, Novak, and O'Brien profess to believe not only in God but, supreme leap of faith, limited nuclear war. As they see it, Jesus really meant to say: "Blessed are the peace specialists."

Their concern, more new right than New Testament, has been the "moral use of power," a concern that they charge Catholic radicals such as the Berrigan brothers with abandoning in favor of either — take your pick — leftist ideology or a simplistic interpretation of the Gospel, two things that, significantly enough, they seem to consider pretty much indistinguishable. Though portraying themselves as ardent supporters of the just war theory, they argue, in fact, for the abandonment of one of the major tenets of just war thinking: its condemnation of the direct killing of noncombatants, something that the more forthright among them — Novak and O'Brien — acknowledge as inevitable given the nature of nuclear war. They contend — or at least they used to contend — that the good represented by preserving American democracy in the face of the Communist threat outweighs the evil represented by the death of a few million or so innocents. And, anyway, they point out with a rectitude that Cromwell before Drogheda would unhesitatingly endorse, these so-called innocents aren't all that innocent anyway since their labor and complicity are what enable their evil leaders to mount so terrible a threat to the free world. Intent as they are on giving the utmost credibility to their argument, they can invariably be counted on as fervent apologists for every twist and turn of American foreign policy. Until two years ago, they had been tireless in accusing the brothers Berrigan of identifying Washington, D.C., as the fountainhead of all iniquity when everyone knew that Moscow was, but recent events have provoked some confusion on the latter point. With a little bit of luck, however, and a few more Saddam Husseins, the Evil Empire that these devout think tank commandos so badly need might arise anew as the entire Third World.

Tranquillitas Ordinis ("Tranquillity of Order"), with blurbs from Cardinal O'Connor and Michael Novak, had made George Weigel the Arnold Schwarzenegger of muscular Christianity. The book solemnly presents the novel — yea, mind-boggling — thesis that American Catholicism once had a rich and nuanced doctrinal tradition on peace and war but rashly abandoned this pearl of great price during the sixties in favor of a simplistic agenda borrowed from the new left.

Procrustes of Attica never had a disciple more apt than Weigel. The Berrigan brothers take up twenty lines in the index, and Weigel quotes them freely, but the bellicose Cardinal Spellman rates but a single line. So it is that just three times in the course of 489 pages, only twice in the main text, does Weigel bother to mention the most powerful American churchman of the mid-twentieth century. Nor does he allow the great man a single quote, a reluctance understandable enough, of course. "My country right or wrong" would hardly bespeak a churchman in touch with a rich and nuanced tradition. Nor does Weigel choose to quote the intemperate language used by Cardinal Gibbons of Baltimore, a predecessor of Spellman as de facto leader of the Church in the United States, exhorting Catholics to support America's entry into World War I, a suicidal conflict that violated every single principle of the just war theory. And while almost every other author, regardless of ideological bent, would simply write "the bombing of Hiroshima," Weigel, pushing disingenuousness to the brink, solemnly informs his readers that on August 6, 1945, a "primitive atomic bomb was dropped on the headquarters of the Japanese army in Hiroshima" (p. 4).

In one section of his book, Weigel offers sketches of six Catholic pacifists: Dorothy Day, Gordon Zahn, Thomas Merton, Philip and Daniel Berrigan, and James Douglass. He is respectful for the most part, especially with Dorothy Day and Gordon Zahn, though at times his respect is hard to distinguish from condescension, as when he concludes his sketch of Dorothy Day by writing: "The enduring truth of Dorothy Day's life rests, though, not in her political judgments, but in her faith that 'all is grace' " (p. 53). The enduring truth is that Dorothy Day's faith clarified her political insight, and her editorials in the *Catholic Worker* condemning saturation bombing in World War II were politically as well as morally sound and everybody else was wrong.

Weigel's treatment of James Douglass is especially interesting since much of it deals not with Douglass himself but with Archbishop Hunthausen, who, according to Weigel, developed his ideas on war and peace under Douglass's "tutelage." Weigel points to Douglass's beginning *The Non-Violent Cross* with a quotation from Frantz Fanon's *The Wretched of the Earth* about how humanity must respond to the need for a redistribution of wealth or else "be shaken to pieces by it." He links this to Hunthausen's charge in his Notre Dame speech that America has amassed nuclear weapons to safeguard its wealth and therein discerns a fearful symmetry: "Frantz Fanon, via classic New Left themes espoused by the Berrigans, through James Douglass, to the archbishop of Seattle, speaking to an adulatory audience at the nation's premier Catholic university: the circle had come complete" (p. 173).

James Douglass did indeed have a strong influence on Hunthausen's thinking, as Hunthausen himself has acknowledged again and again and did so to me. In accomplishing this, however, Douglass began with no special advantage. He was a stranger to Hunthausen, obliged to introduce himself to him. The advantage, in fact, lay with Weigel.

"Let me tell you something," said Hunthausen after I had volunteered the opinion that *Tranquillitas Ordinis* was a thoroughly dishonest book. "When I began to be troubled about my responsibility on this issue, George Weigel was the first one I turned to. I knew George because he was on the staff of the seminary out here. I respected his intelligence, and I sought him out before anybody else. I went to see George. 'I need direction on this issue,' I said. I went to his home two or three times for dinner, and we had long conversations. But I finally had to say to him: 'Respectfully, George, I'm sorry. I can't buy where you are. I just don't feel there is enough of the Lord in what you're talking about. This is not where I feel drawn.' "

Why did James Douglass succeed where George Weigel failed? For one thing, the man to whom they made their respective cases was a man who had been troubled in his heart when he heard the news of the bombing of Hiroshima, a man who had thought to himself: "Gee, I wish we hadn't done that," a sentiment, incidentally, that could hardly have owed much to new left ideology. Weigel was born six years after the bombing of Hiroshima, and Douglass was only ten when it happened. So it seems safe to say that the event left both men untouched. Later, of course, it did have a profound effect on Douglass. Weigel, on the other hand, seems unaware to this day of the human dimensions of what took place. Could anyone troubled in his heart have described the *Enola Gay*'s target as "the headquarters of the Japanese army in Hiroshima"? And no one not troubled in heart over Hiroshima and Nagasaki (the latter a city whose name is so intimately associated with the blood of martyrs and the tragic but glorious history of Christianity in Japan), no matter how great his powers of persuasion, could possibly have had much influence on Raymond G. Hunthausen.

The archbishop of Seattle was, after all, a simple man. Somehow he lacked the imagination to see the problem of nuclear war as a rich mother lode of moral conundrums parried by congenial, attractive people with advanced degrees whose natural habitat is the think tank: gifted creatures who are like rare tropical fish that swish about in aquariums where the temperature is kept at a soothing optimum. It's easy enough to be tolerant in such circumstances, but not if the news of Hiroshima struck you to the heart and the words "nuclear war" evoke not seminars in Berkeley and Cambridge but acres of charred flesh.

I told the archbishop a story I had heard from Gordon Zahn. Before the opening of Vatican II, the English Quaker Douglas Dear had written to Archbishop Thomas Roberts that those who were struggling in the cause of peace deserved "some prophetic gesture" from the Catholic Church on nuclear weapons.

Hunthausen sighed. "Well," he said, "I have to tell you I'm not sure what that prophetic gesture would be, but I know I personally am troubled when I reflect on what I should do. Dan Berrigan had some advice for me recently. Jim Douglass shared something that Dan put into a letter to him, talking about me and in reference to all my . . . my . . . tensions. Dan was rather simplistically suggesting that, fine, if that's what Rome wanted me to do, then I should resign and give myself totally to the peace effort. And the first thing I should do was to find some way of getting myself thrown into jail." Hunthausen laughed. "Well, when you start talking about prophetic actions, I get frightened to death. I guess I'm no different from anybody else.

"Every time I go over to Ground Zero and take part in one of those demonstrations, every time I see some of my friends cross the line and get arrested — like Bill Cate, the Methodist minister who's the director of the Seattle Council of Churches, and his wife — I say, why can't I do that? I get mixed signals in return. You're the archbishop of this diocese, I tell myself, and your responsibilities are primarily to support these people, to proclaim to the rest of the world that this is what Christianity means — to let everybody know how important their sacrifice is. But, then, I can't escape the feeling that I have to remain open in prayer to the possibility of doing something like that myself.

"What I'd like to do — I guess I shouldn't say I'd like to do it — but what I feel a challenge about is to approach influential people in the city — the mayor, bank presidents, and so on down the line — and say, this is where my heart, mind, and convictions are. I don't know where you are, but if you are anywhere near where I am, if together we were to civilly disobey — sit on the tracks or walk across the line — we would make an impression on this city, the kind of impression I think would be necessary."

At times, Hunthausen believes this approach is a cop-out, feeling he should act alone before approaching other leaders in Seattle. His views and approach to this issue continue to evolve, but he remains committed to the search despite the high cost it might incur. "I must pray more about it. I sometimes find myself unwilling to pray about it because of what answers might come back. Prayer, properly understood, makes you vulnerable, makes you realize that you need guidance, knowing you don't know all the answers. There come moments, moments in my life when I think: What am I to do? What am I to tell others? I'm on a Confirmation tour now, and that's what I tell these young people. Please make yourself open to the Spirit. Make God real in your lives. Find out what God wants to do with you and with this world. Don't pay attention to what the world is telling you to do about it.

"There are so many voices. I guess what's needed is a deepening of faith. Prayer is the thing. There is no worthwhile action that doesn't come from prayer. We must be united with the will of the Father's, just as Jesus showed us by his own life. That's what we have to find for ourselves, and it has to be a struggle. Life properly lived is always a struggle in hope, with but a modest degree of support."

A struggle in hope. In the Yorktown jail, Phil Berrigan had called fear "disbelief struggling with belief."

"When people say that I've been of some help, then, it scares me. Because, as I've indicated, I'm aware of my lack of preparation. I try to be comfortable with myself at the same time wishing that I had a whole lot more wisdom. Some say what I've done is in some sense prophetic. I don't see it that way. I've done what was required of me. I don't know if I could fashion something that I considered prophetic and then do it. Somehow I think I have to work toward a conviction — one that derives from who I am, from my sense of what the Lord expects of me — and then do what I do because I'm convinced I'm right."

Like Charlie Liteky, Hunthausen did not want to be in this situation, preferring instead to slip into seclusion somewhere so that he could take up a comfortable prayer life and let someone else accept this responsibility. But he sees his reluctance as part of the growth process. "Something would be wrong if I were comfortable. If I got comfortable in anything the Lord wanted me to do, then I'd have to start worrying."

———————

Before driving me to the airport the next day, Dick Carbray, as was his wont, loaded me with a bundle of clippings, testimonials, dispositions, affidavits, broadsides, and miscellanea lest I pass my time aloft in idleness. What caught my eye at once was a column from the *Seattle Times* by Erik Lacitis. It was headed "Putting Love into Practice."

Lacitis had gotten a phone call, it seemed, from a local eccentric named George Kotelaris who had achieved a measure of fame in Seattle through his fondness for crashing news conferences, civic receptions, weddings, funerals, and other events and snapping pictures of everyone involved — including, at funerals, the deceased. George informed the columnist that "Hunthausen just cleaned up my apartment," and when Lacitis asked if by any chance he meant the archbishop of Seattle, George answered: "Yeah, yeah, who else?"

Lacitis was inclined to be skeptical. George's story turned out to be true, however. The archbishop's office didn't return the journalist's calls, but a local priest was more forthcoming and, in fact, made the cleansing of George's apartment the subject of his sermon the following Sunday.

George, like many eccentrics (he described himself much less pretentiously as "a little nutty"), was a devout Catholic and never missed an ecclesiastical function. The archbishop, taking with good humor George's loud manner, often drove him home afterward. Once, instead of dropping George at the door as he usually did, Hunthausen ventured into his apartment — to be greeted by debris of various sorts, including souvenirs, some perishable, of George's various excursions, piled to a depth of some four feet and never mind the kitchen. Shortly after, George dropped off at the chancery a box of memos from his irate building manager threatening eviction.

Early the next Saturday, Hunthausen, dressed in khaki work pants and accompanied by some volunteers, showed up at George's Augean quarters and set to work on a job that would take much of the day. Lacitis interviewed the manager, and her testimony is perhaps more telling than anything that has been or will be written about His Grace, Raymond G. Hunthausen, archbishop of Seattle:

> I couldn't believe it. I thought of the archbishop as a closed man only involved in big issues. I thought he'd say a few words and then the others would do the work. He got right to it, scrubbing the kitchen floor. He cleaned the toilet which we were going to replace because it was so dirty. He chipped at it with a knife and got it looking like new.

The Admiral's Daughter

Sister Anne Montgomery

It was an overcast Sunday morning in April in New York. The gray bulk of the aircraft carrier *Intrepid* loomed over the Hudson River waterfront hard by a less revered relic, the crumbling ruin of the West Side Highway. The survivor of savage kamikaze attacks off Okinawa, the *Intrepid* had come to rest here at 46th Street and 12th Avenue, a continent and most of an ocean away from where it had won its fame. The impervious sea leaves us no Waterloos, no Gettysburgs, no Verduns, no Omaha Beaches to memorialize. And so, lest the glory of former days be forgotten, the *Intrepid* now functioned as a museum.

Its aviators, who had worn the navy's wings of gold, were gone now. The youngest survivors among them had reached retirement age. The remains of others were lying in cemeteries at the edge of cities and towns scattered throughout America. Still others, those who had taken off from the *Intrepid*'s flight deck more than four decades before never to return, were gone without a trace, their bones dissolved long years before in the everlasting night of the Pacific depths. Their nation had been victorious, but their fate had been the same as that of their adversaries, the Japanese airmen who perished hurling themselves against the gray warships that threatened all that they held precious. For the fallen Americans there was no Yasukuni Shrine at which to be revered. They had no common locus of memory, just a framed photo of a smiling young man on a wall, on a shelf, or on top of a piano in Dubuque, Rochester, San Diego, or wherever.

Now, throughout the great city that they and the slumbering carrier had defended so ably, young men in dark suits and dark ties with features like those of the kamikaze pilots were at work with a dedication perhaps no less fervent. Life was more ambiguous for them, of course, than it had been for their grandfathers. Buying Rockefeller Center could hardly compare with sipping your ceremonial cup of sake before the Shinto altar, your flying helmet bound with the white *hachimaki* bearing the red disk of the sun and inscribed with the battle cry "1,000 Struggles, 1,000 Victories," climbing into your plane, a samurai sword in the cockpit beside you, and waving to your cheering comrades as you taxied into takeoff position. The Japanese, whose heroes were beautiful losers, loved this sort of thing. We Americans, whose heroes were winners, ridiculed it in scatalogical terms. But now that the Japanese had lost so irrevocably, they no longer had the opportunity to die beautifully but had to be content with Rockefeller Center, honeymoons on Guam, and golfing trips to Hawaii. And we Americans, who had won, had to keep on winning. We had to keep on building bigger and better aircraft carriers, fashioning instruments of war so advanced and so awesome in their capabilities as to make the gallant *Intrepid* seem as quaint as a Civil War cannon. Even if we had to let our central cities and their schools go the way of the West Side Highway. And, of course — despite the real or alleged wonders of our killing machines — we also had to oblige some of our young men to die gloriously at regular intervals. Young Americans really don't go for that kind of stuff, but, betrayed by our schools and shut out by our economy, enough of them could always be counted on to join up. Empires needed the disenfranchised. So it had been that the Scotch, the Welsh, the Irish, and the dregs of the slums of London and Liverpool had gone off to die for queen and country in India, the Crimea, Afghanistan, Burma, the Sudan, Zululand, and South Africa, fighting brown men and black men and yellow men and white men with whom they had no quarrel at all, men with whom they had much more in common than with those who sent them to their deaths.

In what would have been the shadow of the *Intrepid*, had there been any sun to cast a shadow, about twenty-five demonstrators were protesting the visit of the battleship *Iowa* to New York Harbor. Cardinal John O'Connor was to take part this Sunday morning in an ecumenical welcoming service on board the *Intrepid*. As usual the police had penned up the demonstrators behind blue sawhorses with the familiar black initials NYPD. As usual the demonstrators were a motley crew. The prize for most exotic might be a toss-up among a genial Buddhist monk from the Mount Nippon Wondrous Law Temple in Manhattan, two quite burly young women with Mohawk haircuts in motorcycle boots and black, studded leather, and me and my two daughters, ten and thirteen, who had taken an early train in from Ridgewood, New Jersey.

The most extraordinary of the protesters, however, was a thin woman in her fifties with fine features and close-cropped gray hair. Her frayed, drab overcoat buttoned against the morning chill did nothing to hide the gauntness of her frame. She was not merely thin. She was one of the thinnest women I had ever seen.

Her face looked familiar, as though I had seen her picture somewhere. I asked John Marth, a member of the Kairos peace group in New York. He told me that the thin woman, who was standing quiet and composed as she talked with some fellow demonstrators, was Sister Anne Montgomery. I recognized the name at once. Anne Montgomery belonged to the Religious of the Sacred Heart. Though their order had been founded in France to educate poor girls, they, like the Jesuits, whose rule they had adopted (they kept it and the Jesuits didn't, ran the ecclesiastical in joke), had gained a reputation for elitism and a predilection for teaching the offspring of the upper middle class. The charge was not altogether fair, but there was probably enough circumstantial evidence in both cases to gain an indictment. Sister Montgomery's order had educated both Ethel Kennedy and Michiko Shinoda, who a year later, in 1989, would become empress of Japan.

Sister Montgomery herself, I well knew, had taken a different direction. She had participated in no less than three Plowshares actions, including the first, and had served three prison terms, one in the women's federal prison in Alderson, West Virginia, where Elizabeth McAlister had been and Helen Woodson still was. Alderson had become a second alma mater for women peace activists, quite a different one from all those colleges of the Sacred Heart in Chicago, Cincinnati, San Diego, Tokyo, and elsewhere. What I didn't know as I watched her from a distance on this April morning, in what would have been the shadow of the *Intrepid*, was that Sister Anne Montgomery was an admiral's daughter, a navy brat. Her father, an aviator, had commanded a carrier in the Pacific and later a carrier division. And her brother, too, had worn the navy's wings of gold.

We talked the next day at a convent on Washington Square, a setting more in keeping with the order's reputation.

Until 1969, Sister Montgomery told me, she had taught at the Academy of the Sacred Heart in Manhattan, a high school that occupied an old mansion at 91st and Fifth, which like this house on Washington Square was a traditional Sacred Heart site. She had for some years previous felt the need to work directly with the poor, and in 1969 she finally left high school teaching to go into a culture program at Hunter College.

"The academy was a good school, but even though it was fully integrated, I felt, you know, that the children in New York who needed good teaching the most were the ones who were getting stuck in the worst of the public schools. The brighter kids could get scholarships to schools like ours, but the ones who were lowest in their eighth-grade classes just had nowhere to go, and that just said something to me: those are the children that need to be taught."

So it was that she went to Hunter and into a course of studies whose focus was building a curriculum, with emphasis on reading skills. Her field had been English, but she had taught just about everything at Sacred Heart and even became a librarian for a while. "They made us do everything in the old days," she said, her voice dropping to an ironic whisper. "You did as you were told."

After a year at Hunter, Sister Montgomery went to Albany to teach at a street academy for dropouts and worked with children whose reading was below grade level. The school was just getting under way, and she and the other teachers had to persuade the New York Board of Regents to recognize it as a high school so that they could award diplomas that would allow their graduates to go on to college. She remembers most of the students as being rather bright young people who had taken to the streets because school had bored them. She enjoyed the atmosphere of freedom at the school and the flexibility of its curriculum.

During her five years in Albany, she became interested in learning disabilities. Though most of her students hadn't done well before because of the way they had been taught, she saw that others didn't learn because they couldn't. She did a year of study and internship in California, and then, after a brief final stint in Albany, she came back to New York City to start a resource center for children with learning disabilities at a parochial school in Harlem.

Even today, when peace work took up most of her time, Sister Montgomery also remained an educator in the more traditional sense. She tutored adults three times a week at a Harlem outreach center run by the Sisters of the Assumption and was helping to organize a high school equivalency program. Her peace work involved teaching people how to speak up for themselves, how to run workshops, and how to do other things to make their influence felt.

Like so many peace activists, Sister Montgomery's commitment was something that had evolved as time went by. "I think I was interested all along," she said. "I realized the Vietnam War was wrong, but we were semicloistered, and I didn't see what I could do other than teaching my kids about social justice."

There was no need to explain this to me. As a Jesuit, I had been on good terms with Sacred Heart nuns in Cincinnati and later in Tokyo. When their parents came to see them on visiting days, the nuns couldn't even eat with them. "We know she does eat," one mother had told me wryly, "but we've never seen her do it."

It was while she was in Albany that Sister Montgomery first found herself confronted with what social justice means in quite specific terms. She saw quite clearly that tax revenues were simply not going to those who needed them most, an injustice she would later encounter in Harlem. She dated her full commitment to peace activism, however, to 1978, the year of the first U.N. session on disarmament.

"I heard Dan Berrigan doing a thing on the Book of Revelation at our Motherhouse on West Ninety-seventh Street, which is right near where he lives. He challenged us to do something." She hadn't known Dan Berrigan before, though they did have a common friend in a nun named Eileen Storey. Berrigan's talk was very influential, leading Sister Montgomery to join the Kairos group, which had been started by Berrigan as a Lenten prayer group and had become a peace group that met regularly. It was at the U.N. that she first participated in civil disobedience. Approaching her first act of civil disobedience, she had envisaged a dramatic confrontation fraught with tension, but it turned out to be quite pedestrian. The police were thoroughly prepared for the demonstrators, with buses lined up to take away those arrested. It was as though the event had been choreographed by the NYPD.

"But, psychologically, getting arrested like that is a big step. You know, you're crossing a line you haven't crossed before. So I never look down on people who do a very low-risk thing at the beginning."

I duly noted, not without a slight twinge, her "at the beginning."

"I think you have to break through something in yourself to do that. But from then, I went from bad to worse." She laughed. Sister Montgomery laughed only when there was good reason to, not wasting energy that could be put to better use.

Her progress downward seemed to have been quite rapid, I observed mildly. She had begun in 1978, and two years later she had been part of the first Plowshares action at King of Prussia.

"Right, I was part of it. Actually it was John Schuchardt who first mentioned it to me during Holy Week of 1980 when I was down at the Pentagon. He's been doing a lot lately with veterans. He's a veteran himself, a former Marine officer. He's a lawyer too, but he's been disbarred of course." Another laugh, very brief.

"So, you know, he suggested it and told me something like that was going to happen without giving any details." Her frequent "you knows" had nothing to do with diffidence but were a form of emphasis. She joined the group, whose membership fluctuated. Then they had to wait for Dan Berrigan, who was in Ireland supporting the fasters dying in British prisons but who had indicated that he wanted to join the group.

I thought of all the patriotic Irish-Americans who were incensed at the brothers Berrigan for being traitors not only to their country but to "their own kind." What would they think if they knew of Dan's support for the ancient cause? One of their heroes, one of mine, Terence MacSwiney, the lord mayor of Cork, had resisted British oppression by going on a hunger strike, as would Gandhi some years later. But MacSwiney would fast until death.

There was one other woman in this historic first Plowshares action, Molly Rush, the founder of the Thomas Merton Peace Center in Pittsburgh. The rest of the group consisted of Dan and Phil Berrigan, John Schuchardt, Carl Kabat, and Elmer Maas. "Elmer's one of the more hidden people in the peace movement but one of the most important. He has the Isaiah Peace Group in New Haven. They are the brains behind all the Trident demonstrations up there. They're over their heads now. The *Pennsylvania*'s just been launched."

Was he a Catholic? I asked, inevitably.

"No. He taught at a small midwestern college. At least I don't think he's Catholic. In a group, all the people are basically Christian, and you're not sure what they started out being. He is utterly dedicated. Peace work is his whole life. He looks like nothing. We call him the "little professor." He knows more about the law than any of us, though he's not a lawyer. He helps groups prepare. He helps them through trials. He's been in two Plowshares actions himself. The first and one of the Tridents — the Trident action that Marcia Timmel was in. So he just keeps going. He has files. All the trial briefs."

The Plowshares Eight, as the King of Prussia group called itself, didn't undergo the kind of intensive preparation that would mark later actions and that Liz McAlister and others had described to me, but most of this first group had had a great deal of experience, Sister Montgomery being the exception. Up to that point, she said, she had spent only one night in jail and she had never had to stand trial for one of her acts of civil disobedience.

She was frightened going into it, she admitted. "But, you know, I think the group was so strong. You know, it was a very good one. And as the trial went on, I learned a lot. I had been afraid, you know — the thing I had been afraid about in prison was not what the guards would do but that the other women would not accept us middle-class white people coming in. But they did. They were just lovely. In the first place, I was older, of course. But, you know, I think poor people understand a lot better what's going on. They don't understand why you go to prison. Why don't you just run away? they say. But the fact that you've done something — they understand that."

You didn't get into trouble in a women's prison, she thought, unless you went out of your way to risk it. Life on the inside was quite different from what most people imagined and feared. "Women can be very supportive. Prison's a very oppressive place. Most women in prison have children — eighty to ninety percent of them. They get harsher sentences than men as they get older, and they get fewer chances for parole, and very few educational opportunities in most prisons — federal prisons especially."

Prison was a great learning experience for her. She had an advantage over other inmates, she said, in that she had in a real sense chosen to be there. Imprisoned peace activists knew that they were in the right place. "We'd formed our consciences," she said, using the traditional expression of Catholic moral theology, which conveys that one has acted only after serious deliberation, taking into account all the factors involved. "It's not the same as somebody having a guilt trip put on them, making them feel that they're bad. And we had a lot of support from outside. We got letters, visitors. You know, it's noisy, it's crowded, I think that's the hardest."

Ironically, it was neither the King of Prussia action itself nor the prison time that followed that proved to be the major ordeal. "What is really deadly in something like this is the trial. It's a very oppressive situation, and you have to know how to handle it. You're in prison and separated from one another, and you have a lot of decisions to make. And unless you have a strong community, it just doesn't go well. I think that the preparation is terribly important."

The right kind of preparation had preceded her two subsequent Plowshares actions. The first was the Trident Nein action, on July 4, 1982, directed against the Trident submarine *Florida* in Groton, Connecticut. Sister Montgomery and eight others had used a canoe to board the *Florida*. They hammered on its missile hatches, poured blood on them, and then renamed the submarine U.S.S. *Auschwitz* with a can of spray paint. Two years later, Easter Sunday, April 22, 1984, she had joined Paul Magno and six others who entered the Martin Marietta facility in Orlando, Florida, where Pershing missile components were manufactured.

She was sentenced to a year for Trident Nein, with three months suspended. The court also ordered her to pay restitution, and, though she didn't comply, she was released after five months for "good time." Her sentence had been somewhat harsher than those given her companions because she was a second offender, but that didn't bother her much. "Actually, it wasn't a bad sentence. As for the Pershing, I got a three-year and a five-year suspended sentence with probation, which I'm now dealing with. They haven't pushed too hard. The judge wants us to pay restitution to Martin Marietta, but the probation officer hasn't made a big fuss over it. With federal time, you usually serve two-thirds of it."

I still couldn't quite adjust to a Sacred Heart nun's being so at ease with such matters, talking about good time and federal time and evaluating sentences with a connoisseur's eye. Nor did her comparative analysis of life in prison strike my ear as any less strange. "County jail is boring because you're waiting to go some place else. You're waiting to be sentenced. You're waiting to be tried. There're no activities. There's little chance to go outdoors, especially for women. They take more care to send men out. You might get out once a week. There's nothing to do. If you're lucky, you get books. So you sit. The only state prison I've been in is Niantic in Connecticut after the Trident action. You have to work once you get to prison. So I usually tutor in the school."

Anne Montgomery's father was Admiral Alfred Eugene Montgomery. Despite his rank, he apparently had not been a happy warrior.

"He never talked about World War II. My mother told me later how nervous he was when he got back from the Pacific. First he was an aircraft carrier commander, and then he became an admiral and commanded the base at Corpus Christi for a while. They trained pilots. And then he went to the Pacific as the commander of a carrier division." It was easy to think of Anne Montgomery's father commanding a carrier force. It was easy, in fact, to think of Anne Montgomery commanding a carrier force.

After a year and a half of service in the Pacific, Admiral Montgomery was injured in an accident, and, though he tried to carry on, navy doctors eventually decreed that he had to return to shore duty, and he finished the war in Hawaii. He never talked about the war with his daughter, but he did tell her of his impressions as an observer of the atomic testing at Bikini

Atoll in 1946. He had found it, he said, an overwhelming experience. Fortunately, he had never had to deal with nuclear weapons as a commander.

Sister Montgomery's brother graduated from the Naval Academy just before the war ended and saw immediate action as a carrier pilot in the Pacific. He survived the war to become a navy test pilot, but he died in a plane crash when he was thirty. It was an accident that occurred during a routine flight, a circumstance that made his death still more of a shock.

Framed photos of a smiling young man on a wall, on a shelf, or on top of a piano in Dubuque, Rochester, and San Diego. Had such a photo also hung from the wall of a cell in Alderson? I wondered.

Anne Montgomery was older than I had taken her to be. She was born in 1926. As it did with the Berrigans, her age gave her an extraordinary perspective on the changes that had taken place in the Catholic Church in the wake of the Second Vatican Council. These changes, however, were occurring at different rates in different places and different situations. Sometimes — quite often — the pace was leaden. Ironically, the Northeast, so liberal in matters secular, had been and still was a bastion of reaction in matters ecclesiastical. Despite the high regard I had always had for her order, I was a bit surprised that the Religious of the Sacred Heart should have accepted with such equanimity Sister Montgomery's veering off in so radical a course of action, especially at an age when she should have been a steadying influence on the younger members of the order. (In the Jesuits, priests her age were designated "patres graviores," often irreverently translated as "heavier fathers" or "fathers nearer the grave.")

"I have been lucky," Sister Montgomery explained, "because the support I have gotten from my congregation has been wonderful. Molly Coakley, who was the provincial when I wanted to work with the poor, was altogether sympathetic. She's since become very involved with Latin America through the Women's Coalition Against Intervention." The term "provincial," much more businesslike than "mother superior," was another mark of Sacred Heart's Jesuit legacy. "I told her I was on the point of leaving if I couldn't change, and she supported me all the way through."

When Sister Montgomery began to become involved in civil disobedience, her superiors did show some alarm because it was an activity unprecedented for Sacred Heart, and the King of Prussia Plowshares had caused a moderate uproar within the order. She had explained what she was going to do ahead of time — an action that might result in a long jail sentence —

but her provincial hadn't fully grasped the significance of what she had heard. After recovering from her surprise, however, she backed Sister Montgomery all the way.

"It's grown so that people are so much more understanding, you know. Just this year, the provincial teams of Canada and the United States asked me to do a three-day retreat with them, which just shows what kind of value they place on it."

It seemed, I said, that the Religious of the Sacred Heart was a much more adaptable order than the Jesuits. Sister Montgomery looked at me for a moment before replying. "Oh God, yes!" she said. "It sure is. Women's orders are in general. I think the Jesuits are going to lose a lot of valuable people."

Maybe they could ask Dan Berrigan, I said, realizing the absurdity of it, to do some recruiting for them.

"But they won't, you see. They don't pay any attention to him. You see, it wouldn't do anyway. He'd recruit people, and then they'd squash them. He tries to help the younger men, but not a lot of people listen. You know, they respect him for who he is, but they don't seem to want to be like him."

Dan Berrigan, however, had once encouraged Sister Montgomery to do some recruiting of a sort among the American hierarchy. "When I was in Niantic Prison, the bishops had just written a second draft of the peace pastoral. It was the worst draft." Indeed it had been. The bishops had excoriated deterrence as "a state of sin" in the first draft, an unwonted show of courage, or slip of the pen, from which they swiftly recoiled in the second draft.

At Dan's suggestion, Sister Montgomery wrote a letter that he arranged to have sent to every bishop in the United States. She received some thirty replies, no more than one out of a dozen, but nonetheless an astounding total. It wasn't every day that a bishop got a letter from a Religious of the Sacred Heart who was doing time.

"Most of them, you know, wrote the usual sort of nonsense. I mean, they were all being sympathetic. I told them I was in jail, you know. I asked them what they were doing. What was the faith basis of it? But there were some very beautiful answers from about ten of them. The usual ones you'd expect. Even O'Connor wrote back. But, you know, I don't think it had much effect on them. But I don't pay much attention, you know. I don't think any changes are going to come from the bishops. I don't think changes will come from any people in authority."

This called into question, it seemed, the educational philosophy of two great religious orders — she belonged to one; I had spent thirteen years in the other — that had sought to influence society by educating its leaders. Should education be abandoned in favor of direct action?

"I think that most people doing civil disobedience also do education of one kind or another. You know, we don't sit around in between. And I would never have been asked to speak to anybody or to write anything if I hadn't acted. So the education has to come out of where you put yourself. I think that a law that is a wrong law has to be broken. Otherwise we betray ourselves. Where does the education lead if it doesn't lead to action?"

She expected nothing from Congress. She expected nothing from politicians, even Jesse Jackson, who was then running for president.

"Even if Jesse Jackson did get elected, he could do nothing about it. They'd kill him if he tried. Look at Carter. He had all sorts of good intentions. But he didn't stand a chance. The president doesn't have that kind of power. And the voters don't have that kind of power. We don't vote for the Pentagon. We don't vote for the CIA."

Perhaps we should just give up, then, on attempting to affect the world, I said. Maybe we should emulate the Desert Fathers, the hermits of the fifth and sixth centuries who fled into the Egyptian desert to escape from the corruption of a decadent Roman Empire.

Sister Montgomery laughed. "I'll give you a very simple answer: I think it's non-Christian to say that there isn't any hope of accomplishing something with the world. No, I would never accept terms like that for a debate. It's setting it on the wrong level. I think we have to speak in terms of faith. I'm up front with people. Faith is where I come from. You know, I keep saying that if we believe, anything is possible."

Faith, she said, did not imply perfection. The Gospel message took into account our weaknesses. One didn't have to be a saint, didn't have to be perfectly nonviolent, before trying to have an effect on the course of events. "Christ came for sinners. He died for sinners. We have to realize what Christianity is all about. And what it's not about is power politics."

Dan Berrigan had said the same thing about expecting nothing from those in power — even, perhaps especially, from those in episcopal power. But still, I thought, a charismatic gesture now and then could help. Like Hunthausen's "Auschwitz of Puget Sound" statement.

"Yes, but Hunthausen would not have said that if Jim Douglass had not been there. The same with Bishop Matthiesen and Larry Rosebaugh."

Leroy Matthiesen, now one of the strongest voices against nuclear weapons among the American hierarchy, was the bishop of Amarillo, where the Pantex facility served as the assembly point for nuclear warhead components shipped from all over the country. Larry Rosebaugh was an Oblate priest who had spent six years in the seventies working for the poorest of the poor in northern Brazil. Dick Carbray had described him to me as "one of the holiest people I've ever met." Dick told me how Rosebaugh had lived on the streets of Seattle while working with the homeless, not going into a shelter until two in the morning and then working all the next day at a Catholic Worker house. When he went to Brazil, he hitchhiked, figuring that if you're going to live with the poor, you just don't hop an airplane. It took him a month to get there, but he'd learned a lot along the way. He was, Dick Carbray said, another Francis of Assisi.

"If Matthiesen hadn't visited Larry in prison, he wouldn't have changed the way he did." Matthiesen hadn't wanted to visit him, she said, but some people whose opinion he respected told him that he should because Rosebaugh was acting on faith, acting on his conscience. "I think Matthiesen was a very open person, but Larry had a strong influence on him. I think the change came just meeting Larry and talking to him."

The bishops, said Sister Montgomery, were very uncomfortable with the whole idea of direct action. "They have to worry about their tax exemptions. And they hate to go beyond dogma. They want to lay out some principles and let it go at that.

"But I'm a hoping individual. I think that the Church is changing. I think it's all coming from the bottom. The women's movement. It will change, and women will celebrate Mass, but it's not because the law's going to be changed — of course it will eventually change, but if we wait for it to change, nothing is going to happen. People think that you have to be patient and wait, but that's not how things work. Even canon law recognizes the process by which things change. If a law isn't practiced, then it ceases to be a law."

The media could be a factor in the process of change, said Sister Montgomery, but she wasn't counting on the media by any means. The media, she said, can be helpful on a local level. She cited the attention the Plowshares Eight had received in Philadelphia and in the local Norristown papers. The letters to the editor, in particular, fostered a dialogue. The same kind of dialogue occurred in Florida and Connecticut despite the bias of the media coverage. It had been evident, she said, that some local people actually came around to a different way of thinking. Nothing had happened before to challenge them.

National coverage, on the other hand, or the lack of it, meant little, she felt. "The *New York Times* is dead silent. You can't get any mention in New York if the action is anywhere else. The *Times* follows the approved line always. And it distorts news. If anybody is any good on the *Times,* they lose out — like Ray Bonner and Sydney Schanberg."

She told me about a young reporter on the metropolitan section of the *Times* who was very sympathetic after the bishops' peace pastoral. He went up to New London to visit a congregation that was holding a discussion on the pastoral and did an article on it. Then he tried to write an article on the Kairos group in Manhattan, but the editors kept postponing it until it finally appeared in truncated form deep in the paper.

"I think it's a matter of policy. There must be a lot of hostility involved, too, the way they treated Dan's book. It was overkill."

Not only had the *Times* panned Berrigan's autobiography, *To Live in Peace,* but its religion editor, Peter Steinfels, the former editor of *Commonweal,* had blasted it in the *Boston Globe.* Nothing irritates a liberal more than a radical. Radicals were always threatening to upset the apple cart of sweet, reasonable intercourse by rudely asking, Whose side are you on anyway?

The struggle that Sister Montgomery and her companions were carrying on was a discouraging one by any standard, a battle being waged in obscurity against fearful odds. So it was that she, like all Catholic peace activists, kept coming back to the issue of faith. "If I didn't have my faith, I couldn't do it. I admire people who can, somebody like Camus, who was supposed to be an atheist. Philip Berrigan is very strong on faith and community. Plowshares actions are actions of a believing community. We can't live isolated. Resistance communities are very important — Kairos, Jonah House, and the others. I think if we didn't have communities, we too would come around to thinking we were nuts because we see everybody else headed the other way.

"Our whole life should be resistance. I try to make mine that way, but what can you do?" The admiral's daughter, the former navy brat, laughed. "I get out of prison, you know, and then I'm back at the supermarket. Ready to gather in the goodies."

The Lost Child

Marietta Jaeger

I hadn't come to Detroit to talk with
Marietta Jaeger. I had come to attend a Pax Christi luncheon honoring
Bishop Thomas J. Gumbleton, a native son of Detroit and one of its
auxiliary bishops. It was an honor well deserved. Gumbleton had waged a
courageous and lonely struggle for more than fifteen years on behalf of
peace and justice. More than five hundred of his admirers had turned out
for the luncheon, filling the tables set up in the auditorium in the Shrine of
the Little Flower in Royal Oak, Michigan, just north of Detroit.

Protesters were marching up and down outside carrying posters alleging
that Gumbleton was un-American, Gumbleton was a pinko, Gumbleton
was a disgrace to the Roman Catholic Church — the familiar terms of
opprobrium marshaled by the untutored right. The protesters were a pretty
glum-looking bunch, including three or four nuns in pre–Vatican II habits.
There didn't seem to be any George Weigels among them; designated
ideologues, after all, have better things to do than to expose themselves to
the elements and to ridicule from hoi polloi who lacked advanced degrees.
The protesters were true believers, strangers to the nuances honed at leisure
at the Heritage Foundation. Their hostility far outreached their powers of
expression, and I felt a little sorry for them. But my dominant mood, I must
confess, was one of wistful irony.

Fifty years earlier, the demonstrators would not have been outsiders here
at the Shrine of the Little Flower. As soon as I found out where the
luncheon was to be held, I began remembering and hearing once more the
voice of Father Coughlin coming from the radio on the shelf in our kitchen
in East Cleveland in 1940. Charles E. Coughlin's fulminations against the

Communist menace and its chief American abettor, fellow traveler Franklin Delano Roosevelt, had been broadcast from the Shrine of the Little Flower, where he was pastor. The anti-Semitic Coughlin had placed great hope in the president until he became convinced that FDR had sold out to the Jews. *Mais ou sont les neiges d'antan?*

Gumbleton, now nearing sixty but trim and youthful looking, had become a bishop two years before his fortieth birthday. He had become a bishop three years before Cardinal Bernard Law of Boston and no less than eleven years before Cardinal John O'Connor of New York. More than two decades later, however, Gumbleton was still an auxiliary bishop of Detroit while O'Connor and Law had long since gone on to greater things. Chances were that Gumbleton would never be anything but an auxiliary bishop. Rome brooks no compromise when it comes to doctrine, but it is fluent in the language of nods and winks when accommodating itself to what it pleases politicians to call political reality. Unfortunately for his career, Gumbleton had never learned the language. He had a different view of reality. So did Raymond G. Hunthausen, but the Vatican had made Hunthausen archbishop of Seattle before it discovered that he did.

My host in Detroit was the Reverend Patrick J. McManamon, S.J., one of the movers and shakers of the Detroit province of the Society of Jesus. Though I really don't have much of a following as a scholastic philosopher, Fr. McManamon happened to be one of my admirers, the only one. Pat had been my study partner at West Baden College in the heart of Indiana long years before. We had spent two years together pondering amid bucolic tranquillity such things as whether the distinction between essence and existence was real or conceptual.

Pat had been especially taken with my affinity for the Arab philosophers of the Golden Age, Thomas Aquinas's worthy adversaries. Long after it had faded from my memory, he would gleefully recount a presentation I had once given on Avicenna, who believed that there was but a single agent intellect for all of us to share. I had obligingly put Avicenna's theory into clearer perspective for my classmates by christening it, so to speak, the dump truck school of cognition: knowledge was the excavation site, each individual mind was a dump truck, and Avicenna's single agent intellect was the steam shovel. Unfortunately, Fr. Schmidt, our metaphysics teacher, didn't share Pat's enthusiasm, and I received no encouragement to do advanced studies in this area.

We hadn't seen each other for about ten years when we met at the 1987 Pax Christi convention in Chicago the year before. Pat had been ill for some time with Parkinson's disease. It had taken its toll on him physically — one arm shook constantly — but we took up where we had left off, more facetious if anything than we had been in antediluvian days at West Baden. It was in the midst of our conversation that my visit to Detroit abruptly took a different turn. Pat pointed out a pleasant-faced middle-aged woman across the room. "Do you see her?" he said. "Her name is Marietta Jaeger. She's somebody you really should talk with."

Marietta Jaeger lived by herself in a devastated section of Detroit's inner city. There was so much open space, whole blocks on which there seemed to be no more than two or three houses still standing, that I felt no great sense of peril the next day as I parked my station wagon in front of a well-kept frame house painted an incongruous pink. She had an apartment in back. The award that Bishop Gumbleton had received the day before was called the Sister Kit Concannon Award, after a saintly nun who had worked in the inner city, and this was where Sister Kit had lived.

Marietta Jaeger was a widow. She earned her living by working part-time for the Episcopal diocese of Michigan. She also gave lectures, gave retreats, and sometimes got herself arrested in nonviolent demonstrations at military bases in Michigan. It had been a very long journey for a middle-class Catholic mother of five children from Farmington Hills, Michigan, and it had begun on a summer morning fifteen years before when the Jaeger family piled into their van, a trailer hooked behind it, to set out for a "once in a lifetime" camping trip to Montana.

In her book *The Lost Child*,* Marietta wrote that at that moment, just before her husband, Bill, started the car, she felt a sudden need for them all to pray aloud together. The Jaegers were not especially religious, and this was by no means a family custom, but she explained to her family that she thought that the occasion demanded something special. In preparing for their trip to Montana, the Jaegers had fallen in love with the state. They were going to investigate the possibilities of settling there permanently.

"This was not only going to be a unique and special time for us," she told her family, "but also maybe the beginning of a new life in a new place. We need God's blessing." The family agreed, and they said some Hail Marys and an Our Father. Marietta felt that something more was called for, however, and though she wasn't at all used to spontaneous prayer she "blurted out" a prayer for the occasion. "Lord, we ask that You bless this vacation, give us good weather and good times, protect us from harm, keep

---

*Marietta Jaeger, *The Lost Child* (Grand Rapids: Zondervan, 1983).

us all safe, and show us what Your will is for us in Montana" (pp. 17–18).

God may have been highly selective, not to say cruel, in responding to Marietta's prayer, but so dramatic were the events that followed that they might give even a determined skeptic pause.

All young children are special, but Susie seems to have been endowed with a grace, in every sense of the word, that was unique. Her mother conveyed this effortlessly in *The Lost Child* by simply recounting ordinary events. In the course of the happy journey out to Montana, the Jaeger family would unwind at rest stops by running around and throwing a Frisbee. Susie, who was tall for seven and very well coordinated, would finish by doing cartwheels all over the place.

There was one extraordinary incident as well, at least in terms of its New Testament resonance. One day, shortly before the family left for Montana, Marietta had been working hard in the garden and had come in, worn out, to get dinner for her family. Susie, seeing how tired her mother was, made her sit down in a chair and then she got a basin of warm water and washed her feet.

On their second night at the campsite in Montana, Marietta came into the tent where Susie was sleeping with her brothers Frank and Joe and her thirteen-year-old sister, Heidi, to kiss them all good night. They were "snuggled side-by-side," she remembered, in their individual sleeping bags, their heads to the back of the tent. The oldest child, sixteen-year-old Dan, was sleeping by himself in the Jaeger's van. When she bent over to kiss them, Marietta could barely reach Susie, who was wedged between Heidi and nine-year-old Joe. Her lips barely brushed her cheek. "Oh, no, Mama," said Susie. She pulled herself out of her sleeping bag, climbed over Heidi, and, putting her arms around her mother, kissed her full on the lips. "There, Mama," she said. "That's the way it should be" (p. 23).

Heidi woke up at five the next morning to feel a cold breeze blowing. The tent had been cut open. She reached out and felt wet grass. There was no trace of Susie except for the teddy bear she had slept with, which lay on the grass outside. The search began. First the Jaegers themselves, including Marietta's mother and father, who had come up from Arizona to join them on their once in a lifetime trip, then local and state law enforcement agencies, and, finally, the FBI. It was to be one of the most extensive searches in the history of Montana.

A week after the kidnapping, the wife of a sheriff's deputy, on duty at the campsite, received a phone call from a man who claimed that he was the kidnapper. To prove it, he said to tell the parents that the girl had "humpy fingernails." When the deputy conveyed this to Marietta and Bill, they stared at each other. Susie had been born with two deformed fingernails. The family had become so used to them that Marietta and Bill had not thought of them as distinctive when they gave the FBI an exhaustive description of Susie. The call had to be authentic.

The kidnapper demanded $50,000 in cash. The Jaegers not only didn't have that kind of money, they knew no one who did, but a friend of a friend, someone who insisted on remaining anonymous, put up the money. But the Jaegers waited in vain for a follow-up call on the ransom demand.

The people of Montana, the state that the Jaegers had once fallen in love with, rallied around the stricken family from Michigan with an extraordinary display of support and affection. Finally, even though it seemed to them that they were abandoning Susie, there was no choice but to return home.

The summer passed with no word from the kidnapper, but then in September he called the Jaeger home. Marietta was out, and Dan took the call, a brief one. The man again identified Susie by her "humpy fingernails" and said that he still wanted to exchange her for a ransom but hadn't figured out how to do it. He would call again, he said. But then there was nothing further.

The months dragged by. In late winter, the FBI reported to the Jaegers that an eighteen-year-old girl had disappeared near the campsite and her charred remains were found on an abandoned farm in the area. They were investigating the case for a possible link with Susie's disappearance. Another element in the investigations was the stabbing death of a boy Susie's age at the same campsite a few years earlier.

Then, exactly one year after Susie was kidnapped, the kidnapper called the Jaeger home a second time, a quite different kind of call. It was in the small hours of the morning on June 26, 1974, the precise time that he had cut the hole in the tent and dragged Susie out into the night, his hand gripping her throat. Marietta stumbled out of bed to answer the phone. She had the presence of mind to turn on the tape recorder.

"A reporter from the Associated Press office in Montana had come to interview me for a story that was to run on the anniversary of Susie's kidnapping," Marietta told me as we sat in the living room of her apartment. "But, by mistake, they ran it a day early, and the kidnapper read it and it challenged him."

Marietta Jaeger was telling a story she had told and retold, one that was all too familiar to her. That would account for her fluency. But there was something more to it than mere fluency. Marietta seemed to be gifted with an extraordinary ability to express herself, not just to convey things clearly but to convey them with a warmth and feeling that demanded a response.

It was a charisma that the world may have little noted during the years she lived in Farmington Hills, but I felt sure it had affected many people since. And one of them was a polite and industrious young man named David, whose pleasant, ordinary demeanor masked a deeply disturbed nature. David was the kind of man who haunts the mind of every mother and father, a man that the media simply term a monster and have done with it. This time, however, thanks to Marietta, the media would be compelled to present something more complex.

She recalled how, after the interview was over and she and the AP reporter were drinking coffee together in her kitchen, he had confessed his inability to understand her faith. He would never be able to set foot in a church again, he told her, if what had happened to Susie had happened to a child of his. "I told him I understood just what he was feeling, but I also felt I had to share with him all the ways the Lord had cared for us during this time. And I said finally — and the story that ran quoted me verbatim — 'I really wish that I could speak to the kidnapper myself. My heart aches for him and how he must feel. But I'm afraid I'll never get the opportunity.' "

Such was Marietta's challenge, a challenge of love delivered to the man she had every earthly reason to hate. And he had risen to it, even if not in the spirit in which she made it.

Marietta described the kidnapper's manner on the phone, smiling faintly. "He was very smug. 'You wanted to talk with me. Okay, here I am. What do you want to talk about? I am the one calling the shots.' "

It seemed incredible to me that she had been able to control herself, but, as Marietta explained, she had traveled a long way since that terrible morning in Montana. "In all this intervening time, this year's period, God had really been doing a number on my heart. Shortly after Susie had been taken, I had come to grips with wanting to kill this man, with revenge. But God had been asking me to surrender, to give up my hatred, to be willing to forgive him. So I had tried to act accordingly all that time. I had tried to think and speak respectfully of the kidnapper and had asked other people to do so in my presence. And I had prayed for him every day.

"So that by the time I was hearing his voice in my ears, I was genuinely concerned about him. He was taken aback by this. It was not the attitude he was expecting, and so he began to back off and to talk about things that he and Susie had done, the friendship that he and Susie had developed. He said that he had come to love her as his own little girl. He was still asking ransom for her, he said. Then in the end, he broke down and wept. He said: 'I wish that this burden could be lifted from me.'

"I really — to my own amazement, really — wished that I could do something to help him. But then he hung up. He realized he had been on the phone for over an hour, and he was terrified that the call had been traced. The rapport of concern and compassion between us had kept him on all that time, and in the process he had inadvertently revealed a lot of information about himself."

After the phone call, the FBI made copies of the tape and distributed them throughout the country. Agents on the scene in Montana realized at once that this new evidence pointed to a young man who had been one of their original suspects. He lived near the campsite, he was a loner, and he had been involved in violent incidents in high school. They began to check on his whereabouts and see if, indeed, he had a child with him.

The FBI had determined that the call had come from Sarasota, Florida. Three weeks later, however, Marietta received a call from the phone company in Montana. They had gotten a complaint from a woman who had received a bill for an hour's long-distance phone call to the Jaegers' number. Marietta referred them to the FBI, and when the FBI interviewed the woman, they learned that the call had come from a cabin she owned, which was far back in the hills. Leading from the cabin, the FBI discovered, were bare telephone wires that anybody with a background in communications would know how to attach a handset to, and directly underneath the wires were truck tire marks made by brand-new tires. The FBI went to the closest tire dealer and discovered that the same young man, David, who had been indicated in the anniversary conversation, had recently bought the kind of tires that had made the tracks. He had also been in the Marines, where he had gained the expertise in communications that would have made such a call possible. Even more telling, David had worked as handyman at the cabin, which was so isolated that most people were unaware of its existence.

The FBI was then able to determine that he had been in the little town in Wyoming from which Marietta's son had received the first phone call in September. As it turned out, David had also been a suspect in the death of the eighteen-year-old girl, since he had been a rejected suitor. But, as he had done when questioned about Susie, David had passed a lie detector test, and the police had released him.

At that point, given this wealth of circumstantial evidence, the FBI went to David and told him that he was a suspect in Susie's disappearance. The young man protested his innocence, but, on the advice of his attorney, he submitted to more lie detector tests, which he again passed with flying colors, doing the same with a truth serum test for good measure. Nevertheless, the psychiatrists and psychologists who had been studying the tapes and other evidence were coming to the conclusion that this clean-cut, highly intelligent young man was seriously ill and a grave menace to the community.

Precisely because David was so dangerous, however, the authorities had to proceed slowly until they could be sure of a successful prosecution. "They needed concrete evidence," said Marietta. "The only concrete evidence they had was that an FBI lab had established that David's voice print on a tape with an FBI man matched the voice on the tape I had made on the anniversary of the kidnapping. That was a new kind of evidence at the time, and they needed a renowned voice print expert to make it credible to the jury. At that time there was just one, at the University of Michigan, but he was tied up in litigation. So we had to wait until he was available."

I couldn't help but recall that J. Edgar Hoover had not shown a like caution a couple of years earlier when, on the word of an informer, he had pushed for the indictment of Philip Berrigan, Elizabeth McAlister, and other Catholic peace activists on the charge of plotting to kidnap Henry Kissinger and bomb the heating tunnels under the Capitol. Hoover knew, of course, that Phil and Elizabeth, whatever else their faults and failings, were not going to murder children if they were acquitted, as indeed they were.

"Because David had broken down during the telephone conversation, the FBI asked me to go out to talk to him in person. A face-to-face conversation might cause him to break down again, they said, and admit what he had done to Susie. By this time it had become clear that there was no little girl there." Marietta's voice suddenly became soft. "In spite of all his talk of exchanging her for ransom, it was clear that she wasn't there.

"So I accepted the opportunity because I felt it was a chance given by God to go out and tell him face to face that I forgave him and, more than that, that God had forgiven him and that God was giving him this opportunity to reconcile all that he had done.

"I had three opportunities to talk with him out in Montana, but he knew I was coming, he had agreed to it, and he had ample opportunity to get up his mental guard. And he was very careful not to incriminate himself. He was very shrewd. He was going to beat this rap. And he was sure that they were not going to pin this on him in court."

In *The Lost Child,* Marietta vividly describes her confrontation with David, a young man whose deep, dark eyes immediately told her that something was terribly wrong with him. She should have been afraid, but she wasn't. She had in fact spent all of the previous night in prayer. Their final parting was especially dramatic:

As David stood up to leave, he reached out to shake hands with me. I grasped his hand with both of mine and tried one last time. "David, I know you're the man who took Susie, and the authorities will be able to prove it in court, but it would be so much better for you if you admit it now. There's no escaping the truth."

"I'm really sorry, Mrs. Jaeger," he replied. "I wish I could help you, but I don't know anything about your little girl." With that, David walked away. It took all the control I had by God's grace to release his hand and allow him out of my sight. (p. 88)

"So I had to come and give the whole thing back to God again, and I went back to Michigan," she recalled. As it turned out, the confrontation had been successful. For a week later David called again. He had come home late one night and pulled down the shades as if he was going to sleep. Then he slipped out the window, cut through a field, took another man's truck, and drove all night to Salt Lake City, where he called her collect the next morning. He wanted to convince her that now she was speaking to the real kidnapper. This man David in Montana who is being considered as the prime suspect, he told her, is not really guilty.

"But I recognized his voice," Marietta said. "It was an extraordinary conversation. And at the end, he said, 'I want you to hear your little girl's voice, but you can't talk with her.' I said okay, and then I heard what sounded like a telephone booth door opening, and then I heard a little girl's voice saying: 'I'm on his lap, Mommy. He's a nice man.' Then he came back on the phone. I knew it wasn't Susie's voice. It was definitely a western-sounding voice. But I wanted to keep him on the phone, and I asked him all kinds of questions about how she looked, what she was wearing, and all that. I knew that they were trying to trace the call. I began to call him David, and that panicked him, threw him into a state of confusion. He began to talk about things that David and I had spoken about the week before in the presence of his attorney and FBI agents, conversations that had been recorded. In his panic, he incriminated himself, and when he realized what he had done, he said: 'You'll never see your little girl alive again,' and he slammed down the phone."

The FBI had traced the call and had agents on the scene, but David eluded them. He jumped into his truck and, traveling by back roads, drove back to Montana. The FBI put out an all-points bulletin for him and for a missing child. (The little girl's voice that Marietta had heard had been on tape, but the FBI didn't determine that until much later.)

"Later that day," said Marietta, "David showed up in town and was immediately approached by the FBI. He said: 'Gee, I've been here all day long. I've been going from job to job, and you've just missed me.' But they knew of course what he had done. And in this tape recording, he had totally incriminated himself. And so they no longer had to wait for the voice expert, and they began to go through the red tape necessary to get a warrant for his arrest. And when it was ready, the head agent called me and told me that David would be arrested in the morning, that I would probably wake up to a host of media people on my doorstep, and not to say anything since I was probably going to be a principal witness in the trial."

The agent in charge, who had become very close to the Jaegers, had more news for Marietta. The family's year and then some of agonizing suspense had finally come to an end. Once the connection had been made between David and Susie and the girl whose remains had been found on the abandoned ranch, the FBI had gone back to the ranch, taking it apart. Every time they found something, they sent it off to the Smithsonian Institution to be examined by anthropologists and biologists. In one of the last bundles they had sent, the Smithsonian had found part of the backbone of a young female child.

"And so it was, finally, the concrete proof of what I had already come to know." Again Marietta's voice dropped. "It wasn't the answer I had prayed for, but God had been faithful to get me through it all. That night was the worst night I spent other than the night that she was taken. Knowing positively that her life had been taken."

David was arrested, still insisting that he was innocent. But when the sheriff and the FBI searched his house, they found irrefutable evidence. Some of the irrefutable evidence was bloodstains. Some of it Marietta did not describe, either in the book or in our interview. The police found it in a freezer, however, a circumstance that leaves little doubt as to its nature. Our minds and our hearts hold back from acknowledging perversities so overwhelming. But in another sense this final horror illustrates just how profound was the charisma that Marietta Jaeger had been gifted with. She had reached this man, a monster so much in control that he had breezed through lie detector and truth serum tests.

"They went back to the jail and confronted him with that evidence in the presence of his attorney," Marietta continued. "At that time in Montana, the penalty for a kidnap-murder was death. And they offered David — and this is what I had asked them to do — they had offered David life imprisonment with a chance for psychiatric help if he would confess. This had been my prayer for David. By this time, I had come to understand that God's idea of justice is not revenge but restoration. I had come to desire this restoration in him.

"If Jesus is the Word of God, then Jesus is the justice of God. And Jesus did not come to punish us, but to restore us. And that's what I wanted for David, because he was a very, very sick young man. So they offered him this opportunity."

David took it. He confessed to killing Susie. He confessed to killing the eighteen-year-old girl. He also confessed to killing the boy stabbed to death at the campgrounds and another boy as well.

David told the police where he had buried Susie's head. Hence there was a skull as well as a piece of backbone in the tiny casket at Susie's funeral.

As it turned out, there was also abundant evidence that David was also responsible for the deaths of many other children throughout the state, but these murders had occurred in counties where the prosecutors refused to yield on the death penalty, so David refused to acknowledge his guilt.

"So much for the deterrent value of the death penalty," Marietta said. "It didn't prevent him from taking the lives of those children. The only deterrent value was a negative one — it prevented the legal resolution of the rest of the murders. And I'm convinced that the concept of capital punishment violates the mandate of forgiveness. All Christians are going to be held accountable for allowing it."

By the time David had finished his confession, it was four o'clock in the morning. And at eight on Sunday morning, they left him alone to eat his breakfast. David, being short enough and clever enough to devise a way to hang himself, committed suicide. "And so . . . so . . . that ended the whole thing. And it wasn't what I wanted for him at all. But God nevertheless had worked in my own heart in terms of the compassion and concern that I had had for him."

David was twenty-six years old.

"He was a very, very intelligent young man, as is often the case with psychotic people. And I believe that there was a part of him that truly, truly grieved for what he had done. But he just was very, very sick. And I'm not sure just how much in control of his behavior he was."

Marietta's concern and compassion through her ordeal seemed astonishing to me. I wondered how her husband, Bill, who had been raised a Lutheran but had no links to any denomination, had reacted to all this.

"Well, my husband was a very brave man and a very stoic man. But he was not in the same place that I was in terms of forgiving. He felt — and I had to struggle with this, too — it's a natural attitude in a parent that you would seem to be betraying your child by being willing to forgive anybody who would do all those things to her. She had been raped. And then . . . when he had cut the tent, he had reached in and strangled her to the point of unconsciousness. And then he pulled her out and carried her to his truck. He drove her to the same abandoned ranch where he'd later take the life of the eighteen-year-old girl, and then he had assaulted her. In the process of that, she had become hysterical, and in an effort to control her he had strangled her again. And then he had dismembered the body, decapitated her. So it couldn't have been any worse."

We like to think that Americans have been spared the kind of horrors that the people of Europe suffered under totalitarian regimes, but some of us have not.

"And for Bill, the thought of forgiving that would be betraying Susie as her father. And that's a very natural human attitude, and that's what I had to struggle with. And yet, he was, you know, a real example of how unforgiveness undoes us." As time went by, Marietta explained, her husband began developing various ailments, first arthritis, then an ulcer. It was only through coming to terms with Susie's death and developing a better attitude toward David that he began to regain his health. But then a fatal heart attack overtook him. Bill had been only fifty-six, relatively young, but who can measure the toll exacted by the trauma that began in the predawn hours of a summer morning during a once in a lifetime vacation?

It was a tragic event that had also left Marietta quite changed. It had, she firmly believed, transformed her relationship with God. "I had been raised to believe that God was a loving father, but I also had been taught that he was a just judge and disciplinarian and that he delighted in hard work and discipline and sacrifice. A real taskmaster. To remain in God's favor you had to toe the line. Then I came into a relationship with a God who to my amazement was just crazy about me and loved me beyond my wildest dreams. And wanted good things for me and joy and gladness."

Marietta had been baptized a Catholic, raised in a Catholic home, and attended Catholic schools. While it was true that she survived the trauma of Susie's death with a firm and joyous faith, she first had to endure a severe crisis of belief. "My intellect wanted to understand why this all happened," she explained. "I've seen that so often. You want to see some sort of divine logic in human disaster. We need to figure that out so that all this pain is not for nothing. So that we can say that it's all in God's will. Well, it's never God's will. I'm absolutely convinced of that. It's not what God wants for his people at all. And God doesn't deliberately send things our way to test our faith or to strengthen our faith." For the first time, her tone was ironic.

"God uses these things to develop our characters and strengthen our faith, but that's not why God allows them."

Pat McManamon had told me about an experience Marietta had when she went to New York to appear on a television program. A woman who had also lost a child had berated her, telling her that her whole reaction was false. I asked her about it. The program, she said, was Geraldo Rivera's show. Not the ideal forum for reasoned discourse.

The program was about capital punishment and in the audience was a woman whose young daughter had gone to the store one night and just disappeared. Seventeen days later her decomposed body was found. Her parents never knew what happened to her or who was responsible. The woman was embittered and in favor of the death penalty.

Marietta had spoken against the death penalty, and, after the program, as the audience was departing, the woman walked past her. Marietta stopped her. "I touched her on the arm and said that I was so sorry about her daughter and that I certainly could relate to her grief. And she looked at me, she glared at me, and she said: 'It's too bad you're not as sorry about your own.'

"And I just felt so bad. Because that's something I have to deal with so much. When I speak against the death penalty, there are some people who seem to think that I must be a failure as a mother and that I couldn't have really loved my daughter if I didn't want to avenge her death." Her voice rose suddenly. "Certainly, I struggled with it. There was a point when I would have happily strangled the kidnapper with my bare hands with a smile on my face. But I'm so grateful that God did not leave me there. Because I see again and again these parents, these people who have lost loved ones through violence. I see how their unforgiveness is undoing them. It really diminishes their lives. They become tormented, embittered, hateful people, and I always say God is the best psychiatrist going. God knows that the only way that we are going to become happy people, whole people, and healthy people is when we learn to forgive. And it certainly comes with a struggle. Meeting Jesus at the Cross and dying to our own feelings. But it also means resurrection — for me as a Catholic. It means resurrection. It means experiencing a peace and a freedom and an inner joy. That just isn't possible otherwise, and I'm so grateful that God did not leave me there."

Appearing on Geraldo Rivera's show had been painful for her. The panel, made up of parents who had lost children to crimes of violence, had been stacked four to one in favor of the death penalty, and, as might be expected, Marietta had little opportunity to say the things she felt had to be said — never mind the distractions and interruptions from commercial breaks and

Geraldo's untiring efforts to whip guests and audience into a frenzy. But despite everything, the show had been the occasion for an immensely consoling experience as well.

As soon as the program was over, Marietta had been whisked out to a waiting limo. When the driver opened the door for her and she took one look into what seemed like a huge cavern, she felt no desire whatsoever to sit there by herself. "So I asked the driver if I could sit in front, and he was delighted to let me do that. And so we discussed capital punishment. He was on the same side as I was. And since I had a couple of hours before my plane left and since I was his last job for the night, he just said, very generously, 'I'm going to give you a tour of New York City.' So he proceeded to show me all the sights, drove me all through New York City, I had a wonderful time. It was just what I needed to kind of put me back together again and just kind of settle me down again. He was a gift from God. What I needed to heal up again. It was wonderful."

It was especially wonderful because Marietta had to get up at six the next morning to give a retreat at a Detroit high school. She had gotten involved in giving retreats when various church groups asked her to share her faith journey with them. These people had all been Protestants. As no Catholic need be told, the Catholic Church is not especially eager to turn an ear to stories of faith told by the laity, especially lay women. And what did Marietta have to offer, after all — a homemaker without even a college degree. It was a pertinent enough question. Marietta herself was the first to ask it, but she was also able to come up with an answer.

"I decided that God wanted something from me that didn't have to do with formal education. So I accepted these invitations. And with my knees knocking, I just told my story. And the more I told the story, the more scriptural principles I began to see in it. I came to see it as a real contemporary parable. The sacrificial lamb, and ransom, and the image of the tent. The tent is a biblical image. I began to see it as a contemporary parable addressed to God's people in the here and now. Calling on them to see areas in which they have been kidnapped from the safety of God's tent and about the attitude of unforgiveness. And I began to see how God spoke through people, through Susie's story, and called them to examine their own lives for areas of unforgiveness.

"Anyhow — as God does things, you know — a speaking ministry evolved. Evolved with no desire or design on my part. I never did anything to promote any of this. I said to God, I'm yours. I know how much pain it causes a parent to have a child kidnapped. And how much it costs and how much it hurts. And I began to see how God was grieving for the children who had been kidnapped from the safety of God's tent. And so I simply offered myself and gave my life to that end. And so I just came to see the rest of my life as an orchestration of God's work."

As time went on, Marietta's concerns broadened. She began giving retreats with a priest concerned about peace and justice. She also starting reading the newspaper with greater care, and she became alarmed and indignant as she began to see that her country was putting more and more money into nuclear arms at the very moment that it was closing the books on welfare programs for children, for the poor, for the homeless. She became aware of the peace community in Detroit, especially the Catholic Worker communities. Slowly, inevitably, Marietta's very personal spiritual journey was leading her toward social action.

"It became clear to me that there was a whole spectrum of violence that a Christian has to say no to. I don't see how these Christians can advocate violence. I just don't see how they reconcile Scripture with that attitude. To me, the same biblical principle applies. If I cannot kill the kidnapper, then neither can we bomb an aggressive nation. And if I have to learn to forgive the kidnapper, then we have to find some way to live at peace and in harmony with those who are in conflict with us. Other than by destroying them. And given the whole cost to the poor and the oppressed of our buildup of nuclear arms, the violence that's being done to those people through it in all its forms, I really felt that God was calling me, in a more public way, to take a stance against violence. Against the violence of nuclear arms, against the violence of our foreign policy in countries like Nicaragua, the passage of the Contra aid bills, and our refusal to take a strong stand on sanctions against South Africa and its practice of apartheid."

When some members of the Michigan legislature attempted to reinstate capital punishment in the state in 1982, Marietta was one of the leaders in the successful campaign to defeat it. She was especially persuasive because her own experience took direct issue with the main arguments of capital punishment's proponents: deterrence and justice for the victims' families. "There are no number of retaliatory deaths," she said, "that are going to compensate me for the loss of my daughter or restore her to my arms. To say that the death of any other person is going to be just retribution is an insult to the inestimable value of her life to me."

We began talking about the effect of history on the choices we make in life. I told her about how anti-abortion activist Joan Andrews was appalled when she learned about the Holocaust in school and the acquiescence of the German people, about how she had begun to read everything that she could get her hands on, and how this knowledge not only intensified her opposition to abortion but gave it a direction that it might not otherwise have taken.

"That's exactly what happened with me," said Marietta of her own emergence as a peace activist. "After what happened with Susie, I remembered reading about the Holocaust in school. I remembered wondering, Why didn't people protest? How could this happen? Why didn't people do something? And then I remembered hearing about how the children in Germany, as they learned about their history, went home to their parents and said, Where were you? How could you have let this happen? And that was one of the things that brought me to the stage where I was willing to take a real public stance and, in fact, become involved in civil disobedience. I don't want my grandchildren coming to me and saying, Where were you when this was happening? Why didn't you do something?

"And I really think that that is what God is calling the Church to do. In these days, to stand up, to take a stand, and be counted as a Christian. The whole of our lives has to be the word of God. Not just our worship, but our work, and our plans, and our play, and our laws, our foreign policies, all that. . . ."

Marietta herself had responded to this call. She had been arrested many times, on one occasion spending thirty days in jail. Her arrests had come for protests against nuclear armaments and against aid to the Contras, one of the latter occurring on the anniversary of Susie's death. Two particular targets of peace activists in the Detroit area, she said, were Wurtsmith Air Force Base and the headquarters of Williams International, a company that had played a crucial role in the development and manufacture of the cruise missile.

Marietta had also gone to Nicaragua. "I've seen for myself what the Contras do. And I've seen for myself the innocent blood that has been shed — the cost and the anguish. And I cannot allow that to be done in my name. I simply refuse to allow that to be done in my name, and I will not wash my hands of it. I will take a public stand against it. So I took my own blood and threw it on the entranceway of the Federal Building." She was now on a year's probation for an arrest at Wurtsmith.

I wondered whether she, like Archbishop Hunthausen, had made tax resistance a part of her opposition to the arms race. She kept her income below a taxable level, she said. She did this in part as a personal challenge to simplify her life, but she also did it to prevent contributing to the "war machine." Her part-time work for the Episcopal diocese also had the advantage of leaving her free for a full round of speaking engagements and retreats.

Marietta's children were all grown. Two sons were married, and she was already a grandmother four times over. The third son was working and going to school, and Heidi, her surviving daughter, who had awakened that terrible morning in Montana to find Susie gone from her side, was in Nicaragua working with an American Jesuit. Heidi was twenty-seven. Tomorrow, Marietta said, was Susie's birthday; she would have been twenty-two.

I asked her about choosing to live in Detroit's inner city, a decision that seemed to entail a frightful risk.

Marietta laughed. "Yes, this is a dangerous neighborhood. But for me — I've lived here five years — but for me, I went out to Montana, which was for me God's country, pure air, water, wonderful people, wide-open spaces. God's country — and the most terrible thing of my life happened there. After that, when you have had to go through that kind of life-and-death situation, the experience becomes a gift to you. It really becomes very freeing. And God has used that to really free me to live down here, without, perhaps, the degree of fear that a lot of other people would experience. After that, what can anybody do to me?"

We finished our conversation, inevitably enough, by talking about the Church and its future. What, I asked, did she want the Church to do?

"I would like to see the Church take a much stronger stand against the policies of our United States. I think for too long we've equated Christianity, Catholicity in fact, with patriotism." It was a stance she felt we ought to rethink. It was clear, she said, that in Jesus' time you could not be one with God and also be one with the state. "And I think that we've compromised our concept of our Catholic faith to accommodate what patriotism demands. Somehow if the government legislates it, then we simply presume that it must be moral, and we don't question it. And I think God is calling us to take all of that and question it and evaluate it against the Word of God. And I praise God for shepherds and leaders like Tom Gumbleton, who is a dear and close friend of mine. And Bishop Colman McGee of the Episcopal diocese. Men who have taken strong and public stands and have been, you know, much persecuted by people of their own constituency. People don't want to be shaken up. They want to just be comfortable and go with the flow.

"But it's clear that if we're going to live a Gospel lifestyle, our life is not going to be comfortable, and we are going to have costs to pay and tasks to do that are going to be inconvenient — at the very least. Think about it — whole books of the New Testament were written while Paul was sitting in the pokey. It comes with a cost. And the Church is called to be prophetic, and, unfortunately, in this world prophets are called to pay a price."

Marietta Jaeger herself had paid an enormous price. And she was still paying it. What she called "one of my great sorrows" had occurred just a few weeks before. She had been invited by the Dutch Reformed Church in Montana to speak on reconciliation. And while she was there she contacted the man who had been the FBI agent in charge of Susie's investigation, a person whom she had gotten very close to in the fifteen months of the investigation and whom she had come to love dearly. "He had grieved terribly when he finally had to resolve the case," Marietta told me. The man, whom she did not name and whose name I didn't ask, was a Catholic, and it was his pastor who had said Susie's funeral Mass.

"But now," said Marietta, "he's the attorney general for the state of Montana. We had lunch together, and when he found out I was involved in peace and justice issues, he stopped eating and looked at me.

"We were now on opposite sides. He had just gone around and told all the judges in Montana that any peace protester that's brought before them should be given the maximum sentence. He would arrest Archbishop Hunthausen, he said, if he set foot in Montana.

"The two of us just sat there and kind of wept across the table from each other."

Laboring Through
the Heat of the Day

Gordon Zahn

That war is too important a matter to be left to the generals is by now a sentiment that even some generals are likely to assent to, albeit reluctantly. As for theology, however, the theologians have been more successful in preserving a monopoly, perhaps because their miscalculations have had less sanguinary consequences, at least in modern times. It happens, nevertheless, that the *Catholic Dictionary of Theology*'s definition of "conscientious objection" — a concept pertinent both war and to theology but one that generals and theologians alike do their best to ignore — was written by a nontheologian, Gordon Zahn. Who is Gordon Zahn?

Dorothy Day had the kind of face that photographers love. She had graceful features, still girlish in old age, but the eyes they framed expressed steely authority as readily as warm compassion. Dorothy knew she was right, and it showed. The Berrigan brothers, too, have faces to be reckoned with: Philip's face is that of the stern patriarch who, trusting in God, fears not to lead his people into the desert, while Daniel's more whimsical crags and creases suggest Elijah as Peter Pan. Even Thomas Merton's bland appearance was redeemed by mobile features, and in his photos a sly irony glints from the corner of the eye, lest piety oppress.

In such company Gordon Zahn, though by all rights a star, has the look of a supporting actor, a Paul Lukas among John Waynes, Jimmy Stewarts, and Joan Crawfords. Like the Berrigans, Zahn had an Irish father and a German mother (as a boy he took his stepfather's name), but, despite the force and eloquence of his prose, his manner betrays no Celtic flare. His is the quiet, methodical determination of Central Europe, formidable enough in its own right. Zahn could be Czinner, the good gray radical, in Graham Greene's *Orient Express* or the socialist in Lina Wertmuller's *Seven Beauties* who tries in vain to talk sense about Mussolini to his feckless fellow prisoner Giancarlo Giannini.

Soft-spoken Gordon Zahn, born in 1918, has eyes that are mild and youthful behind rimless glasses. A stocky man, a bit below middle height, he wears a brush mustache, keeps his gray hair close-cropped, and favors suspenders. Despite his quite unthreatening appearance, despite his being the most loyal of Catholics, Gordon Zahn may have done more to disturb the tranquillity of smug clerics then even Dorothy Day and the Berrigans. Zahn may not have the charisma but he does have the facts, and for three decades he has been a thorn in the side of ecclesiastics who cling, come hell or Vatican II, to the no-spot-or-blemish theory of the Church as bride of Christ, a bit of inspiration they've drawn from the Song of Songs while piously averting their eyes, it's safe to say, from its more celebrated verses. ("Thy breasts are like twin fawns that feed among the lilies.") If Einstein was right in defining genius as the ability to ask the questions that only a child would ask, then Zahn is a genius. His questions, moreover, cause acute embarrassment, another characteristic of the behavior of geniuses and children. Many of them are in effect a variation on "What did you do in the war, Daddy?"

In the early sixties, a time when many of the prelates who ruled the Church in Germany during the Hitler era were passing on to their eternal rewards to the accompaniment of glowing temporal encomia depicting them as adamant foes of the Nazis, Zahn, a professor of sociology at Loyola University, Chicago, published *German Catholics and Hitler's Wars.** The book was a thoroughgoing indictment, all the more devastating for its quietly reasonable tone, of the German Church's wholehearted support for the war. Zahn concluded that "in World War II, the leading spokesmen of the Catholic Church in Germany did become channels of Nazi control over their followers, whether by their general exhortations to loyal obedience to legitimate authority or by their even more direct efforts to rally these followers to the defense of *Volk, Vaterland,* and *Heimat* as a Christian duty" (p. 203). Two years later, he followed it up with the first full-length work in any language on the life and death of the remarkable Austrian peasant Franz Jaegerstaetter, whom the Nazis beheaded because he refused to fight in a war he judged unjust. Zahn gave the sadly apt title *In Solitary Witness* to the Jaegerstaetter book. It was a fitting companion piece to

*Gordon Zahn, *German Catholics and Hitler's Wars* (New York: Sheed and Ward, 1962).

German Catholics and Hitler's Wars and in some ways an even greater embarrassment to the Church in Germany. It was hard to argue that no ordinary person could make a correct judgment on so complex a matter when Jaegerstaetter's death stood as testimony that one ordinary person had in fact done so. *"Contra factum,"* as the Scholastics put it, *"non stat elatio."*

Jaegerstaetter did it, moreover, wholly on his own. Though four Austrian and two German priests perished as he did because they too declared themselves against the war, he knew nothing of their witness, and no priest or bishop he encountered during his time of trial offered him the least support in his decision. His only real sympathizers among those in authority were two army officers, an irony that reflects yet more pitilessly on the willful blindness of the clergy. These two honorable men, once they realized that Jaegerstaetter was wholly sincere, made every effort to save him from the guillotine. All he had to do was to sign a declaration indicating his willingness to serve and he could go home, they assured him, and he would never be bothered again. Jaegerstaetter refused. If he signed the paper, he said, he would be giving his approval to Hitler's crimes. Jaegerstaetter thus lost his head and left his wife a widow and his young children orphans because he refused to sign a piece of paper. An excess of scruples? If so, it was the same one that had afflicted St. Thomas More four centuries earlier, a parallel that no member of the German hierarchy, even to this day, seems to have noted.

It's no wonder that Gordon Zahn should have been drawn to Jaegerstaetter. He, too, came to his conclusions about the morality of war on his own without any help from priests or bishops. The war that forced him to decide, moreover, was the same one. World War II might be fondly remembered by Americans as the last good war, but Zahn, a pacifist, felt that any killing was incompatible with the spirit of the Gospel. Fortunate to be living in the United States rather than Germany, Zahn, instead of losing his head, was obliged to report to a Civilian Public Service Camp for conscientious objectors after his draft number came up in 1944.

Even among fellow Catholics opposed to the war, Zahn was unique, as he explained to James Finn in *Protest: Pacifism and Politics:*

> I came into Civilian Public Service as a conscientious objector, feeling
> that I would be almost alone as a Catholic in the program. I hadn't even
> heard of the *Catholic Worker,* for example, until after I had had my first
> tussle with the draft board. In other words I'd gone, applied as a Catholic
> for this conscientious objection classification, and was told by the local

Catholic pastor, who I believe was chairman of the draft board at that time — or at least sat on it — that it was absolutely impossible for a Catholic to be a conscientious objector. I imagine largely because of his position my first classification was turned down and I had to appeal. And it was while this appeal was in process that somebody pointed out to me there was a group of Catholics that took the same position and were publishing a paper in New York. And that was the first I had *heard* of other Catholics who held this position.

And so when I got into Civilian Public Service, in the Catholic camp, my position is the one that I've described as integralist. It was a humanitarian type of Catholicism: You had on the one hand the nature of war, the spirit of war, the genius of war if you would call it that, and on the other hand the genius or spirit or nature of Christianity. And I just made a judgment — largely emotional, part intellectual, I suppose — that the two were irreconcilable. Then when I was in camp I met educated Catholics who began pointing out that I was holding an untenable position in their eyes, and they instructed me in the traditions of the just war and quite converted me at this point into a traditionalist Catholic pacifist.*

The conversion was short-lived, however. Zahn soon returned to his original position, and, though he was accustomed to going against the tide and didn't need the validation, his kind of pacifism — one based on the whole Gospel and not an exegesis of this or that passage — was recognized by the peace pastoral in 1983 as a wholly orthodox tradition in the Church.

At one point during Zahn's confinement, which lasted until 1946, he was sent to work as an orderly in a facility for the mentally retarded in the Baltimore suburb of Catonsville, where a quarter of a century later the Berrigans would initiate a new era of Catholic protest. It was a type of protest, however, about which Zahn had serious reservations.

On what meat has this our dean of Catholic peace activists fed that he had thus grown so contrary?

Gordon Zahn was born in Milwaukee the year the war to end all wars ended in Europe. His father died when he was a boy, and his mother remarried. Neither his mother nor his stepfather, to whom he says he was never close, influenced his thinking on war and peace, and he believes that they would have disapproved of his refusal to serve in World War II. His mother was

*James Finn, ed., *Protest: Pacifism and Politics* (New York: Random House, 1967), p. 63.

dead two years, however, before the question arose; though his stepfather was still alive, Zahn was on his own by then, having gone to work for a finance company after graduating from high school. Nor did parochial schools influence his thinking. His education was in the Milwaukee public schools, where the German he learned proved sturdy enough to see him through doctoral studies and the years of extensive research required for his books.

Camp life marked Zahn's first association with people who had gone to college, and he decided that he, too, would like to get a college education. A kindred soul, a friend he made during these years, was Richard Leonard. The two, describing themselves as pacifists, wrote to three Catholic colleges: St. John's in Minnesota and two Franciscan colleges in New York State. The latter, despite the well-known sentiments of their order's founder, failed to respond, but St. John's, a Benedictine school, offered them free tuition, and Zahn and Leonard accepted with alacrity. All went well the first year, but then the dean informed Zahn and Leonard that, despite their excellent grades, it was unlikely that they would be allowed to continue at St. John's. It seems that their pacifism had upset the returned veterans on campus and — more significant perhaps — some former military chaplains on the faculty.

"Dick and I slept two nights in a school bus," said Zahn, recalling the incident with calm detachment, "while the community argued about what to do with us. Then after we had gone home, in midsummer, we got telegrams. The abbot proposed that we stay out for a year and then come back on full scholarship after things had settled down. We had been working during the summer, however, and we had enough money for tuition. So we decided to return to St. John's and offered to pay our way."

The innocent gesture set off two more days of argument at St. John's, at the end of which the side favoring Zahn and Leonard — which included the dean, Fr. Martin Schirber, and the renowned liturgist Fr. Godfrey Diekmann and his brother Conrad — decided to capitulate because the issue was tearing the community apart. St. John's thus rejected a future recipient of its Pax Christi Award, but in those heady days, so soon to pass, in which Americans were still savoring their righteous victory over evil, no one saw the need for Pax Christi Awards.

Fortunately, a small diocesan college, St. Thomas in St. Paul, Minnesota, was quite willing to accept pacifist money, and after getting their undergraduate degrees there, Zahn and Leonard went on to do graduate work at Catholic University in Washington, D.C. There they found a benevolent and generous mentor in Monsignor Paul Furfey, one of the rare churchmen of the era who realized the importance of peace studies. Still another happy turn of events was the election to the House of Representatives of a man who had been one of their favorite teachers at St. John's, Eugene McCarthy. Leonard got a job running an elevator in the Capitol, and Zahn worked in McCarthy's office.

Zahn spent the next few years getting his doctorate at Catholic University (his dissertation was on the social backgrounds of American conscientious objectors), after which he went to teach at Loyola, the Jesuit university in Chicago.

"Dick and I were both interested in the same themes — conscientious objection and war and peace — and we always remained so," said Zahn. "We wanted to get college degrees to be more effective in peace and justice work. I don't think we started out intending to be teachers, but then when we saw what teaching was, we decided it was ideal. Dick taught for twenty-five years at LaSalle in Philadelphia. I got more involved in research activities than he did. He got married and started to raise a family, and so he didn't have the freedom I did."

Sociologists, Zahn said, never expressed much interest in his work. "They're still not convinced that anything I've done has been very sociological. My primary career has always been peace work." That has included chairing the American Pax Society with Eileen Egan and serving on the board of its successor, Pax Christi, as well as the boards of the Catholic Peace Fellowship and the Fellowship of Reconciliation.

It hasn't been only sociologists who have been less than enthusiastic about the bent Gordon Zahn's scholarship has taken. Just before *German Catholics and Hitler's Wars* was to be published by the German-based Herder and Herder, Archbishop Samuel Stritch of Chicago, made a cardinal by John XXIII, went to Rome to receive the red hat (one of those consecrated phrases Catholics once loved), and he took with him the president of Loyola, Fr. James McGuire. In the midst of his grand tour, McGuire was invited to meet with three cardinals on a matter of some urgency. One of the three was the recently elevated German Jesuit Augustin Bea, soon to emerge as one of the heroes of Vatican II. (Bea's admirers would take delight in the happy coincidence of a British Empire Airways poster that proclaimed, "BEA Gives You More Freedom." The theme of the Rome meeting, however, had nothing to do with freedom.)

"The cardinals explained to McGuire," said Zahn, "that they were afraid that my book would give aid and comfort to the enemies of the Church and that they wanted me to withdraw it. A book I had worked on for seven years and which had already been accepted for publication! I told McGuire that

I thought their thinking was all wrong. The truth about the German Church in World War II would come out sooner or later, I told him. Better it come out in a book written by a Catholic professor." Fortunately, Zahn had tenure by this time.

Herder and Herder, caving in to ecclesiastical pressure, gave the book to the American Catholic house Sheed and Ward, a move that Zahn took as a change for the better since it gave him the services of Philip Scharper, Sheed and Ward's gifted editor-in-chief.

"The book was already set in type," said Zahn, "when, one Friday, Frank Sheed came in and asked Phil why there was all this fuss about the Zahn book. Phil gave him the proofs, and he read it over the weekend. He came in on Monday and said to Phil: 'This is a book that has to be published.' " No one was more loyal to the Catholic Church than English convert Frank Sheed, who, along with his wife, Maisie Ward, often defended its claim against all comers from a soapbox in Hyde Park. Perhaps, indeed, Sheed's faith in its ability to prevail over the gates of hell exceeded that of the German hierarchy.

Just before the book came out, the student honor society at Loyola, an elite group charged each year with selecting the outstanding faculty member, voted to give the award to Zahn. The administration informed them at once, however, that they were to do nothing of the sort. A Jesuit patiently explained, as only a certain species of Jesuit can patiently explain, that, according to reputable German Catholic journalists, Zahn had dealt with the German hierarchy of the war years in malicious fashion. If the students wouldn't listen to reason, moreover, and if they persisted in giving the teacher of the year award to Zahn, their organization would be disbanded. The students, who included Peter Steinfels, had little choice but to give in, but they later gave Zahn an award of their own devising.

Three years later, in 1962, Zahn left Loyola for the University of Massachusetts. They had made him a generous offer: not only would they pay him $9,000 more than Loyola did, but he would have to teach only two classes, each with no more than twenty-five students. Zahn felt like Bob Cratchit on December 26, even though his Scrooge had not been transformed but superseded. "It sounded pretty wonderful," he recalled. "I offered to stay at Loyola if they were willing to pay half of the difference, but I was pretty sure they wouldn't respond." He was right, needless to say. Zahn's tone became wistful as he reflected. "Loyola wasn't that favorable a situation for me."

His work had, however, gotten support from some members of the Loyola faculty. Especially enthusiastic was the Jesuit John McKenzie, the renowned biblical scholar who would become a peace activist in his own right and, unlike Zahn, take the greatest delight in ruffling episcopal feathers. No one in the administration, however, ever had a word of praise for the author of two of the most significant books of the era, and the American hierarchy too remained silent. Bishops, after all, like members of Congress, have to stick together. So accustomed was Zahn to being ignored that when, some years later, he learned that Bishop Thomas Gumbleton was to introduce a speech of his on Vietnam at Wayne State University, he was apprehensive and quite unprepared for Gumbleton's unstinting praise.

Zahn took advantage of the freedom afforded him by the University of Massachusetts by going to England in 1964 to interview former Royal Air Force chaplains for a third book, *The Military Chaplaincy*, which was published in 1966.

The attitude of air force chaplains in particular was a subject of keen interest to Zahn since the saturation bombings of Europe by the Allied air forces, massacres of unprecedented proportions that by common consent had lengthened the war rather than shortened it, had been direct attacks on the civilian population and, as such, obvious violations of the conditions for waging a just war. But, with two notable exceptions, no Catholic had spoken out authoritatively against these atrocities. John Ford, S.J., a conservative American Jesuit, had duly demonstrated the immorality of saturation bombing in a coolly reasoned 1944 article in *Theological Studies*, but he had seen no need to make a big fuss about it. (Holding the line on artificial birth control was something that engaged Ford's passions to a far greater degree; twenty years later he would be one of the handful of theologians who prevailed upon a wavering Paul VI not to give in.) Dorothy Day, on the other hand, the only other Catholic voice outside the chorus, had vehemently and repeatedly denounced saturation bombing in the *Catholic Worker*.

Either way, no one paid any attention, and the corpses baked to ashes in bomb shelters in Dresden and Hamburg reminded no one of Greer Garson's quietly heroic Mrs. Miniver smiling and hugging her children to her as German bombers droned overhead.

"No one I talked to in the course of my interviews evinced any signs of guilt," recalled Zahn, "at least at first. They considered themselves pastors, they said, just like any other pastors. And as pastors, they thought, they had nothing to do with matters of military policy. They saw as an important part of their role the maintaining of good fellowship and high morale among the men. They knew, of course, that they had an obligation to offer moral guidance, but they saw this as relating to the weaknesses of the flesh."

Gentle as Zahn is, he's never content to let points of this sort slip by uncontested. "I put it to them this way," he said, " 'If a commanding officer ordered a man to procure a woman for him, you'd tell the man that he was morally bound to refuse the order. But if the commander ordered him to wipe out a city — a city like Dresden, packed with women and children fleeing the Russians at a time when victory was certain and the war had only a few months to run — that was another matter entirely.' "

Many of the former chaplains had the grace to be troubled by this line of reasoning. They told Zahn that he was raising questions that had never occurred to them. Questions never raised before! Think of it. Perhaps the mistakes and omissions of theologians even in modern times can, after all, be measured the way those of generals are.

Zahn's presence in England coincided with the discussion of Schema 13, "The Church in the Modern World," at the Vatican Council. Dick Carbray, in Rome as British Archbishop Thomas Roberts's adviser, contacted Zahn and asked him to come to Rome and lend his authority to a lobbying effort in favor of a strong stand against modern war. Zahn's friend Eileen Egan was part of this effort, and so, in a characteristic way, was the indomitable Dorothy Day, who with eighteen other women pacifists from various countries, was in Rome fasting for peace.

"The contents of the Schema," said Zahn, "had been leaked by some bishops who were appalled by its treatment of modern war and conscientious objection. Some Americans, moreover, were arguing, logically enough, that if the just war doctrine was to retain any practical worth, the restrictions against direct assaults on noncombatants had to be dropped. So Dick and the others decided that something had to be done." They invited Zahn to a conference at Oxford at which Archbishop Roberts and Abbot Cuthbert Butler spoke. Butler, a Benedictine who chaired a committee of 150 bishops dealing with the peace and war aspect of the document, started right in on Schema 13, supposedly a forbidden topic, and Roberts, after a proper show of reluctance — he was a Jesuit, after all — eagerly joined in.

"I had, of course, seen a copy of it," said Zahn. "It stated plainly that a citizen could not support any war that was manifestly unjust, but it specified that the presumption of justice had to be with your government, and so you had to go along with it unless there was strong evidence to the contrary. I told the group that I thought that insistence on *manifestly* robbed the statement of all force. Butler responded that there were some things that everyone would agree were manifestly unjust, such as the use of torture. I said that it was interesting that he should bring up torture, since several of the Catholic chaplains I had been talking to, his fellow country-men, had justified the use of torture in interrogations."

The Oxford conference marked the start of a correspondence between Butler and Zahn in which Zahn gave a detailed account of his reservations about Schema 13 and stressed the need to strengthen its support of conscientious objection. Through Butler, Zahn gained the ear of the leadership of the British episcopal conference, verifying Jesus' observation about a prophet not being without honor, save in his own country and among his own people. Later that same year, 1965, Zahn crossed to the continent and spent an eventful week in Rome, though he himself didn't describe it that way.

"Roberts wanted me to write a speech for him, which I did," he said. "I also gave a talk one evening on Jaegerstaetter. Then Butler got me to speak at a luncheon for the British hierarchy. That was the extent of my lobbying."

Zahn's tone was deprecatory. Eileen Egan, however, had already described his efforts to me in rather more positive fashion. "Gordon's talk to the English hierarchy turned some of them around completely," she told me. "A woman journalist I knew came out of the sessions with tears streaming down her face. She said that she had never expected to see such a day."

Whatever the effect of Zahn's eloquence, whatever the effect of the letter drafted by the American pacifists and, translated into Latin by Dick Carbray, sent to every member of Butler's committee, the fact is that the final version of "The Church in the Modern World" contained a strong endorsement of conscientious objection. And, far from accommodating the just war doctrine to a world of nuclear arms by dropping the distinction between combatants and noncombatants, it denounced any attack on population centers with "weapons of mass destruction" as "a crime against God and man himself" which "merits unequivocal and unhesitating condemnation." Though "The Church in the Modern World" stopped short of condemning either modern war or the possession of nuclear weapons, it marked an immense improvement over past statements on the subject of war. The burden of proof, even though it might take a long while for the news to reach the ordinary Catholic in the pew or the Pentagon, had shifted irrevocably from those who would object to war as an instrument of national policy to those who would justify it.

In his treatment of American Catholic pacifists in *Tranquillitas Ordinis,* George Weigel accords ungrudging respect only to Dorothy Day and

Gordon Zahn. He wisely refrains from any direct criticism of Dorothy Day, and he mildly chides Zahn on but a single point: his failure to "take up the cudgels" (a peculiar metaphor, I suggest, vis-à-vis the dean of American Catholic pacifists) against those opponents of the Vietnam War who insisted on spelling America Amerika, equating by implication Nazi Germany and the United States (Weigel, p. 157).

When I mentioned Weigel's tut-tutting relative to the consonant switch, Zahn looked bemused. Not wishing to spend $27.50 on *Tranquillitas Ordinis*, he had only browsed through it at a bookstore and thus had missed Weigel's portrait of him. (It's safe to say that most of us in Zahn's place would have begun by looking in the index.)

"I think Weigel has me tagged as somebody more open than I actually am," said Zahn. Weigel had, in fact, invited him to an affair at the Smithsonian, a "very plush affair" chaired by Cardinal O'Connor, at which Zahn gave a paper on the Catholic peace movement. Michael Novak and James Finn also participated. "I had been bound and determined not to get into any extended discussions because I could see that I would be the token pacifist, but I did anyway. Finn said something I couldn't let pass. He criticized the peace pastoral for saying that pacificism and the just war were currents of Catholic tradition that complement each other. He saw no logic in such an assertion, he said. Then Novak followed it up with a sharper criticism of some sort. I said that I agreed with Jim but for the opposite reason. I couldn't see how the just war theory had anything to do with Christianity as it was at the beginning."

Zahn did praise the pastoral, however, for laying out the conditions for a just war, knowledge, he said, that had been the province of theologians until then, rarely trickling down to ordinary Catholics. Then, speaking of the just war theory, Zahn asked the assembled dignitaries and pundits what they thought of the Grenada invasion, a military adventure that violated at least four of the conditions for a just war, but, despite this, had provoked next to nothing in the way of protest from the American hierarchy. His pointed query was greeted with an awkward silence that was finally broken by Cardinal O'Connor. "He smiled pleasantly," said Zahn, "and said: 'Whenever we discuss these matters, we must make allowances for the charity of Dr. Zahn.' I hadn't intended it as a charitable statement."

The Irish have a facility for getting themselves and others through awkward situations with a joke or pleasant remark, a civilized trait, to be sure. It can be a dangerous knack, however, especially if it's invoked too often at the expense of truth.

Whatever Weigel's reading of Zahn's flexibility, the invitation to the

Smithsonian conference represented the kind of breakthrough that characterized Zahn's method. He stressed education above all else. Now retired from the University of Massachusetts, Zahn lived alone in an apartment in the Prudential Center in downtown Boston and commuted to Charlestown on the trolley to his current base of operations, the Center on Conscience and War. Billed on its stationery as an independent resource agency affiliated with Pax Christi USA, the center occupied a large room with a lofty ceiling in an old elementary school building owned by the Jesuits. The building, which housed various social welfare organizations, was in a bleak neighborhood across from a grim-looking bar, the Celtic Den, which was decorated with shamrocks and a leprechaun, the scene, someone later told me, of at least two murders. Cambridge might border Charlestown, but the groves of academe never seemed more remote.

"The center was started when draft registration began," said Zahn. "Everybody presumed the draft itself would start soon after. Since it didn't, the purpose of the center has changed somewhat. Instead of one-to-one counseling, we're doing more in the way of education work, reaching out to high school and college groups. There is so much hostility and ignorance to overcome. People are so concerned about some boy weasling out of doing his duty that they don't give much thought to those kids who have no fear of serving but have a problem in conscience."

One of Zahn's projects was raising $5,000 to dub into English a German television film about Jaegerstaetter. The film was available with subtitles, but, as he explained, subtitles tended to put off the young people he was trying to reach. Jaegerstaetter's example, he felt, could have a strong effect on the young. As shouldn't be too surprising, given the well-publicized difficulties of high school and college students with a subject as simple as geography, the youth of America have but a tenuous grip on social morality, something bristling with difficulties under the best of circumstances and especially confusing when taken in the abstract. "I'll never forget one boy at a Catholic high school," said Zahn. "He said that all war is wrong but that there were times when we must do what is wrong. Then on another level, you have the Jesuit president of the University of Seattle sending a letter to each incoming freshman urging him to join ROTC."

Zahn has done a lot of thinking on the question of ROTC on Catholic college campuses. "The presidents of the Jesuit universities in the United States have issued a statement calling for the 'strictly conditional acceptance' of ROTC, like, it seems, the pastoral's 'strictly conditional acceptance' of nuclear deterrence. The problem is that they don't specifiy what their conditions are."

Zahn himself had definite ideas about what the conditions should be: (1) Anyone teaching ROTC courses must meet the university's standards. (2) The ROTC program must be ultimately subject to those who run the university. (3) Any ROTC academic course must have a content that meets the school's standards and be open to all. (4) Special courses dealing with the special moral problems that might be faced in the military must be required. (5) If at any point someone decides it's against his conscience, then he is to be allowed to withdraw without penalty, perhaps with the ROTC stipend converting automatically to a student loan.

Zahn stressed that he was opposed to ROTC under any circumstances and that he never hesitated to make that clear. To get Catholic colleges to agree to these conditions, however, would, he said, be a significant break-through. "The Catholic educators who champion ROTC," said Zahn, "invariably argue that it's to the Church's advantage and to the country's advantage to expose future officers to the beneficial effects of a Catholic atmosphere. All right, let's expose them to it, then, and not shield them from it." He and Mike Hovey, his colleague at the center, had discovered from one of their surveys that only one Catholic university, Notre Dame, required its ROTC students to study the peace pastoral.

Zahn was very much a champion of the 1983 peace pastoral, despite his serious reservations about it. For a time at least, it made the morality of war and peace a hot topic. He was like a solitary prospector who finds that the claim he had staked years before has suddenly become a tourist attraction. The man whom Loyola University was quite content to be rid of twenty years before became the man of the hour.

Besides being asked to speak at Weigel's Smithsonian conference, Zahn also received an invitation from the American Catholic Church's Military Ordinate, which exercised authority over all military chaplains. "It came as quite a surprise when I was invited to attend a symposium they were having on the just war theory and pacificism at Georgetown. The main speakers were a General Rowney from the Pentagon and Peter Henriot, the Jesuit from the Center for Concern in Washington. About three hundred fifty chaplains on active duty were there. I gave them a hard-line talk, telling them the chaplain has the obligation to get in there and find out what men are being told to do and to make a decision on the morality of it. And I made frequent reference to the RAF interviews I did when I was writing *The Military Chaplaincy*."

However unpalatable much of Zahn's speech might have been to his audience, one point at least went over well. They took it as an unexpected concession that Zahn felt that servicemen should have a chaplain to attend to their spiritual needs. He was opposed, he explained, to the chaplaincy being militarized, with the chaplain wearing a uniform and getting paid by the government.

General Rowney and Bishop Angelo Accera, an auxiliary bishop from the Military Ordinate, gave speeches attacking the legitimacy of the pacifist tradition in Catholicism. Their speeches, in fact, seemed to have the same source since they made the same points in almost the same words. The level of argument was simply that Catholics who say that there has been an unbroken pacifist tradition extending from the Church Fathers through Francis of Assisi are wrong, and so it's incorrect to speak of the renewal of that tradition since it never existed. Peter Henriot, said Zahn, easily disposed of that one merely by giving the argument from the peace pastoral, which cited Augustine's difficulty in justifying killing for any reason whatsoever before finally reluctantly allowing it in the defense of others, not oneself.

"After it was over, Archbishop Joseph Ryan, the head of the Military Ordinate, came up and threw his arm around my shoulder and said: 'Thank you for coming, Gordon. We have to get together sometime for a talk.' I thought it was just nice, ritual politeness, but, a few months later, Mike and I were going to Washington for a meeting, and I phoned ahead to see if we could get together with Archbishop Ryan. It turned out that we got the red carpet treatment at their place in Silver Spring, Maryland. They gave us a tour, and then Ryan and two auxiliaries took us to lunch."

Archbishop Ryan told Zahn and Hovey that their presence at the symposium had destroyed the stereotypes that many chaplains had of peace activists. They videotaped the program and sent it around the world, Ryan said, and the response had been tremendous, though Zahn was inclined to think that that was more due to Rowney's contribution than his own.

Ryan went so far as to express the hope that Zahn and Hovey would participate in the next year's symposium. "We're not going to convert each other," Zahn admitted, "but it's opening a level of dialogue that I for one would never have thought possible. They're putting something together for chaplains, and they asked me to contribute an article and a peace bibliography. It's incredible. It was such a friendly meeting. And we had been trying to get in touch with them for years."

Another issue the Center on Conscience and War had taken up under Zahn's direction was the laws on selective conscientious objection, something that the American hierarchy had been critical of since 1968, though in its usual dithering manner. According to the law, a moral objection to a particular war is not enough to qualify one for conscientious objector status. One has to be against all wars. While Cardinal Joseph Bernardin, the head of the Bishop's Conference, was enthusiastic about Mike Hovey's proposal to do something about it, Zahn saw it as an area that most people don't seem to care all that much about. He had had trouble publishing articles on the subject, he said, and a conference he and Hovey held at Catholic University Law School, to which Selective Service failed to send a representative as promised, laid a large egg.

In Spike Lee's much-discussed film *Do the Right Thing*, one peripheral character, slightly demented perhaps, keeps trying to sell people a copy of a photograph that allegedly depicts Martin Luther King, Jr., and Malcolm X together. It would be much less of a problem to turn up a photo of Gordon Zahn and the Berrigan brothers together, but he and they nonetheless stand on opposite sides of an issue that divides the Catholic peace movement.

As unswerving as Zahn has been in his pacificism and as evil as he thinks the arms race is, he has never broken the law nor does he advocate doing so. "I have full respect for people who feel that that is what they must do, someone like Dan Berrigan. I would not criticize Plowshares people for doing what they're doing. I do object to the claims made by some that civil disobedience is the only form that activism may take. I am willing to give them whatever moral support I can. But my definition of an activist would include somebody who would come in here two days a week and watch our telephones because we're away. Anybody who does something."

Zahn recounted a conversation that had given him some pain. It occurred while he was riding to the airport with Marcia Timmel after the 1987 Pax Christi convention in Chicago. The dates set for the convention the following year were August 5–7, straddling the anniversary of the bombing of Hiroshima, a time that's invariably the occasion for demonstrations and acts of civil disobedience. Zahn mentioned to Marcia that the dates were inconvenient for him since he wanted to be in Austria on August 9 to join in a pilgrimage to mark the thirty-fifth anniversary of the death of Franz Jaegerstaetter. "She said, yes," said Zahn, "they certainly are inconvenient. Unless they change them, no activist will be able to come to the convention. That really got me."

I had to suppress a smile. The remark was vintage Marcia.

Some thought should also be given, Zahn said, to the economics of resistance. "It cost forty thousand dollars to run this place for a year. Yet how much money does it take for five hundred people to go to the Nevada desert test site to get arrested? And how much of the Plowshares funds are drained off on court costs and the like? Then there's also a drain on leadership.

"The Berrigans — the Baltimore Four, the Catonsville Nine — they accomplished something," said Zahn. "But it's the replications that weaken everything. How many Plowshares have there been? Who knows? They're reported. The trial is reported, and then they fade. People can't even remember the names. People could be active outside of prison in other forms of activities. Many get lost. One young man came out of prison a total wreck. He came up to me after a talk I gave at the Catholic Worker house in New York, and I thought he was some derelict who had walked in off the street. He has nothing to do with the Church anymore. Getting arrested has been romanticized. We haven't come to giving little medals for these things, but at times it seems that it's the only way you can prove to people that you're committed. Why haven't you been in prison?

"I admit that what I do is not the sort of stuff to make headlines, such as you'd get if you damage a nose cone. I admire the people who do it. It's just that I'm not sure it's the best thing they should be doing. But it's their own decision. Jim Harney, a priest from Boston, came back after being one of the Milwaukee Fourteen, and we had a long talk. I think it was meant as a recruiting talk. And I made it quite clear that I felt that that kind of thing had a diminishing impact. Each proliferation, even with larger numbers, doesn't have the effect you want. It turns people off, in fact.

"There were people in Milwaukee who supported me through my conscientious objection against a popular war even though they didn't agree with me. One woman who worked in a defense factory sent me her Army-Navy E pin. It wasn't the sort of thing to wear in a CO camp, of course. But the letters I got from Milwaukee after the Milwaukee Fourteen were quite different. No one has a right to do this, they said. And these letters were from people opposed to the Vietnam War, who supported my peace position. This kind of thing, they thought — burning draft files — was an affront to all authority. The message gets across that these people are breaking laws and defacing property. Another aspect I mentioned to Jim was that destroying draft records was like playing God. The draft board is going to fill its quotas in any case. They're simply going to pick young men whose records weren't destroyed." Zahn sighed. "But I'm not going to mount a soapbox to state my opposition."

I had been present at the speech that Zahn had given at the Catholic Worker. After describing his own history and the work that he was doing now, he spoke of the future of the Catholic peace movement. For it to be what it should be, he said, it must remain thoroughly Catholic, and it must not dissipate its energy by going off in various directions. The focus must always be on peace, however worthy other causes were. Ideas such as that, however, sensible as they seemed, were not welcome in all circles of the Catholic peace movement.

"There are those opposed to the Catholic peace movement," said Zahn, "who come right out and charge that Catholic liberals — the Catholic Worker movement, Pax Christi — have weasled on the abortion issue." Though the charge came from the far right, there was, unfortunately, some validity to it, he thought, because of the liberal affinity for freedom of conscience.

Given his total rejection of war, Zahn could hardly be called a centrist, but his essentially conservative Catholicism, his rejection of civil disobedience as a strategy, and his willingness to strive for the possible en route to the ideal all conspired to make him open to criticism from the left as well as from the right.

He had had an article on abortion rejected recently by the *Catholic Worker*. Instead of running his article, the editors had had a woman on their staff do a basic we-are-against-abortion-but essay, with most of it devoted to the hard cases always cited by those in favor of abortion. Zahn had responded with a letter that evoked Dorothy Day's unswerving opposition to World War II, a conflict for which there was no dearth of justifying arguments. The letter wasn't published.

The *Catholic Worker* also failed to publish an open letter that Zahn sent about certain liturgical irregularities at a Catholic Worker house. "I had heard various reports," he said, "and I had talked to someone who was very disturbed by what was going on. Liturgies were being celebrated by a nun, by lay people, by non-Catholics. The Catholic Worker movement had always been Catholic in the strictest sense of the word. The idea was to abide by the rules and not go off on your own."

The editors at the *Catholic Worker* had told him that the article was beautifully done but that he should get a theologian to address the issue of invalid liturgy. It was interesting, I thought, that the *Catholic Worker* had never suggested that Zahn seek a theologian's opinion to buttress his eloquent arguments against war. After that, *America* too rejected the article. *Commonweal* finally took up the issue Zahn had raised, though without printing Zahn's article in its entirety. As the *Catholic Worker* essay had suggested, *Commonweal* obtained the services of a theologian, who delivered the expected abstract on-the-one-hand-this, on-the-other-hand-that evaluation.

As willing as Zahn was to compromise on matters of tactics and strategy, he would not give an inch when it came to doctrine and principle. It was the kind of conservatism that struck a chord with me. It took very little accommodation, I thought, before we found ourselves on the way to becoming good liberals and subscribing to an array of dogmas fully as rigorous and much less reasonable than those we had left behind. But how strong one's faith had to be to take such a stand!

It seemed a lonely struggle, then, but never in the course of our conversations did Zahn's voice betray either discouragement or indignation. At the most there was a note of sadness, and that but once or twice, at not being understood.

"Maybe the recognition Mike Hovey and I get at the center may not mean much in the long run," he said as we walked along the promenade of the Prudential Center after our final conversation. I was on my way to catch a trolley to the train station. "But at least somebody is bringing up these issues in forums where they weren't brought up before.

"We could do more if we had more people. There's an awful lot of work for a two-man staff. Actually, just one. Mike's the only one getting paid. My initial idea was to retire from teaching altogether, but I still teach part-time, two or three times a week, and what I get from that goes into our work."

How about personal expenses? I asked.

"Well, I don't have a family, and my pension takes care of my needs. As for tax resistance," he said, turning to a subject that interested him more than his needs, "I've never been able to convince myself on that, whether partial or complete. If it's partial, then the part you pay goes for what you're against. If you make it total, they come and get it eventually, plus a penalty. What I say — and maybe it's a cop-out — is to give more to peace activities than they take from you for war activities. That you can do, and you can get a deduction for it, too. I've been called in sometimes, but I've always had the receipts to prove it."

Perhaps it was the talk of money, a major concern of mine, if not of my companion, that caused Zahn to take notice of the expensive shops that lined our way. Prosperity was in the air. The bloom was not yet off the Massachusetts economic resurgence, a boom fueled by Reagan-inspired military extravagance that — an irony unfortunate in more than one respect — was about to propel an unimpeachably liberal governor into the Democratic nomination for president.

Zahn turned back to me, smiling a boyish, conspiratorial smile. "I guess you and I don't have much to do with places like this," he said.

I remembered something from my Jesuit past. For a half hour every day in the novitiate we had to read from a vast work — four volumes covered in dark green oilcloth — called *The Practice of Christian Perfection* — by a seventeenth-century Portuguese Jesuit named Alphonsus Rodriquez. Rodriquez's standard narrative style was turgid, but he enlivened it from time to time with often pithy anecdotes not of his creation ("wherein the preceding is illustrated by various and sundry examples"). It was one of these that I thought of now. A Desert Father, the holy abbot Arsenius, never failed to take in the bazaar in Alexandria every time he got to the big city. Why? Well, as Fr. Rodriquez, or his translator, put it: "Arsenius would rejoice in his heart at the sight of all the things of which he had no need."

Rodriquez was gone now, gone with the wind of Vatican II, all those thick green oilcloth-bound volumes swept away. But Gordon Zahn was here beside me, his face lit with a rare smile. Sober, reasonable Gordon, with his short haircut, his gray suit, his rimless glasses. And while Gordon lived, so lived Arsenius — and Eutychius and Pancratius, and, patron saint of flagpole sitters, Simon Stylites, and Francis of Assisi and all the other holy screwballs of ages past. Two thousand years after Golgotha, despite the initial odds, the foolishness of the Cross seemed to be pulling still further ahead of the wisdom of men.

Not many people noticed of course, but that was always the problem, wasn't it?

A Grave
Beside the Road

William P. Ford

The photo I saw in *The New York Times* in January of 1983 showed a stocky man in shirtsleeves standing beside a road, his back to the camera. He was looking down at the ground as though lost in thought. As news photos go, it seemed too lackluster to have made the grade. It was a symbolic picture, however, the kind that usually involves heads of state or bereaved family members.

I knew the man in the picture. We had talked at length the year before, and we would do so again many more times over the next several years. He wasn't a head of state. He was William P. Ford, a Wall Street lawyer from Montclair, New Jersey. The picture had been taken in El Salvador, and the road ran through the province of La Paz to a village called San Pedro Nonualco. On the night of Monday, December 2, 1980, five Salvadoran National Guardsmen in civilian clothes had casually murdered his sister Ita and three other American women on the spot where Bill Ford was standing. The other three were Maura Clarke, a Maryknoll nun like Ita, Dorothy Kazel, an Ursuline nun, and Jean Donovan, a lay volunteer.

After sexually assaulting the women according to custom, the soldiers had shot each of them through the head; a gaping exit wound had destroyed Jean Donovan's face. It was the kind of thing that happened every day in El Salvador, but this was the first time it had happened to any North American women.

After a milkman making his rounds on the morning of December 3 had discovered the bodies, the National Guard, with a belated concern for tidying up, ordered some peasants to bury the bodies. The peasants, their reverence for the women contending no doubt with the fear that they might soon join them, had clothed one of the bodies with the jeans the soldiers had torn off, but in their haste they put them on backward. And so the ravaged bodies had lain buried beside the road to San Pedro Nonualco for two days, until Thursday, when they were dragged out into the bright sunlight of midday while cameras whirred and clicked and a horrified and enraged American ambassador looked on. Jean and Dorothy had had dinner with him and his wife on the last night of their lives, and they had gone directly from the embassy to the airport to pick up Ita and Maura, who were returning from a Maryknoll conference in Managua.

As it happened, His Excellency Robert White was the last American ambassador to El Salvador capable of moral indignation, or at least the last willing to express it. It was an indulgence that was to end his State Department career, but the scene he witnessed that day, so thoroughly recorded by the cameras, has had a significant effect on American foreign policy.

Ita Ford was from Brooklyn, Maura Clarke from Queens, Dorothy Kazel from Cleveland, and Jean Donovan from Westport, Connecticut. (The lone lay woman among the four, Jean had given up a successful business career to join the Cleveland mission team in La Libertad.) Today Ita and Maura, in accordance with the traditions of America's first missionary order, lie in graves in the blood-soaked soil of Chalatenango Province in the north, a province still bitterly contested more than a decade later. Their cemetery is crowded and garishly decorated. Dorothy lies in a section set aside for the Ursulines in a tranquil and spacious cemetery in a Cleveland suburb, her grave just a few yards from that of my Aunt Helen, who, in her more than sixty-five years as an Ursuline, never had an assignment that took her away from Cleveland. Irrepressible Jean lies in the family plot in Sarasota, Florida, where her parents now live.

Like Jesus, these four women went about doing good. Like Jesus, they made enemies in high places. Like Jesus, they were humiliated and cruelly put to death by soldiers. Like Jesus, they lay two nights in a grave. No glorious resurrection followed, but the witness of their broken, violated bodies was powerful enough in its own right. Today in towns and cities throughout the United States, there are thousands of young men, and women too, going about their lives who themselves would be lying in graves decorated each Memorial Day if Ita, Maura, Dorothy, and Jean were not in theirs.

They — or still younger men — might find their way there yet, but, up to now at least, no administration, not even Bush's, has dared to send American boys to die for allies who have been rash enough to make so obvious a display of their inhumanity. We have sent money, however, lots of money. And so the passion of El Salvador goes on. Today the Savior still hangs from the cross, held fast by nails that represent our tax dollars at work.

The deaths of the four women strongly affected me. Fifteen years earlier, as a Jesuit seminarian in Japan, I had in various ways been groping uncertainly toward the same kind of ideal that they had embraced with such conviction. Inspired by the Priest Worker movement in France — suppressed by the Vatican because the priests had gotten on much too well with their supposed mortal enemies, the Communists — I had lived in flophouses in the notorious Kamagazaki district of Osaka and worked as a day laborer. But it was the wrong time and the wrong country, and, as it turned out, I was the wrong person.

Though I myself had failed, I wanted very much to write about these women who had succeeded — not according to the wisdom of men, of course, but according to the foolishness of the Cross. The problem was to find an opportunity, and it didn't look as though one would ever come my way. In February of 1982, however, while I was working as a movie critic for National Catholic News Service, the release of a film called *Missing* finally gave me the chance I had been waiting for.

Though *Missing* was an American film, its director was the controversial Greek Costa-Gavras, who had gained fame in the late sixties with *Z*, a film about the assassination of a liberal politician in his native land. *Missing* also deals with an actual political crime: the arrest and murder of a young American named Charles Horman by Chilean security forces in the aftermath of Augusto Pinochet's bloody 1972 coup against the government of Salvador Allende. Jack Lemmon plays the victim's father, Edmund Horman, who goes to Chile to try to find him, and Sissy Spacek plays his son's wife. That *Missing* should have seen the light of day was extraordinary. Like the tragedy that would be enacted eight years later on the road to San Pedro Nonualco, Charles Horman's murder was the kind of thing, rife with explosive political implications, that Hollywood scrupulously averts its eyes from.

Costa-Gavras's film accused the American government not only of encouraging and supporting Pinochet's coup and of turning a blind eye to the bloody repressions that followed — charges that not even the State Department could deny with any show of conviction — but, by implication at least, of complicity in young Horman's death.

Naturally, the film was controversial, and I took some flak from the Catholic right for a sympathetic interview with Costa-Gavras in the *National Catholic Reporter*. No one, however, dared criticize me for interviewing Bill Ford in connection with *Missing.* For as Ford would put it on another occasion: "What's the percentage in arguing with somebody whose sister's been murdered?"

The idea for interviewing Ford came to me as I watched *Missing* at an early preview. There were some remarkable similarities, I thought, between his own experiences and those of the elder Horman, especially their running encounters with the tender mercies of the Department of State. Our ambassadors in Latin America, Robert White being a rare exception, had long enjoyed the style of imperial consuls, and neither they nor their superiors in Washington took kindly to confrontations with outraged taxpayers who had somehow gotten the idea that government was the servant of the people. Ford had become the primary spokesman for the families of the four women. Working with Maryknoll priests and sisters on the eastern seaboard, a well-organized group who knew how to attract public attention, he had in the fourteen months since his sister's death become a thorn in the side of the Reagan administration. Ford liked to bring his children with him when he traveled to Washington to sit down with State Department officials and other bureaucrats because, he said, it unnerved them to have to lie in front of children.

It wasn't just a matter of justice for the four women now. Ford was working for nothing less than justice for the people of El Salvador. I had met him at a rally in New Jersey and, presuming on this brief acquaintance, I gave him a call. So it was that my wife and I met Bill and Mary Anne Ford outside of a movie theater on East 3rd Street in New York City in early March of 1982 to see a final screening of *Missing* before its release.

Watching *Missing* with Bill Ford sitting next to me was a different experience from seeing it on my own, especially during one lengthy sequence in which Horman and his daughter-in-law search for young Horman's body in a hospital morgue filled with bodies. But it was a movie, after all, however disturbing its theme, and, as a movie, it had a beginning, a middle, and an end. It conveyed an esthetic sense of order that was satisfying. Jack Lemmon and Sissy Spacek and John Shea, as the victim, were glamorous and charismatic figures. One could mourn Shea's death, but one knew he'd appear again, handsome and charming, in other movies. *Missing* entertained as a good movie should. There was none of the messy and frustrating loose ends that life entails. Afterward we had sodas and sundaes at an ice cream parlor next door. As we knew all too well, we lived in a world in which terrible things happened, but in agreeable company in such a setting, the fashionable East Side, the horrors of life didn't seem all that real.

When I talked with Ford in his office the next day, however, the mood was quite different. Ford was once more the earnest, reserved man I had met at the rally. Once again he had to re-create an extremely painful event, an ordeal he was willing to go through only out of a sense of duty and a desire for justice. There was more to his determined air than that, however. Bill Ford was plainly a man who did not suffer fools gladly, a man used to succeeding in what he set out to do. The office in which we sat in the Wall Street firm of Ford Marrin Esposito and Witmeyer was emblematic of the bright American success story that Bill Ford's life had been until December 2, 1980.

The Fords had come from the Bay Ridge section of Brooklyn, the same Bay Ridge of *Saturday Night Fever*. Bill was the oldest of three children. His father was an insurance agent for John Hancock, his mother a teacher in the New York public schools. Besides Ita, the youngest, there was another sister, Irene. Bill had gone to Brooklyn Prep, where, before him, the author of *The Exorcist*, William Peter Blatty, had come to revere the Jesuit order. Ford's zeal for things academic was less than fervent at this stage of his life, as I would later learn from a friend, and his mother, Mildred, had to make a few trips to school to confer with his teachers. From Brooklyn Prep he went to Fordham University and then to pursue a law degree at St. John's University. Apparently he had picked up his academic pace quite a bit in the intervening years. For when he left St. John's, he went to work for the prestigious law firm of Mudge Rose Guthrie Alexander and Ferdon, which numbered Richard Nixon and John Mitchell among its alumni. In the early seventies, he and some colleagues left to form their own firm, an accomplishment Ford shrugged off by saying: "Well, we saw what they were doing, and we didn't see why we couldn't do it as well on our own."

Though he now lived in Montclair and though he would in years to come send his children to Dartmouth, Smith, Sarah Lawrence, Holy Cross, and Virginia, Bill Ford struck me as very much the kind of tough, urban Irish-American who thrived in New York City. Though his voice was more cultured, his speech rhythms were reminiscent of James Cagney's, growing staccato with a rising inflection when he wanted to make sure you understood what he meant.

Missing spoke even more directly to Bill Ford than I had imagined it would. Before going to El Salvador, Ita had spent seven years in Chile, and she had been in Santiago in 1972 when Pinochet's forces struck.

"Obviously when you watch something like that," he said, "you wonder what happened to Ita — you wonder what happened to her before she died." He paused. "You just realize the overwhelming sense of violence, the overwhelming sense of evil. I never had that feeling watching a film before, but of course I never watched a film in which I've had such a sense of involvement. I was horrified, but I was glad to see a movie like this shown in New York."

He spoke of the trip that he and his wife took to Chile to see Ita in 1976, four years after the coup, and of being startled at the sight of soldiers with submachine guns at the airport. The atmosphere of terror and menace in *Missing* caught the mood of the city, he said. He and Mary Anne stayed in the *bandera*, the shantytown outside of Santiago where Ita worked. The Fords had five children by then, but whenever they tried to guess the age of the undersized children in the *bandera*, they would be off by as much as five years: a thirteen-year-old looked like an eight-year-old. The police and soldiers came through in trucks like an army of occupation. "When you see a policeman in New York," said Ford, "you might get nervous if your car is overparked, but you don't think of him as the enemy."

It was an incident, however, that occurred when Ford and his wife were dining out in Santiago with Ita that brought the terror home most forcefully. A curfew was in effect, and the moment the lights in the restaurant blinked in warning an hour before the curfew was to begin, Ita jumped up and said that it was time to go. Ford protested that he hadn't finished his wine yet, but Ita insisted that they couldn't delay a moment. Then on the ride back to the *bandera*, she grew more and more nervous, and she asked her brother to drive faster because if they didn't get there by curfew, police or soldiers might open fire on the car. "I didn't believe it," said Ford. "I felt like, you know, 'Civis Romanus sum.' I was an American, and nobody was going to push me around." But his sister's anxiety finally convinced him the danger was quite real. Four years earlier, just at the time of the coup, Ita had had to make her way through a city swept by gunfire to get to the airport to return to the United States for her father's funeral. It was an experience so traumatic that it had affected her physically, and she suffered a permanent loss of much of her peripheral vision.

The house Ita lived in had been ransacked by the police more than once. She had also been a friend of Dr. Sheila Cassidy, a British woman working among the poor of Santiago who had been imprisoned and tortured by the security forces. The reaction of the British government, said Ford, had been in striking contrast to the American government's reaction to Charles Horman's disappearance. The British recalled their ambassador and lodged the strongest imaginable diplomatic protest.

Ford's reception in Washington after Ita's death, he said, was, initially at least, much more positive than the polite brush-off that Horman's father had received. Their circumstances were different, of course. Horman's son was missing and Ford's sister had been brutally murdered, an undeniable atrocity that had outraged many congressional representatives. "But when it came to the State Department, the treatment we got was very much the same. Our group got a lot of sympathetic murmurings but virtually no information. Even now we've had no contact with Secretary of State Haig. We write Haig and we get answers from somebody else."

Alexander Haig, whose brother was a Jesuit, was a "devout Catholic," the term used by the media to describe any member of the Church of Rome in public office who has never been indicted for indecent exposure or white slavery, and when he left government service, the Church honored him by making him a member of the Knights of Malta, a fraternal order made up of rich and powerful Catholic lay men throughout the world. The Knights of Malta are by no means to be confused with the egalitarian, even plebeian, Knights of Columbus. The Knights of Malta don't support charitable causes by standing around in front of supermarkets and jingling cans filled with coins. They sit down and, with quiet dignity, make out checks for sums recommended by their accountants.

Haig's elevation, duly noted in the media, may have inspired Mario Puzo when he wrote the opening scene of *Godfather III*, which depicts Michael Corleone's becoming a commander of the fictional order of St. Sebastian. The parallel is not as remote as a noncynic might hope. For Alexander Haig, devout Catholic and future Knight of Malta, revealed a Corleone-like tolerance for murder most foul in sharing his thoughts with the House Committee on Foreign Affairs on March 18, 1981. "I would like to suggest," he told the committee members, "that the vehicle the nuns were riding in may have tried to run a roadblock or may have accidentally been perceived to have been doing so, and there may have been an exchange of fire."

"When Haig gave his famous account to a congressional committee," said Ford, "it was four months after the event, and he already had been given the FBI report which states plainly that they each had been shot through the head at close range."

Haig soon had cause to regret his ponderous attempt to be disingenuous. Some of the less domesticated elements of the press gleefully seized upon it to write about pistol-packing nuns. Another Reagan administration luminary, Jeane Kirkpatrick, also had occasion to bite her tongue relative to the atrocity on the road to San Pedro Nonualco.

Kirkpatrick, not a Catholic but a member of the faculty of Georgetown, a Jesuit university, was our ambassador to the United Nations at the time.

She had endeared herself to the right, especially to Reagan, by her fervent and abrasive anticommunism and, in particular, by her ingenuity in devising a theory that postulated a distinction between totalitarian regimes (that is, Communist) and authoritarian (not Communist). Though both types were nondemocratic, the United States, she contended, should adopt a benign attitude toward the latter because there was hope that they would evolve into something better. As for Communist regimes, there was no hope of their changing, and so we had to tough it out with them. Even at the time, Kirkpatrick's theory had, at best, slight claim to intellectual respectability. Events in China and Eastern Europe would eclipse it at the end of the decade, and our splendid little war in the Gulf would turn it on its head, but it made Jeane Kirkpatrick famous. Ronald Reagan loved it. Not only did it have the immense attraction of being easily grasped, it sanctified some glaring inconsistencies in American foreign policy.

Kirkpatrick did not endear herself to Bill Ford and the other relatives of the slain women. The victims, she told a reporter from the *Tampa Tribune*, were not what they had seemed to be. "The nuns," she said, "were not just nuns. The nuns were also political activists." This was a truth, Madame Ambassador explained in her best schoolmarm manner, "that we have to understand much more clearly than we have." Ita, Maura, Dorothy, and Jean had been asking for it, in other words, just as the three civil rights workers murdered in Mississippi in 1964 had been asking for it. Blaming the victims is a harsh and cruel tactic in any circumstances, but for a woman to blame the victims of rape seemed especially malicious. Maybe it was a belated sense of shame, in fact, and not sheer expediency that prompted Kirkpatrick to deny her statement the next day, but in any event the reporter had gotten it on tape.

One scene in *Missing* that had especially stirred Ford's indignation was one in which State Department officials present the victim's father with a bill for shipping his son's body home. Eight years later, the State Department would inform Jean Donovan's parents that it would cost $3,500 to ship her body home. How, precisely, did the Donovans intend to make payment? they wanted to know. But there was no more talk of bills, said Ford, when Congressman Benjamin Gilman, a Republican from New York, went down to the State Department and raised hell.

"I got the very definite impression," said Ford, "that there are a lot of very unfeeling people in the State Department who are not really concerned about the death of Americans but only about this mindless and morally bankrupt policy that they are pushing. The death of the women is a mere distraction, a blip on the screen. They're concerned only about not embarrassing their client government. That, of course, was the message of Costa-Gavras's movie."

Another moment in the film that struck home with painful effect came when the ambassador finally tells Horman that if his son hadn't been involved, he would have been back in the United States quite unconcerned about events in Chile. "I'm sorry to say that in my case that's true," Ford said. "If Ita hadn't been murdered, I would have been sitting quietly making soft, clucking noises about what's going on in El Salvador without being moved to take any action. I just hope that the American people . . . that nobody has to suffer the kind of tragedy I did to get involved."

He hoped that *Missing* would have a wide audience and that it would make those who saw it stop and think about how their government was conducting itself in other parts of the world. "I think our government works fine here in the United States," he explained, "where it has to contend with a critical press, with one party watching the other. But, unfortunately, when we leave these shores, when we get out of sight, we tend to become like the people we're fighting."

The Catholic Church in the United States was, he felt, attempting to make Catholics somewhat aware of what was going on, but even though the bishops were ahead of their own people on this issue, they weren't doing nearly as much as they should. He believed that a pastoral letter should be read from every pulpit in the country denouncing the government for its support of a regime that murdered American missionaries as well as thousands of its own people, a slaughter financed by American tax dollars. The bishops had to be unmistakably clear.

"I think that this is a long way of saying that I'm basically an optimistic person. I think that you have to believe what Anne Frank said: that, in spite of everything, down deep people are good, or at least most of them are." He paused for a moment, thinking. Then he smiled for the first time. "If you see Costa-Gavras again, tell him I said thanks."

A year later, in March of 1983, I made another trip down to Wall Street, the place synonymous with power, to talk about the powerless. El Salvador, as Ford's picture in the *New York Times* had indicated, was still in the news, and the killing was still going on. The bishops, who unlike the prophets of old liked to think of themselves as team players, hadn't come out with the pastoral letter he wanted (nor have they yet). The five guardsmen charged with murdering Ita, Maura, Dorothy, and Jean had been in jail for two years, but they hadn't been brought to trial.

The trip to El Salvador two months before had been the first of many that Bill Ford would make to the country where his sister died. It had been a painful experience for him, he said, especially going to Chalatenango Province, where Ita and Maura had worked and where they lay buried. But he now better understood Ita's love for El Salvador and its people. He had also come away struck with the courage of those who were determined to make things better. "It's one thing," he said, "to live in El Salvador like Ambassador Dean Hinton, with a bodyguard and bulletproof car, but it's quite another to go out every day unprotected, knowing that the government is at best unhappy with you because you're working with the poor. Knowing you might not come home."

He had spent six days there, accompanied by Michael Posner of the Lawyers Committee for International Human Rights and Scott Greathead, first assistant attorney general of the state of New York. Their purpose was to investigate the state of the case against the five guardsmen arrested for the murders. What they learned was disheartening.

"The case is going nowhere — unless it's sideways over a cliff. The authorities are not interested, they're not concerned, they're not competent. And this despite the fact that this trial is supposed to be a showcase. The Salvadoran government simply does not seem to have gotten the message that the American government is seriously concerned. They've gotten the message rather that the U.S. is obsessed with Communism and that if the guerrillas can be tagged Communists, anything goes."

The FBI, he said, had not volunteered any of the evidence it had gathered. This material includes such valuable information as forensic evidence, lie detector test results, and evidence of death threats against the women. El Salvador's attorney general had made no effort to obtain this material and, yet worse, the judge appointed to try the case wasn't aware of its existence. Not only had the FBI not volunteered to give this evidence, which it admitted was more complete than that of any other agency, but it had refused to meet with the families of the women. The families, in turn, had sued the Defense Intelligence Agency and the CIA under the Freedom of Information Act, but national security, they were told, would be jeopardized if the FBI turned over the material.

Ford was not impressed with the zeal of the Salvadoran attorney general, Mario Adalberto Rivera, a nephew of Archbishop Arturo Rivera Damas, Archbishop Oscar Romero's successor. The attorney general's being a relation of the archbishop of San Salvador, a man once passed over for the see in favor of Romero because the Vatican and the local hierarchy had feared he was too far to the left, said nothing about his political orientation. Among the upper class of El Salvador everybody was related.

"Rivera didn't engage in conversation with us. He answered specific questions. It was obvious that he was meeting me only because he had been pressured. He told us that he believed that God himself had chosen him to handle this case. At one time he had been assigned to it as a judge, but he dropped off because of ill health. Now his health seems to have improved.

"He's a member of one of the right-wing parties, who have no interest in seeing the case brought to trial. So if he believes he's been placed there by God to try the case, it's probably because he believes that God doesn't want it to proceed. He didn't know where the files were. He's never visited the site of the murder. The autopsy reports have been lost. Other than offering some platitudes on vigorous prosecution, he had no theory of the case. The case is in shambles, and I told him that."

Ford smiled wearily at the suggestion that the Salvadoran government in its own self-interest should just try the five men, execute them, and have done with it. "I used to wonder myself why they just didn't have a lottery and shoot the five losers. But the problem is that there's blood on everybody's hands. Our understanding is that the five have been told that if they keep their mouths shut, the case will eventually go away. A lot of people know what a lot of other people have done. If these men are brought to trial and start naming names, the whole house of cards might come down."

The State Department showed hardly more zeal to prosecute the case than the Salvadoran government except for once every six months when it had to find some reason to tell Congress that progress was being made toward true democracy in El Salvador so that American military aid could continue. At such times, Ford got several phone calls from State Department officials assuring him of their everlasting concern. "Once they even asked me for advice on what evidence to ask the FBI for. I told them I thought the question was a bit ironic coming from a government that hasn't itself given me any information." Actually, said Ford, the State Department would like the trial to go forward and have the five convicted simply because then they could point to the conviction as evidence that El Salvador was a functioning democracy after all. Without at least the prospect of a trial, that was something that was going to be hard to prove.

At no time did the State Department betray the least hint that it entertained any suspicions that the soldiers might have been acting under orders when they murdered the women. This tranquillity, Ford explained crisply, was based on a single answer to a single question put to a single guardsman.

He was asked if he had been ordered to detain the women, and his negative response was true according to the polygraph. But no one at the State Department had seen the entire polygraph, said Ford, just this one portion of it.

Not a single lawyer Ford had talked to in El Salvador, aside from the attorney general, believed that only these five men were involved. Even the Salvadoran military men he had talked to had told him with unexpected frankness that five enlisted men would not have killed four North American women without having been ordered to do so, especially since the crime involved leaving their posts and changing into civilian clothes. There was no direct evidence, but a murder such as this could simply not have occurred in a Salvadoran context without orders having been issued.

As might be expected, American officials on the scene were not especially happy to see Ford and his companions, particularly the ambassador. "Hinton's attitude was that people like me put him in a very bad position. Because of us he has to lie. El Salvador is a very bad place. People are being murdered all the time, everywhere. He said that they obviously didn't like to have to say every six months that progress was being made around here, but they had to do it. The law says so."

Ford wasn't given to dramatic flair, but he was able to achieve the effect he wanted with ease. There was no change of facial expression, but there was a hardening of tone and a slight rise in pitch.

"But the law, of course, doesn't say you have to lie. The law says that unless you certify that progress is being made, there'll be no more aid. And the administration wants the aid to continue. So Hinton has to lie. He has to say that progress is being made because communism has to be stopped. And by the way, nobody from the embassy actually goes out and counts bodies. They depend on reports in the newspapers."

The press in El Salvador was firmly under the control of the government. The archdiocese of San Salvador was forced to buy an ad to get into print the pope's letter to the Salvadoran bishops urging them to be peacemakers and asserting that the country's conflicts were rooted in social problems. In all but one of the papers, the letter appeared way back in the classified section. The next day the advertising manager of the paper that had featured it more prominently was murdered. "Was there any connection between the murder and the placement of the ad?" asked Ford. "Well, there are a lot of priests in El Salvador who think that there was. And it's from these papers that the U.S. gets its information."

Perhaps the most affecting and difficult experience Bill Ford had had while in El Salvador had been a visit to a prison. "The prison is like a tourist attraction. Everything was arranged by the embassy, and an embassy official accompanied us. The inside of the prison was controlled by inmates, and there were pictures of Archbishop Romero all over. In an American prison, you can feel the tension, but that wasn't the way it was here. The warden took us through, and people would come up to him and complain about one thing or another, ask for more food or some other kind of food, or something. There were places set aside for conjugal visits."

Despite this relaxed atmosphere, Ford saw prisoners who had been tortured with hydrochloric acid because they had been accused of being Communists. The warden took care to make clear to his visitors that the military had tortured these prisoners before they were brought there, and the prisoners later confirmed this. They said that they felt very lucky since most of those arrested with them had been killed.

The embassy had taken the risk of letting them see these torture victims, Ford surmised, because there were enough Americans already well aware that this kind of thing was going on and the State Department could thus give the impression that they were aware of the problem and coping with it. If so, the arrogance of the young State Department official who had accompanied them dispelled any such illusions. "On the way back," said Ford, "we asked him what he thought about the men who had been tortured. He said they were liars, but when we pressed him about the actual scars they had, he said they were leftists, after all, implying that they got what they deserved. This young man was becoming like the kind of people we were supposed to be fighting — like becoming a Nazi to beat the Nazis." I couldn't help but be reminded of *The Time's Discipline* where Philip Berrigan and Liz McAlister quote a prophetic statement of Josef Goebbels, Hitler's minister of propaganda: "Even if we lose, we shall win, for our ideals will have penetrated the hearts of our enemies."*

No American in any official capacity in El Salvador had ever given voice to any sort of moral indignation over what had happened to Ford's sister and her three companions. "They all consider it a political problem," he said, "pure and simple. And that's the way they're dealing with it. The death of the women means nothing to them. Their only concern is damage control.

"But, you know," he went on somewhat ruefully, "the deaths of thirty-five thousand Salvadorans passed almost unnoticed. It took the death of these four women to get our attention. And that includes me."

As I had the previous year, I asked him about the awareness and involve-

*Philip Berrigan and Liz McAlister, *The Time's Discipline* (Baltimore: Fort Kamp, 1989), p. 21.

ment of the Church outside of El Salvador. He answered, as he had before, that the American bishops, though they hadn't been as forceful as he would have liked, were still far ahead of the rest of the American Church. He was a "bit surprised," he said, that the Vatican hadn't spoken out more strongly. "But I'll tell you who's dynamite on this — nuns. They've gotten the message that it's the religious women who are the main targets in situations like this. They're not in the churches functioning, as one priest put it, as sacrament machines. They're less tied to institutions, and they're out among the people. They're the ones who are at risk."

There were no longer any Maryknollers in El Salvador by 1983 (they would return in four years), but the work of Ita and Maura was being carried on by Salvadoran Sisters of the Assumption. They had originally withdrawn from Chalatenango because of the danger, but they had returned after the deaths of the two women. The Cleveland mission, to which Dorothy and Jean had belonged, was still carrying on as well in La Libertad.

Bill Ford, too, was carrying on, but he didn't see himself as laboring under any great burden. He was fortunate, he said, to be working for himself and to have the freedom to be able to devote a significant amount of time to this mission that he felt obliged to pursue.

It was evident, I said, that he viewed what happened as something more than a personal tragedy. Ford didn't answer immediately and, when he did, his tone of voice was almost harsh because of the emotion he was holding in check. Irishmen don't mind showing their feelings, but they want to be damn good and ready. "Well, let's put it this way: what does the death of these women mean? Are we just going to throw up our hands and say we're overwhelmed by the presence of evil? Are we just going to be quiet about it whether these five guys are convicted or not convicted? I think the lives and deaths of these four women have meant a lot to a lot of people."

He stopped for a moment.

"There is no question that I think I know Ita better now than before she was killed." All trace of harshness was gone from his voice now, and he was speaking softly. "She was a very deep person. I've gone back and I've reread her letters. I've read a number of things she wrote that I hadn't seen before. It would be presumptuous of me to say that I was carrying on Ita's work. But to the extent that I can draw attention to the cause for which Ita lived and died, then I think that's something I must do."

He was never tempted, then, to give up the struggle?

This time there was no pause. "How could I? Think of it — there were just these two women, Maura and Ita, working with those thousands of refugees. They certainly would have been more justified in giving up, but they stayed at it because they thought they were making a difference. If I threw up my hands and then met Ita again, how could I justify myself?"

Ita Ford. Ita. Her name was that of an Irish saint. I kept wondering what she had really been like. I thought of Dana Andrews in *Laura,* the detective who falls in love with a murdered woman. Holden Caulfield was right; the movies do ruin you. But maybe they don't after all, at least not the movies of the forties that J. D. Salinger was thinking of. Romantic and melodramatic though they were, the emotions they evoked were genuine enough. They were at least as good an education for life as was school, maybe better — just as long as you didn't come to believe in happy endings. Ita, unlike Laura, was really dead. She'd never step through a doorway like Gene Tierney wondering what all the commotion was about. Nor did Ita leave a stylish portrait in oils. Just the usual snapshots, so aptly named for the hurried glimpses they give into our busy lives. With Ita, however, reality far outdid the movies. Ita was a heroine in the true sense, the kind of heroine that American Catholics once thought you could no longer be, the kind we encountered as children reading the lives of the saints, the kind whose courage and selfless love might have stirred Ita herself when she was a schoolgirl in Brooklyn.

I felt awkward about asking her brother what Ita had been like, but once I did ask his wife, Mary Anne, a warm and voluble woman. Mary Anne smiled. "She was a pixie," she said. It was hard to think of a sister of Bill Ford as a pixie, but all the snapshots bore out Mary Anne's description. Short hair, elfin features, slim — Ita still had a girlish look in the last pictures, taken when she was forty.

When Ita died, Bill and Mary Anne Ford's six children ranged from John, a newborn baby, to eighteen-year-old Miriam. Of all the children, Miriam had known Ita the best. She had been only a baby when Ita entered Maryknoll, but then her aunt had gotten sick and dropped out of the order for a few years. During this time she had worked as an editor of children's books, and she had had an apartment in Greenwich Village to which Miriam sometimes went to spend the weekend. Miriam would help with the cooking when guests came for dinner and to listen to records. Since Miriam was tall for her age and Ita small, they could wear each other's clothes, and some of the last photos taken of Ita in El Salvador show her in one of Miriam's shirts.

It was to Miriam that I next talked. When I did, however, there was a more pressing reason than getting to know more about Ita. In the spring of 1983, Smith College decided to give Jeane Kirkpatrick an honorary degree and invited her to speak at its commencement. Kirkpatrick agreed to come, but then she changed her mind when college officials told her that they could not "guarantee her safety." It seemed that a group of malcontents on campus were raising a fuss, and even the liberal press, delighted with the opportunity to demonstrate the purity and consistency of its principles, had come down on the side of Madame Ambassador. As it happened, however, one of the ringleaders of the opposition, though the media for the most part missed the significance of it, was Miriam, a twenty-one-year-old senior.

Miriam had been shocked when she heard about Kirkpatrick's getting an honorary degree. "I felt it as a personal insult. Here it would be graduation, the last event of my life as a student at Smith, and this woman would be getting honored. It seemed to mock everything that my family and I stood for and that we had been working for."

Contrary to the media versions of the controversy, most of which were of the free-speech-imperiled-at-Smith genre, Miriam and her group were not protesting Kirkpatrick's speaking at Smith but her getting an honorary degree. (Ironically enough, Kirkpatrick didn't speak but did get her degree in absentia.)

The protesters didn't threaten to disrupt the ceremonies in any way but expressed their disagreement in a very reasonable manner. The Smith student paper ran a debate on the issue. Miriam wrote an article, and someone presented the pro-Kirkpatrick side. And there was a teach-in attended by more than 250 students. The protesters asked the trustees of Smith to consider the place of morality in politics. "For it wasn't just what Mrs. Kirkpatrick said about my aunt and the other women," Miriam explained, "but her whole outlook toward the rest of the world. We felt that it was up to us who represented the future to stand up and say: 'No, we don't want a person like this to be honored at a time when we're being honored.' So I don't think it's we who are against free speech. I think it's those who say we have no right to protest who are."

Two days after the Fords learned of Ita's death, Mary Anne received a postcard from her, hastily written just before she boarded the plane at Managua that would take her back to San Salvador. It was a just a postcard, with no great stylistic merit perhaps, and not at all pious and edifying in a conventional sense, but in the annals of the martrys Ita's postcard is worthy to stand beside the letters of Ignatius of Antioch and Jean de Brébeuf and Isaac Jogues.

Nicaragua
Dec. 1, 1980
Felicidades (Congratulations), as they say here. With you I celebrate birth and new life — because at this point that's all I know. The message I received was that "a child has been born," and that's good enough for me! When I get near a phone that works, I'll get filled in on the particulars.
Love to all,
Ita

The birth of a son and brother and the death of a beloved sister and aunt, extremes of joy and sorrow, came almost together to the Fords of Montclair at the end of 1980. "I believe there's a meaning to things," said Miriam. "The terrible thing that happened has brought us into contact with all sorts of good people and with families who have suffered as we have. It was a little hard at first for us to realize that it wasn't just our personal tragedy — that thousands and thousands of other people had been killed — but then we came to understand that. And now we feel we have an obligation to take up where she left off. So that no one else is killed."

After graduation Miriam spent four months in Bolivia working with Maryknoll lay missioners, and she later accompanied her father on one of his trips to El Salvador. In the course of the latter, the two of them were detained for questioning at an army post for two hours in Chalatenango Province by an arrogant teenage lieutenant, a brother in arms of her aunt's killers.

And, of course, more people were killed, thousands more, and yet every six months the State Department duly testified that it was convinced that good faith efforts were being made by the Salvadoran government to bring the slaughter of the innocent under control, and every six months Congress would nod its head and bless more guns and bullets.

In May of 1984, justice of a sort was done in El Salvador. The five guardsmen were finally brought to trial, convicted, and sentenced to thirty years. There was no formal death penalty in El Salvador, perhaps because the masters of the country were quite content with the ample opportunities they had to invoke it informally.

Napoléon Duarte, an honorable man and a personable graduate of the University of Notre Dame fluent in English, had been elected president in

March of 1984. The colonels, of course, still ran the country, and Duarte, whom they had kept from the presidency after he had won at the ballot box in an earlier election, was willing to go along with the charade for reasons that will forever be disputed. He was now dying of cancer, the president from central casting, the kind of Latin American politician that the State Department would have prayed for had it prayed. But he was still there, however diminished, to edify the uncritical in both houses of Congress. God was in his heaven and all was right with El Salvador as far as the Reagan administration was concerned. It was a position that the media didn't bother to dispute. There was, to be fair, a sameness to Latin American atrocities that became tedious after a while (unless, of course, your loved ones happened to be among the victims), and so El Salvador had disappeared from the news.

In January of 1989, I talked again with Bill Ford in the living room of his home in Montclair, the prosperous suburb of Newark in which Liz McAlister's sister and her family lived and in which the Gilbreths of *Cheaper by the Dozen* fame had flourished in the twenties. Bill Ford's house was of that era, big and old-fashioned and comfortable. It had to be big even though Bill and Mary Anne had only half as many offspring as the Gilbreths. Both families had highly successful fathers, loving mothers, and intelligent and vibrant children. But how right everything had seemed with the America of the Gilbreths and how wrong so much seemed with the America of the Fords.

Nine years had passed since the event that Bill Ford invariably referred to as "the deaths of the women." In the light of events at home and abroad, there was an obvious question to ask, unkind perhaps but inevitable: Had the deaths of the women made any difference?

Ford answered by making a distinction, showing that the labor of the Jesuits at Brooklyn Prep and Fordham had not been in vain. "You could talk about this in terms of whether or not the deaths of the women made a difference in the United States. You can talk about it as to whether or not it has made any difference in El Salvador, whether or not it has made a lasting difference in the lives of the families."

There were myriad aspects to what had happened and what had come of it, and even he, who was so close to it, couldn't begin to account for all of them. But one thing that he became surer and surer of as time went by, he said, was that the lives and the deaths of the women meant a great deal to a great number of people. "I continually meet people who say that hearing about what happened to the women was either a turning point or an important point in their lives. It made them refocus what they were thinking and what they were doing."

The deaths of the women made a difference in the United States, he believed, because at least annually, the anniversary of their deaths, there were commemorative services throughout the country that made people think about El Salvador.

In El Salvador itself, he said — to which he had gone every year since 1983 — it seemed at first that the deaths of the women had made no difference. The army went on waging war against its own people with North American arms and munitions, slaughtering them without remorse because they saw them as agents of a foreign power. Yet the truth was that the deaths of the women had made a great deal of difference in El Salvador. They focused so much attention on El Salvador that it became impossible to intervene militarily, and so they prevented the government of the United States from making things still worse.

Ford always said "United States," never "America." In simpler times, we North Americans were quite sure that we had an exclusive claim to the word in its pristine state and it was up to those other people to qualify it.

The United States government had not, he said, fulfilled the promises it had made after the deaths of the women that the judicial system would be reformed and that the authority of Salvadoran civil government would be restored.

"I guess this is a long way of saying that it's a complicated situation, and I think what most gratifies me and the members of my family is that there is still attention being paid to this situation in the United States even if it hasn't stopped the guns and bullets going to El Salvador.

We then began talking about the role of the Church and about the conspicuous absence of any substantial protest from the Vatican on the death of Archbishop Romero, the first Roman Catholic archbishop killed in eight centuries, since St. Thomas à Becket. Nor did Henry II's barons cut down the archbishop of Canterbury while he was saying Mass. Had Becket been at the altar, they probably would have held their swords until he finished. But neither superstition nor piety restrains the assassins of our century.

"The silence of the Vatican, the silence of the institutional Church, in the face of Romero's death is scandalous," said Bill Ford, who, I remembered, had pronounced himself merely "a bit surprised" six years before. In the intervening years, he had had ample time to observe the lethal effects of the Vatican's silence. The old men in Rome, safe and secure themselves, have done their best to ignore the deaths of the women and would prefer to keep on doing so. Romero's death, of course, was something they hadn't been able to ignore, but they had done the next best thing. The Vatican was quick to admonish those who would make too much of Romero's death, lest it be used for "political purposes."

Heedless of Rome's pleasure or Rome's displeasure, the common people of El Salvador had already conferred sainthood on their martyred archbishop. Romero's picture was spread over the walls of prison cells. His tomb in the cathedral was covered with tiny plaques, each an expression of gratitude for answered prayers and favors received.

Charlie Liteky, I recalled, had expressed himself very strongly on Archbishop Rivera Damas, Romero's successor. I told Ford that Liteky had called him a fence-sitter.

Ford paused for a long moment before answering. "I would have a different view. Damas is a man who in many respects was out front before Romero. Romero was chosen as a conservative to be the bishop over Damas. They thought Damas was too liberal, too advanced a social thinker." Damas had to be concerned about the real limits of the Church's power and the systematic slaughter of his people. He was a man who had lived in a pressure cooker for twenty-five years. "It's true, I suppose, that you could argue that he should be doing a lot more, but he has done a lot, and for all practical purposes he's done it by himself, without the support of his eight brother bishops, at least two of whom are colonels. There have been at least two instances in which Damas has issued pastoral letters, and the other bishops have come out within a week with counter-pastoral letters, contradicting him."

Ford had touched on something that went to the heart of El Salvador's agony and the agony of Latin America in general. Despite the justly celebrated preferential option for the poor, the ringing declaration at Medellín, Colombia, in 1968 that put the Church in Latin America on the side of the oppressed, not every bishop, it seemed, had endorsed the Medellín accord in his heart. More and more of them, as the years went by, were making no secret of their own preferential option, which was for the good old days when colonels and prelates feted each other and gave each other medals for services rendered to God, country, and family — their families.

To make matters worse, the Vatican under John Paul II had, wittingly or unwittingly, endorsed this betrayal of Medellín by consistently ordaining conservative bishops and appointing the most reactionary to important sees. So it was that the saintly apostle of the poor, Helder Camara, archbishop of Recife in impoverished northern Brazil, was replaced with a man more sensitive to the prevailing winds from Rome than to the needs of his people.

An event that occurred in Honduras in 1975, like the murder of Romero and the murders of the four women five years later, threw into stark relief not only the warped priorities of the Vatican's Latin American policy but the indifference of the government of the United States to any repression, no matter how savage, carried out in the name of anticommunism. And though the Olancho Massacre, as it came to be called, was little noted nor long remembered in this country, it, like the murder of Ita, Maura, Dorothy, and Jean, involved the shedding of American blood.

Olancho is a rural area of Honduras whose principal crop is bananas. The rock-bottom wages that the plantation owners paid the peasants of Olancho had made the area extremely attractive to United Brands — better known to fame as United Fruit or El Pulpo, the octopus. The bishop of Olancho, Nicholas D'Antonio, was an American Franciscan who, ironically, came from New York just like United Brands. D'Antonio and his fellow Franciscans, together with lay workers and other priests and religious in Olancho, had roused the wrath of the plantation owners by helping the peasants to form a union, a heinous offense against tradition for which they were denounced as Communists. D'Antonio was in the United States on a fundraising trip in June of 1975 when the plantation owners and their hired guns, backed by the Honduran army, launched a violent and furious assault on all those who threatened their way of life. The most infamous of the atrocities that resulted was the Olancho Massacre. It might not seem like much as massacres go — nine people died (separate incidents claimed five more victims) — but what set the Olancho Massacre apart was its style.

In one night of horror presided over by a plantation owner, soldiers and the plantation owner's thugs tortured, mutilated, and finally murdered a Colombian Jesuit named Ivan Betancur and a newly arrived Franciscan from Wisconsin named Jerome Cypher. To find a parallel to what the Franciscan and the Jesuit suffered at the hands of baptized Catholics, one would have to go back three centuries to the martyrdom of Betancur's brother Jesuits St. Jean de Brébeuf and St. Isaac Joges at the hands of the Iroquois. In the course of the night, moreover, the torturers also roasted five peasants to death in bread ovens and raped at leisure two young women who had been kidnapped with Betancur (one of whom was engaged to his brother). The next morning, these staunch anti-Communists finished off their work by throwing their victims down an abandoned well — the two women still alive — and sealing the grave with dynamite.

Besides the death of an American, there were other similarities to the atrocity that would take place in El Salvador five years later. The soldiers drove the jeep in which Betancur and the women had been riding off the road some distance from the scene of the crime and set fire to it, and the grave of the victims was discovered because of courageous peasants. In the case of the Olancho Massacre, the peasants showed an awesome determination as well as courage. They had to dig for eight days before they uncovered the bodies.

This was Latin America where the standards for atrocities are very high, but, even so, the grisly evidence was compelling enough to embarrass even the government of Honduras, especially since Honduran officials had explained the disappearances of Betancur and Cypher to the Colombian and United States embassies (and also to Betancur's mother, who had arrived from Colombia for a visit on the day of her son's murder) by assuring all concerned that the priests had taken to the hills to join the guerrillas. The owner of the bread ovens corroborated the peasants' account, a bit of good citizenship that didn't go unrewarded. He was shot to death two days later.

The plantation owner, whose son happened to be married to the daughter of the general whose turn it was that year to be president of Honduras, was exonerated in the trial that followed (while awaiting judgment, he lived in a small brick house built for him in the prison courtyard), and a young officer and the local official who had ordered the kidnapping of Betancur were given ten years each. The owner of the bread ovens wasn't around to testify, of course, a salutary lesson not lost on the witnesses for the prosecution.

The government of Colombia broke diplomatic relations with Honduras. The government of the United States did not. The Vatican, never one to linger over disedifying incidents, ordered D'Antonio not to return to Honduras and, in due time, relieved him of his duties as bishop of Olancho though it let him keep the title.*

While it's true that, according to tradition, one pope was crucified upside down on Vatican Hill, that was a long time ago. Nothing so unseemly had happened in recent memory, nor, as far as I know, has any official of the Roman Curia had his testicles slashed off, his eyes gouged, or his fingernails pulled out.

So it was that tranquillity and good order prevailed once more in Olancho. United Brands was able to keep undercutting competitors who bought bananas on the Florida market, and the bishop of Olancho took his memories with him into exile in New Orleans.

*Penny Lernoux, *The Cry of the People*, p. 107ff.

Several years later, I had the opportunity to strike up a conversation with Archbishop Philip Hannan of New Orleans at a Washington reception. "I see Bishop D'Antonio is one of your bishops," I said. Hannan, a stalwart and handsome man, had jumped into Normandy as a chaplain with the 82nd Airborne. A vigorous anti-Communist, he had been one of the foremost opponents of the adoption of the 1983 peace pastoral. I couldn't help but wonder what he and D'Antonio talked about, but I merely made some innocuous observation on how terrible were the events of June 1975.

"Yes," said Hannan, shaking his head. "He's a man who has experienced death, and that has a lasting effect on people." Hannan himself had evidently seen his share of death in Normandy — dead American paratroopers, most of them even younger than Jerome Cypher had been. Then he looked directly at me, his expression sad and incredulous. "Do you know what he said to me?"

I didn't.

"He said to me that even if the Communists took over, the situation couldn't get any worse. Can you imagine that?"

Bill Ford had made his trips to El Salvador under the auspices of the Lawyers Committee for Human Rights. The Lawyers Committee had undertaken to represent the four families and had been a major force behind their ability to keep reminding their fellow Americans of what had happened on the road to San Pedro Nonualco, bringing to bear on it the kind of sustained public attention that the death of Jerome Cypher had not gotten.

"The families believe, and I believe," said Ford, "that the deaths of the women should be remembered as a sign of what can continue to happen unless the situation is changed." Ford paused. He frowned slightly and his words, always deliberate, became more so. "I think — after the deaths of the women — I understand better the insistence of the Jews that the Holocaust never be forgotten. Because if things like that are forgotten, they can happen again.

"I also believe that the deaths of the women, because the acts were so outrageous, presents, in a sense, a constant challenge to those people in the United States who want to impose a military solution on El Salvador. And I believe that the memory of the dead women should be used to shield the Salvadoran people from further violence."

Ford paused once more. Years had passed, and yet he still had to keep in check a surge of emotion that threatened the calm surface of his narration. "Since these women lived for and died for the people of El Salvador — those of us who are left behind should use their memories on behalf of these people."

Ford spoke. He wrote. He saw himself as trying in some small way to be a presence among those who were trying to stop the violence and the killings. He did it, he said, because there was no question in his mind as a citizen of the United States that the fundamental cause of the violence and the killings was his own government. "The government of the United States," he said, "has put the tools of violence into the hands of people who are butchers."

The problem he continually ran up against in speaking to groups, he said — particularly men and women his own age — was that so many Americans were still frightened by the word *Communist*. They might, recently at least, be willing to give Russian Communists the benefit of the doubt because they were so far away, but Communists in their own backyard were something else again. So fearful were they that it didn't seem to bother them at all that their government was cooperating in the butchering of thousands of innocent men, women, and children in a supposed crusade against communism in Central America. Their unwillingness to see reason never ceased to amaze Ford.

I remembered a story told to me by Jim Harney, the man who had failed to convert Gordon Zahn to civil disobedience. Harney was a priest of the archdiocese of Boston who, as one of the Milwaukee Fourteen, had spent two years in prison for burning draft records. He was a tall man with a lantern jaw and classic black Irish features set off with a drooping mustache. He laughed easily, but there was a certain melancholy cast to his eyes that bespoke just as surely his Celtic heritage. No longer a priest in the formal sense, Harney was nonetheless a man with a mission. He was the photographer whose picture of a big-eyed Salvadoran child was paired on a poster with the famous quote of Dorothy Day "When they come for the innocent, if it's not over your dead body, cursed be you and your religion." Harney went to El Salvador, took pictures of what he saw, and then came back to give slide lectures. He'd pass the hat after the lectures, and when he had gotten enough money, he'd take another trip to El Salvador and take more pictures.

Once, when visiting a Catholic girls' school in the United States, he told his audience how a Salvadoran soldier had thrown a grenade into a crowd of peasants and it had exploded inside a baby's carriage. One, at least, of his schoolgirl audience took the story right in stride. She didn't even bother arguing that it was sad indeed about the poor baby, but things like that happened in war. No, no, this sweet young thing, the product of Catholic education, was made out of sterner stuff than that. "Well," she told Harney, "that baby could have grown up to be a Viet Cong."

Harney's vignette made one wonder if there was any chance at all of making headway against such entrenched ignorance, but Ford remained hopeful. It was hard to tell, he said, from talk to talk, from encounter to encounter, how much he was getting across, but it would be inexcusable not to keep trying. "To the extent that you're out there speaking, even if only one person in ten or one person in a hundred thinks about what you say or is impressed with what you say, you have done something. At the very least, somebody is out there saying something. There is a voice, an undercurrent of sound out there, one that says what's going on is wrong. If we get discouraged and say that our voices mean nothing, if we lapse into silence, then we are approving what's happening." The "we" included Ford's eighty-five-year-old mother, who was part of a women's group that gave presentations two or three nights a week in schools and retreat houses in Brooklyn and Queens.

Bill Ford's most recent trip to El Salvador, his seventh, had been the previous fall, September of 1988. Mary Anne accompanied him for the first time. It took them two days to get to Chalatenango. Even though they had safe-conduct passes, the guards wouldn't let them past the checkpoint twenty miles out of San Salvador. The same people stopped them at the same checkpoint the second day, but finally the young lieutenant in charge told them they could go as long as they were out of the area by six o'clock. "After six he wouldn't be responsible for us," Ford recalled. "Not that he was going to be responsible for us in any event."

Chalatenango, Ford said, was the name of both the province and its capital, a good-sized town. The town was some fifty miles north of San Salvador by way of the worst road that he had ever seen. The government had a garrison there, but the control of the countryside went back and forth. The province had just been made a separate diocese, and the new bishop was a protégé of Rivera Damas. His appointment had come as something of a surprise, a liberal who had somehow slipped through the Vatican's net.

Ford and his wife had ample opportunity while waiting at the checkpoint both days to get a firsthand view of oppression at work in a very personal way. Buses filled with peasants pulled up, and the young soldiers, some of them no more than thirteen or fourteen, forced everybody to get off, using their rifles like cattle prods on men and women of all ages. When the couple finally reached Chalatenango, the first thing Bill and Mary Anne did was to visit the graves of Ita and Maura. "The cemetery is unbelievably crowded," he said. "You and I are now sitting in a room about ten by twelve feet. Well, there might be fifteen people buried in an area this size. Goats and pigs wander through. Some of the graves are garishly decorated, but it seems a very peaceful place."

A peaceful place, but how very far from Bay Ridge.

They then drove into the town and went to the house where Maura and Ita had worked. By now it had started to pour rain, and the driver of their rented van was getting very nervous. There had been an attack on the supposedly impregnable garrison a few days before, and he wanted to get back to San Salvador before dark, but the Fords persuaded him to wait. They were given a warm reception by the two Salvadoran Assumption sisters who had come up from the capital to carry on the work of Ita and Maura. The nuns had known the slain women. "They took us into their chapel. The chapel is very small, and it has just four straight chairs in it. There's a crucifix on the wall about two feet or so from the floor. There's no Eucharist, and the only other decorations are four two-by-three-inch photographs of the four women." Ford's voice showed the effect of strong feeling. "If you're sitting in one of the chairs, which are very low, the crucifix and the pictures would be about eye level. And there's nothing else in the room. Nothing at all. The nuns told us that they spend a couple of hours a day in there, reading and praying. It was clear to us that prayer was the source of the courage that it took to stay in Chalatenango and carry on."

As usual, Ford and the other members of the Lawyers Committee on International Human Rights made the required official stops in the course of the trip. One of these, however, to the headquarters of an elite brigade in San Salvador, turned out to be of some interest.

"The colonel who commands this brigade — his name is Zepeda — is one of the up-and-coming younger army officers, sort of the Salvadoran Pete Dawkins. As you walk into his headquarters, there are these signs on the wall from Josephus and Herodotus about how our obligation is to kill our enemies to the last man. These are the generic statements. But then when you walk around the corner to the next room, there is a detailed list and pictures of these enemies, men like Guillermo Ungo and Reuben Zamora, men who are operating aboveground, carrying on legitimate political activities. The context in which the army regards these people — never mind what the laws say — became quite clear to me when I was down there."

The colonel and other officials as well agreed to see them because John

Lindsay was part of their delegation. However fleeting other forms of celebrity might be, being mayor of New York City seemed to set a man apart from ordinary mortals forever — at least outside of New York.

"Colonel Zepeda was obviously more intelligent than most of the thugs that we saw walking around in uniforms. He told us that it was true that El Salvador was a poor place, but the poor were happy and content until they were stirred up by these outsiders. He was a good Catholic, and he realized that low-intensity warfare was immoral because it would continue for ten years and bleed the country. The only true moral course, then, was to just go out and kill them all. It would be kinder. It would get it all over at once. We have to go out and take care of them, he said, these outsiders and those peasants among us who have been poisoned by them."

Zepeda's mind-set was quite typical, said Ford. For him and his comrades, it was no civil war. They were the defenders of the faith, the defenders of tradition, and the enemy were outsiders who had provoked ignorant peasants to rebel.

There was one encounter, however, that did have a lighter side, at least relatively speaking. Bill's delegation met with the government's Human Rights Commission, which, said Ford, was to human rights as military intelligence was to intelligence. Its members, nevertheless, were quite eager to meet with the distinguished visitors from North America and tell them all about their educational efforts. The main thrust of these, it turned out, was to warn the populace about the lethal effects of liberation theology, and they were very proud of a pamphlet they were putting together that drew heavily on essays of Cardinal Joseph Ratzinger on this theme.

"We told them," said Ford, "that we understood that they get 90 percent of their funding from the United States government. Was that true? They said yes, it was true. Then they turned white when we told them they were in violation of the law of the United States by using this money to promote a religious point of view and that we would have to report them. They hastened to assure us that the funds for this were donated and it was just a small part of what they were doing and so on and so forth."

In the course of our conversation, I had kept coming back to the matter of risk. Now I put it more bluntly. It seemed to me, I said, that Ford was taking a big chance every time he went down there. Moral niceties were never a primary concern of the guerrillas either. They could kill him, knowing that his death would be blamed on the government forces, and gain a big propaganda boost.

Bill Ford took a long time to answer. When he did his voice was raised slightly and had an aggressive pitch to it. A lawyer's counterthrust. "Well,

I suppose that's a possibility. But it's also possible to get run over crossing the street in Montclair." He paused and then went on, now brisk and businesslike. "Now if I were a constant pain in the ass to them, that would be an entirely different situation. But a guy who comes in once a year, who doesn't speak Spanish very well, so he won't be heard on local news stations, and if he's heard at all, he's heard in the U.S. . . . . I mean I'm just a curiosity down there." I didn't press the point. When we first talked, eight years before, he hadn't known Spanish at all.

The delegation also visited the new ambassador, William Walker. He struck Ford as being less ideological than his predecessor, Erwin Corr, whose office had been bedecked with Marine Corps memorabilia, not the most tasteful ambience in a Central American context.

The United States embassy in San Salvador was like a fortress, he said. The Salvadoran guards outside were not allowed inside with their weapons. Visitors had to go through several checkpoints and submit to body searches. Inside the building, there were heavy doors every ten feet or so along the corridor, and much of every visit was taken up waiting for doors to open and close.

Ambassador Walker seemed quite reasonable, and he told the delegation that he was new and that he was going to try to meet people "at the center." In the course of previous visits, Ford had met embassy personnel who he felt would have fit right in at the Reichstag. They felt that they had a problem to deal with, and the best way to deal with it was to wipe out their enemy. One of his trips had occurred right after a major earthquake, and Ford's delegation asked the chief of mission, John Delury, if any United States aid was going to be diverted from the military to earthquake relief, and he answered absolutely not. Putting military pressure on the guerrillas was of primary importance.

"It's clearly a bunker mentality at the embassy," said Ford. "They insist that the American missionaries there aren't aware of what's going on, but the missionaries are living among the people, and the diplomats are living in a bunker. If a couple at the embassy are Catholic and they want to get married, a Maryknoll priest has to come to the embassy to give them instructions. The Maryknoll parish in San Salvador is off limits because it is in a guerrilla-infested neighborhood."

Archbishop John R. McGann and Bishop Thomas Gumbleton were the main sources of support for the families of the slain women among the North American hierarchy, Ford said. McGann, the bishop of Rockville

Centre on Long Island, was by no means a peace and justice activist in season and out like auxiliary bishop Thomas Gumbleton of Detroit. A warm and kindly man who fit the old-fashioned image of a Catholic priest, McGann usually avoided politics, but if there was a clear-cut moral issue involved, he didn't hesitate to speak in unequivocal fashion, a trait that was definitely not the American episcopal style. McGann had expressed disapproval of American military aid to El Salvador in a pastoral letter a few years before, and Bill Ford had sat next to him at his press conference on that occasion. Much more controversial was his homily at the funeral of former CIA director William J. Casey in May of 1987 at the height of the Iran-Contra scandal.

While praising Casey, whom he had known for thirty years, as "a devoted public servant" and as a man who had been tireless in his dedication to the diocese and to charitable works, Bishop McGann felt compelled to express his "fundamental disagreement" with Casey over the cause to which this devoted public servant had given his last full measure of devotion, and he condemned "the violence wrought in Central America by support of the Contras." He went on to tell the stunned mourners, who included the president of the United States, that Casey had found "incomprehensible" the ethical questions "raised by me as his bishop . . . about our nation's defense policy since the dawn of the nuclear age." Among those who expressed their indignation in print at McGann's striking departure from the innocuous piety deemed proper on such occasions were William F. Buckley, Jr., and Jeane Kirkpatrick. Whatever the tenor of her remarks to the press after the death of the four women in 1980, Madame Ambassador had since become a convert, it seemed, to "De mortuis nihil nisi bonum."*

Every once in a while there was a memorial Mass for the women at St. Patrick's Cathedral in New York, but Ford acknowledged that his group hadn't really looked for any regular, systematic support from the American bishops. "Maybe we should," he said, "but we figure they have their own problems. Hickey in the early days was good. He was very moved by the death of Jean Donovan." Cardinal James Hickey of Washington, the man irreverent Bob Begin had characterized as as liberal as an ambitious man can be, had good cause to be moved by Jean's death. As bishop of Cleveland in 1979, he had urged her to stay longer in El Salvador than she had originally intended. It was in Hickey's house, Ford said, that he had met Napoléon Duarte.

Duarte, Ford said, was a good man whom the true rulers of El Salvador

*William F. Buckley, Jr., ". . . And the Bishop's Misreading," *Washington Post*, May 16, 1987; Jeane Kirkpatrick, "Intrusion of Politics," *Washington Post*, May 18, 1987.

had used as a cover to keep doing whatever they wanted to do. "Tens of thousands of people were being killed while he was president. For anybody to believe that he was just this genial graduate of Notre Dame was wrong. For Hesburgh to anoint him and say that he was a good man was wrong. It showed a great misconception on Hesburgh's part about what was actually going on in El Salvador."

The impeccable liberal credentials of Notre Dame's president, Fr. Theodore Hesburgh, didn't inhibit Ford in the least.

Duarte had more power than he was willing to use, said Ford. Duarte was the reason that the Reagan administration was able to get so much aid for the Contras. He was from Notre Dame. He was affable. He spoke English fluently. Congress loved him. He wasn't a thug like the notorious Roberto D'Aubisson, the former head of the far-right ARENA party who, everyone seemed to agree, had ordered the assassination of Archbishop Romero. "Duarte could have insisted that the army clean house. He could have said he wasn't going to ask for another nickel in American aid until the officers who were butchering the people were removed. But I guess he thought he couldn't challenge the Army. And he wanted to stay president."

Ford was afraid ARENA might win the elections that were coming up in March of 1989 because the corrupt, stife-ridden Christian Democrats were split into two factions, and so it would turn out. ARENA would gain an absolute majority, and Alfredo Cristiani would succeed the dying Duarte.

The more things changed, the more they remained the same in El Salvador. Ford and his companions had begun their struggle eight years before to see that justice was done on behalf of their slain loved ones, but then they very soon came to see that there was no way they could do so without also seeking justice for the oppressed people for whom Ita, Maura, Dorothy, and Jean had lived and died. How true that insight had been! For now even the partial justice done on behalf of the four women seemed in danger of becoming undone. The convicted guardsmen were still in prison, but they might not long remain so. One amnesty petition after another was being filed in their behalf.

Ford and the Lawyers Committee delegation had met with the judge to whom these petitions were being directed. She assured them that she would never grant the killers amnesty, but she told them that she had asked for a transfer and, if she didn't get it, she was going to resign. The death threats had become too much for her.

The judge who had presided over the guardsmen's trial, Bernardo Rauda, had been demoted afterward and sent to Chalatenango. Since he didn't have a car, he had to ride the bus two hours each way from San

Salvador. "There's a very clear message in that," said Ford. "People who preside over trials like this get punished."

I asked Bill Ford about the attitude of the Ford children toward institutions, such as the government and the Church, in the light of all that had happened.

Ford paused before answering. "My kids are more politically aware than most. Nobody in the family believes that the Church, as a church, has turned its back, and that may be just because of the immediate and whole-hearted support we got from Maryknoll. There is no resentment. No bitterness. Look at Salvador. The thousands of families who have had to mourn by themselves. We didn't have to do that."

The institutional Church did have problems, he said, and a lot of them came from people like him, who wouldn't go away when they disagreed, people who weren't as dependent on the Church as their fathers and grandfathers had been. When Ford's grandfather came over from Ireland, he got his first job through a priest. His own situation was much different, and if he and his wife were dissatisfied with the local parochial school, they would take their children out the next day. The Church, he thought, had to do much more to make itself significant to people like him. And he himself, he realized, had to do his share since it wasn't just the problem of bishops and priests.

"I do think that the Church would be better off if it realized that the government was . . . not its enemy maybe . . . but that the government was its adversary. I think that there is still too much of this business of flag and faith. If the Church were more willing to confront the government on a number of issues — social justice issues — if they were as vigorous on the social justice as they were on some of the other issues, they might give people a clearer choice as to what they should do.

"A lot of the FBI agents doing surveillance of Catholic peace activists are Catholics. A lot of Catholics are in the military, many of them down there advising the Salvadoran military. We are in danger of becoming like the Church of England — an arm of the government."

When I talked with Bill Ford for the last time, in May of 1991, the tenth anniversary of the deaths of the women had come and gone. There had been the usual services the previous December to mark the deaths of Ita, Maura, Dorothy, and Jean, including one in Sacred Heart Cathedral in Newark and one my wife and I attended in Cleveland (our home once more). But since it was the tenth anniversary, there had also been a special commemorative forum for the relatives of the victims in Washington, D.C., the see of Cardinal Hickey, who had sent Jean Donovan to El Salvador.

Besides the Fords, Ray and Pat Donovan, Jean's parents, her brother, Michael, and his wife were there, and so were Dorothy Kazel's brothers and sisters from Cleveland and Maura Clarke's nieces. It was a weekend of prayer and reflection. After it was over there was an ecumenical service at the chapel of Trinity College. There were no bishops in attendance, and there was no media coverage, but the weekend had been a moving experience for the families of the women.

One of those who attended, though he wasn't related to Ita, Maura, Dorothy, or Jean, was himself bereaved — bereaved in such a way that he was able to empathize with those who mourned the four as almost no one else could. He was a Spanish Jesuit named Jon Sobrino, and he was the sole survivor of the seven Jesuits who had been on the faculty of San Salvador's University of Central America. For as incredible as it might seem, the masters of El Salvador had once more outdone themselves in arrogant cruelty.

On the morning of November 16, 1989, a unit of government soldiers had broken into the Jesuit residence of the University of Central America and murdered Jon Sobrino's six companions: Ignacio Ellacuría, Ignacio Martín-Baró, Segundo Montes, Joaquín Lopéz y Lopéz, Juan Ramón Moreno, and Amando López, and their cook, Elba Ramos and her teenage daughter Celina Ramos. Sobrino, whose writings on liberation theology had gained him an international reputation and, no doubt, a place near the top of the military's hate list, had escaped the slaughter because he had been on a speaking tour in Southeast Asia.

The government had at first denied involvement, but few even pretended to take its protestations seriously, not even among the true believers in the Pentagon and the Department of State. Then in January of 1991, President Cristiani had announced that a Colonel Guillermo Alfredo Benavides and three other officers and five soldiers had been formally charged in the murders. And there the matter stood with no further progress to date. Benavides was the highest ranking member of the Salvadoran military ever charged with a crime, but would even a colonel dare commit such an act on his own?

Colonel Juan Orlando Zepeda, the Salvadoran Pete Dawkins, whom Ford had described to me two years before, had indeed gone on to greater things, as Ford had predicted. The man who quoted Josephus and Herodotus was now a general in charge of the defense of the capital, a command area that included, needless to say, the University of Central America.

It wasn't the first time that blood had been shed at the university. Immediately after Reagan's first victory in November of 1980, the colonels and generals had celebrated by sending a death squad into the university to shoot down six prominent opposition leaders who were meeting there. (It was the night before their funeral Mass in the cathedral that another death squad, five National Guardsmen in civilian clothes, had stopped a white van not far from the airport. Jean Donovan, the driver of the van, had visited her uncle's family in Cleveland in October, and, before returning to El Salvador, she had urged them not to vote Republican. They had laughed, not taking her seriously, and they had voted Republican as they had always done.)

Bill Ford had made two more trips to El Salvador since 1989. His son Bill, a twenty-seven-year-old graduate of Dartmouth, had accompanied him on the second, in July of 1990. This time Ford hadn't gone with a Lawyers Committee delegation, and the trip had struck a somewhat different chord. The BBC was making a television documentary on the deaths of the Jesuits, and they had asked Ford to participate along with Jon Sobrino and an American Jesuit from Fordham named Dean Brackley, who had come down to replace one of the slain men.

"I guess the most moving part of this trip was to be taken on a tour of the University of Central America by Jon Sobrino and be shown the places where the Jesuits were murdered." Unless I was mistaken, Ford now made less effort to disguise his emotions than he had in years past. "To be shown where they're now buried. To be shown the rooms where these men lived. To be shown where they were shot down, and then to be taken to where their bodies were found. They've made the place where the bodies were found into a rose garden. The women are represented by yellow roses, the Jesuits by red. And then to be told the gardener of the rose garden was the husband and father of the two women who died. . . ."

Sobrino told Ford how he had seen a picture in a newspaper in Thailand of one of the bodies. Intent on delivering a message to him, the soldiers had dragged one of the dead Jesuits into Sobrino's room. He knew it was his room because the body was at the base of a bookcase, and he recognized the books as his own.

After Sobrino had shown Ford and his son the chapel, he led them out of the university through a house where the Jesuits had lived. They were walking through the living room when Sobrino stopped and said to them: "You know, my brothers and I spent hours here, doing puzzles, watching television, you know, just being with each other. And now my family is gone."

He had come from Spain at the age of nineteen, Sobrino said, with four of the slain Jesuits. He had grown up with them, and now they were gone. "It was very moving," said Ford, "To be in the presence of a man who had seen all that."

Sobrino had a prophetic vision about El Salvador, said Ford — about El Salvador being ground down, about the lack of compassion and the distorted values of North Americans who wanted the coffee or whatever else was to be had and gave no thought to the peasants who had labored to produce it.

The Jesuits had left two of the rooms untouched after the killings, and in one of them was a picture of Archbishop Romero with a bullet hole through the heart. "After that," said Ford, "a soldier had turned a flame thrower on the picture, and the frame is burnt and the glass looks like ice that has melted and then refrozen." Ford paused and then spoke slowly, stressing each syllable. "The picture itself, except for the bullet hole, is absolutely undamaged." The FBI wanted to examine the picture and try to find out how it could have remained unscorched, but the Jesuits wouldn't let them touch it."

The trip had had a strong effect on young Bill Ford, though he hadn't said much at the time. He taught at St. Mary's High School in Jersey City, whose students were mostly boys and girls from poor families, about a third of them refugees from Central America. He was asked to give a talk on his experiences in El Salvador at a Mass at which new students were inducted into a volunteer program, and he invited his father to attend. "As I sat there listening to him talk," said Ford, "I thought, 'My God, Bill, you've got to stop. It's too long.' Because he was going on for twenty-five or thirty minutes. But at the end these kids just stood up in the pews and cheered."

One experience that must have figured prominently in the account Ford's son gave to the boys and girls of St. Mary's was his trip with his father to Chalatenango to visit his aunt's grave.

"It's always moving to visit the cemetery," said Bill Ford, recalling the July visit with the young man who had been a boy of eleven when Ita died, "even though it's so crowded and has all those decorations. You know, as the years go by, I find myself more and more in awe of Ita, Maura, Dorothy, and Jean. What they did was put themselves in a position of helplessness. And it's very hard for North Americans to put themselves in a position of helplessness."

Epilogue

Bob Begin is still with the West Side Ecumenical Ministry on Clinton Street. We have occasion to work together in getting minority students into John Carroll University, where I've worked since my return to Cleveland in 1989.

Bill and Judy Corrigan still live on Clinton Street. In 1989, Bill was elected to a municipal judgeship with special jurisdiction over housing cases. His honesty and probity on the bench and his vigor in going after absentee landlords gratify many and astound the rest.

Marcia Timmel and Paul Magno had a second child in 1990, a girl whom they named Ariel, and now they face a crisis.

Two years ago, they moved the Olive Branch Catholic Worker House from the north side of Washington to an area closer to the center of the city, a section where drug traffic and its accompanying dangers are even more prevalent. There is at least one murder a month in their immediate neighborhood. The reign of terror climaxed in late 1991 when a ten-year-old boy was shot dead in their front yard after being caught in a crossfire between rival drug dealers. Sarah, now five, and Ariel had been playing there just a few minutes before.

In an attempt to be more "inclusive," moreover, the Olive Branch community had invited two street people who had worked at their soup kitchen to live with them, an experiment that all agreed turned out to be disastrous.

So it was that in December of 1991 Marcia took Sarah and Ariel and moved in with friends in a safer area of the city.

Marcia still faces a court hearing in connection with her participation in a demonstration in front of the White House in opposition to the Persian Gulf War.

Dan Berrigan persists in being Dan Berrigan, to the delight of some and the mingled scorn and discomfiture of others.

Among his other transgressions — most of which stem from the Kairos group's constant witness against the Riverside Research Institute, a flourishing weaponry think tank located behind the Port Authority Bus Terminal in Manhattan — he has been arrested twice for participating in actions against abortion clinics, and he faces a hearing in Rochester.

In August of 1991, Dan, together with Sister Anne Montgomery, John Marth, and other members of the Kairos group were arrested at a "die-in" on board the aircraft carrier *Intrepid* as a protest against an "obscene" exhibit extolling the prowess of American arms in the Persian Gulf.

Elizabeth McAlister and **Philip Berrigan's** book *The Time's Discipline* was published in 1989. It is a collection of searingly personal essays on the Beatitudes and the terrible price they demand.

Phil received a six-month sentence for the Nuclear Navy Plowshares. He and Liz, carrying on as always, have had numerous skirmishes with the law since 1988. Liz was arrested at John Hopkins's Applied Physics Laboratory on December 5, 1991, and at the U.N. on March 26, 1991, for a demonstration calling for an end to sanctions against Iraq and for aid to Iraqi children. In October of 1991, she spent ten days in jail for spray-painting "Hiroshima" and "Nagasaki" on the sidewalk in front of the Pentagon on August 9.

On Easter Sunday, March 31, 1991, the third anniversary of the Nuclear Navy Plowshares, Phil and three companions — Tom Lewis of the Catonsville Nine; Barry Ross, a psychiatrist from Cambridge, Massachusetts; Kathy Boylan, who runs a shelter for Central American refugees on Long Island; and Daniel Sicken, an engineer from Vermont — enacted the familiar Plowshares disarmament rituals on board the Aegis missile cruiser the *Gettysburg,* a sister ship of the *Vincennes,* which shot down the Iranian airliner in the Persian Gulf in 1989.

Brand new at a cost of one and a half billion dollars, the *Gettysburg* lay unguarded at its dock at the Bath Iron Works in Bath, Maine, one of the nation's largest shipyards. After Phil and his companions had finished their action, they tried in vain to arouse the security guards by ringing the ship's bell. When this failed, Phil and Tom had to go to the front gate and bring back the unfortunate watchman, who was quite taken aback to see so expensive a piece of government property stained with blood and festooned with banners.

At its initial hearing the group drew a sympathetic judge who allowed them to remain at liberty while awaiting trial. At the September trial, the prosecutor acquiesced to a motion that the charges be dropped, most likely because the circumstances were so embarrassing to the government.

On December 29, 1991, Phil was arrested with Felton Davis, a Catholic Worker from New York City, for pouring blood on the pillars of the White House. They were released on their own recognizance, and no date for a trial has been set.

Frida Berrigan, looking forward to graduating from high school in June of 1992, was busy during the school year filling out applications for college.

Frida has been arrested several times — once at the White House in the company of her brother, Jerry, and Dr. Benjamin Spock and once on the roof of the Applied Physics Laboratory at Johns Hopkins with Jerry and her sister, Katy.

Jerry Berrigan, like Frida a veteran of several arrests, spent his junior year, 1991–92, in Germany on a scholarship from the German government. He lived with a German farm family and, by all reports, became quite fluent in German, something not at all surprising to anyone familiar with Jerry's zeal to communicate under any and all circumstances.

Katy Berrigan is in middle school. She read a poem on the roof of the Applied Physics Laboratory on Martin Luther King Day before her arrest in January of 1990.

John Heid and **Dale Ashera-Davis** are still dedicated peace activists and are still frequently arrested, though they no longer live at Jonah House.

Charlie Liteky continues to let himself be led by the Spirit, even though it leads him where most of us would prefer not to go.

On December 20, 1991, Charlie was released after serving all of a six-month sentence in the federal prison in Allenwood, Pennsylvania, for an action directed against the School of the Americas at Fort Benning, Georgia, a training facility for Latin American officers and troops. On November 16, 1990, the anniversary of the murder in El Salvador of the six Jesuits and their cook and her teenage daughter (an atrocity that may well have been carried out on the orders of graduates of the School of the Americas), Charlie, his younger brother Patrick, and Roy Bourgeois, a

Maryknoll priest, entered the headquarters of the School of the Americas and threw blood over the photos and award cases that made up the school's hall of fame.

In the trial that took place in March of 1991, the defendants were forbidden to discuss their motivation, and the judge kept from the jury the knowledge that Charlie had won the nation's highest honor in Vietnam.

At the sentencing the following June, Patrick, like Charlie, got six months, and Roy Bourgeois, whose name is wholly at variance with his politics and who had long been a thorn in the side of the authorities at Fort Benning, got sixteen months.

Sister Margaret McKenna has performed quite a bit more than the 240 hours of public service given her by Judge Tommy Miller, along with two years' probation, in 1988. Exuberant as ever despite the ravages of Lyme disease, Sister Margaret is the director of a social service agency in a bleak area of North Philadelphia, and one of her major tasks is getting enough money to keep it going. When the conditions are right, she says, she'll probably get herself a new right knee, and she's looking forward to the increased mobility it will give her.

Greg Boertje received six months for the *Iowa* action. After he was released he went to prison on a thirty-six-month sentence for the Epiphany Plowshares and for his failure to appear for sentencing. Greg served twenty-seven months in three federal prisons, his two moves resulting from his involvement in protests that threatened the good order of his host institutions.

Greg returned to Jonah House in December of 1990 and, after telling his parole officer that he had no intention of reporting to him, immediately took up where he left off. Among other occasions, he was arrested at the White House in October of 1991 and, with Liz McAlister, at the demonstration at the Johns Hopkins Applied Physics Laboratory on December 5, 1991.

Andrew Lawrence received six months from Judge Tommy Miller. He was arrested several times after his release, but now he is seriously considering marriage and the responsibilities that such a step will entail.

Joan Andrews married Christopher Bell in June of 1991. Her husband is a pro-life activist who has established homes for pregnant women in New Jersey; Joan and he live in one of the homes in Hoboken and are looking for a place of their own.

Joan has been arrested countless times since 1988, and twice at least she has come close to being sent back to Pittsburgh and another confrontation with Judge Novak. On one occasion she was in jail for six months in Youngstown, Ohio, and marshals came from Pittsburgh to pick her up. What saved her was the legal expertise of a local lawyer whom John Broderick persuaded to help; the man was firmly pro-choice, but Joan's obvious sincerity won him over. A second narrow escape occurred in July of 1991 in New York City. The officer in charge at the police station she was taken to told her that he was sure that he would find all sorts of outstanding warrants if he checked his computer but, just for that reason, he wasn't going to do it. Two months later, at the hearing, Broderick was able to spirit Joan out of the courthouse one jump ahead of Novak's marshals.

As might be expected, Novak remembers her well, and whenever he sentences friends of hers, he tells them that he expects to see her again before too long. Joan for her part has gone through a struggle of conscience, wondering at times if she should go back and perform a rescue in Pittsburgh and confront Novak once more. But, so far at least, her friends have been able to persuade her that her mission for now is to carry the rescue message overseas, and she has done so in Brazil (where abortion is illegal but nonetheless a flourishing industry), Spain, Poland, and Yugoslavia.

She is the happiest she has ever been, she told me, and she asked me to pray that at forty-three she still might have a baby. In any event, she and her husband intend to adopt children, preferably ones with handicaps. Her plans for motherhood, however, won't preclude her participation in rescues. Christopher has promised to take care of the children should she be sent to prison.

Archbishop Raymond G. Hunthausen retired as archbishop of Seattle on his seventieth birthday in August of 1991. He gave no reason for retiring five years earlier than the mandatory seventy-five, but health may have been a factor.

Hunthausen, as always an exception among the American hierarchy, issued an unqualified denunciation of the Persian Gulf War in late 1990. He also attracted some media attention in his final year as archbishop of Seattle by declaring that he would ordain no more male deacons until the Church reconsidered its prohibition of the priesthood for women. He continues to withhold fifty percent of his income tax to protest military expenditures.

There was no need for Hunthausen to move out of the magnificent episcopal residence to make way for the new archbishop of Seattle. He had never moved in, and he continues to live in the small rectory beside the cathedral.

George Kotelaris, whose apartment Hunthausen cleaned, died in 1990, and the archbishop said his funeral mass. The cathedral was filled with mourners. It was exactly George's kind of event, and, under other circumstances, he would have been snapping pictures of the participants.

Sister Anne Montgomery has been involved in two Plowshare actions since 1988, though in neither case did she serve any time in jail.

In December of 1990, after war in the Persian Gulf became inevitable, she went to Iraq as a member of the Gulf Peace Team, and she and her companions set up a camp on the border of Iraq and Saudi Arabia. After ten days, however, the Iraqi army ordered them back to Baghdad. Before she and her group were evacuated to Jordan, she experienced the first of the air assaults against the city.

In September of 1991, she made another visit to Iraq, after being arrested with Dan Berrigan on the *Intrepid,* and she wrote an article for the *Catholic Worker* on the appalling conditions in Iraq, the major victims of which are the children. Despite all the propaganda about smart bombs and surgical strikes, what the American military did, she said, was destroy the infrastructure of the country, causing immense suffering and death. The sanctions, furthermore, make things still worse, and the people suffer greatly, especially from the lack of adequate medical care.

Sister Montgomery and Eileen Storey, a Sister of Charity who accompanied her, have prepared a slide show on Iraq, and they are writing a book called *Victory of Grass.*

Just before Christmas of 1991, Sister Montgomery returned from a trip to Panama, the scene of another triumph of American arms. She still tutors adults in Harlem.

Marietta Jaeger still lives in inner-city Detroit and carries on her witness against violence in all its forms. Her daughter Heidi returned from Nicaragua with a Nicaraguan husband, and they and their infant son live upstairs.

In June of 1991, Marietta, worn down by all her activity, got an opportunity for some rest and recuperation at a small resort operated by a California-based foundation dedicated to supporting peace activists. As Providence would have it, the resort was located in Montana not far from the campground where the tragedy took place and the little town where Susie is buried. So it was that Marietta was able to visit Susie's grave on the eighteenth anniversary of her death.

For a second time, she renewed her friendship with the man who had been the FBI agent in charge of the investigation and later the attorney general of Montana. He is now retired. This time they knew where each of them stood and what to avoid, and there was no tension in their cordial exchange.

Gordon Zahn, at seventy-four, is still writing and speaking about peace.

In June of 1991, lack of funds forced the closing of the Center on Conscience and War in Charlestown across from the Celtic Den. Gordon still hasn't been able to raise the $5,000 necessary to dub the German television film on Franz Jaegerstaetter, who, were it not for Gordon, might have been forgotten.

Fortkamp will soon publish his autobiography, *A Vocation of Peace,* and he is almost finished with a book called *Catholic Conscientious Objection in Perspective.*

William P. Ford remains unsanguine about peace in El Salvador despite the official proclamation of it that came on New Year's Day 1992. Nor does he consider the September 28, 1991, conviction of a colonel and a lieutenant in the murders of the six Jesuits and their housekeeper and her daughter as a resounding victory for justice. (Had it been that resounding, the presiding judge would not have immediately left the country for an extended "study tour" in Europe.)

The eighties began with the assassination of the archbishop of San Salvador and the murder of the four churchwomen, and they ended with the murder of the six Jesuits and the two women. Those who gave the orders in both instances are still in power, and as long as they are, and as long as the United States bankrolls them, there can be no true peace. The specter of the Third World in arms may well replace the specter of international communism as the threat against which we must keep on arming ourselves and our proxies so that they can keep their own people under control.

Since it is impossible to get a straight answer out of anyone in El Salvador, says Ford, there is no way of knowing if the five guardsmen who murdered Ita, Maura, Dorothy, and Jean are still in prison, much less the conditions under which they're being held, which could include furloughs and weekends off. Nor is there any guarantee that the colonel and the lieutenant convicted in the Jesuit murders will not soon be given amnesty. Bill Ford, it seems, still hasn't made his last trip to El Salvador.

Helen Woodson is serving the seventh year of her twelve-year sentence. She has been transferred, as Liz McAlister predicted, to the new federal maximum-control prison for women in Marianna, Florida.

Helen recently petitioned the court to take away all of her "good time," the credit that counts toward an early release. The court granted her petition, and now the government is appealing the decision.

Acknowledgments

I want, first of all, to thank my wife, Rosemary, who proofread the entire manuscript and who has cheerfully endured much because of this project. Without her, I never would have been able to carry it through.

Of all the others I have to thank, two stand out. One is Ana Carrigan, filmmaker and author, a volatile mixture of Irish and Latin American, who made the marvelous documentary *Roses in December* on the life and death of Jean Donovan and later wrote *Salvador Witness*, a biography of Jean. It was Ana who urged me to write a book on the Catholic Church in the United States, a topic that at first blush I didn't find all that exciting, and brought me together with John Herman, now editorial director at Ticknor & Fields. John responded enthusiastically to the ideas I offered and kept faith with me during a long and difficult period. Without his kindness and unfailing encouragement I never would have been able to finish the book that he enabled me to begin.

After these three, I owe the greatest thanks to my editor at Ticknor & Fields, Jane von Mehren, who subjected my hapless manuscript to all sorts of cruel and unusual scrutiny until I coerced it into a narrative, cutting much of what Sean O'Casey would have called all that blather while retaining just enough to manifest, at least to the elect, my ethnic heritage.

I also want to thank Walter F. Murphy, whose inspiration had everything to do with my hitting upon the theme of this book and whose warm friendship and support helped me see it through to completion; John O'Neil, another good and faithful friend whose support has been indispensable to me (and who, I hope, will look benignly upon my little jokes about the Knights of Malta and a few others as well); Faith Hamlin, my agent, whose first name is singularly appropriate for her vocation, especially vis-à-vis me; and Leone and Pat Marinello, whose confidence in my abilities has remained steadfast over the years despite the lack of much empirical data to sustain it.

In many respects, of course, my greatest debt — one all Americans share, whether they realize it or not — is to the gallant men and women I've written about in these pages: Americans of extraordinary faith and courage in a supposedly cynical age devoid of heroes. And the debt extends not only to them but to many, many more whose lives I haven't even touched on here, men and women like Richard Cowden-Guido, Fr. Carl Kabat, Rich Miller, Katya Komisaruk, Larry Morlan, Jean and Joe Gump, Jerry Ebner, and George Ostensen, all of whom are in prison or have recently been released.

Michael Gallagher
Cleveland
January 6, 1992

Index

Abortion: Andrews's opposition to, 157, 158–59, 160–61, 161–62, 163–66, 167–68, 176, 189 (*see also under* Andrews, Joan); Daniel Berrigan's action against, 298; in Canada, 168; and Catholic liberals, 260; and Catholic Worker movement, 32; double message on, 171; and Jesse Jackson candidacy, 143; as killing precedent (Andrews), 168; and Network organization, 95; and *Roe vs. Wade*, 2, 30; by Marcia Timmel, 35; Timmel's program against, 39; Zahn article on, 260

Accera, Bishop Angelo, 257

Afterlife, Begin on, 28–29

Alacoque, Saint Margaret Mary, 36

Alderson prison for women, 68, 215

Alinsky, Saul, 6–7

Allende, Hortensia, 195

Allenwood prison, 52–53, 299

Alter, Archbishop Karl J., 39–40

Ambition: of priests to be bishops, 6–7; and Timmel's view of Glenmary, 40

America (Jesuit magazine), 53–54, 260

Anarchy, Judge's accusation of, 152

Anderson, William H., 157

Andrews, Bill, 160

Andrews, Joan, 3, 155–56, 160–61,

300–301; cancer suffered by, 155, 162–63; and civil rights movement, 188–89; early life of, 156–57, 159–60, 180; imprisonment of, 3, 56, 106, 155, 157–58, 164, 169–70, 172, 173, 175–76; Pennsylvania sentencing of, 175–86; personal influence of, 169; relationship of with Marine, 174; release of, 187–88

IN ANTI-ABORTION MOVEMENT: direct action, 157, 158, 161–62, 163–67, 176, 184, 189; on friends' indifference, 171; and Holocaust comparison, 156–57, 171, 173, 240–41; as inspiration, 173; and noncooperation, 167–68, 170–73, 181; number of convictions, 185

Andrews, John, 160

Andrews, Miriam, 161, 174

Andrews, Susan (later Susan Brindle), 154, 155, 156–57, 161, 175, 186, 188

Antigone (Sophocles), 66, 186

Appalachia, and Timmel, 38

Arms race: Begin vs. businessman on, 25; Philip Berrigan on, 136. *See also* Nuclear weapons

Ashera-Davis, Dale, 59, 63, 132, 299

Atlantic Life Community, 49, 76

Augustine, Saint, and pacifism, 257